It Takes A Village Academy
18 K 563
5800 Tilden Avenue
Brooklyn, NY 11203

History Alive!

The Medieval World and Beyond

Student Edition

Teachers' Curriculum Institute

Managing Editor: Laura Alavosus
Developmental Editor: John Bergez
Production Editor: Mali Apple
Editorial Assistant: Anna Embree
Art Director: Tim Stephenson
Production Manager: Lynn Sanchez
Senior Graphic Designer: Christy Uyeno
Graphic Designers: Katy Haun, Paul Rebello, Don Taka
Photo Editor: Lindsay Kefauver
Audio Director: Katy Haun
Operations Manager: Ellen Mapstone

 Teachers' Curriculum Institute
P.O. Box 50996
Palo Alto, CA 94303

ISBN 1-58371-376-X
8 9 10 -WC- 09 08 07

Program Directors

Bert Bower

Jim Lobdell

Author

Wendy Frey

Contributing Writers

Lillian Duggan

Rena Korb

Joan Kane Nichols

Joy Nolan

Curriculum Developers

Joyce Bartky

Terry Coburn

Anne Maloney

Steve Seely

Kelly Shafsky

Reading Specialist

Kate Kinsella, Ed.D.
Reading and TESOL Specialist
Department of Secondary Education
College of Education
San Francisco State University
San Francisco, California

Teacher Consultants

Randi Gibson
Stanford Middle School
Long Beach Unified School District
Long Beach, California

Jana Kreger
Hanover Middle School
Hanover School District
Hanover, Massachusetts

Dawn Lavond
SC Rogers Middle School
Moreland School District
San Jose, California

Michal Lim
Borel Middle School
San Mateo Foster City Elementary
School District
San Mateo, California

Alana D. Murray
Parkland Middle School
Montgomery County Public Schools
Rockville, Maryland

Stevie Wheeler
Rincon Middle School
Escondido Union School District
San Diego, California

Scholars

Dr. Ayad Al-Qazzaz
Professor of Sociology
California State University Sacramento,
California

Dr. William H. Brennan
Associate Professor of History
University of the Pacific
Stockton, California

Dr. Philippe Buc
Professor of Medieval History
Stanford University
Palo Alto, California

Dr. Eun Mi Cho
Department of Special Education
California State University Sacramento,
California

Dr. Tom Conlan
Assistant Professor of History
Bowdoin College
Brunswick, Maine

Dr. Thomas Dandelet
Department of History
University of California
Berkeley, California

Dr. James A. Fox
Department of Anthropological Sciences
Director of the Center for Latin
American Studies Stanford University
Palo Alto, California

Gloria Frey
Ethical Culture Schools
New York, New York

Christopher Gardner
Western Civilization Post-Doctoral
Fellow
George Mason University
Arlington, Virginia

Dr. Bruce Grelle
Department of Religious Studies
Director, Religion and Public Education
Resource Center
California State University
Chico, California

Dr. Kan Liang
Director, Asian Studies
Associate Professor of History
Seattle University
Seattle, Washington

Dr. Merrick Posnansky
Professor Emeritus
Departments of History and
Anthropology
University of California
Los Angeles, California

Dr. John Rick
Department of Anthropological Sciences
Stanford University
Palo Alto, California

Dr. Melinda Takeuchi
Professor of Japanese Art and Culture
Stanford University
Palo Alto, California

Dr. Allen Wittenborn
Professor of Asian Studies
San Diego State University
San Diego, California

Assessment Consultant

Julie Weiss
Curriculum and Assessment Specialist
Elliot, Maine

Music Consultant

Melanie T. Pinkert, Ethnomusicologist
Bethesda, Maryland

Geography Specialist

Mapping Specialists
Madison, Wisconsin

Internet Consultant

Amy George
Weston, Massachusetts

Diverse Needs Consultants

Erin Fry
Glendora, California

Colleen Guccione
Naperville, Illinois

Welcome to *History Alive! The Medieval World and Beyond*

History Alive! The Medieval World and Beyond was developed by middle school teachers at Teachers' Curriculum Institute (TCI). We, Bert Bower and Jim Lobdell, are two former high school teachers who started TCI. Our goal is to help students like you succeed in learning about history in a way that is fun and exciting. With the help of teachers from around the nation, we've created the TCI Approach to learning. This chapter explains how the TCI Approach will make medieval history come alive for you.

The TCI Approach has three main parts. First, during class you'll be involved in a lot of exciting activities. For example, you'll learn about medieval towns in Europe by bringing to life various places, like a legal court and a medieval fair. You'll participate in the gold and salt trade of West Africa to understand how Ghana became a powerful kingdom. You'll explore the world of Japanese samurai by visiting a "samurai school" of training. Every lesson is built around an activity like these.

Second, during and after these activities, you get to read this book. You'll discover that your reading connects closely to the activities that you experience. We've worked hard to make the book interesting and easy to follow.

Third, during each lesson you'll write about your learning in your Interactive Student Notebook. You'll end up with your very own personal account of medieval history.

With the TCI Approach, you'll not only learn more about history than ever before, but you'll have fun doing it. Let's take a closer look at how this approach will help you learn medieval history.

Two teachers, Bert Bower (above) and Jim Lobdell (below), started TCI. They work with teachers and students like you to develop new ways to learn history.

Researchers have found that students learn best when they are given the opportunity to use their multiple intelligences, work cooperatively with their peers, and build on what they already know.

Theory-Based, Active Instruction

History Alive! The Medieval World and Beyond is probably unlike any other history program you have ever encountered. Perhaps you have been in history classes where you listen to the teacher and then read a textbook and answer chapter questions. Does this approach make you excited about learning history? Most students would say no, and educational researchers would tend to agree. Researchers have discovered new ways of reaching all students in the diverse classroom. This program relies on three of their theories.

Students learn best through multiple intelligences. Howard Gardner, an educational researcher, discovered that people use their brains in very different ways to learn the same fact or concept. From this discovery, he created a theory called *multiple intelligences*. There are seven intelligences. You can think of them as different ways of being smart—with words, with pictures, with numbers, with people, with your body, with music and rhythms, and with who you are. Everyone has multiple intelligences. Using one or more of these ways of being smart can help make learning easier.

Cooperative interaction increases learning gains. Through research, Elizabeth Cohen discovered that students learn more when they interact by working in groups with others. Interactive learning includes working with your classmates in many kinds of activities. You'll work in groups, do role plays, and create simulations. This kind of learning requires you and your classmates to share ideas and work together well.

All students can learn via the spiral curriculum. Researcher Jerome Bruner believed that learning isn't just up to students. Teachers need to make learning happen for all students. Bruner believed, as the TCI Approach does, that all students can learn through a process of step-by-step discovery. This process is known as a spiral curriculum.

These three theories are the foundation of the TCI Approach. Putting them into practice in *History Alive! The Medieval World and Beyond* gives you what you need to succeed.

Standards-Based Content

A lot of people care about what you are learning in history. These people include your parents, your school administrators, your teachers, and even your state and national elected officials. In fact, if you're like students in most states, you take tests at the end of the year to measure your progress.

Most end-of-year tests are based on standards. Standards are the key pieces of information about history that elected officials think are important for you to remember. When you read most standards, you might scratch your head and think, "These seem really hard to understand, and they're probably even harder to learn and remember." There's no need to worry about that with *History Alive! The Medieval World and Beyond.* Every lesson is based on standards. So every day, while you're having fun learning medieval history, you are also learning key standards.

You'll be recording everything you learn in your Interactive Student Notebook. When it's time to prepare for tests, your notebook will make it easy to review all the standards you've learned.

In fact, students across the nation using the TCI Approach are getting better scores than ever on standardized tests. A big reason for this success is that the TCI Approach is based on interactive learning. That means you won't just read about history. You'll be actively involved in experiencing it and recording what you learn. Now let's look at what you'll do during each part of a lesson with the TCI Approach.

History Alive! The Medieval World and Beyond has been carefully developed to provide the information and learning you need to succeed on state tests.

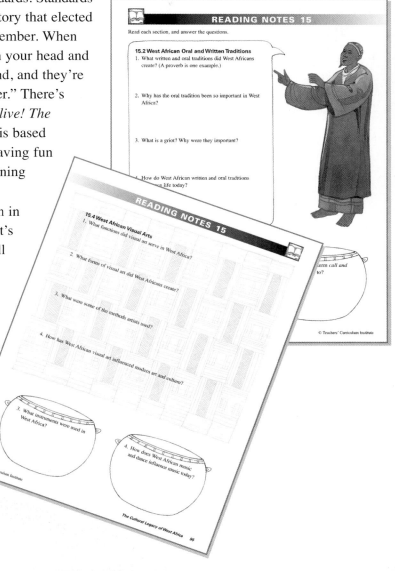

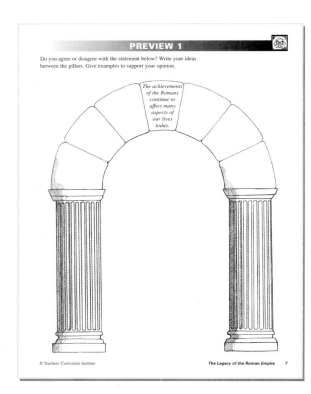

Do you agree or disagree with the statement below? Write your ideas between the pillars. Give examples to support your opinion.

The achievements of the Romans continue to affect many aspects of our lives today.

© Teachers' Curriculum Institute

The Legacy of the Roman Empire 7

Preview assignments like the one shown here help introduce you to new topics.

Preview Assignments

With the TCI Approach, learning starts even before you begin studying. Most of the lessons in *History Alive! The Medieval World and Beyond* begin with a Preview assignment. Previews are short assignments that you complete in your Interactive Student Notebook. They allow you to make a personal connection to what you will study.

After you complete a Preview assignment, your teacher will hold a brief class discussion. Several students will share their answers. Your teacher will then reveal how the assignment "previews" what is to come in the lesson.

Here are some examples of the kinds of Preview assignments you will complete:

- Before learning about the rise of the Byzantine Empire in Chapter 6, you will play a game exchanging colored tokens. You will compare your experience to the system of trade in the Byzantine city of Constantinople.

- Before learning about the influence of Islam on West Africa in Chapter 14, you will complete a spoke diagram. You will use the diagram to show ways your community has been influenced by cultures from other parts of the world.

- Before learning about China's foreign policies in Chapter 19, you will complete a T-chart on policies toward your neighbors. You will hear and note arguments for both sides.

- Before learning about the rise of Japan's warrior class in Chapter 22, you will examine a list of skills and knowledge for American soldiers. You will give your opinion about which are most important for their training.

Preview assignments like these will spark your interest and get you ready to tackle new concepts. Next come the exciting activities that make up the heart of each lesson. As you're about to see, these activities draw on many ways of being smart—our multiple intelligences.

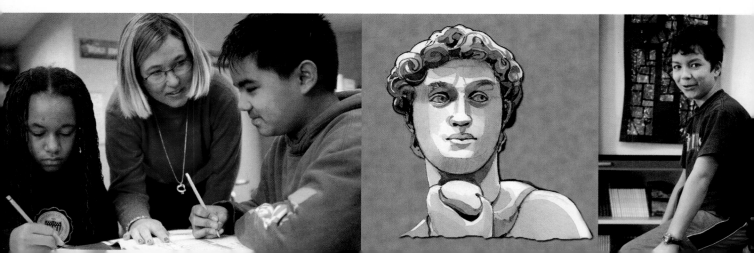

Multiple-Intelligence Teaching Strategies

The teaching strategies in the TCI Approach are based on hands-on learning. Every lesson in *History Alive! The Medieval World and Beyond* is built around a fun and exciting activity. We mentioned some examples earlier. Here are some other things you and your classmates will do to experience medieval history:

- For Chapter 3, you'll take a walking tour of medieval sites in Europe to see the influence of the Roman Catholic Church on daily life.
- For Chapter 16, you'll become Chinese government officials to debate how people are chosen to serve the emperor.
- For Chapter 27, you'll pretend to be museum curators designing exhibits on the achievements of the Maya, Aztecs, and Incas.

Activities like these will challenge you to use your multiple intelligences. Think about times when learning new things has been easier for you. Were you looking at pictures about the new ideas? Were you writing about them? Does acting out an event help you to better understand what happened? Studying history is a lot easier and more fun when you learn new ideas in ways that best suit your learning styles. Here is a list of the different intelligences:

- Linguistic (word smart)
- Logical-mathematical (number/reasoning smart)
- Spatial (picture smart)
- Body-kinesthetic (body smart)
- Musical (music smart)
- Interpersonal (people smart)
- Intrapersonal (self smart)

While you're engaged in fun and exciting activities, you'll also be reading this book to learn more about medieval history. The next page explains why this book is so easy to read.

Using your multiple intelligences helps you learn and remember what you study.

You'll use *History Alive! The Medieval World and Beyond* during classroom activities. You'll be turning to it over and over again to find the information you need to know.

Considerate Text

The TCI Approach is all about being successful and having fun while you learn. You're about to discover that *History Alive! The Medieval World and Beyond* is interesting to read and easy to understand. That's because this book is "reader friendly," which is another of saying that it makes readers want to read it. Some people call this *considerate text*. The writers of this book considered your needs as a reader and made sure you would have fun reading.

Here are some of the ways this book is considerate of all levels of readers:

- Each chapter is organized around key concepts. Introduction and summary sections point out the big ideas in the chapter.
- Each chapter begins with a graphic organizer—a picture that represents the main ideas of the chapter. The graphic organizer also appears in the Reading Notes in your Interactive Student Notebook. It will help you remember key ideas long after you've read the chapter.
- Short chapters make it easier for you to understand and remember what each one is about.
- Each section has a clear focus and a subtitle that provides an outline for your reading. Research shows that presenting new information in easy-to-manage chunks makes it easier to understand.
- Important new words are in bold type. These words are defined in the margins and in the Glossary at the back of the book.
- Photos and illustrations provide additional information about the topic on the page. A great way to check your understanding is to ask yourself, "How does this picture show what I just read?"

Most importantly, *History Alive! The Medieval World and Beyond* is as exciting to read as a good story. The next section explains a special way of taking notes that will help you remember what you read.

Graphically Organized Reading Notes

Note taking is very important in the TCI Approach. As you read this book, you'll complete Reading Notes in your Interactive Student Notebook. You'll answer important questions, find main ideas, and connect new ideas to what you already know.

You'll record key ideas on the Reading Notes pages in your Interactive Student Notebook. This will help you remember what you learned long after the lesson is over.

Your Reading Notes will leave you with a picture in your mind of each chapter's key ideas. The graphic organizers at the start of each chapter will be a visual reminder of what you read. In your Reading Notes, you'll use those same graphic organizers to help you record key ideas. For example, in Chapter 24, you'll be taking notes on a diagram of a Mexican flag. You will use the colors, sections, and symbols to show how the Aztecs created an empire. For Chapter 28, you will take notes around a flowering plant. The plant represents the roots and growth of the Renaissance. For Chapter 35, you'll use a picture of Enlightenment thinkers in an 18th-century French salon. You'll take notes about each thinker's ideas on sunrays that "shine" from their heads.

Completing your Reading Notes will help you study in two ways. First, it will encourage you to think carefully about what you read. Second, recording key ideas will help you remember them for a long time.

There's one more part of the TCI Approach that will help you remember the important ideas you are learning. Read the next page to find out.

PROCESSING 2

Think about which individuals or groups in our society are most similar to the various social classes in European feudal society. List those modern groups or individuals next to each level of feudal society, and draw symbols to represent them. Then list some of their similarities and differences.

Social Classes in Feudal Europe	Individuals or Groups in Our Society	Similarities and Differences Between These Two Groups
Monarch		Similarities: Differences:
Lords		Similarities: Differences:
Knights		Similarities: Differences:
Peasants		Similarities: Differences:

© Teachers' Curriculum Institute

In Processing assignments, you'll show that you understand the new ideas of the lesson.

Processing Assignments

At the end of each lesson, you'll complete a Processing assignment in your Interactive Student Notebook. Here you'll show that you understand the key concepts of the lesson.

These pages encourage you to relate ideas to one another. You'll make connections between the past and present. You'll show your understanding of concepts by creating illustrations, diagrams, flowcharts, poetry, and cartoons. As one student said, "It's really cool to have a place in our notebooks where we can record our own ideas. It makes learning history a lot more fun."

Here are some examples of the kinds of Processing assignments you'll complete:

- In Chapter 6, you will study important events, people, and places in the Byzantine Empire. In the Processing assignment, you will create a real estate advertisement to encourage people to move to Constantinople, the capital city of the empire.

- In Chapter 9, you will learn about the main beliefs and practices of Islam. In the Processing assignment, you'll write a newspaper story about a day in the life of a Muslim teenager.

- In Chapter 30, you will create a gallery of sculptures for key figures of the Renaissance. In the Processing assignment, you'll decide where to best seat each individual for a lively dinner party.

Students across the country report that their Processing assignments have helped them understand and remember what they have learned. As a result, they are earning higher test scores.

Multiple Intelligence Assessments

Do you dread taking chapter and unit tests? If so, maybe you feel that most tests don't let you show what you've learned. The tests for *History Alive! The Medieval World and Beyond* are different. They let you show how well you understand each lesson's key ideas.

These tests also allow you to use your multiple intelligences. Each test has some of the usual multiple-choice questions. These will help prepare you for taking more formal tests. But other parts of the assessments will challenge you to use more than just your "word smart" intelligence. They'll give you a chance to shine if you are good in other areas, such as reading maps, using charts and graphs, drawing, understanding music, or analyzing historical paintings. You may also be asked to show how well you read. You'll be invited to express your ideas and your understanding of historical events in writing, too.

The secret to doing well on tests is preparation. You have the perfect tool for this purpose: your Interactive Student Notebook. Right there on those pages are your notes about all the key ideas in each chapter. Students who study their Reading Notes and Processing assignments before a test usually earn good scores.

Success on tests is important, but the most important thing of all is learning. We've designed our tests to assess not just your understanding but to help you remember key ideas. That's because the lessons you learn from medieval history can help you make sense of your world and guide your future decisions. We hope that what you learn in *History Alive! The Medieval World and Beyond* will remain with you for years to come.

Your teacher may give you test pages to complete at the end of a lesson. These tests include questions with multiple-choice answers as well as questions that let you draw or write your answers.

UNIT 1

Europe During Medieval Times

UNIT 2

The Rise of Islam

UNIT 3

The Culture and Kingdoms of West Africa

UNIT 4

Imperial China

UNIT 5

Japan During Medieval Times

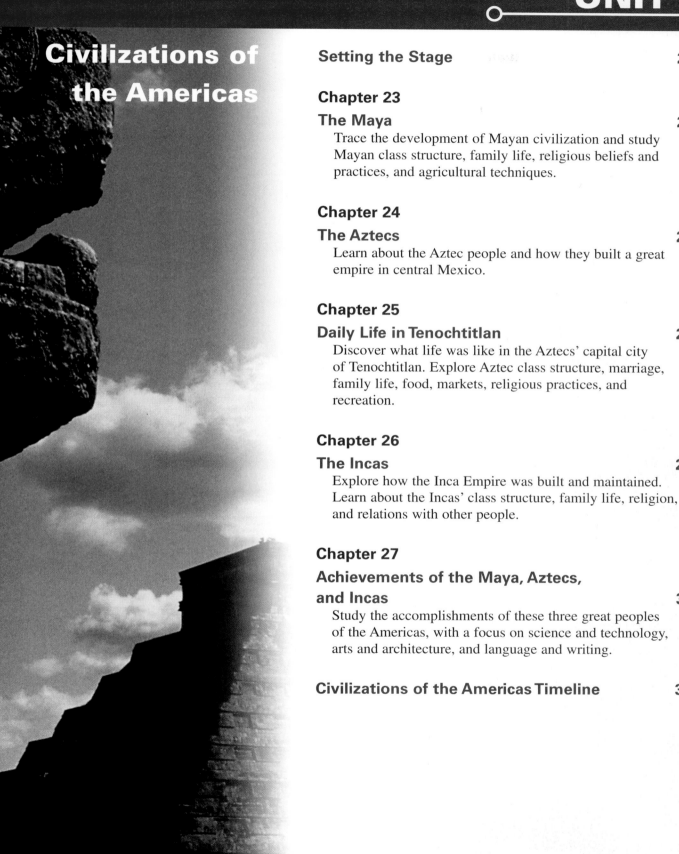

UNIT 6

Civilizations of the Americas

UNIT 7

Europe's Renaissance and Reformation

Europe Enters the Modern Age

Introduction

Welcome to *History Alive! The Medieval World and Beyond.* The word *medieval* refers to the period between ancient and modern times. In this book, you'll explore this period in Europe, Asia, Africa, and the Americas. You'll sometimes go beyond the medieval period to look at what happened before and after it.

Studying history involves figuring out what happened in the past, and why. People who study history are a lot like detectives. They ask questions and study clues. They form hypotheses, or educated guesses. Then they test their ideas against the evidence.

Many scholars study the past. Among these "history detectives" are archeologists and historians. Scholars like these are interested in much more than names and dates. They try to understand people's cultures and ways of life. They study values, beliefs, customs, political systems, and much more.

Archeologists study the distant past by examining objects that people left behind. These objects are called *artifacts.* They can include anything that people made or used. Some examples are clothing, tools, buildings, weapons, and coins. Clues like these can tell us a great deal about what cultures were like before they had written records.

Historians both record and interpret the past. They try to understand how events are connected by tracing their causes and effects. Historians are most interested in the last few thousand years, when people began leaving written records.

Historians use two types of sources to study the past. Primary sources come from the period being studied. Often they are written documents such as diaries, letters, and official records. Artifacts and works of art are also primary sources.

Secondary sources are materials that interpret primary sources. For instance, a historian might write someone's biography, or life story. To do so, the historian might use primary sources such as letters and diaries. The biography itself is a secondary source. Other people can learn useful things from the historian's work.

History is like a mystery that never ends. That's because scholars' ideas about the past change as they learn more. In this book, you'll join the history detectives in exploring the past. You'll study clues and weigh the evidence. You'll make and defend your own educated guesses. You'll see for yourself that history is very much alive!

UNIT 1

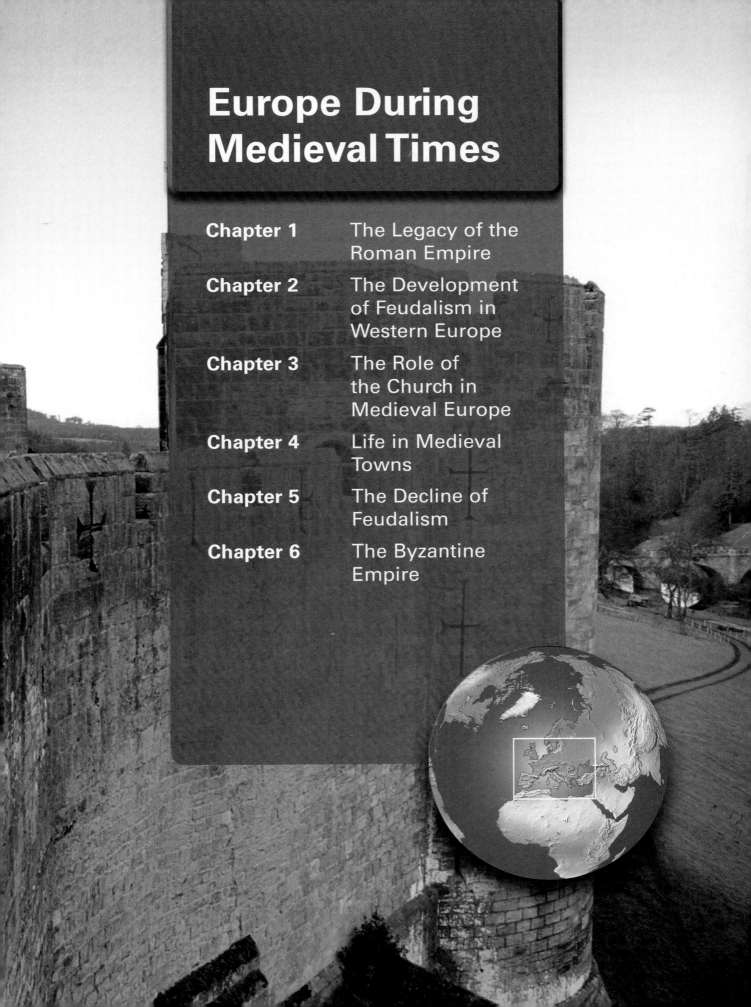

Europe During Medieval Times

Setting the Stage

Europe During Medieval Times

We will begin our study of the medieval world with the continent of Europe. Our study of this region will include England, the continent of Europe, and the Byzantine Empire (which straddled Europe and Asia).

Europe is bounded by seas and oceans and threaded with rivers. During medieval times, these waterways allowed people to travel more easily through Europe, but they also made settlements along coastal areas vulnerable to attack by invaders. Mountain ranges—like the Pyrenees, Alps, and Carpathian Mountains—helped protect settlements but also acted as barriers to travel and trade.

The period of time we call *medieval* began with the fall of the Roman Empire and lasted until about 1450 C.E. (C.E. means Common Era, and B.C.E. means Before the Common Era). Toward the end of this period, many Europeans felt they were living in a time of dramatic change. They began referring to the centuries since the fall of Rome as the Middle Ages. We still use this term today.

Historians divide the European Middle Ages into three periods:

- *Early Middle Ages*: From about 476 to 1000 C.E.
- *High Middle Ages*: From about 1000 to 1300 C.E.
- *Late Middle Ages*: From about 1300 to 1450 C.E.

Europe During Medieval Times

4

The Early Middle Ages began after the fall of the Roman Empire in the west. The Roman Empire had unified Europe. After the empire ended, western Europe fell into chaos. People spoke different languages and could not communicate as easily. Fewer travelers braved the ruined roads. Force became the law of the land. In the east, however, the Byzantine Empire survived Rome's fall.

By the start of the High Middle Ages, about 1000 C.E., life had become more stable. Many separate European kingdoms (such as England, France, the Papal States, and the Holy Roman Empire) had formed in the west.

During the High Middle Ages, most people in western Europe lived in the countryside under an economic and political system called *feudalism*. Under feudalism, a king (sometimes a queen) ruled the kingdom. The king granted land to nobles in exchange for military service. Peasants worked the land for the nobles.

The Late Middle Ages were a time of transition. Trade between the west and the east flourished once more, as it had under the Roman Empire. As a consequence, people in western Europe began moving from the countryside into towns. This led to many other changes.

Let's start our exploration of the Middle Ages with a close look at the Roman Empire. Why did it fall? What influence did it have on western civilization?

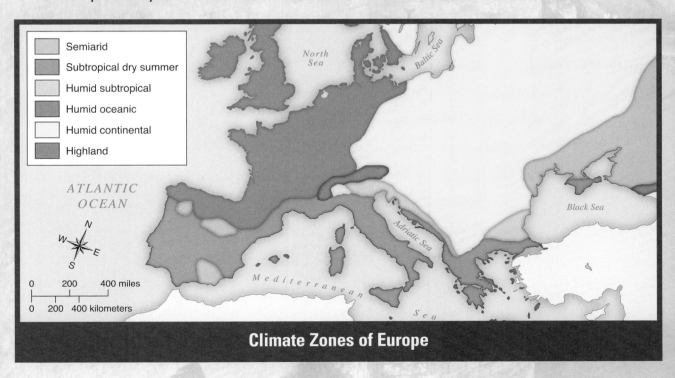

Climate Zones of Europe

Semiarid

Subtropical dry summer

Humid subtropical

Humid oceanic

Humid continental

Highland

ATLANTIC OCEAN

North Sea

Baltic Sea

Black Sea

Adriatic Sea

Mediterranean Sea

0   200   400 miles

0   200   400 kilometers

The oldest of ancient Rome's great roads, the Appian Way ran from Rome to southern Italy.

The Legacy of the Roman Empire

1.1 Introduction

"All roads lead to Rome" boasted the ancient Romans. For 500 years, from about 27 B.C.E. to 476 C.E., the city of Rome was the capital of the greatest empire the world had ever seen. Road markers for thousands of miles showed the distance to Rome. But more than roads connected the empire's 50 million people. They were also connected by Roman law, Roman customs, and Roman military might.

At its height, around 117 C.E., the **Roman Empire** spanned the whole of the Mediterranean world, from northern Africa to the Scottish border, from Spain to Syria. During this time, the Roman world was generally peaceful and prosperous. There was one official language and one code of law. Roman soldiers guarded the frontiers and kept order within the empire's boundaries. Proud Romans believed that the empire would last forever.

But the empire did not last. By the year 500, the western half of this great empire had collapsed. For historians, the fall of Rome marks the end of the ancient world and the beginning of the Middle Ages.

As one historian has written, "Rome perished, yet it lived on." The medieval world would pass on many aspects of Roman culture that still affect us today.

In this chapter, you will discover how and why the Roman Empire fell. Then you will learn how Rome's influence lives on in **art, architecture** and **engineering, language** and **writing,** and **philosophy, law,** and **citizenship**.

Use this drawing as a graphic organizer to help you explore Roman influences on modern life.

In 410 C.E., a Germanic tribe attacked Rome, the capital of the western part of the Roman Empire.

1.2 The End of the Roman Empire in the West

Rome's first emperor, Caesar Augustus, ended 100 years of civil war and expanded the boundaries of the empire. When he died in 14 C.E., few Romans could imagine that the empire would ever end. Yet by the year 500, the western half of the empire had collapsed. What caused the fall of the mighty Roman Empire?

Problems in the Late Empire

There was no single reason for the end of the Roman Empire. Instead, historians point to a number of problems that combined to bring about its fall.

Political instability. Rome never solved the problem of how to peacefully transfer political power to a new leader. When an emperor died, ambitious rivals with independent armies often fought each other for the emperor's crown.

Even when the transfer of power happened without fighting, there was no good system for choosing the next emperor. Often the Praetorian Guard, the emperor's private army, chose the new ruler. But they frequently chose leaders who would reward them rather than those who were best prepared to be emperor.

Economic and social problems. Besides political instability, the empire suffered from economic and social problems. To finance Rome's huge armies, its citizens had to pay heavy taxes. These taxes hurt the economy and drove many people into poverty. Trade also suffered.

For many people, unemployment was a serious problem. Wealthy families used slaves and cheap labor to work their large estates. Small farmers could not compete with the large landowners. They fled to the cities looking for work, but there were not enough jobs for everyone.

Other social problems plagued the empire, including growing corruption and a decline in the spirit of citizenship. Notorious emperors like Nero and Caligula wasted large amounts of money. A rise in crime made the empire's cities and roads unsafe.

Weakening frontiers. A final problem was the weakening of the empire's frontiers. The huge size of the empire made it hard to defend. It sometimes took weeks for leaders in Rome to communicate with generals. By the 300s C.E., Germanic tribes were pressing hard on the western borders of the empire. Many of these people settled inside the empire and were recruited into the army. But these soldiers had little loyalty to Rome.

The Fall of Rome   In 330 C.E., the emperor Constantine took a step that changed the future of Rome. He moved his capital 850 miles to the east, to the ancient city of Byzantium. He renamed the city New Rome. Later it was called Constantinople. (Today it is known as Istanbul, Turkey.)

After Constantine's reign, power over the vast empire was usually divided between two emperors, one based in Rome and one in Constantinople. Rome became the capital of just the western part of the empire.

The emperors in Rome soon found themselves threatened by invading Germanic tribes. In 410 C.E., one of these tribes attacked and looted Rome itself. Finally, in 476, the last emperor in the west was driven from his throne. The western half of the empire began to dissolve into separate kingdoms ruled by different tribes.

In the east, the empire continued for another 1,000 years. Today we call this eastern empire the Byzantine Empire, after Byzantium, the original name of its capital city. You will learn more about the Byzantine Empire in Chapter 6.

In western Europe, Rome's fall did not mean the end of Roman civilization. The influence of Rome lived on through the medieval period and all the way to our time. As you read about the legacy of the Romans, think about how ideas and events from the distant past still affect us today.

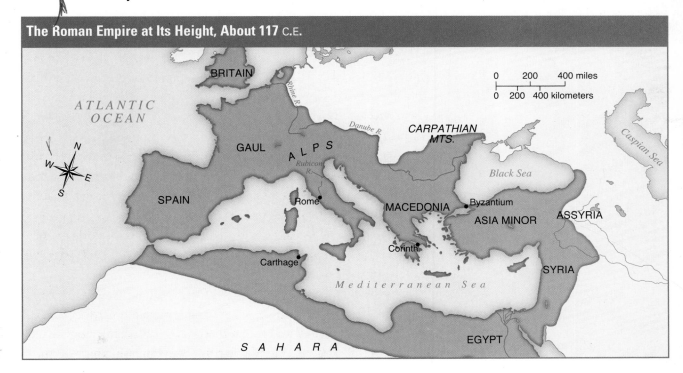

The Roman Empire at Its Height, About 117 C.E.

1.3 The Legacy of Roman Art

The Romans adopted many aspects of other cultures and blended them into their own culture. This was true of Roman art. The Romans were especially influenced by the art of the Greeks. In fact, historians often speak of "Greco-Roman" art. Rome played a vital role in passing on this tradition, which has had a major influence on western art.

The Romans added their own talents and tastes to what they learned from other cultures. For example, they imitated Greek sculpture, but Roman sculptors were particularly good at making lifelike busts and statues.

Romans were also great patrons (sponsors) of art. Wealthy families decorated their homes with statues and colorful **murals** and **mosaics.** Roman artists were especially skilled in painting **frescoes,** scenes painted on the moist plaster of walls or ceilings with water-based paints. Roman frescoes often showed three-dimensional landscapes. Looking at one of these frescoes was almost like looking through the wall at a view outside. You've probably seen similar murals in restaurants, banks, and other buildings.

American artists have often adopted a Roman style to add nobility to sculptures and paintings of heroes. Shown here is a Roman statue of the emperor Augustus and an American statue of George Washington. In what ways are they alike?

The Romans also brought a sense of style and luxury to everyday objects. For example, they made highly decorative bottles of blown glass. A bottle for wine might be made in the shape of a cluster of grapes. They also developed the arts of gem cutting and metalworking. One popular art form was the cameo. A cameo is a carved decoration showing a portrait or a scene. The Romans wore cameos as jewelry and used them to decorate vases and other objects. You can find examples of all these art forms today.

A thousand years after the fall of the empire, Roman art was redis-covered during the period called the Renaissance. You will learn about this time in Unit 7. Great artists like Michelangelo revived the Greco-Roman style in their paintings and sculptures.

A good example is the famous ceiling of the Sistine Chapel in Rome. Painted by Michelangelo in the 1500s, the ceiling shows scenes from the Bible. A Roman would feel right at home looking up at this amaz-ing creation. Tourists still flock to Rome to see it.

Roman art has continued to influence painters and sculptors. Roman styles were especially popular during the early days of the United States. Americans imitated these styles to give their art dignity and nobility. Today you can see a number of statues in Washington, D.C., that reflect a strong Roman influence.

Mosaics, such as this one from Pompeii, decorated the walls of wealthy Roman homes. They often showed scenes of Roman life.

1.4 The Legacy of Roman Architecture and Engineering

The Romans were skilled and clever builders. In their architecture and engineering, they borrowed ideas from the Greeks and other peoples. But the Romans improved on these ideas in ways that future engineers and architects would imitate.

Architecture   The Romans learned how to use the arch, the vault, and the dome to build huge structures. A **vault** is an arch used for a ceiling or to support a ceiling or roof. A **dome** is a vault in the shape of a half-circle that rests on a circular wall.

Roman baths and other public buildings often had great arched vaults. The Pantheon, a magnificent temple that still stands in Rome, is famous for its huge dome. The Romans used concrete to help them build much bigger arches than anyone had attempted before. Concrete is made by mixing broken stone with sand, cement, and water and allowing the mixture to harden. The Romans did not invent the material, but they were the first to make widespread use of it.

The Romans also invented a new kind of stadium. These large, open-air structures seated thousands of spectators. The Romans used concrete to build tunnels into the famous stadium in Rome, the Colosseum. The tunnels made it easy for spectators to reach their seats. Modern football stadiums still use this feature.

The grand style of Roman buildings has inspired many architects through the centuries. Medieval architects, for example, frequently imitated Roman designs, especially in building great churches and **cathedrals**. You can also see a Roman influence in the design of many modern churches, banks, and government buildings. A fine example is the Capitol building, the home of the U.S. Congress in Washington, D.C.

Another Roman innovation that has been widely copied is the triumphal arch. This is a huge monument built to celebrate great victories or achievements. A famous example is the Arc de Triomphe (Arch of Triumph) in Paris, France. This monument

vault an arched structure used to hold up a ceiling or a roof
dome a roof shaped like a half-circle or hemisphere
cathedral a large and important church

The Pantheon still stands in Rome as an immense tribute to the legacies of Roman architecture.

The ruins of the Roman Colosseum, where gladiators fought for the entertainment of spectators, still stand in Rome today.

celebrates the victories of the French emperor Napoleon in the early 1800s. Today it is the national war memorial of France.

Engineering   The Romans changed engineering as well as architecture. They were the greatest builders of roads, bridges, and **aqueducts** in the ancient world.

More than 50,000 miles of road connected Rome with the frontiers of the empire. The Romans built their roads with layers of stone, sand, and gravel. Their techniques set the standard of road building for 2,000 years. Cars in some parts of Europe still drive on freeways built over old Roman roads.

The Romans also set a new standard for building aqueducts. They created a system of aqueducts for Rome that brought water from about 60 miles away to the homes of the city's wealthiest citizens, as well as to its public baths and fountains. The Romans built aqueducts in other parts of the empire as well. The water system in Segovia, Spain, still uses part of an ancient Roman aqueduct. Roman arches from aqueducts can still be found in Europe, North Africa, and western Asia.

aqueduct a pipe or channel built to carry water between distant places

What features of Roman architecture can you spot in the U.S. Capitol building?

Romans wrote in all capital letters, as seen on this Roman distance marker from 217 C.E.

1.5 The Legacy of Roman Language and Writing

An especially important legacy of Rome for people in medieval times was the Romans' language, Latin. After the fall of the empire, Latin continued to be used by scholars and the Roman Catholic Church. Church **scribes** used Latin to record important documents. Educated European nobles learned Latin so they could communicate with their peers in other countries.

Latin remains extremely influential today. Several modern European languages developed from Latin, including Italian, Spanish, and French. English is a Germanic language, but it was strongly influenced by the French-speaking Normans, who conquered England in 1066 C.E. English has borrowed heavily from Latin, both directly and by way of French. In fact, we still use the Latin alphabet, although Latin has 23 letters and English has 26.

You can see the influence of Latin on many of the words we use today. For example, our calendar comes from the one adopted by the Roman ruler Julius Caesar. The names of several months come from Latin. *August* honors Caesar Augustus. *September* comes from Latin words meaning "the seventh month." (The Roman new year started in March, so September was the seventh month.) *October* means "the eighth month." Can you guess the meanings of *November* and *December*?

scribe a person trained to write or copy documents by hand

Many English words start with Latin prefixes. A prefix is a combination of letters at the beginning of a word that carries its own meaning. Attaching a prefix to a root word creates a new word with a new meaning. In fact, the word *prefix* was formed this way. It comes from *pre* ("in front of") and *fix* ("fasten" or "attach"). The chart below on the right shows other examples.

As you can see from the chart below on the left, other English words come from Latin root words. For instance, *manual* and *manipulate* are derived from the Latin word *manus,* meaning "hand."

Even Latin **proverbs** are still in use. For example, look at the reverse side of a U.S. penny. There you'll see the U.S. motto *E pluribus unum* ("Out of many, one").

Finally, we still use Roman numerals. The Romans used a system of letters to write numbers. The Roman numerals I, V, X, L, C, D, and M represent 1, 5, 10, 50, 100, 500, and 1,000 in the Roman number system. You may have seen Roman numerals used on clocks, sundials, and the first pages of books. You might also spot Roman numerals on buildings and in some movie credits to show the year in which they were made.

proverb a popular saying that is meant to express something wise or true

Latin Roots Used in English Words		
Latin Root	**Meaning**	**English Word**
anima	life, breath, soul	animal
civis	citizen, community	civic
lex, legalis	law, legal	legislature
manus	hand	manual
militare	to serve as a soldier	military
portare	to carry	portable
unus	one	united
urbs	city	suburb
verbum	word	verbal

Latin Prefixes Used in English Words		
Latin Prefix	**Meaning**	**English Word(s)**
in, im, il	not	inactive, impossible, illogical
inter	among, between	international
com, co	together, with	communicate, cooperate
pre	before	precede
post	after, behind	postpone
re	back, again	remember
semi	half	semicircle
sub	under, less than, inferior to	submarine
trans	across, through	transportation

1.6 The Legacy of Roman Philosophy, Law, and Citizenship

Roman **philosophy,** law, and ideas about citizenship were greatly influenced by the Greeks. But the Romans made contributions of their own that they passed on to future generations.

A Philosophy Called Stoicism   A Greek school of thought that became especially popular in Rome was Stoicism. Many upper-class Romans adopted this philosophy and made it their own.

Stoics believed that a divine (godly) intelligence ruled all of nature. A person's soul was a spark of that divine intelligence. "Living rightly" meant living in a way that agreed with nature.

To the Stoics, the one truly good thing in life was to have a good character. This meant having virtues such as self-control and courage. Stoics prized duty and the welfare of the community over their personal comfort. Roman Stoics were famous for bearing pain and suffering bravely and quietly. To this day, we call someone who behaves this way "stoic."

The emperor Marcus Aurelius was a devoted Stoic. He wrote about his philosophy of life in a book called *Meditations*. Many people are still inspired by the ideas in this book.

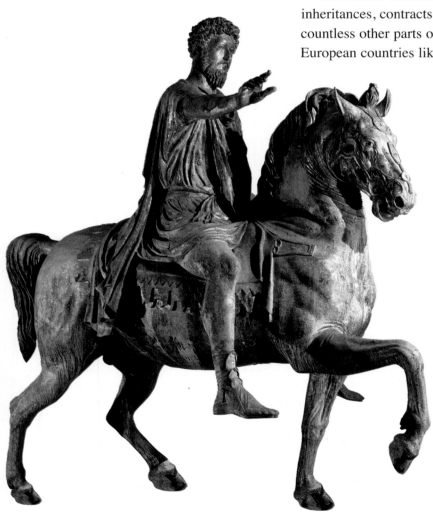

Law and Justice   Roman law covered marriages, inheritances, contracts (agreements) between people, and countless other parts of daily life. Modern legal codes in European countries like France and Italy are based in part on ancient Roman laws.

Another legacy of the Romans was the Roman idea of justice. The Romans believed that there was a universal law of justice that came from nature. By this natural law, every person had rights. Judges in Roman courts tried to make just, or fair, decisions that respected people's rights.

Like people everywhere, the Romans did not always live up to their ideals. Their courts did not treat the poor or slaves as equal to the rich. Emperors often made laws simply because they had the power to do so. But the ideals of Roman law and justice live on. For example, the ideas of natural law and natural rights are echoed in the Declaration of Independence. Modern-day judges, like judges in Roman courts, often

make decisions based on ideals of justice as well as on written law. Similarly, many people around the world believe that all humans have basic rights that no written law can take away.

Citizenship   When Rome first began expanding its power in Italy, to be a "Roman" was to be a citizen of the city-state of Rome. Over time, however, Rome's leaders gradually extended citizenship to all free people in the empire. Even someone born in Syria or Gaul (modern-day France) could claim to be a Roman. All citizens were subject to Roman law, enjoyed the same rights, and owed allegiance (loyalty) to the emperor.

The idea of citizenship as both a privilege and a responsibility has descended from Roman times to our own. While most people in the United States are citizens by birth, many immigrants become citizens by solemnly promising loyalty to the United States. Regardless of where they were born, all citizens have the same responsibilities. For example, they must obey the law. And all enjoy the same basic rights spelled out in the Constitution and its amendments, including the Bill of Rights.

U.S. citizens enjoy the right to vote thanks to the ideas of citizenship that began in Roman times.

1.7 Chapter Summary

In this chapter, you explored the rich legacy of ancient Rome. The Roman Empire fell more than 1,500 years ago, but it left a lasting mark on western civilization. We can see Rome's influence today in our art, architecture and engineering, language and writing, philosophy, law, and ideas about citizenship. In the next chapter, we'll look at the society that developed in western Europe in the centuries after Rome's fall.

CHAPTER 2

◀ This page from an illuminated manuscript shows a typical day on a feudal manor.

The Development of Feudalism in Western Europe

2.1 Introduction

In the last chapter, you learned about the rich legacy of the Roman Empire. The fall of the Roman Empire in 476 C.E. marks the beginning of the Middle Ages. In this chapter, you will learn about the system of **feudalism** that developed in Europe during the Middle Ages.

Recall that historians divide the Middle Ages into three periods. The Early Middle Ages lasted from about 476 to 1000 C.E. The High Middle Ages lasted from about 1000 to 1300. The Late Middle Ages lasted from about 1300 to 1450.

The Early Middle Ages began with the fall of Rome. The Roman Empire had unified much of Europe for about 500 years. After the empire collapsed, life was dangerous and difficult in western Europe. People worked hard simply to survive and to have enough to eat. They also needed to protect themselves from conquest by invading barbarians and nearby kingdoms.

These challenges gave rise to the economic and political system historians call *feudalism*. In the feudal system, people pledged loyalty to a **lord**—a ruler or a powerful landholder. In return, they received protection from the lord. **Knights,** or armed warriors, fought on behalf of their lords. **Peasants** worked the land. At the bottom of the system were serfs, peasants who were not free to leave the lord's land.

In this chapter, you will learn more about the difficulties people faced during the Early Middle Ages. Then you will learn about the rise of feudalism. Finally, you will explore what daily life was like for people living under feudalism.

Use this illustration as a graphic organizer to help you understand the system of feudalism.

In 800 C.E., Charlemagne was crowned Holy Roman emperor by Pope Leo III.

2.2 Western Europe During the Middle Ages

For 500 years, much of Europe was part of the Roman Empire. The rest of the continent was controlled by groups of people that the Romans called **barbarians**. When Rome fell to invading barbarians in 476 C.E., Europe was left with no central government or system of defense. Many invading groups set up kingdoms throughout western Europe. These kingdoms were often at war with one another. The most powerful rulers were those who controlled the most land and had the best warriors.

Charlemagne's Empire One powerful group during this time was the Franks (from whom modern-day France takes its name). The Franks were successful because they had developed a new style of warfare. It depended on troops of knights, heavily armed warriors who fought on horseback. To get and hold power, a ruler needed the services and loyalty of many knights. In return for their loyalty and service, the ruler rewarded knights with land and privileges.

One of the early leaders of the Franks was an ambitious young warrior named Clovis. In 481 C.E., at the age of 15, Clovis became king of the Franks. Five years later, he defeated the last great Roman army in Gaul. During his 30-year reign, he led the Franks in wars that widened the boundaries of the Frankish kingdom.

Clovis also helped lead the Franks into **Christianity**. Clovis married a Christian woman, Clotilda, and eventually was baptized into the **Roman Catholic Church**. Many of his followers became Christians as well.

The most important leader of the Franks was Charlemagne (Charles the Great). This impressive king ruled for over 40 years, from 768 to 814. Writings from that period say that he was six feet four inches tall—extremely tall for his time—and "always stately and dignified." Legend has it that he read very little and couldn't write, yet he loved to have scholarly works read to him. He encouraged education and scholarship, making his court a center of culture. Most important, he unified nearly all the Christian lands of Europe into a single empire. One of the poets at his court called him the "King Father of Europe."

Charlemagne built his empire with the help of a **pope**—Leo III, the leader of the Catholic Church in Rome. As you will learn in the next chapter, the church was a central part of society during this time. For Charlemagne, the blessing of the church sent the message "God is on my side." For his part, Leo needed the support of someone with an army. In return for Charlemagne's help, the pope crowned him Holy Roman emperor in 800 C.E.

Charlemagne's empire survived many barbarian attacks. After his death in 814, however, it quickly fell apart. The weak rulers who followed him could not defend the empire against new waves of invasions. Still, these kings helped prepare the way for feudalism by following Charlemagne's example of rewarding knights with land and privileges in return for military service.

A Need for Order and Protection   In the 9th and 10th centuries, western Europe was threatened by three main groups. Muslims, or followers of the religion of Islam, advanced from the Near East and northern Africa into what is now Spain. Magyars, a central Asian people, pressed in from the east. And Vikings swept down from present-day Norway and Denmark.

The Vikings were fierce warriors who struck fear into the people of Europe. At times their intent was to set up colonies. But they were best known for their terrifying raids on towns and villages.

Imagine a Viking attack. The people of the village are at early morning church services when an alarm

A fleet of Viking ships attacked the walled city of Paris in 885 C.E.

bell starts to peal. Vikings! Long, shallow wooden boats have brought the Vikings close to shore. Now they leave their boats and run toward the town with swords and axes raised over their heads. People are running in all directions. Several villagers who try to resist are killed. Others are seized by the Viking raiders and taken back to the ships.

Clearly, the people of western Europe needed ways to defend themselves. To protect themselves and their property, they gradually developed the system we call *feudalism*. Let's find out how it worked.

Knights fought on foot and horseback to defend their king's castle and land.

2.3 Feudalism: Establishing Order

By the High Middle Ages (about 1000 C.E.), Europeans had developed the system of feudalism. The feudal system provided people with protection and safety by establishing a stable social order.

Under this system, people were bound to one another by promises of loyalty. In theory, all the land in the kingdom belonged to the **monarch** (usually a king but sometimes a queen). A great deal of land was also owned by the church. The king kept some land for himself and gave **fiefs,** or grants of land, to his most important lords, who became his vassals. In return, each lord promised to supply the king with knights in times of war. A lord then enlisted lesser lords and knights as *his* vassals. Often these arrangements were written down. Many of these contracts survive to this day in museums.

At the bottom of the social system were peasants. Lords rented some of their land to peasants who worked for them. Some peasants, called *serfs,* were "tied" to the land they worked. They could not leave the lord's land, and they had to farm his fields in exchange for a small plot of land of their own.

Most lords and wealthier knights lived on **manors,** or large estates. A manor included a castle or manor house, one or more villages, and the surrounding farmland. Manors were in the country, far from towns. That meant the peasants had to produce everything the people on the manor needed. Only a few goods came from outside the manor, such as salt for preserving meat, and iron for making tools.

During the Middle Ages, people were born into a social class for life. They had the same social position, and often the same job, as their parents. Let's take a closer look at the classes in feudal society.

monarch a ruler, such as a king or queen
fief land granted by a lord to a vassal in exchange for loyalty and service
manor a large estate, including farmland and villages, held by a lord

2.4 Monarchs During Feudal Times

At the very top of feudal society were the monarchs, or kings and queens. As you have learned, medieval monarchs were feudal lords. They were expected to keep order and to provide protection for their vassals.

Most medieval monarchs believed in the **divine right of kings,** the idea that God had given them the right to rule. In reality, the power of monarchs varied greatly. Some had to work hard to maintain control of their kingdoms. Few had enough wealth to keep their own army. They had to rely on their vassals, especially **nobles,** to provide enough knights and soldiers. In some places, especially during the Early Middle Ages, great lords grew very powerful and governed their fiefs as independent states. In these cases, the monarch was little more than a figurehead, a symbolic ruler who had little real power.

In England, monarchs became quite strong during the Middle Ages. Since the Roman period, a number of groups from the continent, including Vikings, had invaded and settled England. By the mid–11th century, it was ruled by a Germanic tribe called the Saxons. The king at that time was descended from both Saxon and Norman (French) families. When he died without an adult heir, there was confusion over who should become king.

William, the powerful **Duke** of Normandy (a part of present-day France), believed he had the right to the English throne. But the English crowned his cousin, Harold. In 1066, William and his army invaded England. William defeated Harold at the Battle of Hastings and established a line of Norman kings in England. His triumph earned him the nickname William the Conqueror.

When William conquered England, he brought feudal institutions from Europe with him. Supported by feudalism, strong rulers brought order to England. In fact, by the start of the High Middle Ages, around 1000 C.E., the feudal system had brought stability to much of Europe. Let's take a closer look at what daily life was like for people during this time.

divine right of kings the belief that God gives monarchs the right to rule

noble a person of high rank by birth or title

duke the highest type of European noble, ranking just below a prince

William, Duke of Normandy, depicted on the French tapestry below, became known as William the Conqueror after he seized the English throne.

2.5 Lords and Ladies During Feudal Times

Like monarchs, lords and ladies were members of the nobility, the highest-ranking class in medieval society. Most lived on manors. Some lords had one manor, while others had several. Those who had more than one manor usually lived in one for a few months and then traveled with their families to the next.

Lords and ladies were served elaborate meals at feasts, or banquets. Often musicians and jesters entertained them while they ate.

Manor Houses and Castles

Many of the people on a manor lived with the lord's family in the main house, or manor house. Built of wood or stone, manor houses were surrounded by gardens and outbuildings, such as stables. They were protected by high walls and, sometimes, a **moat**.

The manor house was the center of the community. In times of trouble, villagers entered its walls for protection. Its great hall served as the manor court. It was also a place for special celebrations and feasts, such as those given at Christmas or after a harvest.

Kings and queens, high-ranking nobles, and wealthy lords lived in even grander structures: castles. Castles were built for many purposes. One of a castle's main functions was to serve as a home. Castles were also one of the most important forms of military technology. With their moats and strong walls and gates, they were built to provide protection for those who lived in them. Finally, their large size and central locations made castles strong visual reminders of the **hierarchy** within a kingdom and the strict barriers between classes.

The earliest medieval castles were built of wood and surrounded by high wooden fences. The strongest part, the *motte,* was built on a hilltop. A walled path linked the motte to a lower enclosed court, the *bailey,* where most people lived. After about 1100 C.E., most castles were built of stone to resist attacks by flaming arrows and stronger siege weapons.

Castles gradually became more elaborate. Many had tall towers for looking out across the land. The main castle building had a variety of rooms, including storerooms, a library, a dining hall, bedrooms for distinguished guests, and the lord and lady's quarters.

moat a deep, wide ditch, often filled with water

hierarchy a system of organizing people into ranks, with those of higher rank having more power and privileges

The Responsibilities and Daily Life of Lords and Ladies

It was the lord's responsibility to manage and defend his land and the people who worked it. The lord appointed officials to make sure villagers carried out their duties, which included farming the lord's land and paying rent in the form of crops. Lords also acted as judges in manor courts and had the power to fine and punish those who broke the law. Some lords held posts in the king's government. In times of war, lords fought for their own higher-ranking lords or at least supplied them with a well-trained fighting force.

In theory, only men were part of the feudal relationship between lord and vassal. However, it was quite common in the Middle Ages for noblewomen to hold fiefs and inherit land. Except for fighting, these women had all the duties that lords had. They ran their estates, sat as judges in manor courts, and sent their knights to serve in times of war.

Noblewomen who weren't landowners were still extremely busy. They were responsible for raising and training their children and sometimes the children of other noble families. Ladies were also responsible for overseeing their household or households. Some households had hundreds of people, including priests, master hunters, and knights-in-training called *pages* and *squires,* who assisted the knights. There were also cooks, servants, artists, craftspeople, and grooms. Entertainment was provided by musicians and jesters ("fools" who performed amusing jokes and stunts).

When they weren't hard at work, lords and ladies enjoyed hunting and hawking (hunting with birds), feasting and dancing, board games such as chess, and reading. Ladies also did fine embroidery, or decorative sewing.

Although nobles and monarchs had the most privileged life in medieval times, their lives were not always easy or comfortable. Lit only by candles and warmed by open fires, manor homes and castles could be gloomy and cold. There was little or no privacy. Fleas and lice infected all medieval buildings. People generally bathed only once a week, if that. Clothes were not washed daily either. Diseases affected the rich as well as the poor. And, of course, war was a great and ever-present danger.

A lady had servants to help her with her personal needs as well as the care of her large household.

2.6 Knights During Feudal Times

Knights were the mounted soldiers of the medieval world. In general, knights had to have some wealth, as a full suit of **armor** and a horse cost a small fortune. Knights were usually vassals of more powerful lords.

Becoming a Knight The path to becoming a knight involved many years of training. A boy started as a page, or servant. At the age of seven, he left home and went to live at the castle of a lord, who was often a relative. Nearly all wealthy lords had several pages living in their castle. A page learned how to ride a horse and received religious instruction from the local priest or friar.

During this first stage of training, pages spent much of their time with the ladies of the castle. They were expected to help the ladies in every way possible. The ladies taught pages how to sing, dance, compose music, and play the harp. These skills were valued in knights.

After about seven years as a page, a young boy became a squire. During this part of his training, he spent most of his time with the knight who was his lord. He polished the knight's armor, sword, shield, and lance. He helped care for his horse. He even waited on him at mealtime, carrying water for hand washing, carving meat, and filling his cup when it was empty.

Most importantly, squires trained to become warriors. They learned how to fight with a sword and a lance, a kind of spear that measured up to 15 feet long. They also learned how to use a battle-ax and a mace (a club with a heavy metal head). They practiced by fighting in make-believe battles. But squires also went into real battles. A squire was expected to help dress his lord in armor, follow him into battle, and look after him if he was wounded.

In his early 20s, if he was deserving, a squire became a knight. Becoming a knight could be a complex religious event. A squire often spent the night before his knighting in prayer. The next morning, he bathed and put on a white tunic, or long shirt, to show his purity. During the ceremony, he knelt before his lord and said his vows. The lord drew his sword, touched the knight-to-be lightly on each shoulder with

armor a covering, usually made of metal or leather, worn to protect the body during fighting

Before a joust or tournament, knights received gifts, or tokens of support, from the ladies of the manor.

Knights in a joust tried to knock each other off their horses.

the flat side of the blade, and knighted him. Sometimes, if a squire did particularly well in battle, he was knighted on the spot.

The Responsibilities and Daily Life of Knights Being a knight was more than a profession. It was a way of life. Knights lived by a strong code of behavior called **chivalry**. (*Chivalry* comes from the French word *cheval,* meaning "horse.") Knights were expected to be loyal to their church and their lord, to be just and fair, and to protect the helpless. They performed acts of gallantry, or respect paid to women. From these acts, we get the modern idea of chivalry as traditional forms of courtesy and kindness toward women.

Jousts and tournaments were a major part of a knight's life. In a joust, two armed knights on horseback galloped at each other with their lances held straight out. The idea was to unseat the opponent from his horse. Jousts could be done as a sport, for exercise, or as a serious battle. A tournament involved a team of knights in one-on-one battle.

Knights fought wearing heavy suits of armor. In the 11th century, armor was made of metal rings linked together. By the 14th century, plate armor was more common and offered better protection.

The institution of knighthood lasted until about the 17th century, when warfare changed with the growing use of gunpowder and cannons. Knights, who fought one-to-one on horseback, were no longer effective.

Next let's turn to daily life for the vast majority of the medieval population: the peasants.

chivalry the medieval knight's code of ideal behavior, including bravery, loyalty, and respect for women

2.7 Peasants During Feudal Times

Most people during the Middle Ages were peasants. They were not part of the feudal relationship of vassal and lord, but they supported the entire feudal structure by working the land. Their labor freed lords and knights to spend their time preparing for war or fighting.

During medieval times, peasants were legally classified as free or unfree. These categories had to do with how much service was owed to the lord. Free peasants rented land to farm and owed only their rent to the lord. Unfree peasants, called *serfs,* farmed the lord's fields and could not leave the lord's estate. In return for their labor, they received a small plot of land of their own to farm.

The daily life of peasants revolved around work. Most peasants raised crops and tended livestock (farm animals). But every manor also had carpenters, shoemakers, smiths (metalworkers), and other skilled workers. Peasant women worked in the fields when they were needed. They also cared for their children and their homes.

In addition to the work they performed, serfs owed the lord numerous taxes. There was a yearly payment called "head money," which was a fixed amount per person. The lord could also demand a tax known as

Men and women worked side by side in the fields.

tallage whenever he needed money. When a woman married, she, her father, or her husband had to pay a fee called a *merchet*.

Serfs were also required to grind their grain at the lord's mill (the only mill in the village). The miller kept portions of the grain for the lord and for himself. Lords could keep any amount they wanted. Serfs found this practice so hateful that some of them hid small hand mills in their houses.

Most peasants lived in small houses of one or two rooms. A typical house was made of woven strips of wood covered with straw or mud. Peasants had little furniture or other possessions. There was a hearth fire in the middle of the main room, but often no chimney, so it was dark and smoky inside. An entire family might eat and sleep in one room that sometimes also housed their farm animals.

Peasants ate vegetables, meat such as pork, and dark, coarse bread made of wheat mixed with rye or oatmeal. During the winter, they ate meat and fish that had been preserved in salt. Herbs were used widely, in part for flavor and in part to lessen the taste of the salt or to disguise the taste of meat that was no longer fresh.

Peasants' homes were small and crowded with people and animals.

2.8 Chapter Summary

In this chapter, you learned about life during feudal times. The fall of the Roman Empire led to a time of uncertainty and danger. The feudal system arose as a way of protecting property. It was based on oaths of loyalty. Kings and queens gave fiefs, or grants of land, to lords, their most important vassals. In exchange, lords promised to supply monarchs with knights in times of war. At the bottom of the social structure were peasants.

Daily life was quite different for the various social classes. Monarchs, lords, and ladies oversaw their lands and the people who worked them. They lived in manor homes or castles. Knights were the soldiers of the medieval world. They were skilled warriors who went through years of training. Peasants labored to farm the land and to make most of the necessary articles of life.

One common link for people in western Europe during the Middle Ages was the Catholic Church. In the next chapter, you'll learn more about the church and explore its impact on the medieval world.

CHAPTER 3

The Role of the Church in Medieval Europe

3.1 Introduction

In the last chapter, you learned about the rise of feudalism in western Europe. In this chapter, you will explore the influence of the **Roman Catholic Church** during the High Middle Ages, from about 1000 to 1300 C.E.

The church was the **center of medieval life** in western Europe. Almost every village and town had a church building. Larger towns and cities had a cathedral. Church bells rang out the hours, called people to worship, and warned of danger.

The church building was the center of community activity. Religious services were held several times a day. Town meetings, plays, and concerts were also held in churches. Merchants had shops around the square in front of the church. Farmers sold their produce in the square. Markets, festivals, and fairs were all held in the shadow of the church's spires (towers).

During the Middle Ages, the church provided education for some, and it helped the poor and sick. The church was a daily presence throughout a person's life, from birth to death. In fact, religion was so much a part of daily life that people determined the proper time to cook eggs by saying a certain number of prayers!

People also looked to the church to explain world events. Storms, disease, and famine were thought to be punishments sent by God. People hoped prayer and religious devotion would keep away such disasters. They were even more concerned about the fate of their souls after death. The church taught that salvation, or the saving of a person's soul, would come to those who followed the church's teachings.

Christian belief was so widespread during this time that historians sometimes call the Middle Ages the "Age of Faith." It's no wonder that the church's power rivaled that of kings and queens.

In this chapter, you'll learn how the church began and how it grew. Then you'll discover how the church affected people's daily lives during the High Middle Ages.

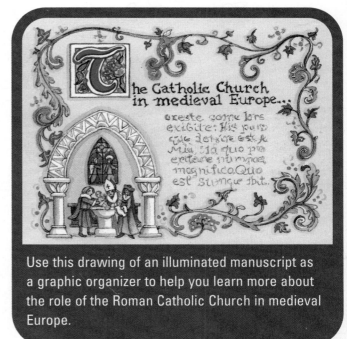

Use this drawing of an illuminated manuscript as a graphic organizer to help you learn more about the role of the Roman Catholic Church in medieval Europe.

The pope was the most powerful official of the Roman Catholic Church. This painting of the procession of Pope Lucius III was created in the year 1183 and shows the pope, cardinals, archbishops, bishops, and priests in their various garments and levels of finery.

3.2 The Christian Church Takes Shape

The Christian religion is one of the most important legacies of ancient Rome. Christians are followers of Jesus, who, according to Christian Scripture, was put to death on a Roman cross in the first century C.E. Christians believe that Jesus was the son of God, that God sent him to Earth to save people from their sins, and that he rose from the dead after his crucifixion.

Initially, the Romans **persecuted** Christians for their beliefs. Yet the new religion continued to spread. In 313 C.E., the emperor Constantine issued a decree that allowed Christians to practice their religion freely. In 395 C.E., Christianity became the recognized religion of the Roman Empire.

At the start of the Middle Ages, all Christians in western Europe belonged to a single church, which became known as the Roman Catholic Church. After the collapse of Rome, the church played a vital role in society. In part, it was one of the few ties that people had to a more stable time. The church provided leadership and at times even organized the distribution of food. **Monasteries,** or communities of **monks,** provided hospitality to refugees and travelers. Monks also copied and preserved old texts, and in this way helped keep learning alive. The spread of monasteries, and the preaching of missionaries, helped bring new converts to the Christian faith.

The Organization of the Roman Catholic Church Over time, church leaders in western Europe developed an organization that was modeled on the structure of the old Roman government. By the High Middle Ages, they had created a system in which all members of the **clergy** had a rank. The pope, who was the bishop of Rome, was the supreme head of the Roman Catholic Church. He was assisted and counseled by high-ranking clergymen called *cardinals*. Cardinals were appointed by the pope and ranked just below him in the church hierarchy.

Archbishops came next. They oversaw large or important areas called *archdioceses*. Below them were bishops, who governed areas called *dioceses* from great cathedrals. Within each diocese, local communities called *parishes* were served by priests. Each parish had its own church building.

The Increasing Power of the Church   During the Middle Ages, the church acquired great economic power. By the year 1050, it was the largest landholder in Europe. Some land came in the form of gifts from monarchs and wealthy lords. Some land was taken by force. The medieval church added to its wealth by collecting a *tithe*, or tax. Each person was expected to give one tenth of his money, produce, or labor to help support the church.

The church also came to wield great political power. Latin, the language of the church, was the only common language in Europe. Church officials were often the only people who could read. As a result, they kept records for monarchs and became trusted advisors.

At times, the church's power brought it into conflict with European monarchs. One key struggle involved Pope Gregory VII and Henry IV, the Holy Roman emperor.

Gregory was elected pope in 1073. An ambitious leader, he undertook several reforms, such as forbidding priests to marry and outlawing the selling of church offices (official positions). He also banned the practice whereby kings could appoint priests, bishops, and the heads of monasteries. Only the pope, said Gregory, had this right.

Gregory's ruling angered Henry IV. Like rulers before him, Henry considered it his duty (and privilege) to appoint church officials. He called a council of bishops and declared that Gregory was no longer pope. Gregory responded by **excommunicating** Henry. This meant Henry was thrown out of the church and, therefore, could not gain salvation. Gregory also said that Henry's subjects were no longer obliged to obey him.

The pope's influence was so great that Henry begged forgiveness and was readmitted to the church. For the moment, his action amounted to recognizing the pope's authority, even over an emperor. But future rulers and popes would resume the fight over the rights of the church versus those of the state.

excommunicate to formally deprive a person of membership in a church

In the winter of 1077, Henry IV traveled to northern Italy to beg forgiveness from Pope Gregory. Legend has it that the pope let Henry stand barefoot in the snow for three days before he forgave him.

3.3 Sacraments and Salvation in the Middle Ages

Most people in medieval Europe believed in God and an afterlife, in which the soul lives on after the body's death. The church taught that people gained salvation, or entry into heaven and eternal life, by following the church's teachings and living a moral life. Failing to do so condemned the soul to eternal suffering in hell.

To believers, hell was a real and terrifying place. Its torments, such as fire and demons, were pictured in vivid detail in many paintings.

The church taught its members that receiving the seven sacraments was an essential part of gaining salvation. **Sacraments** were sacred rites that Christians believed brought them grace, or a special blessing from God. The sacraments marked the most important occasions in a person's life.

The sacrament of baptism welcomes a child into the church. Baptism is the first important sacrament of a Christian's life. It is required in order to receive the other sacraments.

sacrament a solemn rite of Christian churches

The Seven Sacraments	
Baptism	Entry into the church. To cleanse a person of sin, a priest pours water gently over his or her head at the baptismal font, the basin that holds the baptismal water.
Confirmation	Formal declaration of belief in God and the church.
Eucharist	A central part of the mass, the church service in which the priest consecrates (blesses) bread and wine. In Catholic belief, the consecrated bread and wine become the body and blood of Christ.
Matrimony (marriage)	A formal union blessed by the church. After being married by a priest, a couple signs their names in a registry, or book of records.
Holy Orders	The sacrament in which a man becomes a priest.
Penance	Confession of sins to a priest in order to receive God's forgiveness. Today Catholics call this sacrament *reconciliation*.
Extreme Unction	A blessing in which a person in danger of death is anointed (blessed with holy oil) by a priest. Today this rite is known as the *sacrament* (or anointing) *of the sick*.

3.4 Pilgrimages and Crusades

During the Middle Ages, religious faith led many people to perform extraordinary acts of devotion. For example, most Christians hoped to go on a **pilgrimage** at some point in their lives. Pilgrims traveled long distances to visit holy sites such as Jerusalem (where Jesus Christ was killed) and Rome. They also visited churches that housed **relics,** such as the cathedral at Canterbury, England.

Pilgrims went on these journeys to show their devotion to God, as an act of penance for their sins, or in hopes of being cured of an illness. A pilgrimage required true dedication, because travel was difficult and often dangerous. Most pilgrims traveled on foot. Because robbers were a constant threat, pilgrims often banded together for safety. Sometimes they even hired an armed escort. On popular pilgrimage routes, local rulers built special roads and bridges. Monks set up hostels (guest houses) spaced a day's journey apart.

Geoffrey Chaucer wrote a popular book of verse about pilgrims called the *Canterbury Tales*. Chaucer lived in England from about 1342 to 1400. His amusing "tales" are stories that a group of pilgrims tell to entertain each other as they travel to the shrine of Saint Thomas Becket in Canterbury. Among Chaucer's pilgrims are a knight, a miller, a cook, and a prioress (the head of a **convent,** or community of **nuns**).

A second type of extraordinary service involved fighting in the crusades. The crusades were military expeditions to the land where Jesus had lived, which Christians called the Holy Land. During the seventh century, this part of the Near East had come under the control of Muslims. Jerusalem, which was a holy city to Jews, Christians, and Muslims alike, became a Muslim city. Between 1095 and 1270, Christians in western Europe organized several crusades to recover Jerusalem and other sites of pilgrimage.

Some people went on crusades to seek wealth, and some to seek adventure. Some went in the belief that doing so would guarantee their salvation. But many crusaders also acted from deep religious feeling. You will learn more about the crusades in Unit 2.

pilgrimage a journey to a holy site

relic an object considered holy because it belonged to, or was touched by, a saint or other holy person

convent a community of nuns; also called a *nunnery*

nun a woman who has taken a sacred vow to devote her life to prayer and service to the church

Pilgrims believed their journeys of devotion earned good graces in the eyes of God. These beliefs served to strengthen the power of the church.

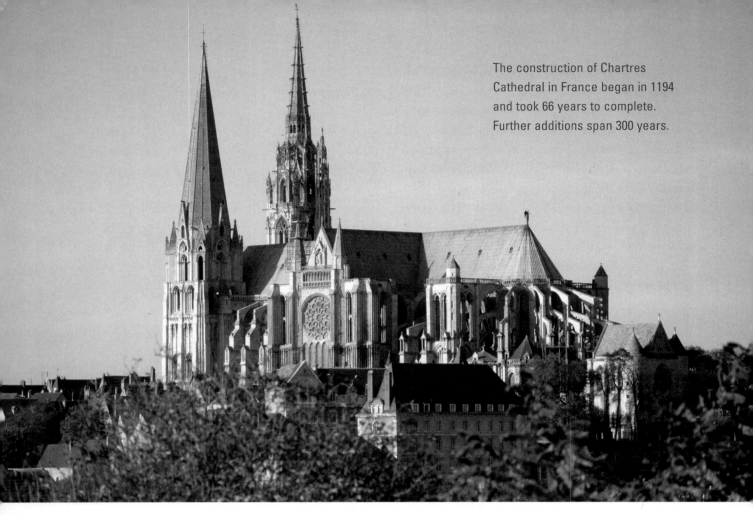

The construction of Chartres Cathedral in France began in 1194 and took 66 years to complete. Further additions span 300 years.

The gargoyles on Gothic cathedrals were often carved in the shape of hideous beasts.

3.5 Art and Architecture

During the Middle Ages, most art was made for a religious purpose. Paintings and sculptures of Christ and Christian saints were placed in churches to help people worship. Since most people did not know how to read, art helped tell the story of Christ's life in a way everyone could understand.

Medieval art and architecture found their most glorious expression in cathedrals, the large churches headed by bishops. (The word *cathedral* comes from the Latin word *cathedra,* meaning the throne upon which the bishop sat.) Cathedrals were built to inspire awe. For centuries, they were the tallest buildings in towns. Often they were taller than a 30-story building today. Most were built in the shape of a cross, with a long central section called the *nave* and shorter arms called *transepts*.

The cathedrals built between 1150 and 1400 were designed in the Gothic style. Gothic cathedrals looked like they were rising to heaven. On the outside were stone arches called *flying buttresses*. The arches spread the massive weight of the roof and walls more evenly. This building technique allowed for taller, thinner walls and more windows.

Gargoyles are a unique feature of Gothic cathedrals. Gargoyles are stone spouts projecting from the rain gutters of the roof. They were usually carved in the form of beasts. In medieval times, some people thought gargoyles were there to warn them that devils and evil spirits would catch them if they did not obey the church.

The immense space inside a Gothic cathedral was lined with pillars and decorated with religious images. Beautiful stained glass windows let in colorful light. Stained glass windows are made from pieces of colored glass arranged in a design. The pictures on medieval stained glass windows often taught people stories from the Bible.

Cathedrals were visible expressions of Christian devotion. They were mostly constructed by hand. On average, it took from 50 to 100 years to complete a cathedral. In some cases, the work took more than 200 years.

The interiors of Gothic cathedrals have similar features. The nave and a transept passage, or aisle, form a cross shape. The nave leads to the altar area. Beautiful stained glass windows and ribbed vaults are overhead.

3.6 Education

During the Middle Ages, most schooling took place in monasteries, convents, and cathedrals. This pattern was established under Charlemagne, who encouraged the church to teach people to read and write. During his reign, scholars developed a new form of writing that helped make reading easier. Instead of writing in all capital letters, as the Romans did, scholars began to use lowercase letters, too. We still use this system today.

In medieval times, the clergy were the people most likely to be educated. Most of the students in church schools were sons of nobles who were studying for careers in the clergy. They spent much of their time memorizing prayers and passages from the Bible in Latin.

university a school of advanced learning

rhetoric the study of persuasive writing and speaking

theology the study of God and religious truth

natural law the concept that there is a universal order built into nature that can guide moral thinking

Students at the University of Paris wore scholars' caps and gowns. This illustration from 1400 shows some students carrying scepters of the church.

Starting in the 1200s, cathedral schools gave rise to **universities**. Students in universities studied Latin grammar and **rhetoric,** logic, geometry, arithmetic, astronomy, and music. Books at that time were hand copied and rare, so teachers often read to students.

Ancient texts were greatly respected in the universities, but the church was sometimes uneasy about them. The church taught people to be guided by faith. Ancient writers like the Greek philosopher Aristotle taught that reason, or logical thinking, was the path to knowledge. Church leaders feared that studying such writers might lead people to question the church's teachings.

Thomas Aquinas, an Italian scholar of philosophy and **theology,** tried to bridge the gap between reason and faith. Aquinas greatly admired Aristotle. He saw no conflict between faith and reason, because he believed that both were gifts of God. Reason, he believed, helped people discover important truths about God's creation. Faith, meanwhile, revealed its own truths about God.

Aquinas wrote logical arguments in support of his faith to show how reason and religious belief worked together. For example, his concept of **natural law** stated that there was an order built into nature that could guide people's thinking about right and wrong. Natural law, he said, could be discovered through reason alone. Since God had created nature, natural law agreed with the moral teaching of the Bible.

Aquinas's teachings brought ancient philosophy and Christian theology together. His teachings were later accepted and promoted by the church.

In the Middle Ages, Carnival and Lent were important holidays. Lent was a period of 40 days just before Easter when people were especially pious and gave up luxuries, like meat and some drinks. Before the start of Lent, Christians would celebrate with a three-day festival, as shown here in a painting by the artist Breughel.

3.7 Holidays

The people of medieval Europe looked forward to the many festivals and fairs that marked important days of the year. Most of these celebrations were connected in some way to the church. Almost every day of the year was dedicated to a Christian saint, an event in the life of Jesus, or an important religious concept. In fact, our word *holiday* comes from "holy day."

Two of the greatest medieval holidays were Christmas and Easter. Christmas is the day when Christians celebrate the birth of Christ. During the Middle Ages, Christmas celebrations lasted for 12 days. There were no Christmas trees, but people of all social classes decorated their homes with evergreens, holly berries, and mistletoe. On Christmas day, they attended church. Then they enjoyed a great feast, which was often given by the lord of the manor for everyone.

Easter is the day when Christians celebrate the Resurrection. In Christian belief, the Resurrection is Christ's rising from the dead. For medieval Christians, Easter was a day of church services, feasting, and games. Often the games involved eggs, a symbol of new life.

Music, dancing, and food were all part of medieval holidays and festivals. People sang folk songs and danced to the music of wooden pipes and drums. They drank wine and ale (a strong beer), and they ate baked and fried foods.

Other favorite holiday entertainments included bonfires, acrobats and jugglers, and dancing bears. Plays were also popular. During church services on special days, priests sometimes acted out Bible stories about the life of Jesus. By the 13th century, plays were often held outdoors in front of the church so more people could watch. In some English villages, *mummers* (traveling groups of actors) would give elaborate performances with masks, drums and bells, dances, and make-believe sword fights.

Work was especially important to St. Benedict, who wrote "To work is to pray."

3.8 Monks, Nuns, and Mendicants

Religion was important to all Christians in the Middle Ages. Some men and women, however, solemnly promised to devote their lives to God and the church.

The Monastic Way of Life Monks were men who joined monasteries, communities devoted to prayer and service to fellow Christians. This way of life is called **monasticism**.

Men became monks for many reasons. Some were seeking refuge from war, sickness, or sinfulness. Some came to study. Some were attracted by a quiet life of prayer and service.

The man who developed the monastic way of life in western Europe was Saint Benedict. In the sixth century, he founded a monastery in Italy. His followers became known as the Benedictines. They followed Benedict's "Rule," or instructions. Benedictines made three solemn vows, or promises: poverty (to own no property), chastity (never to marry), and obedience (to obey their leaders).

Monks spent their lives in prayer, study, and work. They attended eight church services every day. Other duties included caring for the poor and sick, teaching, and copying religious texts. Since most monasteries were self-sufficient, monks spent much of their time working. They farmed their land, tended their gardens, raised livestock, and sewed clothing.

Most monasteries were laid out around a *cloister*, a covered walkway surrounding an open square. On the north side was the church. On the south side were the kitchen and dining hall. On the third side was the dormitory, or sleeping quarters. Monks slept in small cells, often on beds of wood.

The library writing room, called the *scriptorium*, was on the fourth side of the cloister. Here the monks copied books by hand and created beautiful **illuminated manuscripts**. By copying rare documents, monks kept knowledge of the past alive. Much of what we know today, about both the Middle Ages and ancient times, comes from their work.

Monastic life was one of the few opportunities open to medieval women who did not wish to marry. Women who became nuns lived in convents (also called *nunneries*). These communities were run in the same way as monasteries. Nuns did many of the same types of work that monks performed.

monasticism a way of life in which men and women withdraw from the rest of the world in order to devote themselves to their faith

illuminated manuscript a handwritten book decorated with bright colors and precious metals

Many nuns became important reformers and thinkers. For example, Hildegard, of Germany, founded a convent and wrote many letters to popes and other church officials. She also wrote books in which she criticized some of the practices of the church.

Both monks and nuns joined **religious orders**. Each order had its own distinctive rules and forms of service. The Benedictines were one such group.

Mendicants   Some people wanted to live a religious life without the seclusion of the monastic orders. A famous example is Francis of Assisi. Francis was born to a wealthy Italian family, but he gave up his money to serve the poor. He founded the Franciscans, an order that is also called the Little Brothers of the Poor.

Instead of living in monasteries, Franciscan **friars** traveled among ordinary people to preach and to care for the poor and sick. They lived in complete poverty and had to work or beg for food for themselves and the poor. For this reason, they were also called *mendicants,* a word that means "beggar." With his friend Clare, Francis founded a similar order for women called the Poor Clares.

Francis, who loved nature, believed that all living things should be treated with respect. He is often pictured surrounded by animals. To many people, his example of faith, charity, and love of God represents an ideal form of Christian living.

religious order a brotherhood or sisterhood of monks, nuns, or friars

friar a member of a certain religious order devoted to teaching and works of charity

Francis of Assisi lived a simple life with great respect for all living things. Here he is shown preaching to the birds.

3.9 Chapter Summary

During the Middle Ages, the Roman Catholic Church played a central role in the lives of people in western Europe. More than just a religious institution, the church acquired great political and economic power.

The church's sacraments marked all the most important occasions of life. Many people expressed their faith by going on pilgrimages or fighting in the crusades. The church's influence can also be seen in art and architecture, education, holidays, and the founding of religious orders.

In the later parts of the Middle Ages, more and more people lived in towns rather than on manors in the countryside. In the next chapter, you'll explore daily life in medieval towns.

CHAPTER 4

◀ Merchants offer their wares to shoppers in a 13th-century marketplace.

Life in Medieval Towns

4.1 Introduction

In the last chapter, you learned about how the Roman Catholic Church influenced life in medieval times. In this chapter, you will find out what **daily life** was like for people living in towns during the later Middle Ages, from about 1000 to 1450 C.E.

At the start of the Middle Ages, most people lived in the countryside, either on feudal manors or in religious communities. But by the 12th century, towns were growing up around castles and monasteries and along trade routes. These bustling towns became centers of trade and industry.

Almost all medieval towns were surrounded by thick stone walls for protection. Visitors entered through gates in the walls. Inside the walls, homes and businesses lined unpaved streets. Since few people could read, signs with colorful pictures hung over the doorways of shops and businesses. Open squares in front of public buildings such as churches served as gathering places.

Most streets were very narrow. Often the second stories of the houses were built projecting out over the first story, so very little daylight filtered down to the streets. Squares and streets were crowded with people, horses, and carts— as well as cats, dogs, geese, and chickens. There was no garbage collection, so residents threw their garbage into nearby canals and ditches, or simply out the window. As you can imagine, most medieval towns were filled with unpleasant smells.

In this chapter, you'll first learn about the growth of medieval towns. Then you'll look at several aspects of daily life in these towns. You'll explore **guilds, trade** and **commerce, homes and households, disease** and **medical treatment, crime and punishment,** and **leisure and entertainment**.

Use this drawing as a graphic organizer to help you learn more about daily life in medieval European towns.

4.2 The Growth of Medieval Towns

In the ancient world, town life was well established, particularly in Greece and Rome. Ancient towns were busy trading centers. But after the fall of the Roman Empire in the west, trade with the east suffered, and town life declined. In the Early Middle Ages, most people in western Europe lived in scattered communities in the countryside.

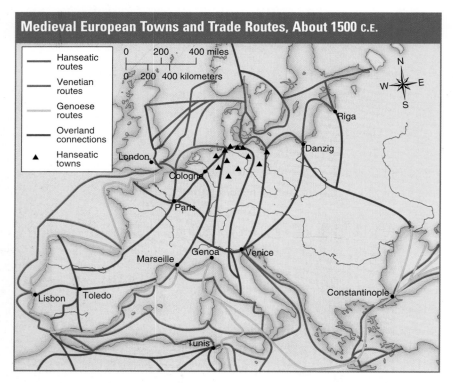

Medieval European Towns and Trade Routes, About 1500 C.E.

- Hanseatic routes
- Venetian routes
- Genoese routes
- Overland connections
- ▲ Hanseatic towns

0   200   400 miles
0   200   400 kilometers

N W E S

London, Cologne, Paris, Marseille, Genoa, Venice, Lisbon, Toledo, Tunis, Riga, Danzig, Constantinople

The trade routes shown here were used by people from Venice, Genoa, and Hanseatic towns. Hanseatic towns were part of a group called the Hanseatic League. Merchants in this group worked together to make trade safer and easier.

By the High Middle Ages, towns were growing again. One reason for their growth was improvements in agriculture. Farmers were clearing forests and adopting better farming methods. As a result, they had a surplus of crops to sell in town markets. Another reason was the revival of trade. Seaport towns like Venice and Genoa in Italy served as trading centers with the east. Within Europe, goods often traveled by river, and many towns grew up near these waterways.

Many of the merchants who sold their wares in towns became permanent residents. So did people practicing various trades. Some towns grew wealthier because local people specialized in making specific types of goods. For example, towns in Flanders (present-day Belgium and the Netherlands) were known for their fine woolen cloth. The Italian city of Venice was known for making glass. Other towns built their wealth on the banking industry that grew up to help people trade more easily.

At the beginning of the Middle Ages, towns were generally part of the **domain** of a feudal lord—whether a monarch, a noble, or a high-ranking church official. As towns grew wealthier, town dwellers began to resent the lord's feudal rights and his demands for taxes. They felt they no longer needed the lord's protection—or his interference.

In some places, such as northern France and Italy, violence broke out as towns struggled to become independent. In other places, such as England and parts of France, the change was more peaceful. Many towns became independent by purchasing a royal **charter**. The charter granted them the right to govern themselves, make laws, and raise taxes. Free towns were often governed by a mayor and a town council. Power gradually shifted from feudal lords to the rising class of merchants and craftspeople.

domain the land controlled by a ruler or lord

charter a written grant of rights and privileges by a ruler or government to a community, class of people, or organization

4.3 Guilds

Medieval towns began as centers for trade, but they soon became places where many goods were made. Both trade and the production of goods were overseen by organizations called **guilds**.

There were two main kinds of guilds, merchant guilds and craft guilds. All types of craftspeople had their own guilds, from cloth makers to cobblers (who made shoes, belts, and other leather goods) to the stonemasons who built the great cathedrals.

Guilds provided help and protection for the people doing a certain kind of work, and they maintained high standards. Guilds controlled the hours of work and set fair prices. They also dealt with complaints from the public. If, for example, a coal merchant cheated a customer, all coal merchants might look bad. The guilds therefore punished members who cheated.

Guild members paid dues to their guild. Their dues paid for the construction of guildhalls and for guild fairs and festivals. Guilds also used the money to take care of members and their families who were sick and unable to work.

It was not easy to become a member of a guild. Starting around the age of 12, a boy, and sometimes a girl, became an **apprentice**. An apprentice's parents signed an agreement with a master of the trade. The master agreed to house, feed, and train the apprentice. Sometimes, but not always, the parents paid the master a sum of money. Apprentices rarely got paid for their work.

At the end of seven years, apprentices had to prove to the guild that they had mastered their trade. To do this, an apprentice produced a piece of work called a "master piece." If the guild approved of the work, the apprentice was given the right to set up his or her own business. Setting up a business was expensive, however, and few people could afford to do it right away. Often they became **journeymen** instead. The word *journeyman* does not refer to a journey. It comes from the French word *journee,* for "day." A journeyman was a craftsperson who found work "by the day" instead of becoming a master who employed other workers.

guild an organization of people in the same craft or trade
apprentice a person who works for an expert in a trade or craft in return for training
journeyman a person who has learned a particular trade or craft but has not become an employer, or master

The cobblers working in this shoemaker's shop were probably journeymen working for the master of the shop.

4.4 Trade and Commerce

What brought most people to towns was business—meaning trade and **commerce**. As trade and commerce grew, so did towns.

At the beginning of the Middle Ages, most trade was in luxury goods, which only the wealthy could afford. People made everyday necessities for themselves. By the High Middle Ages, more people were buying and selling more kinds of goods. These included everyday items, like food, clothing, and household items. They also included the specialized goods that different towns began producing, such as woolen cloth, glass, and silk.

Most towns had a market, where food and local goods were bought and sold. Much larger were the great merchant fairs, which could attract merchants from many countries. A town might hold a merchant fair a couple of times a year. The goods for sale at large fairs came from all over Europe and the east.

With the growth of trade and commerce, merchants grew increasingly powerful and wealthy. They ran sizable businesses and looked for trading opportunities far from home. Merchant guilds came to dominate the business life of towns and cities. In towns that had become independent, members of merchant guilds often sat on town councils.

Not everyone prospered, however. In Christian Europe, there was often prejudice against **Jews**. Medieval towns commonly had sizable Jewish communities. The hostility of Christians, sometimes backed up by laws, made it difficult for Jews to earn their living. They were not allowed to own land. Their lords sometimes took their property and belongings at will. Jews could also be the targets of violence.

One opportunity that was open to Jews was to become bankers and moneylenders. This work was generally forbidden to Christians, because the church taught that charging money for loans was sinful. Jewish bankers and moneylenders performed an essential service for the economy. Still, they were often looked down upon and abused for practicing this "wicked" trade.

commerce the buying and selling of goods

Jew a descendant of the ancient Hebrews, the founders of the religion of Judaism; also, any person whose religion is Judaism

During the Late Middle Ages, marketplaces provided townspeople with food and goods from local farmers and faraway merchants.

4.5 Homes and Households

Medieval towns were typically small and crowded. Most of the houses were built of wood. They were narrow and could be up to four stories high. As wooden houses aged, they tended to lean. Sometimes two facing houses would lean so much they touched across the street!

Rich and poor lived in quite different households. In poorer neighborhoods, several families might share a house. A family might have only one room where they cooked, ate, and slept. In general, people worked where they lived. If a father or mother was a weaver, for example, the loom would be in the home.

Wealthy merchants often had splendid homes. The first level might be given over to a business, including offices and storerooms. The family's living quarters might be on the second level, complete with a *solar*, a space where the family gathered to eat and talk. An upper level might house servants and apprentices.

The Meal at the House of Epulone was painted by artist Carlo Saraceni around the year 1600. The family appears to be wealthy, with an outdoor space in which to gather and be entertained by lute players.

Even for wealthy families, life was not always comfortable. Rooms were cold, smoky, and dim. Fireplaces were the only source of heat as well as the main source of light. Windows were small and covered with oiled parchment instead of glass, so little sunlight came through.

Growing up in a medieval town wasn't easy, either. About half of all children died before they became adults. Those who survived began preparing for their adult roles around the age of seven. Some boys and girls attended school, where they learned to read and write. Children from wealthier homes might learn to paint and to play music on a lute (a stringed instrument). Other children started work as apprentices.

In general, people of the Middle Ages believed in an orderly society in which everyone knew their place. Most boys grew up to do the same work as their fathers. Some girls trained for a craft. But most girls married young, some as early as 12, and were soon raising children of their own. For many girls, their education was at home, where they learned cooking, cloth making, and other skills necessary to run a home and care for a family.

4.6 Disease and Medical Treatment

Unhealthy living conditions in medieval towns led to the spread of many diseases. Towns were very dirty places. There was no running water in homes. Instead of bathrooms, people used outdoor privies (shelters used as a toilets) or chamber pots that they emptied into nearby streams and canals. Garbage, too, was tossed into streams and canals or onto the streets. People lived crowded together in small spaces. They usually bathed only once a week, if that. Rats and fleas were common, and they often carried diseases. It's no wonder people were often ill.

Many illnesses that can be prevented or cured today had no cures in medieval times. One example is **leprosy**. Because leprosy can spread from one person to another, lepers were ordered to live by themselves in isolated houses, usually far from towns. Some towns even passed laws to keep out lepers.

Common diseases that had no cure included measles, cholera, and scarlet fever. The most feared disease was **bubonic plague,** also called the Black Death. You'll learn more about this disease and its impact on Europe in the next chapter.

No one knew exactly how diseases like these were spread. Unfortunately, this made many people look for someone to blame. For example, after an outbreak of illness, Jews were sometimes accused of poisoning wells.

Although hospitals were invented during the Middle Ages, there were few of them. When sickness struck, most people were treated in their homes by family members or, sometimes, a doctor. Medieval doctors believed in a mixture of prayer and medical treatment. Many treatments involved herbs. Using herbs as medicine had a long history based on traditional folk wisdom and knowledge handed down from ancient Greece and Rome. Other treatments were based on less scientific methods. For example, medieval doctors sometimes consulted the positions of the planets and relied on magic charms to heal people.

Another common technique was to "bleed" patients by opening a vein or applying leeches (a type of worm) to the skin to suck out blood. Medieval doctors believed that "bloodletting" helped restore balance to the body and spirit. Unfortunately, such treatments often weakened a patient further.

leprosy a skin and nerve disease that causes open sores on the body and can lead to serious complications and death

bubonic plague a deadly contagious disease caused by bacteria and spread by fleas

This doctor is treating patients by "bleeding" them. It was believed that this technique removed contaminated blood from the body and would restore health.

4.7 Crime and Punishment

Besides being unhealthy, medieval towns were noisy, crowded, and often unsafe. Pickpockets and thieves were always on the lookout for travelers with money in their pouches. Towns were especially dangerous at night, because there were no streetlights. Night watchmen patrolled the streets with candle lanterns to deter, or discourage, criminals.

People accused of crimes were held in dirty, crowded jails. Prisoners had to rely on friends and family to bring them food or money. Otherwise, they might starve. Wealthy people sometimes left money in their wills to help prisoners buy food.

In the Early Middle Ages, trial by ordeal or combat was often used to establish an accused person's guilt or innocence. In a trial by ordeal, the accused had to pass a dangerous test, such as being thrown into a deep well. Unfortunately, a person who floated instead of drowning was declared guilty, because he or she had been "rejected" by the water.

In a trial by combat, the accused person had to fight to prove his or her innocence. People believed that God would make sure the right party won. Clergy, women, children, and disabled people could name a champion to fight for them.

Punishments for crimes were very harsh. For lesser crimes, people were fined or put in the stocks. The stocks were a wooden frame with holes for the person's legs and sometimes arms. Being left in the stocks for hours or days was both painful and humiliating.

People found guilty of serious crimes, such as highway robbery, stealing livestock, treason, or murder, could be hanged or burned at the stake. Executions were carried out in public, often in front of large crowds.

In most parts of Europe, important lords shared with kings the power to prosecute major crimes. In England, kings in the early 1100s began setting up a nationwide system of royal courts. The decisions of royal judges contributed to a growing body of **common law**. Along with an independent judiciary, or court system, English common law would become an important safeguard of individual rights. Throughout Europe, court inquiries based on written and oral evidence eventually replaced trial by ordeal and combat.

The introduction of a court system to judge crimes and punishment was a great improvement over trials by ordeal and combat.

common law a body of rulings made by judges that become part of a nation's legal system

4.8 Leisure and Entertainment

Although many aspects of town life were difficult and people worked hard, they also participated in many leisure activities. Medieval people engaged in many of the same activities we enjoy today. Children played with dolls and toys, such as wooden swords and hobbyhorses. They rolled hoops and played games like badminton, lawn bowling, and blind man's bluff. Adults also liked games, such as chess, checkers, and backgammon. They might gather to play card games, bet on rolls of dice, or go dancing (although the church frowned on these activities).

Townspeople also took time off from work to celebrate special days, such as religious feasts. On Sundays and holidays, animal baiting was a popular, though cruel, amusement. First a bull or bear was fastened to a stake by a chain around its neck or a back leg, and sometimes by a nose ring. Then specially trained dogs were set loose to torment the captive animal.

Fair days were especially colorful. Jugglers, dancers, clowns, and **minstrels** entertained the fairgoers. Guild members paraded through the streets, dressed in special costumes and carrying banners.

Guilds also put on **mystery plays** in which they acted out stories from the Bible. Often they performed stories that were appropriate to their guild. In some towns, for instance, the boat builders acted out the story of Noah. In this story, Noah had to build an ark (a boat) to survive a flood that God sent to "cleanse" the world of people. In other towns, the coopers (barrel makers) acted out this story. The coopers put hundreds of barrels filled with water on the rooftops. Then they let the water out to represent the 40 days of rain the story tells about.

Mystery plays gave rise to another type of religious drama, the **miracle play**. These plays dramatized the lives of saints. Often they showed the saints performing miracles, or wonders. For example, in England it was popular to portray the story of St. George, who slew a dragon that was about to eat the daughter of a king.

Mystery and miracle plays were performed by guild members to entertain townspeople with dramatizations of stories from the Bible or the lives of saints.

minstrel a singer or musician who sang or recited poems to music played on a harp or other instrument

mystery play a type of religious drama in the Middle Ages based on stories from the Bible

miracle play a type of religious drama in the Middle Ages based on stories about saints

The church eventually disapproved of both mystery and miracle plays, but people still enjoyed seeing them acted out in the streets or the public square.

4.9 Chapter Summary

In this chapter, you learned about daily life in towns in the High and Late Middle Ages. At the beginning of the Middle Ages, most people lived in the countryside. By about 1200, however, towns were growing. Farmers came to towns to sell their crops, and the revival of trade brought merchants with many kinds of goods to sell.

As trade and commerce grew, so did towns. Many became powerful and wealthy enough to purchase their independence from their feudal lords. Guilds, especially the merchant guilds, became leading forces in their communities.

Life in towns was crowded, noisy, and dirty. Diseases spread rapidly, and many people could not be cured with the medical knowledge of the time. Crime was also a problem, and it was punished harshly. Despite these hardships, many types of leisure activities made life more enjoyable for town dwellers, including games, fairs, and religious plays put on by guilds.

The growth of towns, and of an economy based on trade and commerce, represented a significant change in people's way of life. Many historians believe that these developments prepared the way for sweeping change at the end of the Middle Ages. In the next chapter, you'll learn about the decline of feudalism.

As towns grew, farmers brought their crops to sell at the town marketplace.

CHAPTER 5

◀ In this illuminated manuscript, the
Horseman of Death represents the plague.

The Decline of Feudalism

5.1 Introduction

In the last chapter, you learned about daily life in medieval towns. Now you will explore key events that contributed to the **decline of feudalism** in the 12th through the 15th centuries.

There were many causes for the breakdown of the feudal system. In this chapter, you will focus on three: political changes in England, a terrible disease, and a long series of wars.

In England, several political changes in the 12th and 13th centuries helped to weaken feudalism. A famous document known as the **Magna Carta,** or Great Charter, dates from this time. The Magna Carta was a written agreement that limited the king's power and strengthened the rights of nobles. As feudalism declined, the Magna Carta took on a much broader meaning and contributed to ideas about individual rights and liberties in England.

The disease was the **bubonic plague,** or Black Death. The plague swept across Asia in the 1300s and reached Europe in 1347. Over the next two centuries, this terrifying disease killed millions in Europe. It struck all kinds of people—rich and poor, young and old, town dwellers and country folk. Almost everyone who caught the plague died within days. In some places, whole communities were wiped out. The deaths of so many people led to sweeping economic and social changes.

Between 1337 and 1453, France and England fought a series of wars known as the **Hundred Years' War**. This conflict changed the way wars were fought and shifted power from feudal lords to monarchs and the common people.

How did such different events contribute to the decline of feudalism? In this chapter, you'll find out.

Use this illustration as a graphic organizer to help you learn more about how key events contributed to the decline of feudalism in western Europe.

5.2 Political Developments in England

There were many reasons for the decline of feudalism in Europe. In one country, England, political developments during the 12th and 13th centuries helped to weaken feudalism. The story begins with King Henry II, who reigned from 1154 to 1189.

Henry II's Legal Reforms   Henry made legal reform a central concern of his reign. For example, he insisted that a jury formally accuse a person of a serious crime. Cases were then tried before a royal judge. Henry's reforms strengthened the power of royal courts at the expense of feudal lords. In time, trial by judges and juries replaced trial by ordeal and combat.

Henry's effort to strengthen royal authority led to a serious conflict with the church. In 1164, Henry issued the Constitutions of Clarendon, a document that he said spelled out the king's traditional rights. Among them was

King John's acceptance of the Magna Carta has been illustrated and painted many times since the historic event. He is often shown signing his name with a pen. In fact, he did not. He stamped his royal seal on the document to show his agreement.

the right to try clergy accused of serious crimes in royal courts rather than in church courts.

Henry's action led to a long, bitter quarrel with his friend Thomas Becket, the Archbishop of Canterbury. In 1170, four knights, perhaps seeking the king's favor, killed Becket in front of the main altar of Canterbury Cathedral. Becket's tomb soon became a popular destination for pilgrimages. In 1173, the church proclaimed him a saint. Still, most of the Constitutions of Clarendon remained in force.

King John and the Magna Carta   In 1199, Henry's youngest son, John, became king. John soon made powerful enemies by losing most of the lands the English had controlled in France. He also taxed his barons heavily and ignored their traditional rights, arresting opponents at will. In addition, John quarreled with the church and collected large amounts of money from its properties.

In June 1215, angry barons forced a meeting with King John in a meadow called Runnymede, beside the River Thames. There they insisted that John put his seal to the Magna Carta, or Great Charter.

The charter was an agreement between the barons and the king. The barons agreed that the king could continue to rule. For his part, King John agreed to observe common law and the traditional rights of barons and the church. For example, he promised to consult the barons and church officials before imposing special taxes. He also agreed that "no free man" could be jailed except by the lawful judgment of his peers or by the law of the land. This idea eventually became a key part of English common law known as **habeas corpus**.

In many ways, the Magna Carta protected the rights and privileges of nobles. Later, it took on a much broader meaning as people in England came to regard it as one of the foundations of their rights and liberties.

King Edward I and the Model Parliament

In 1295, Edward I, King John's grandson, took a major step toward including more people in government. Edward called together a governing body called the Model Parliament. It included **commoners** and lower-ranking clergy as well as church officials and nobles.

The Impact of Political Developments in England

These political changes contributed to the decline of feudalism in two ways. Some of the changes strengthened royal authority at the expense of nobles. Others weakened feudalism by shifting power to common people.

The Magna Carta established the idea of rights and liberties that even the king cannot violate. It also affirmed that monarchs should rule with the advice of the governed. Henry II's legal reforms strengthened English common law and the role of judges and juries. Finally, Edward I's Model Parliament gave a voice in government to common people as well as lords. All these ideas became part of the tradition that later gave rise to modern democratic institutions.

habeas corpus the principle that accused persons cannot be held in jail without the consent of a court

commoner a person who is not of noble rank

This 14th-century illuminated manuscript shows King Edward I sitting over his parliament. The King of Scots is seated to his right, and the Prince of Wales is seated to his left.

5.3 The Bubonic Plague

We've looked at how political developments in England helped to weaken feudalism in that country. Another reason for the decline of feudalism was the bubonic plague, which affected all of Europe. The bubonic plague first struck Europe from 1347 to 1351. It returned about every decade into the 15th century, leaving major changes in its wake.

Historians think the plague began in central Asia, possibly in China, and spread throughout China, India, the Near East, and Europe. The disease traveled from central Asia to the Black Sea along the Silk Road (the main trade route between east and west). It was probably carried to Italy on a ship. It then spread north and west, throughout the continent of Europe and England.

The Black Death   Symptoms, or signs, of the plague included a fever, vomiting, fierce coughing and sneezing fits, and egg-sized swellings or bumps. The name Black Death probably came from the black and blue blotches that appeared on the skin of many victims.

The dirty conditions in which people lived contributed significantly to the spread of the bubonic plague. The bacteria that caused the disease were carried by fleas that fed on the blood of infected rodents, like rats. When the rats died, the fleas jumped to other animals and people. During the Middle Ages, it was not unusual for people to go for many months without a change of clothing or a bath. Rats, covered with fleas, often roamed the floors of homes looking for food. City streets were filled with human waste, dead animals, and trash.

At the time, though, no one knew where the disease came from or how it spread. Terrified people falsely blamed the plague on everything from the positions of the planets to lepers and Jews.

Persecution of the Jews did not begin with the plague. Prejudice against Jews had led England to order all Jews to leave the country in 1290. In France, the same thing happened in 1306 and again in 1394. But fear of the plague made things worse. During the Black Death, many German cities ordered Jews to leave.

The Impact of the Plague   The plague took a terrible toll on the populations of Asia and Europe. China's population was reduced by nearly half between 1200 and 1393, probably because of the plague and

The Spread of the Plague in the Fourteenth Century

0   750   1,500 miles

0   1,500 kilometers

1346–1348
Plague enters and spreads through Europe

1330s–1340s
Plague crosses Asia along trade routes

1346–1351
Muslim merchants help carry plague to Egypt and Arabia

ENGLAND
GERMANY
London
Cologne
Paris
FRANCE
Venice
Genoa
Kaffa
ITALY
Black Sea
SPAIN
Constantinople
ASIA MINOR
Mediterranean Sea
NORTH AFRICA
EGYPT
Red Sea
ARABIAN PENINSULA
INDIA
CHINA

famine. Travelers reported that dead bodies covered the ground in Central Asia and India.

Some historians estimate that 24 million Europeans died as a result of the plague—about a third of the population. The deaths of so many people speeded changes in Europe's economic and social structure that contributed to the decline of feudalism.

Trade and commerce slowed almost to a halt during the plague years. As Europe began to recover, the economy needed to be rebuilt. But it wouldn't be rebuilt in the same way, with feudal lords holding most of the power.

After the plague, there was a shift in power from nobles to the common people. One reason was that the need for workers was high, but there were fewer workers because so many people had died. The workers who were left could therefore demand more money and more rights. In addition, many serfs abandoned feudal manors and moved to towns and cities, seeking better opportunities. This led to a weakening of the manor system and a loss of power for feudal lords.

After the plague, a number of peasant rebellions broke out. When nobles tried to return to the way things had been, resentment exploded across Europe. There were peasant revolts in France, Flanders, England, Germany, Spain, and Italy.

The most famous of these revolts was the English Peasants' War in 1381. The English rebels succeeded in entering London and presenting their demands to the king, Richard II. The leader of the rebellion was killed, however, and after his death the peasants' revolt lost momentum. Still, in most of Europe the time was coming when serfdom would end.

During the plague, a dancing mania spread among those who remained healthy—expressing their joy of life during those black times.

5.4 The Hundred Years' War

Between 1337 and 1453, England and France fought a series of wars over the control of lands in France. Known as the Hundred Years' War, this long conflict helped to weaken feudalism in England and France.

English kings had long claimed lands in France as their own fiefs. French kings disputed these claims. When Philip VI of France declared that the French fiefs of England's King Edward III were part of his own realm, war broke out in France.

Early English Successes   Despite often being outnumbered, the English won most of the early battles of the war. What happened at the Battle of Crecy shows why.

Two quite different armies faced each other at the French village of Crecy in 1346. The French had a feudal army that relied on horse-mounted nobles, or knights. French knights wore heavy armor, and they could hardly move when they were not on horseback. Their weapons were swords and lances. Some of the infantry, or foot soldiers, used **crossbows,** which were effective only at short ranges.

In contrast, the English army was made up of lightly armored knights, foot soldiers, and archers armed with **longbows**. Some soldiers were recruited from the common people and paid to fight.

The English longbow had many advantages over the crossbow. Larger arrows could be notched and fired more quickly. The arrows flew farther, faster, and with greater accuracy. At Crecy, the longbow helped the English defeat the much larger French force.

The French Fight Back   The French slowly chipped away at the territory the English had won in the early years of the war. In 1415, after a long **truce,** King Henry V again invaded France. This time the English met with stronger resistance. One reason was that the French were now using more modern tactics.

The king was recruiting his army from commoners, paying them with money collected by taxes, just as the English did.

Another reason for better French resistance was a new sense of national identity and unity. In part the French were inspired by a 17-year-old peasant girl, today known as Joan of Arc. Joan claimed that she heard the voices of saints urging her to save France. Putting on a suit of armor, she went to fight.

crossbow a medieval weapon made up of a bow that was fixed across a wooden stock (which had a groove to direct the arrow's flight) and operated by a trigger

longbow a large bow used for firing feathered arrows

truce an agreed-upon halt in fighting

At the Battle of Crecy, the English army's light armor and longbows triumphed over the French knights' heavy armor and crossbows.

In 1429, Joan led a French army to victory in the Battle of Orleans. The next year, the "Maid of Orleans" was captured by allies of England. The English accused Joan of being a witch and a **heretic,** and burned her at the stake.

Joan of Arc's heroism changed the way many French men and women felt about their king and nation. Twenty-two years after Joan's death, the French finally drove the English out of France. Almost 500 years later, the Roman Catholic Church made Joan a saint.

heretic a person who holds beliefs that are contrary to the teachings of a church or other group

The Impact of the Hundred Years' War   The Hundred Years' War contributed to the decline of feudalism by helping to shift power from feudal lords to monarchs and common people. During the war, monarchs on both sides had collected taxes and raised large professional armies. As a result, kings no longer relied on nobles to supply knights for the army.

In addition, changes in military technology made the nobles' knights and castles less useful. The longbow proved to be an effective weapon against mounted knights. Castles became less important as armies learned to use gunpowder to shoot iron balls from cannons and blast holes in castle walls.

The new feeling of nationalism also shifted power away from lords. Previously, many English and French peasants felt more loyalty to their local lords than to their king. The war created a new sense of national unity and patriotism on both sides.

In both France and England, peasants bore the heaviest burden of the war. They were forced to fight in the army and to pay higher and more frequent taxes. Those who survived the war, however, were needed as soldiers and workers. For this reason, the common people emerged from the fighting with greater influence and power.

Joan of Arc, a 17-year-old peasant girl, inspired the people of France to fight for their country. She is honored for her heroism to this day. A late 19th-century artist painted this scene called *Entrance of Joan of Arc into Orleans on 8th May 1429.*

5.5 Chapter Summary

In this chapter, you've explored three key events that contributed to the decline of feudalism. Political developments in England helped shift power to the king and the common people. After the bubonic plague, the need for workers to rebuild Europe led to a shift in power from feudal lords to the common people. The Hundred Years' War brought a rise in national feeling in both England and France. It also reduced the importance of nobles and knights on the battlefield.

This chapter ends your study of the Middle Ages in western Europe. In the next chapter, you'll travel east to explore the Byzantine Empire.

A modern drawing re-creates the city of Constantine during the Byzantine Empire.

CHAPTER 6

The Byzantine Empire

6.1 Introduction

In the last chapter, you learned about the decline of feudalism in western Europe. In this chapter, you will learn about the **Byzantine Empire** in the east. This great empire straddled two continents, Europe and Asia. It lasted from about 500 to 1453 C.E., when it was conquered by the Ottoman Turks.

The Byzantine Empire was the continuation of the Roman Empire in the east. As you learned in Chapter 1, in 330 C.E. the emperor Constantine moved his capital from Rome to the ancient city of Byzantium. The city was an old Greek trading colony on the eastern edge of Europe. Constantine called his capital New Rome, but it soon became known as **Constantinople** (Greek for "Constantine's City").

After Constantine's reign, control of the huge empire was usually divided between two emperors. One was based in Rome, and one in Constantinople. After the fall of Rome, the eastern half of the empire continued for another 1,000 years. Today we call this eastern empire the Byzantine Empire, after Byzantium, the original name of its capital city.

East and west remained connected for a time through a shared Christian faith. But the church in the east developed in its own unique way. It became known as the **Eastern Orthodox Church**. Over time, Byzantine emperors and church officials came into conflict with the pope in Rome. The conflict eventually led to a permanent split between the Eastern Orthodox Church and the Roman Catholic Church.

In this chapter, you'll learn about the Byzantine Empire, one of its greatest emperors, and its distinctive church. Let's begin by exploring the empire's capital—the fabulous city of Constantinople.

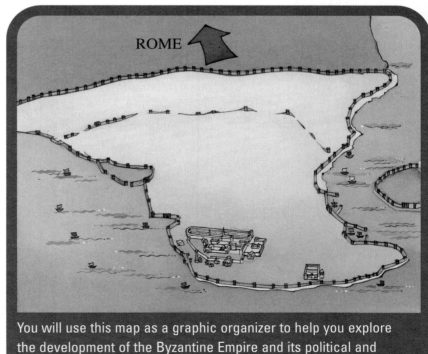

You will use this map as a graphic organizer to help you explore the development of the Byzantine Empire and its political and religious traditions.

6.2 Constantinople

Constantinople was more than 800 miles to the east of Rome. Why did Constantine choose this site to be the capital of the Roman Empire?

One reason was that the site was easy to defend. It was surrounded on three sides by water. The Byzantines fashioned a chain across the city's harbor to guard against seafaring intruders. Miles of walls, fortified by watchtowers and gates, made invasion by land or sea difficult.

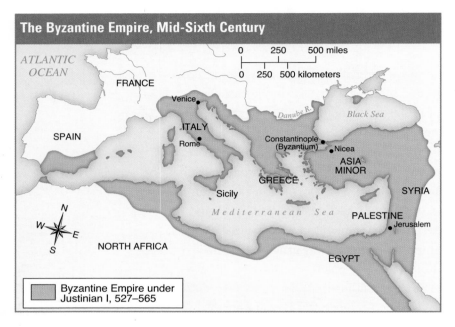

The Byzantine Empire, Mid-Sixth Century

ATLANTIC OCEAN

FRANCE

Venice

ITALY
Rome

SPAIN

Danube R.

Black Sea

Constantinople
(Byzantium)

Nicea

ASIA
MINOR

GREECE

Sicily

SYRIA

Mediterranean Sea

PALESTINE

Jerusalem

NORTH AFRICA

EGYPT

0   250   500 miles
0   250   500 kilometers

N W E S

Byzantine Empire under
Justinian I, 527–565

Constantinople also stood at the crossroads of Europe and Asia, and the many sea and overland trade routes linking east and west. Under the Byzantines, this location helped make the city, and some of its citizens, fabulously wealthy. For more than 700 years, Constantinople was the richest and most elegant city in the Mediterranean region. Ivory, silk, furs, perfumes, and other luxury items flowed through its markets. A French soldier who saw the city in 1204 exclaimed, "One could not believe there was so rich a city in all the world."

Constantinople's location made it easy to defend from attacks by land or sea. It was also an important location for trade routes linking east and west.

At its height, Constantinople was home to around one million people. The city's language and culture were Greek, but traders and visitors spoke many languages. Ships crowded the city's harbor, loaded with goods. The city streets, some narrow and twisting, some grand and broad, teemed with camel and mule trains.

Life in Constantinople was more advanced than in western Europe. The city boasted a sewer system, rare in medieval times. Social services were provided by hospitals, homes for the elderly, and orphanages.

Despite the luxuries enjoyed by the rich, many people lived in poverty. The emperor gave bread to those who could not find work. In exchange, the unemployed performed such tasks as sweeping the streets and weeding public gardens.

Almost everyone attended the exciting chariot races at a stadium called the Hippodrome. Two chariot teams, one wearing blue and the other green, were fierce rivals. In Constantinople and other cities, many people belonged to opposing groups called the Blues and Greens after the chariot teams. At times the rivalry between Blues and Greens erupted in deadly street fighting. But in 532, the two groups united in a rebellion that destroyed much of Constantinople. You'll find out what happened in the next section.

6.3 The Reign of Justinian I

One of the greatest Byzantine emperors was Justinian I, whose long reign lasted from 527 to 565. But Justinian's reign nearly came to an abrupt end much sooner. In January 532, the emperor and his beautiful wife, Theodora, were attending the chariot races at the Hippodrome. In the past, Blues and Greens at the races had often fought with each other. This time, however, both groups were upset over the arrests of some of their members. To Justinian's horror, they united in denouncing him. Fighting broke out, spilled into the streets, and escalated into a full-scale rebellion.

The rioting continued for a week while Justinian and Theodora hid in the palace. Much of the city was in flames. Justinian's advisors wanted him to flee the city. Theodora, however, urged him to stay and fight. With her encouragement, Justinian put down the revolt. According to the official court historian, Procopius, 30,000 people were killed in the fighting. Constantinople lay in ruins.

Justinian was determined to rebuild the city on an even grander scale than before. He put huge sums of money into **public works**. Soon Constantinople had new bridges, public baths, parks, roads, and hospitals. The emperor also built many grand churches, including the magnificent Hagia Sophia ("Holy Wisdom"). Today this great cathedral is one of the most famous buildings in the world.

During rioting in Constantinople, Theodora encouraged her husband, Emperor Justinian I, to stay and fight for his city.

Besides rebuilding Constantinople, Justinian tried to reclaim some of the empire's lost territory. He launched military campaigns that, for a time, won back parts of North Africa, Italy, and southeastern Spain.

Justinian is most famous, however, for creating a systematic body of law. Under his direction, a committee studied the thousands of laws the Byzantines had inherited from the Roman Empire. They revised outdated and confusing laws. They also made improvements, such as extending women's property rights. The result of their work is known as Justinian's Code. It became the basis for many legal codes in the western world.

Procopius, the court historian, wrote glowing accounts of Justinian's achievements. But he also wrote the *Secret History,* in which he called the emperor "a treacherous enemy, insane for murder and plunder." Throughout Byzantine history, distrust and divisions often plagued the imperial court. Justinian's court was no exception.

The Hagia Sophia was built between the years 532 and 537. Its architectural features have inspired the design of many Orthodox churches.

6.4 The Eastern Orthodox Church

To the Byzantines, Christianity was more than a religion. It was the very foundation of their empire.

When Constantine built his new capital, he intended it to be the religious center of the empire as well as the seat of government. Constantine himself tried to settle religious disputes by calling bishops together in council.

Over time, the Byzantine church became known as the Eastern Orthodox Church. The word *orthodox* means "in agreement with right belief." The medieval Eastern Orthodox Church was based on a set of beliefs that its leaders traced back to Jesus Christ and to the work of bishops in early Christian councils.

The Role of the Eastern Orthodox Church in the Empire   Religion and government were more closely linked in the Byzantine Empire than in the west. The Byzantines viewed the emperor not just as the head of the government but as the living representative of God and Jesus Christ. This meant that church and state were combined into one all-powerful body.

The state religion also united people in a common belief. The Eastern Orthodox Church played a central role in daily life. Most people attended church regularly. Religious sacraments gave shape to every stage of the journey from birth to death. Monasteries and convents cared for the poor and the sick. These institutions were supported by wealthy people and became quite powerful. Let's look at some of the practices of Eastern Orthodoxy.

Church Hierarchy   Like Roman Catholic clergy, Orthodox clergy were ranked in order of importance. In Byzantine times, the emperor had supreme authority in the church. He chose the **patriarch** of Constantinople, who ranked next to him in matters of religion.

patriarch in the Eastern Orthodox Church, the bishop of an important city

Unlike the pope in the west, the patriarch did not claim strong authority over other patriarchs and bishops. Instead, he was "first among equals." The patriarch of Constantinople (which today is Istanbul, Turkey) still holds this honor.

Orthodox priests served under patriarchs and other bishops. Unlike Roman Catholic priests, who were not allowed to marry, many Orthodox priests were married. Bishops, however, could rise only from the ranks of unmarried clergy.

Liturgy and Prayer   The Orthodox church service corresponding to the Roman Catholic mass was the Divine Liturgy. Both the clergy and worshippers sang or chanted the liturgy. The **liturgy** was conducted in Greek or in the local language of the people.

Orthodox Christians also prayed to saints. Two saints were particularly important in Byzantine times. Saint Basil promoted charity and reformed the liturgy. Saint Cyril helped create the Cyrillic alphabet, which allowed scholars to translate the Bible for people in eastern Europe to read.

Architecture and Art   Christian faith inspired magnificent works of architecture and art in the Byzantine Empire. With its square base and high dome, Hagia Sophia served as a model for many Orthodox churches. The architecture of the church also reflects Orthodox views. The simple base represents the earthly world. Upon it rests the "dome of heaven." Rich decorations on the inside were meant to remind worshippers of what it would be like to enter God's kingdom.

Building on the Greek love of art, the Orthodox church used many images in its services and prayers. Byzantine artists created beautiful **icons,** which were usually painted on small wooden panels. Artists also fashioned sacred images as mosaics and painted them in murals.

An image of Christ as the Pantocrator, or ruler of all, gazed down from the dome of all Orthodox churches. Christ was usually shown holding a gospel and giving a blessing. Most churches also placed an icon of Jesus' mother, Mary (called the Theotokos, or god-bearer) and the Christ child over the altar.

Many Byzantines believed that sacred pictures helped bring them closer to God. But icons also became a source of violent disagreement, as you will see next.

liturgy a sacred rite of public worship

icon a type of religious image typically painted on a small wooden panel and considered sacred by Eastern Orthodox Christians

The architecture of Greek Orthodox monasteries copied the features of the Hagia Sophia. The simple bases and domed roofs echoed Orthodox views of life rooted in the earth with the "dome of heaven" above.

6.5 Conflict Between East and West

Medieval Europe and the Byzantine Empire were united in a single faith, Christianity. Over the centuries, however, cultural, political, and religious differences brought the two parts of the old Roman Empire into conflict.

The two regions had been quite different even in the days of the old Roman emperors. The eastern half of the empire had many cities, much trade, and great wealth. The western half was mostly rural and agricultural, and not nearly as wealthy.

Other differences became more pronounced after the fall of Rome. Byzantine culture was largely shaped by its Greek heritage. The west was influenced by Frankish and Germanic cultures. In Constantinople, people spoke Greek. In the west, Latin was the language of scholars, diplomats, and the church.

Perhaps most important was the conflict that developed between the churches of east and west. After the fall of Rome, popes gradually emerged as powerful figures in western Europe. The popes claimed supreme religious authority over all Christians. The emperors and patriarchs of the east resisted such claims.

Other differences added to the conflict. Let's look at three major disagreements and how they led to a split in the Christian church.

Iconoclasm The first major disagreement concerned religious icons. Many Christians in medieval times used images of Jesus, Mary, and the saints in worship and prayer. Some Christians in the east, however, believed that people were wrongly worshipping the icons themselves as if they were divine. In 730 C.E., Byzantine emperor Leo III banned the use of religious images in all Christian churches and homes.

The policy of iconoclasm ("icon smashing") led to the destruction of much religious art. Throughout Christian lands, people cried out in protest. In Rome, popes were angry because Leo's order applied to parts of Italy that were under Byzantine control. Pope Gregory III even excommunicated the emperor.

The Byzantine Empire lifted its ban on icons in 843. But the dispute over iconoclasm had caused a major split between the east and west. It also helped drive popes in Rome to look for support and protection against enemies.

After many disagreements between the Byzantine Empire and Pope Leo IX, Pope Leo excommunicated Cerularius, the patriarch of Constantinople. Cerularius then excommunicated the leaders of the Roman Catholic Church from the Eastern Orthodox Church.

The Crowning of a Holy Roman Emperor Another major disagreement occurred in 800 C.E. At the time, Empress Irene was the ruler of the Byzantine Empire. Because she was a woman, Pope Leo III did not view her as a true ruler. More important, the pope needed the protection of a strong leader to help defend the church in the west.

As you learned in Chapter 2, Leo decided to crown Charlemagne, the king of the Franks, as Holy Roman emperor. The pope's action outraged the Byzantines, who felt that they were the rightful rulers of the Roman Empire.

The Final Break Matters between east and west came to a head in 1054. The patriarch of Constantinople, Cerularius, wanted to reassert Byzantine control of the church. He closed all churches that worshiped with western rites. Pope Leo IX was furious. He sent Cardinal Humbert to Constantinople. The cardinal marched up to the altar of Hagia Sophia. In front of everyone, he laid down a bull (a proclamation by the pope) excommunicating Cerularius.

Cerularius responded by excommunicating the cardinal. This was only a symbolic act, for the patriarch did not have that power. But it showed that the split, or **schism,** between east and west was complete. Despite future attempts to heal the division, the Eastern Orthodox Church and the Roman Catholic Church were now separate churches.

> **schism** a formal division in a church or religious body

The division between the Eastern Orthodox and Roman Catholic Churches lasted until 1964. Pope Paul VI and Patriarch Athenagonas met in Jerusalem and made a formal statement that undid the excommunications of 1054.

6.6 Chapter Summary

In this chapter, you learned about the Byzantine Empire and the Eastern Orthodox Church. After the fall of Rome, the eastern half of the Roman Empire lived on with its capital at Constantinople. Today it is referred to as the Byzantine Empire. Destroyed by rioting in 532, Constantinople was rebuilt by the emperor Justinian I.

The Byzantine Empire was a Christian state. The Eastern Orthodox Church was at the center of daily life and inspired great art and architecture.

Byzantine emperors and patriarchs clashed with popes in Rome over a number of issues. These disagreements led to a schism between the Roman Catholic Church and the Eastern Orthodox Church. In Unit 2, you will read more about the fate of the Byzantines.

Medieval Europe Timeline

About 800
Scholars in Charlemagne's schools begin to write with lowercase letters.

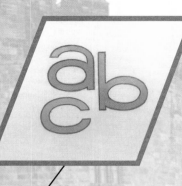

1054
A schism leads to two separate Christian churches: Roman Catholic and Eastern Orthodox.

800
C.E.

900
C.E.

1000
C.E.

1100
C.E.

1194
Construction of the present-day Chartres Cathedral begins in France.

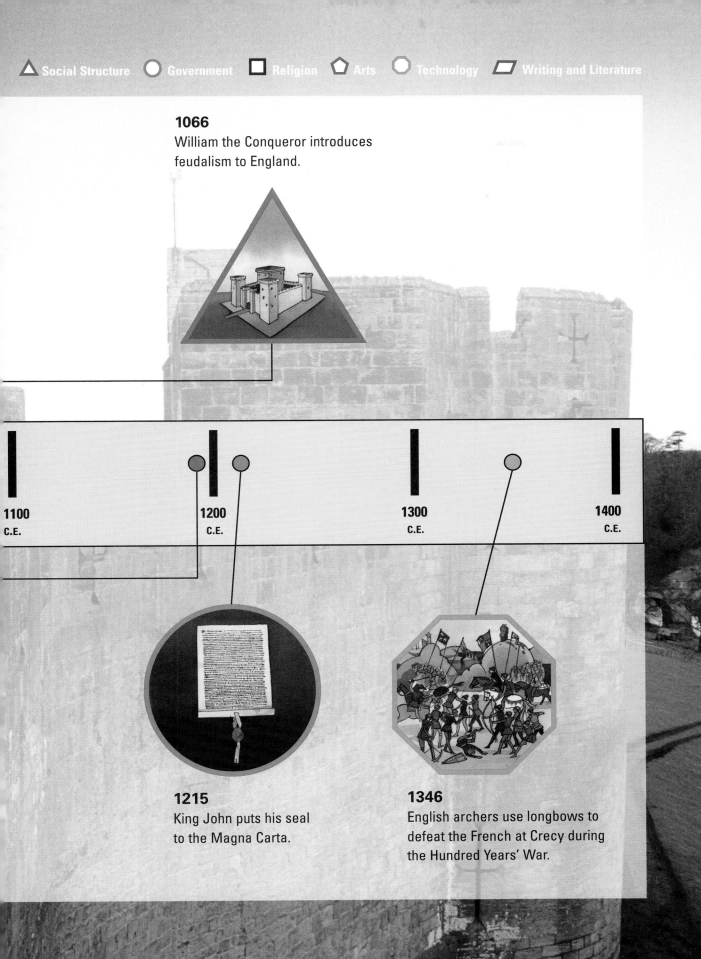

1066
William the Conqueror introduces feudalism to England.

1100
C.E.

1200
C.E.

1300
C.E.

1400
C.E.

1215
King John puts his seal to the Magna Carta.

1346
English archers use longbows to defeat the French at Crecy during the Hundred Years' War.

UNIT 2

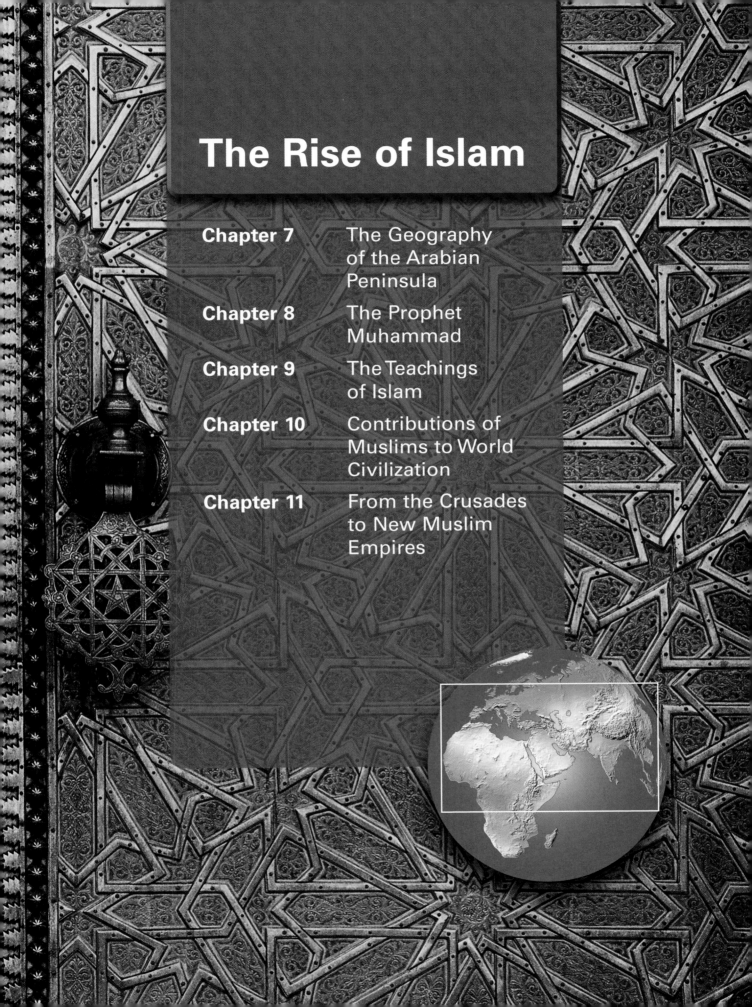

The Rise of Islam

Setting the Stage

The Rise of Islam

In the last unit, you learned about Europe and the Byzantine Empire. In this unit, you will explore rise of Islam and the history of Muslim empires, from about 600 to 1500 C.E. Islam is one of the world's major religions, and those who practice the religion are called Muslims.

Islam began in Arabia, a peninsula of southwest Asia between the Red Sea and the Persian Gulf. The Arabian Peninsula is part of the region known as the Middle East. Today the peninsula includes the countries of Saudi Arabia, Yemen, Oman, Qatar, Bahrain, Kuwait, and the United Arab Emirates.

Most of the people living on the Arabian Peninsula when Islam arose were Arabs. Arabs also lived in other places. What all Arabs shared was a common language, Arabic.

In the early 600s C.E., an Arab man named Muhammad introduced Islam to the people of the Arabian Peninsula. His followers became known as Muslims. Among other things, Muslims believe there is one God (the Arabic word for God is Allah) and that Muhammad is his prophet.

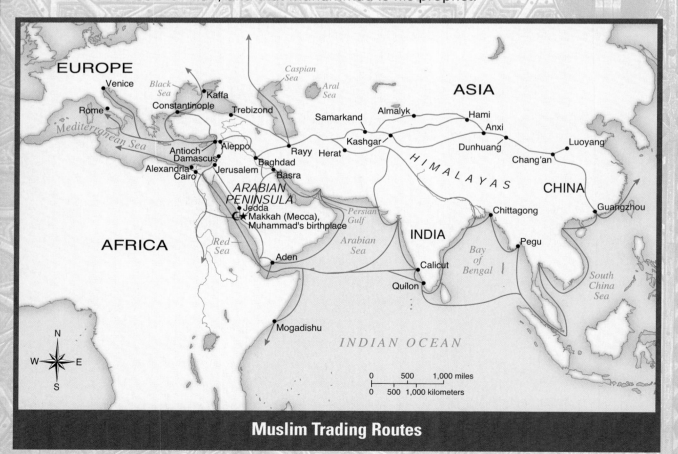

Muslim Trading Routes

Although the first Muslims lived in Arabia, Islam spread throughout the Middle East, North Africa, Persia (now called Iran), and other parts of Asia and Europe. Many non-Arabs became Muslims. In fact, today Arabs are a small minority of Muslims worldwide.

If you look at a map of the Middle East, you will see that the Arabian Peninsula is located at the crossroads of North Africa, Europe, and Asia. Arab Muslims were very active traders. It's not surprising, then, that one of the ways Islam spread was along Muslim trading routes. You'll learn more about the spread of Islam in this unit.

In this unit, you will also learn about Muhammad, the teachings of Islam, and some of the contributions Muslims have made to world civilization. You will take a close look at the crusades, a series of religious wars that European Christians waged against Muslims during medieval times. You'll also find out how Islam and Muslim societies continued to thrive and spread after the crusades.

Let's start our explorations with a closer look at the geography of the Arabian Peninsula, where Islam first arose.

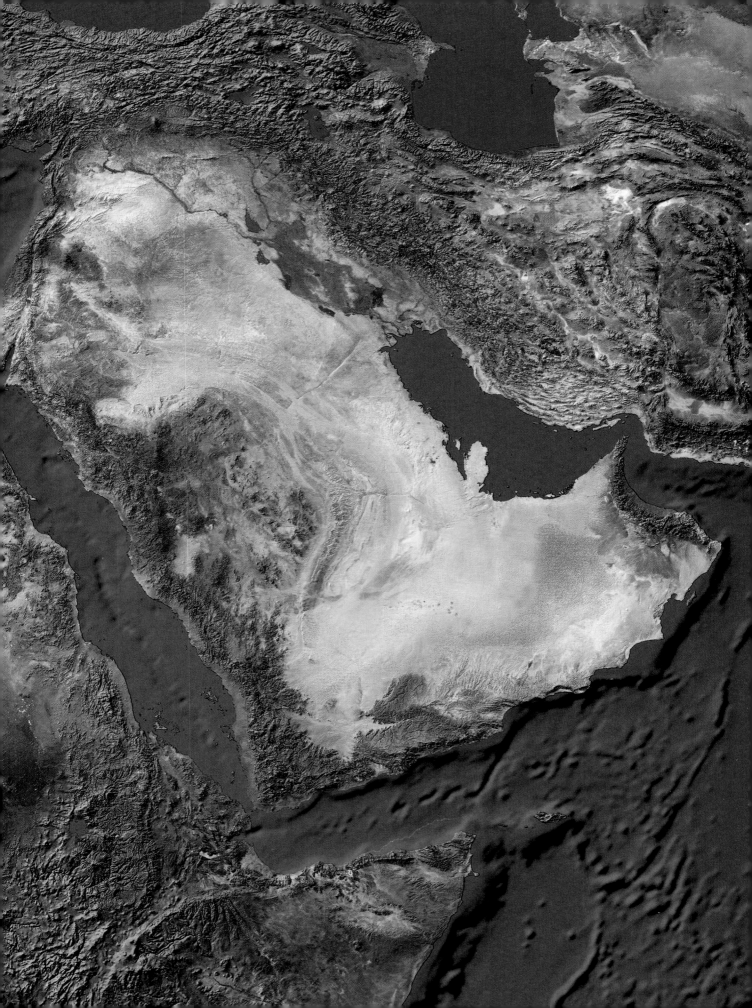

CHAPTER 7

◀ ◀ This photograph of the Arabian Peninsula was taken from a satellite in space.

The Geography of the Arabian Peninsula

7.1 Introduction

Our study of Islam begins with the **Arabian Peninsula,** where Islam was first preached. The founder of Islam, Muhammad, was born on the peninsula in about 570 C.E. In this chapter, you'll learn about the peninsula's **geography** and the ways of life of its people in the sixth century.

The Arabian Peninsula is in southwest Asia, between the Red Sea and the Persian Gulf. It is often called Arabia. Along with North Africa, the eastern Mediterranean shore, and present-day Turkey, Iraq, and Iran, it is part of the modern Middle East.

Most of the people living in Arabia in the sixth century were Arabs. Some Arabs call their homeland al-Jazeera, or "the Island." But it is surrounded by water on only three sides. The Persian Gulf lies to the east, the Red Sea to the west, and the Indian Ocean to the south. To the north are lands bordering the Mediterranean Sea. These lands serve as a land bridge between Africa, Asia, and Europe.

Imagine that you are flying over the Arabian Peninsula. As you look down, you see vast **deserts** dotted by **oases**. **Coastal plains** line the southern and western coasts. **Mountain ranges** divide these coastal plains from the deserts.

The hot, dry Arabian Peninsula is a challenging place to live. In this chapter, you will study the geography of Arabia and its different **environments**. You'll see how people made **adaptations** in order to thrive there.

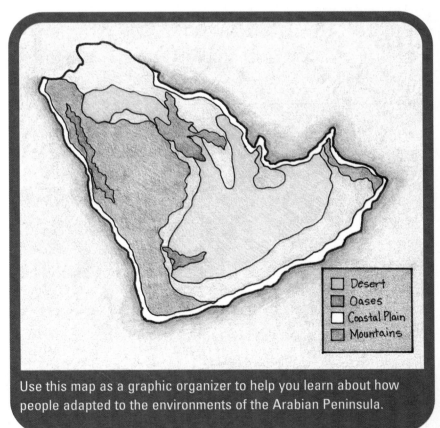

☐ Desert
☐ Oases
☐ Coastal Plain
☐ Mountains

Use this map as a graphic organizer to help you learn about how people adapted to the environments of the Arabian Peninsula.

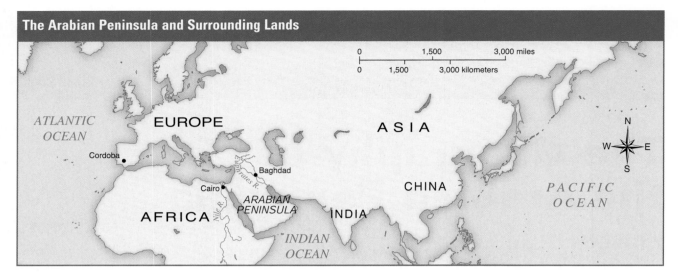

7.2 The Importance of the Arabian Peninsula and Surrounding Lands

Arabia lies at the crossroads of Asia, Africa, and Europe. In ancient times, great civilizations grew up in the lands around Arabia. To the northeast, Sumerians built their complex civilization along the valleys of the Tigris and Euphrates rivers in present-day Iraq. To the west, the Egyptians built their society on the banks of the Nile River in North Africa. Later, the Greeks, Romans, and Persians all had a major influence on the Middle East.

A great deal of trade passed through this region. Traders carried silk from China and jewels, cotton, and spices from India. From Africa came ivory and gold. The Romans sent glass and gold east to China.

As early as 2000 B.C.E., the people of Arabia served as middlemen in the trade between these lands. Arab traders used camels to carry goods through the desert in **caravans**. Along the coasts, merchants sent ships to distant marketplaces. Serving as a link between such diverse regions exposed Arabia to new goods and ideas. Arabs also shared their own knowledge along these trade routes.

The influence of Arabia became far more powerful with the rise of Islam. From its central location in Arabia, Islam spread rapidly throughout the Middle East, North Africa, and parts of Europe. Great cities like Cordoba in Spain, Cairo in Egypt, and Baghdad in present-day Iraq became important centers of the Islamic world.

Knowledge, ideas, technology, and goods flowed through Arab lands. For example, Arabs brought knowledge of paper making to Europe from China. Europe also benefited from ancient Greek learning that was preserved and enhanced by Arab scholars. And Islam itself would become one of the largest and most influential religions in the world.

What was the birthplace of Islam like? In the rest of this chapter, we'll look at Arabia's geography.

caravan a group of people traveling together for mutual protection, often with pack animals such as camels

76   Chapter 7

7.3 The Desert

About three quarters of the Arabian Peninsula is covered by desert. Besides vast seas of sand, the desert includes plains and **plateaus**.

Environment   The hot, dry desert environment is very harsh. Summer temperatures often rise above 120 degrees Fahrenheit. Winter and nighttime temperatures can drop below freezing. Annual rainfall does not surpass more than 3 to 4 inches, and droughts can last for years. When the rain comes, it often falls as violent storms, sometimes causing flash floods. These infrequent waters cause clumps of grass and pockets of low shrubs to spring to life.

The desert is often swept by windstorms. Powerful winds may flare up suddenly, causing blinding sandstorms. The winds transform the landscape, sometimes creating sand dunes that rise 800 feet into the sky.

Adaptations   Many Arabs in the sixth century lived in towns and villages. Others, however, were **nomads**. Arab nomads, called Bedouins, migrated through the desert raising sheep, goats, and camels. Upon finding a place for their herds to graze and drink, they set up tents. They moved on when the animals had eaten most of the vegetation.

The camel—called the "ship of the desert"—was the Bedouins' main method of transportation. Camels could survive for days without water, eat almost anything, and carry heavy loads for long distances.

Bedouins clothed themselves in loose-fitting long gowns and cotton headdresses to protect against dust, heat, and flies. They got almost everything they needed from their herds. They drank milk, made yogurt and cheese, and sometimes ate meat. The animals provided wool and hair for clothing, blankets, and tents, as well as leather hides. To obtain other items, like grain or weapons, Bedouins traded their animal products with merchants from the towns.

Some Bedouins controlled the valuable trade routes that linked towns and villages. Merchants operated caravans that carried goods across the desert. Sizable towns, like Makkah (Mecca) in western Arabia, developed as markets and resting places for the caravans.

plateau a raised area of flat land

nomad a person who moves from place to place, often in search of water and vegetation

The harsh desert environment covers much of the Arabian Peninsula. The deserts include plains and plateaus like those seen below.

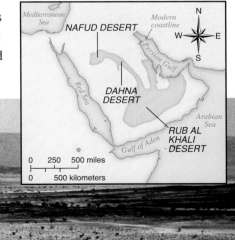

The Geography of the Arabian Peninsula   77

Oases provide water and plant life in the desert environment. Adaptations for living in the desert revolve around oases.

7.4 The Oases

The desert is dotted with oases, areas where fresh water is available. Oases are important because they provide plant life and shade as well as water.

Environment   Oases occur in areas where water has been trapped under the ground. The water seeps to the surface as a spring or waterhole. On these fertile lands, plant life sprouts up, particularly grass and shrubs. Oases vary in size, ranging from a few acres to large areas of land.

Adaptations   For centuries, nomads traveled from oasis to oasis in search of water and vegetation for their herds. Realizing they could grow crops at the oases, some nomads gave up their wandering lifestyle to become **sedentary**. To obtain more water for the crops they planted, they dug wells deep into the ground.

Oasis dwellers grew fruits such as dates and peaches, and grains to make bread. The date palm tree thrived in Arabia, and it became an invaluable resource. Palm leaves offered shade, while dates were a source of food. Farmers used palm wood to build homes. They used leaves for thatch roofs, fibers for rope, hollowed-out trunks for irrigation pipes, and various parts of the tree to fuel fires. The date palm was so useful that it was called "the mother and aunt of the Arabs."

A number of towns developed around oases, linked by tracks through the desert. Many of these towns evolved into small trading centers. Farmers **bartered** (traded) their crops for the goods the nomads brought, like milk, meat, and camel hair. Nomads either used these crops themselves or traded them elsewhere in the region. In time, merchants became an important part of town life.

sedentary permanently settled in one place

barter to buy and sell by trading goods or services rather than money

7.5 The Coastal Plain

Arabia's coastal plain runs along the coasts of the peninsula. The coastal plain separates inland plateaus from the Red Sea, the Arabian Sea, and the Persian Gulf.

Environment   Arabia's coastal plain ranges between 5 and 40 miles inland. It ends at a series of rocky cliffs. The air is damp and moist, and rain falls regularly. Several dry riverbeds cut through the coastal plain and periodically fill with water. The coastal plain also has a few natural harbors.

Adaptations   Unlike the dry desert, the coastal plan is suitable for farming. For centuries, farming communities thrived in southern Arabia. People built deep wells, dams, and systems to **irrigate** the land. They conserved rainwater in canals and reservoirs. In what is now Yemen, the great Marib Dam brought water to fields that grew food for 300,000 people. This dam survived for about 1,000 years. In about 580 C.E., the walls broke, and waters flooded the land.

In the sixth century, most people on the coastal plain were farmers. They grew crops such as grains, fruits, and vegetables. They also collected fragrant tree sap to make myrrh and frankincense, which Europeans used as incense, perfumes, and medicine.

There were also traders on the coastal plain. They sent their goods by caravan to towns like Makkah or to seaports. From ancient times, ships had stopped at such port cities as Aden (at the southern tip of Arabia). In this way, the people of the coastal plain traded with merchants from places like India, East Africa, and the lands along the Red Sea and the Persian Gulf. The combination of farming and trade led to the rise of powerful kingdoms in southern Arabia in ancient times.

irrigate to bring water to a dry place in order to grow crops

The coastal plain environment extends from the coast inland. Coastal plains receive plenty of rain and are suitable for farming.

7.6 The Mountains

Arabia's largest mountain ranges run along the western and southern edges of the peninsula. They divide the coastal plain from the desert.

Environment   Arabia's mountains rise from 1,000 to 12,000 feet high. These craggy mountain ranges have a very different climate from the rest of the peninsula. Moist winds from the Indian Ocean bring as much as 20 inches of rain each year to the mountains. The rain and elevation help keep temperatures in the mountains cool. In the winter, frost may form. Ancient dry riverbeds cut down the sides of the mountains and fill with water during rainstorms.

Adaptations   People have lived in Arabia's mountains for thousands of years. Isolated from the rest of the peninsula, they developed ways of life that endure to this day. For instance, it is likely that mountain dwellers in the sixth century lived in houses made of mud bricks. People in this region today still live in this type of dwelling.

In the sixth century, many people lived in the Asir Mountains in the southwest. These people farmed on the steep slopes by creating steplike **terraces,** or flat areas. They probably made the terraces by building low stone walls around narrow strips of land. The terraces enlarged the space that was usable for farming. Terrace walls also conserved water by keeping it from running off the fields.

Farmers also constructed dams and irrigation systems. They stored extra rainwater in underground storage containers, leather bags, and hollowed-out trees.

Farmers in the mountains relied on many different crops. They grew fruits, like melons and pomegranates. They also grew trees to produce frankincense and myrrh. They probably used manure and ashes from cooking fires to fertilize the soil.

terrace a flat strip of ground on a hillside used for growing crops

Mountain ranges separate the coastal plain and desert environments of the Arabian Peninsula. People have lived in these mountains for thousands of years.

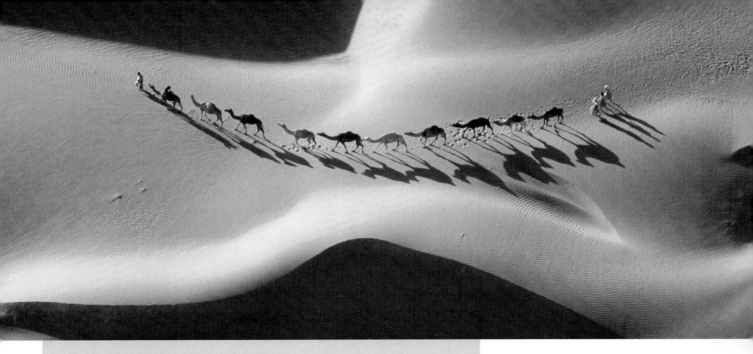

7.7 Chapter Summary

In this chapter, you learned about the geography of the Arabian Peninsula, the birthplace of Islam. You also found out how people on the peninsula adapted to their environments.

Arabia and nearby lands are at the crossroads of Asia, Africa, and Europe. Arabia played a key role in the exchange of goods and ideas among these regions. With the rise of Islam in the 600s C.E., Arabia would have a major influence on distant societies. Islamic culture spread from Arabia through the Middle East, North Africa, and parts of Europe.

Desert stretches over much of Arabia. The desert is a place of fiery heat, bitter cold, and little water or plant life. Still, people learned how to survive and even thrive in this barren region. Nomads raised animals that could survive in the desert and moved from place to place to find vegetation for their livestock.

Some people gave up the nomadic life to settle in the desert oases. Most people on the oases were farmers, but towns also grew up and became centers of trade.

Unlike the desert, the wet coastal plain in the south and west is quite fertile. Here farmers grew crops, and traders sent items to distant lands. To water their crops, farmers built irrigation systems. Port cities became trading centers.

Arabia's mountains run between the coastal plain and the desert. In these tall peaks, people lived off the land by creating terraced fields. This adaptation allowed them to make better use of the steep slopes.

The founder of Islam, Muhammad, came from Makkah, an ancient holy place and trading center in western Arabia. In the next chapter, you will learn about Muhammad and the faith he introduced to the world.

Camel caravans cross the desert carrying goods for trade. Camels are well suited to desert life because of their ability to travel for days without water.

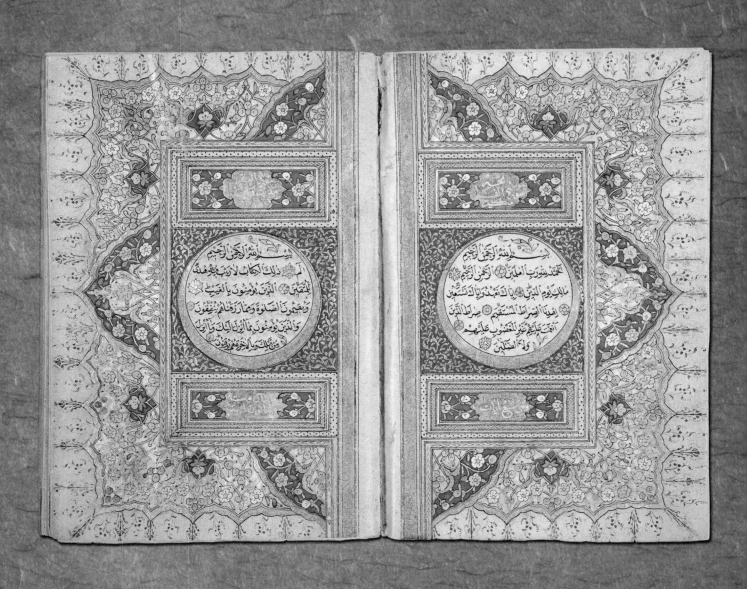

CHAPTER 8

◀ ◀ The Qu'ran is the holy book of Islam.
Its pages record Muhammad's teachings.

The Prophet Muhammad

8.1 Introduction

In Chapter 7, you learned about the geography of the Arabian Peninsula, where **Muhammad** was born in about 570 C.E. Muhammad taught the faith called **Islam,** one of the great religions of the world. In this chapter, you will learn about his life and the early spread of Islam in the 600s and 700s C.E.

Muhammad's birthplace, Makkah (Mecca), was an ancient place of worship. According to Arab and Muslim tradition, many centuries before Muhammad was born, it was here that God tested the faith of the **prophet** Abraham by commanding that he leave his wife Hagar and baby son Ishmael in a desolate valley. As Abraham's wife desperately searched for water, a miracle happened. A spring bubbled up at her son's feet. This spring became known as Zamzam. Over time, people settled near it, and, according to the Qur'an, Abraham built a house of worship called the Ka'ba.

By the time of Muhammad's birth, Makkah was a prosperous city that stood at the crossroads of great trade routes. Many people came to worship at the Ka'ba. But instead of honoring the one God of the Abrahamic faiths, the worshippers at the Ka'ba honored the many traditional gods who had shrines at the Ka'ba.

According to Islamic teachings, Muhammad was living in Makkah when he experienced his own call to prophethood. Like Abraham, according to religious Scriptures, Muhammad proclaimed belief in a single God. At first the faith he taught, Islam, met with resistance in Makkah. But Muhammad and his followers, called **Muslims,** eventually triumphed. Makkah became Islam's most sacred city, and the Ka'ba became a center of Islamic worship.

In this chapter, you will explore Muhammad's life. You will learn how Islam quickly spread throughout Arabia and beyond. As you will see, within a century of Muhammad's death, a great Muslim empire stretched from North Africa to central Asia.

Use this illustrated manuscript as a graphic organizer to help you learn about Muhammad's life and teachings.

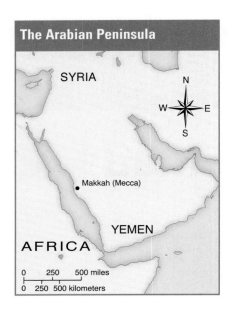

The Arabian Peninsula

SYRIA

Makkah (Mecca)

YEMEN

AFRICA

0   250   500 miles
0   250 500 kilometers

clan a group of related families
polytheist a person who
believes in more than one god
tribe a social group that shares
a common ancestry, leadership,
and traditions

8.2 Arabia During Muhammad's Time

Islam has its roots in Arabia, where Muhammad was born. To understand Islam's beginnings, we first need to look at the world in which Muhammad grew up.

The town of Makkah, Muhammad's birthplace, was located in a dry, rocky valley in western Arabia. Unlike oasis towns, Makkah did not have agriculture. Instead, it gained wealth as a trading city. Merchants traveling along caravan routes stopped at the city's market and inns. They bought spices, sheepskins, meat, dates, and other wares from townspeople and nomads.

By the late 6th century C.E., when Muhammad was born, Makkah was a prosperous city. Merchant families brought goods into Makkah from faraway places. Merchants grew wealthy through trade with Yemen (southern Arabia), Syria, and Africa. Over time, a handful of families had come to rule the city. These families would not share their fortune with the weaker, poorer **clans** who lived in the city.

Makkah was also a religious center. The Ka'ba, a cube-shaped shrine, was said to have been built by Abraham for God centuries before. In Muhammad's day, according to Islamic teaching, most Arabs were **polytheists** (people who believed in many gods), and the Ka'ba housed hundreds of statues of gods. Pilgrims from all over Arabia came to Makkah to worship.

Many Arabs, however, lived in the desert rather than in towns. There was no central government in Arabia. Instead, Arabs pledged loyalty to their clans and larger groups called **tribes**. Sometimes tribes launched raids on other tribes to capture territory, animals, goods, watering places, and even wives. When someone was killed during a raid, his family was honor-bound to avenge that death.

Although Arabs on the peninsula were not united as a nation, they shared ties of culture, especially language. Arabic poetry celebrated the history of the Arab people, the beauty of their land, and their way of life. Poets and singers from different tribes competed at gatherings held at the markets and during pilgrimages.

This was the culture into which Muhammad was born. Let's turn now to the story of his life and how he changed his world.

In the late sixth century, Makkah was a wealthy trading city with a busy marketplace.

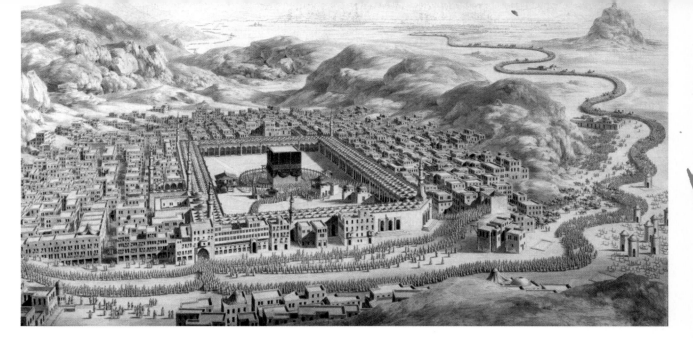

8.3 Muhammad's Early Life

Around 570 C.E., a boy named Muhammad was born in Makkah. Muhammad's early life was a humble one. Few people who were not members of his clan, the Hashim, noted his birth. His father had already died, and the clan was poor.

Following custom, Muhammad's mother sent her baby to live with a nomad family in the desert. There the young boy learned about Arab traditions, such as being kind to strangers and helping orphans, widows, and other needy members of society.

When Muhammad was about five or six, he returned to the city and his mother. They had little time together, because she soon died. Muhammad was left in the care of his grandfather, Abd al-Muttalib, a highly regarded leader of the Hashim clan. Upon Abd al-Muttalib's death, Muhammad's uncle, Abu Talib, a respected merchant himself, took charge of the orphan. Abu Talib also became head of the clan.

As a boy, Muhammad watched his family's flocks of sheep and goats. When he was about 12 years old, he accompanied his uncle on a trading journey. They traveled far north to Syria. On this journey, Muhammad gained his first exposure to places outside of the Arabian deserts.

As Muhammad grew up, he took on more duties and made more trading journeys. He became a trader who enjoyed a reputation throughout Makkah for his honesty. People called him al-Amin, which means "the Trustworthy."

Muhammad was still a young man when he began managing caravans for a widow named Khadijah, who ran a trading business. Muhammad earned her great profits. Impressed with his abilities and honesty, Khadijah proposed marriage. Muhammad accepted her offer, and at around age 25 he married Khadijah. Muhammad and Khadijah had several children, but only their daughter Fatimah had children of her own. She continued the bloodline of Muhammad.

The Ka'ba shrine in Makkah was surrounded by homes. In Muhammad's time, people came from all over Arabia to worship at Makkah.

The Hira Cave is where, according to Islamic teachings, Muhammad was first visited by the angel Gabriel.

8.4 The Call to Prophethood

For the next 15 years, Muhammad made his living as a merchant. Although he enjoyed success in business, he also cared about spiritual matters. He often spent time at prayer in the mountains around Makkah.

In about 610 C.E., Muhammad went to pray in a cave in the mountains. It was there, according to Islamic teachings, that he received the call to be a prophet, or messenger of God, whom the Arabs called Allah.

Muhammad later described the remarkable events of that night. He told that he received a visit from the angel Gabriel. Muhammad described how Gabriel told him several times to "recite." Muhammad asked what he was to recite, and Gabriel answered:

Recite—in the name of thy Lord!
Who created man from blood coagulated
Recite! Thy Lord is wondrous kind
Who by the pen has taught mankind
Things they knew not.

Muhammad left the cave, quaking with fear. But Gabriel spoke to him again, declaring, "You are the messenger of God."

At first, Muhammad feared that he might be going mad. But, according to Muslim tradition, Khadijah consoled Muhammad and expressed her faith that God had chosen him as a prophet to communicate his words to the people.

Khadijah became the first **convert** to Islam. The faith of Islam is based on **monotheism,** or the belief in a single God. This God, Muhammad taught, was the same God of Abraham, Moses, and Jesus. Through Gabriel, God told Muhammad to teach others about treating people with compassion, honesty, and justice.

According to Muslim tradition, Gabriel continued to reveal messages from God over the next 22 years. At first, Muhammad confided these messages only to his family and friends, including his cousin Ali and a close companion, Abu Bakr. Gradually, a small group of followers developed at Makkah. They were called Muslims, which means "those who surrender to God." For Muslims, Islam was a way of life and the basis for creating a just society.

Though Muhammad apparently could neither read nor write, he said that the messages from Gabriel were imprinted on his mind and heart. His followers also memorized them. Eventually, some followers wrote down these words and collected them in the Qur'an (also spelled Koran), the holy book of Islam. The poetic beauty of this book helped attract new believers to Islam.

8.5 Muhammad's Teaching Meets with Rejection

Around 613 C.E., Muhammad began to preach to other Makkans. He taught that people must worship one God, that all believers in God were equal, and that the rich should share their wealth. He urged Makkans to take care of orphans and the poor, and to improve the status of women.

Some members of Muhammad's clan became Muslims. People from other clans and social classes also joined him. Most Makkans, however, rejected Muhammad's teachings. Makkah's leaders did not want to share their wealth. They also feared that if Muhammad grew stronger, he would seize political power. Merchants worried that if people stopped worshiping their gods, they might stop making pilgrimages to Makkah. Muhammad's monotheistic teachings also disturbed Arabs who did not want to give up their gods.

To prevent the spread of the prophet's message, some Arabs called Muhammad a liar. Some tortured his weaker followers. Despite this treatment, the Muslims would not give up their faith. Muhammad was also protected by Abu Talib, the head of the Hashim clan. Anyone who harmed a member of the clan would face Abu Talib's vengeance.

As the number of Muslims grew, the powerful clans of Makkah started a **boycott** to make Muhammad's followers give up Islam. For three years, the Hashim clan suffered as Makkans refused to do business with them. Although they were threatened with starvation, the boycott failed to break their will. These difficult years, however, took their toll on Abu Talib and Khadijah. In 619, these trusted family members died.

While these losses were terrible for Muhammad, that year he reported a miraculous event. The Qur'an tells the story of the Night Journey in which a winged horse took Muhammad to Jerusalem, the city toward which early Muslims had directed their prayers. There he met and prayed with earlier prophets, like Abraham, Moses, and Jesus. The horse then guided Muhammad through the seven levels of heaven, and Muhammad met God. To this day, Jerusalem is a holy city for Muslims.

As-Akhar rock is thought to be where, according to Muslim tradition, Muhammad ended his Night Journey to Jerusalem and was led to heaven. An eight-sided, domed monument now marks the spot over the rock.

boycott a refusal to do business with an organization or group

The Prophet's Mosque in Madinah holds Muhammad's tomb.

8.6 From the Migration to Madinah to the End of His Life

With Abu Talib's death, Muhammad lost his protector. As Muslims came under more attacks, Muhammad sought a new home. Then a group of Arab pilgrims from a town called Yathrib visited Makkah and converted to Islam. They asked Muhammad to move to Yathrib to bring peace between feuding tribes. In return, they pledged their protection.

In 622, Muhammad and his followers left Makkah on a journey known as the *hijrah*. Yathrib was renamed Madinah (also spelled Medina), short for the "City of the Prophet." The year of Muhammad's hijrah later became the first year in the Muslim calendar.

In Madinah, Muhammad developed a new Muslim community as more Arabs converted to Islam. Muslims pledged to be loyal and helpful to each other. They emphasized the brotherhood of faith over the ties of family, clan, and tribe. Muhammad also asked his followers to respect Christians and Jews. Like Muslims, these "People of the Book" believed in one God.

The Makkans, however, still felt threatened. In 624, fighting broke out between the Muslims and Makkans. The Muslims successfully attacked a caravan on its way to Makkah. A few years later, the Makkans staged a **siege** of Madinah, but failed to capture the city.

Meanwhile, Muhammad convinced other tribes to join the Muslim community. As Islam spread across Arabia, the Makkans made a truce with the Muslims. In 628, they agreed to let Muhammad make the pilgrimage to their city the following year. In 630, however, they broke the truce. As Muhammad's army marched toward Makkah, the city's leaders surrendered without a battle. Muhammad and his followers destroyed the idols (statues of gods) at the Ka'ba and rededicated the shrine to Allah. Muhammad also forgave his former enemies. The war had ended.

In March 632, Muhammad led his final pilgrimage. In the town of his birth, he delivered his Last Sermon. He reminded Muslims to treat each other well and to be faithful to their community. Shortly after his return to Madinah, Muhammad died.

siege an attempt to surround a place and cut off all access to it in order to force a surrender

8.7 The Four Caliphs

When Muhammad died, most of central and southern Arabia was under Muslim control. After the prophet's death, his companions had to choose a new leader to preserve the community. They picked Abu Bakr, Muhammad's friend and father-in-law.

Abu Bakr became the first **caliph,** or Muslim ruler. He and the three leaders who followed him came to be known to a large group of Muslims as the "rightly guided" caliphs. These caliphs were said by this group of Muslims to have followed the Qur'an and the example of Muhammad. The Muslim government was called the *caliphate*.

When some tribes tried to break away, Abu Bakr used military campaigns to reunite the community. Under his leadership, Muslims completed the unification of Arabia. Then they began to carry the teachings of Islam beyond the Arabian Peninsula.

After Abu Bakr died in 634 C.E., Caliph Umar expanded the Muslim empire. In addition to spreading the faith of Islam, conquest allowed Muslims to gain new lands, resources, and goods.

By 643, the Muslim empire included lands in Iraq, Persia, the eastern Mediterranean, and North Africa. Umar set up governments and tax systems in these **provinces**. He also let Jews and Christians worship as they liked. In Egypt, treaties allowed for freedom of worship in exchange for the payment of tribute. Later, Muslims completed similar treaties with the Nubians, a people who lived to the south of Egypt.

Upon Umar's death in 644 C.E., Uthman became caliph. Uthman was a member of the Umayyad clan. He helped unite Muslims when he selected an official edition of the Qur'an. But he also awarded high posts to his relatives. People in the provinces complained that they were ruled unfairly. Discontent spread, and rebels killed Uthman in 656.

Ali ibn Abi Talib, Muhammad's cousin and son-in-law, reluctantly agreed to become the fourth caliph. Some Umayyads challenged his rule, drawing the Muslim community into a civil war. Ali sent forces against them. When he ended the rebellion through negotiation, some of his supporters disapproved of his action. In 661, one of them murdered Ali.

The fourth caliph in the Muslim government fought against rebellious Muslims who challenged his rule.

caliph a title taken by Muslim rulers who claimed religious authority to rule

province a division of a country or an empire

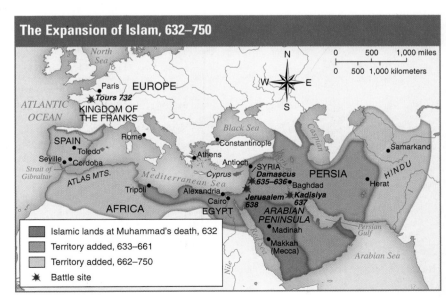

The Expansion of Islam, 632–750

North Sea

ATLANTIC OCEAN

Paris · EUROPE
★ Tours 732
KINGDOM OF THE FRANKS
Rome
SPAIN
· Toledo
Seville · · Cordoba
Strait of Gibraltar
ATLAS MTS.
Tripoli
AFRICA

Black Sea

Constantinople
Athens
Antioch
Cyprus
Mediterranean Sea
Alexandria · Cairo
EGYPT

Caspian Sea

Samarkand

SYRIA
Damascus ★ 635–636 · Baghdad
Jerusalem ★ Kadisiya
638   637
ARABIAN PENINSULA
· Madinah
· Makkah (Mecca)
Red Sea

PERSIA
Herat ·
HINDU

Persian Gulf

Arabian Sea

0   500   1,000 miles
0   500 1,000 kilometers

■ Islamic lands at Muhammad's death, 632
■ Territory added, 633–661
■ Territory added, 662–750
★ Battle site

8.8 The Umayyad Dynasty

Soon after Ali's death, Mu'awiyah, the leader of the Umayyads, claimed the caliphate. Most Muslims, called the Sunnis, came to accept him. But a minority of Muslims, known as the Shi'a, or "party" of Ali, refused to do so. They believed that only people directly related to Muhammad through his son-in-law Ali should be caliph. The split between the Sunnis and Shi'a lasts to this day.

Mu'awiyah put down a revolt by Ali's supporters. He held on to the role of caliph. He also founded the Umayyad **dynasty**. In 661, the Umayyads moved their capital to Damascus, Syria. From there, the caliphs ruled the huge Muslim empire for close to 100 years. To maintain control, they kept large armies posted at **garrison** towns.

Slowly, the lands of the Muslim empire took on more elements of Arab culture. Muslims introduced the Arabic language. Along with Islam, acceptance of Arabic helped unite the diverse people of the empire. In addition, Arabs took over as top officials. People bought goods with new Arab coins. While the Muslims did not force people to convert to Islam, some non-Arabs willingly became Muslims.

The Muslim empire continued to expand. The Umayyad caliphs sent armies into central Asia and northwestern India. In 711, Muslim armies began their conquests of present-day Spain. However, at the Battle of Tours in 732, forces under the Frankish king Charles Martel turned the Muslims back in west-central France. This battle marked the farthest extent of Muslim advances into present-day France.

Muslims held on to land in Spain, where Muslim states lasted for almost 800 years. Muslims in Spain built some of the greatest cities of medieval Europe. Their capital city, Cordoba, became a center of learning where Muslim, Jewish, and Christian scholars shared ideas. Through their work, Muslim Spain made amazing advances in arts, science, technology, and literature. You will learn more about the accomplishments of Islamic civilization in Chapter 10.

dynasty a line of rulers descended from the same family
garrison a place where a group of soldiers is stationed for defensive purposes

The first two caliphs, Abu Bakr and Umar, are buried on either side of Muhammad's tomb.

8.9 Chapter Summary

In this chapter, you learned about the life of Muhammad and the early spread of Islam. Muhammad and his followers unified Arabia. Within 100 years, Muslims created a great empire.

When Muhammad was born, Arabia was not a united country. Tribes raided each other and fought over the region's scarce resources. Arabs did, however, share economic ties through trade, as well as the Arabic language and culture.

Born in Makkah, Muhammad was, according to Muslim tradition, a successful merchant known for his honesty. He was also a spiritual man. After a dramatic experience during a night of prayer in 610, he gradually came to accept his calling as a prophet. Muhammad described how he continued to receive revelations from the angel Gabriel. His teachings were gathered in the Qur'an, the holy book of Islam.

Muhammad taught that there was only one God. He also taught equality. He told his followers to share their wealth and to care for the less fortunate in society. He preached tolerance for Christians and Jews as fellow worshipers of the one true God.

Many people in Makkah opposed Islam. In 622, Muhammad and his followers moved to Madinah. There Muhammad established a Muslim community. By the time of his death in 632, people throughout central and southern Arabia had accepted the teachings of Islam and the Qur'an as the words of God.

The caliphs who followed Muhammad greatly expanded the lands under their rule despite struggles over leadership and even civil war. In 661, the Umayyads moved their capital to Syria. By the mid 700s, the Muslim empire included Spain, North Africa, the Middle East, and part of central Asia and India.

Along with the Arabic language, the acceptance of Islam helped unify this vast empire. In the next chapter, you will learn more about the core beliefs of the Islamic faith.

Muslims continued to follow Muhammad's teachings as Islam spread throughout the Middle East and beyond.

CHAPTER **9**

The beliefs and practices of Islam are a way of life for Muslims.

The Teachings of Islam

9.1 Introduction

In Chapter 8, you learned about the prophet Muhammad and the early spread of Islam. Now you will take a closer look at the Islamic faith.

If you visited any city in a Muslim country today, you would notice many things that reflect the teachings of Islam. Five times a day, you would hear a call to prayer throughout the city. While some people hurry to houses of worship, called *mosques,* others simply remain where they are to pray, even in the street. You would see people dressed modestly and many women wearing a head scarf. You would find that Muslims do not drink alcohol or eat pork. You might learn how Muslims give money to support their houses of worship and many charitable works. Soon you would come to understand that Islam is practiced as a complete way of life.

In this chapter, you will explore the basic beliefs and practices of Islam. You will learn more about the holy book called the **Qur'an**. Together with the **Sunnah** (the example of Muhammad), this book guides Muslims in the **Five Pillars of Faith**. The Five Pillars are faith, prayer, charity, fasting, and making a pilgrimage to Makkah. You will also study the idea of **jihad**. Jihad represents Muslims' struggle with internal and external challenges as they strive to please God. Finally, you will examine **shari'ah,** or Islamic law.

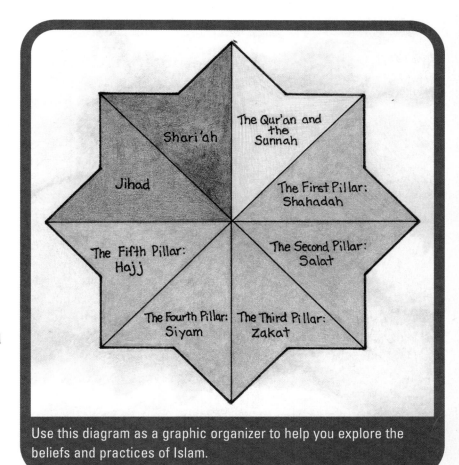

Use this diagram as a graphic organizer to help you explore the beliefs and practices of Islam.

The Islamic community has spread throughout the world. These Muslims in Cairo, Egypt, prepare to pray on a sidewalk by facing toward Makkah.

9.2 Background on Islam

Since the time of Muhammad, Islam has had a huge impact on world history. From Arabia, Islam spread rapidly throughout the Middle East, across North Africa to Spain, and across central Asia nearly to China. In addition to sharing a common faith, Muslims also belonged to a single Islamic community, called the *ummah*. The Islamic community blended many peoples and cultures.

Islam now has more followers than any religion except Christianity. One out of five people in the world are Muslims. Most people in the Middle East and North Africa are Muslim, but Muslims live in nearly every country of the world. In fact, the majority of Muslims are Asian. And Islam is the fastest-growing religion in the United States.

Islam, Judaism, and Christianity have much in common. Members of all three faiths are monotheists (they believe in one God). All three religions trace their origins to the prophet Abraham. Their scriptures, or sacred writings, all include such figures as Adam, Noah, and Moses. Muslims believe that all three religions worship the same God.

As you learned in Chapter 8, Muslims consider Jews and Christians to be "People of the Book." The Jewish Bible, called the **Torah,** is known as the Old Testament in the Christian Bible. The New Testament of Christianity includes, among other writings, the gospels that tell of the life and teachings of Jesus. Muslims believe that these holy books, like the Qur'an, came from God. The Qur'an states that God "earlier revealed the Torah and the Gospel as a source of guidance for people."

For Muslims, however, the Qur'an contains God's final revelations to the world. They believe that its messages reveal how God wants his followers to act and worship. In the rest of this chapter, you'll learn more about the ideas that have shaped the Muslim faith.

Torah the Jewish scriptures, or Bible. The word Torah is often used to mean to the first five books of the Bible, traditionally said to have been written by Moses.

9.3 The Qur'an and the Sunnah

Two foundations of Islam are the Qur'an and the Sunnah. Through the Qur'an, God describes his laws and moral teachings, or the "straight path." The Qur'an holds a central position for Muslims everywhere, guiding them in all aspects of their lives.

The Qur'an contains passages that Muhammad is believed to have received from the angel Gabriel. Muhammad and his followers recited and memorized these verses. As Muhammad could apparently not read or write, scribes wrote down these passages. The Arabic of the Qur'an is notable for its great beauty.

In about 651 C.E., Caliph Uthman established an official edition of the Qur'an. He destroyed other versions. The Qur'an used today has remained largely unchanged since then.

Muhammad called the Qur'an Allah's "standing miracle." Muslims honor the spoken and written Qur'an. They do not let copies of the sacred book touch the ground or get dirty. Most Muslims memorize all or part of the Qur'an in Arabic. Its verses accompany Muslims through their lives, from birth to death.

The Sunnah ("practice") is the example that Muhammad set for Muslims during his lifetime. What Muhammad did or said in a certain situation has set a precedent, or guide, for all Muslims. For instance, Muhammad told his followers to make sure their guests never left a table hungry. He also reminded children to honor their parents when he said, "God forbids all of you to disobey your mothers." For Muslims, the Sunnah is second only to the Qur'an in religious authority.

Within 200 years after Muhammad's death, thousands of reports about the prophet had traveled throughout Muslim lands. Scholars looked into each story. They placed the stories they could verify into collections. Called **hadith** (tradition), these accounts provided written evidence of Muhammad's Sunnah as seen in his words and deeds. They continue to have this role today.

The most basic acts of worship for Muslims are called the Five Pillars of Faith. The Qur'an provides general commands to perform these five duties. The Sunnah explains how to perform them using Muhammad's example. Let's look next at each of the five pillars.

hadith accounts of Muhammad's words or actions that are accepted as having authority for Muslims

These girls in Bangladesh are reading the Qur'an to learn how to perform the basic acts of Muslim worship, called the Five Pillars of Faith.

9.4 The First Pillar: Shahadah

The first Pillar of Faith is *shahadah,* the profession (declaration) of faith. To show belief in one God and in Muhammad's prophethood, a Muslim says, "There is no god but God, and Muhammad is the messenger of God."

The first part of the shahadah affirms monotheism. Like Christians and Jews, Muslims believe that one all-powerful God, whom they call Allah, created the universe. They believe that the truth of one God was revealed to humankind through many prophets. These prophets include Adam, Noah, Moses, and Jesus, who appear in Jewish and Christian scriptures. The Qur'an honors all these prophets.

The second part of the shahadah identifies Muhammad as God's messenger. According to this statement, Muhammad announced the message of Islam, which was God's final word to humankind.

The meaning of shahadah is that people not only believe in God, but also pledge their submission to Him. For Muslims, God is the center of life. The shahadah follows Muslims through everyday life, not just prayers. Parents whisper it into their babies' ears. Muslims strive to utter the shahadah as their last words before death. Students taking a difficult test say the shahadah to help them through the ordeal.

In addition to the reality and oneness of God, Muslims accept the idea of an unseen world of angels and other beings. According to their faith, God created angels to do His work throughout the universe. Some angels revealed themselves to prophets, as Gabriel did to Muhammad. Other angels observe and record the deeds of each human being.

Muslims also believe that all souls will face a day of judgment. On that day, God will weigh each person's actions. Those who have lived according to God's rules will be rewarded and allowed to enter paradise. Those who have disbelieved or done evil will be punished by falling into hell.

A muezzin is a person who calls Muslim people to prayer from a mosque's tower, or minaret.

9.5 The Second Pillar: Salat

The second Pillar of Faith is *salat*, daily ritual prayer. Muhammad said that "prayer is the proof" of Islam. Salat emphasizes religious discipline, spirituality, and closeness to God.

Throughout Muslim communities, people are called to prayer five times a day: at dawn, noon, midday, sunset, and after nightfall. A crier, called a *muezzin* (or *mu'addin*), chants the call to prayer from the tall minaret (tower) of the mosque.

Before praying, Muslims must perform ritual washings. All mosques have fountains where worshipers wash their hands, face, arms, and feet. With a sense of being purified, Muslims enter the prayer area. There they form lines behind a prayer leader called an **imam**. The worshipers face the *qibla*, the direction of Makkah. A niche in a wall marks the qibla. People of all classes stand shoulder to shoulder, but men stand in separate rows from women.

This mosque has two minarets. Muezzins climb up into them to chant their calls to prayer out over the town.

The imam begins the prayer cycle by proclaiming "Allahu akbar!" ("God is most great!"). The worshipers then recite verses from the Qur'an and kneel before God.

While praying at a mosque is preferable, Muslims may worship anywhere. In groups or by themselves, they may perform their prayers at home, at work, in airports, in parks, or on sidewalks. A qibla compass may help them locate the direction of Makkah. Some Muslims carry a prayer rug to have a clean spot to pray. Some make additional prayers by using prayer beads and reciting words describing God's many characteristics.

Unlike Christians and Jews, Muslims do not observe a sabbath, or day of rest. On Fridays, however, Muslims gather at a mosque for midday congregational prayer. The worshipers listen to a Qur'an reading and the imam's sermon. After saying prayers together, some return to their regular business. For others, Friday is a special day when people meet with family and friends.

imam a leader of prayer in a mosque

9.6 The Third Pillar: Zakat

almsgiving the giving of money, food, or other things of value to the needy

The third Pillar of Faith is *zakat,* or **almsgiving** (giving to those in need). In Chapter 8, you learned that Muhammad told wealthy people to share their riches with the less fortunate. This practice remains a basic part of Islam.

The word *zakat* means "purification." Muslims believe that wealth becomes pure by giving some of it away and that sharing wealth helps control greed. Zakat also reminds people of God's great gifts to them.

Through zakat, Muslims give to the poor or needy.

According to the teachings of Islam, Muslims must share about one fortieth (2.5 percent) of their income and possessions with their poorer neighbors. They are encouraged to give even more. Individuals decide the proper amount to pay. Then they either give this sum to a religious official or distribute it themselves.

Zakat helps provide for many needs. In medieval times, zakat often went to constructing public fountains so everyone had clean water to drink or to inns so pilgrims and travelers had a place to sleep. If you walk down a busy street in any Muslim town today, you will see the fruits of zakat spending everywhere. Zakat pays for soup kitchens, clothing, and shelter for the poor. Orphanages and hospitals are built and supported through zakat. Poorer Muslims may receive funds to pay off their debts. Zakat provides aid to stranded travelers.

Zakat also helps other good causes that serve the Muslim community. For instance, zakat can cover the school fees of children whose parents cannot afford to send them to Muslim schools. It can be used to pay teachers.

Zakat is similar to charitable giving in other faiths. For instance, Jews and Christians also ask for donations to support their houses of worship and charitable activities.

9.7 The Fourth Pillar: Siyam

The fourth Pillar of Faith is *siyam*, or fasting (going without food). Muslims were not the first people to fast as a way of worshiping God. Both the Old and New Testaments praise the act. But the Qur'an instructs Muslims to fast for an entire month during **Ramadan,** the ninth month of the Islamic calendar.

According to Islamic teachings, Ramadan was the month that God first revealed His message to Muhammad. Muslims use a lunar calendar (one based on the phases of the moon). A year on this calendar is shorter than a 365-day year. Over time, as a result, Ramadan cycles through all the seasons of the year.

During Ramadan, Muslims fast from the break of dawn to the setting of the sun. Pregnant women, travelers, the sick, the elderly, and young children do not have to fast.

During the daylight hours on each day of Ramadan, Muslims do not eat any food or drink any liquid, including water. It is considered time to begin fasting when a person standing outside can tell a white thread from a black thread. Muslims then break their fast, often with dates and other food and beverages—as Muhammad did—and perform the sunset prayer. After a meal shared with family or friends, Muslims attend special prayer sessions. Each night a portion of the Qur'an is read aloud. By the end of Ramadan, Muslims have heard the entire holy book.

Ramadan the ninth month of the Islamic calendar, during which Muslims are required to fast

The holy month of Ramadan ends with a celebration that includes a feast of special foods.

The holy month of Ramadan encourages generosity, equality, and charity within the Muslim community. Fasting teaches Muslims self-control and makes them realize what it would be like to be poor and hungry. Well-off Muslims and mosques often provide food for others. During Ramadan, Muslims also strive to forgive people, give thanks, and avoid arguments and bad deeds.

At the end of Ramadan, Muslims remember Gabriel's first visit to Muhammad. A celebration called Eid al-Fitr takes place when Ramadan ends. People attend prayers. They wear new clothes, decorate their homes, and prepare special foods. They exchange gifts and give to the poor.

9.8 The Fifth Pillar: Hajj

The fifth Pillar of Faith is *hajj*, the pilgrimage to the holy city of Makkah. In the Islamic year's 12th month, millions of believers from all over the world come together at Makkah. All adult Muslims who can do so are expected to make the hajj once during their lifetime. By bringing Muslims from many places and cultures together, the hajj promotes fellowship and equality.

In Makkah, pilgrims follow what Muslims believe are the footsteps of Abraham and Muhammad, and so draw closer to God. For five days, they dress in simple white clothing and perform a series of rituals, moving from one sacred site to another.

Upon arrival, Muslims announce their presence with these words: "Here I am, O God, at thy command!" They go straight to the Great Mosque, which houses the Ka'ba. As you learned in Chapter 8, Muslims believe that Abraham built the Ka'ba as a shrine to honor God. The pilgrims circle the Ka'ba seven times, which is a ritual mentioned in the Qur'an. Next, they run

Pilgrims to the holy city of Makkah circle the Ka'ba seven times as directed in the Qur'an.

along a passage between two small hills, as did Hagar, Abraham's wife, when she searched for water for her baby Ishmael. As you may remember, Muslims believe that a spring called Zamzam miraculously appeared at Hagar's feet. The pilgrims drink from the Zamzam well.

Later, pilgrims leave Makkah to sleep in tents at a place called Mina. In the morning they move to the Plain of Arafat to pray until sunset, asking God's forgiveness. Some climb Mount Arafat, where Muhammad preached his Last Sermon. After spending another night camped in the desert, they reject evil by casting stones at pillars representing Satan.

Afterward, pilgrims may celebrate with a four-day feast. In honor of Abraham's ancient sacrifice, as recounted in religious Scriptures, they sacrifice animals, usually sheep or goats, and share the meat with family, friends, and the poor. Then, having completed the hajj, they don their own clothes again. Before leaving Makkah, each pilgrim circles the Ka'ba seven more times. Muslims around the world celebrate this "farewell" day as Eid al-Adha.

9.9 Jihad

The word *jihad* means "to strive." Originally in Islam, it meant physical struggle with spiritual significance. The Qur'an tells Muslims to fight to protect themselves from those who would do them harm or to right a terrible wrong. Early Muslims considered their efforts to protect their territory and extend their rule over other regions to be a form of jihad. However, the Qur'an forbade Muslims to force others to convert to Islam. So, non-Muslims who came under Muslim rule were usually allowed to continue practicing their faiths.

Although the Qur'an allows war, it sets specific terms for fighting. Muhammad told his followers to honor agreements made with foes. Muslim fighters must not mutilate (remove or destroy) the dead bodies of enemies or harm women, children, old people, and civilians. Nor should they destroy property, orchards, crops, sacred objects, or houses of worship.

Jihad originally meant a physical struggle against enemies while striving to please God. Sometimes it may be a struggle within an individual to overcome spiritually significant difficulties.

Jihad represents the human struggle to overcome difficulties and do things that would be pleasing to God. Muslims strive to respond positively to personal difficulties as well as worldly challenges. For instance, they might work to become better people, reform society, or correct injustice.

Jihad has always been an important Islamic concept. One hadith, or account of Muhammad, tells about the prophet's return from a battle. He declared that he and his men had carried out the "lesser jihad," the external struggle against oppression. The "greater jihad," he said, was the fight against evil within oneself. Examples of the greater jihad include working hard for a goal, giving up a bad habit, getting an education, or obeying your parents when you may not want to.

Another hadith says that Muslims should fulfill jihad with the heart, tongue, and hand. Muslims use the heart in their struggle to resist evil. The tongue may convince others to take up worthy causes, such as funding medical research. Hands may perform good works and correct wrongs.

9.10 Shari'ah: Islamic Law

The body, or collection, of Islamic law is called *shari'ah,* the "path to be followed." It is based on the Qur'an and the Sunnah. Shari'ah covers Muslims' duties toward God. It guides them in their personal behavior and relationships with others. Shari'ah promotes obedience to the Qur'an and respect for others.

In Madinah's Muslim community, Muhammad explained the Qur'an and served as a judge. After his death, the caliphs used the Qur'an and the Sunnah to solve problems as they arose. As the Muslim empire expanded, leaders faced new situations. Gradually, scholars developed a body of Islamic law. By the 12th century, several schools of Islamic law had emerged.

Islamic law guides Muslim life by placing actions into one of five categories: forbidden, discouraged, allowed, recommended, and obligatory (required). Sometimes the

A shari'ah court is shown on this page from an illuminated manuscript dated 1334 C.E.

law is quite specific. Muslims, for instance, are forbidden to eat pork, drink alcohol, or gamble. But other matters are mentioned in general terms. For example, the Qur'an tells women to "not display their beauty." For this reason, Muslim women usually wear different forms of modest dress. Most women cover their arms and legs. Many also wear scarves over the hair.

Shari'ah also covers Muslims' duties toward other people. These duties can be broadly grouped into criminal, commercial, family, and inheritance law.

In a shari'ah court, a *qadi* (judge) hears a case, including witnesses and evidence. Then the qadi makes a ruling. Sometimes the qadi consults a *mufti,* or scholar of law, for an opinion.

Islamic law helped Muslims live by the rules of the Qur'an. By the 19th century, however, many Muslim regions had come under European rule. Western codes of law soon replaced the shari'ah except in matters of family law. Today, most Muslim countries apply only some parts of Islamic law. But shari'ah continues to develop in response to modern ways of life and its challenges.

9.11 Chapter Summary

In this chapter, you learned about the basic beliefs and practices of Islam. One of the world's major religions, Islam has more followers today than any faith except Christianity.

Islam, Judaism, and Christianity share many similarities. People of these faiths believe in one God and possess holy books. Muslims accept the Jewish and Christian scriptures as earlier revelations by God. For Muslims, however, the Qur'an contains God's final messages to humanity.

The Qur'an guides Muslims on how to live their lives. Additional guidance comes from the Sunnah, the example of Muhammad. The hadith (tradition) provides a written record of sayings and deeds of the prophet.

Islam is a way of life as well as a set of beliefs. Muslims follow the Five Pillars of Faith. The five pillars are shahadah (profession of faith), salat (daily worship), zakat (almsgiving), siyam (fasting), and hajj (the pilgrimage to Makkah).

Muslims also have the duty of jihad, or striving militarily or personally to please God. Shari'ah, or Islamic law, helps Muslims live by the teachings of the Qur'an. It includes practices of daily life as well as the duty to respect others.

Islam expanded rapidly in the century following the death of Muhammad. In the next chapter, you will learn about some of the great accomplishments of Islamic civilization.

Mosques are centers of worship for Muslims.

CHAPTER 10

◄ This mosque in Cordoba, Spain, displays distinctive Muslim architecture and design.

Contributions of Muslims to World Civilization

10.1 Introduction

In Chapter 9, you learned about Islam, the Muslim faith. In this chapter, you will study many contributions made by Muslims to world civilization.

By 750 C.E., Muslims ruled Spain, North Africa, the Middle East, and much of central Asia. Over the next 500 years, many cultural influences blended in this vast region. Arabs, Persians, Turks, and others all helped to build Islamic civilization.

The Islamic world was rich, diverse, and creative. Rulers encouraged scholarship and art. Great cities flourished as centers of culture. Muslims learned from the ancient Greeks, the Chinese, and the Hindus of India. They preserved old learning and made many striking advances of their own. Scholars traveled and exchanged ideas across the Islamic world, from Spain to Baghdad (in present-day Iraq). By spreading knowledge and ideas, they had a deep impact on other cultures.

You can still see signs of this influence today. For instance, Muslims introduced many foods to other parts of the world. Among them were sugar (*al-sukkar* in Arabic), rice (*al-ruzz*), and oranges (*naranj*). *Mattress* and *sofa* are both from Arabic. *Pajamas* and *tambourine* are derived from Persian words. The Arabic numerals (1, 2, 3, …) we use today were brought to Europe by Muslims.

In this chapter, you will explore Muslim contributions to world civilization. You'll study Muslim achievements in **city building** and **architecture, scholarship** and **learning, science** and **technology, geography** and **navigation, mathematics, medicine, literature** and **bookmaking, art** and **music,** and even **recreation**. Let's begin by looking more closely at the flowering of Islamic culture following the Arab conquests of the 7th and 8th centuries.

Use this illustrated map as a graphic organizer to help you discover and remember Muslim contributions to world civilization.

10.2 The Flowering of Islamic Civilization

Abbasid member of a Muslim ruling family descended from Abbas, an uncle of Muhammad

Fatimid dynasty a Muslim ruling family in Egypt and North Africa that was descended from Fatimah, Muhammad's daughter

Harun al-Rashid, the fifth caliph of the Abbasids, created a lavish court at Baghdad. He presented this jeweled water jug to Charlemagne, emperor of the Holy Roman Empire.

As you have learned, Islam began in Arabia. By the middle of the 8th century, Arab conquests had created a vast Muslim empire. Spain, North Africa, and much of western and central Asia came under Muslim rule. Over the next 500 years, Islamic civilization flowered throughout this huge area.

As a political unit, however, the empire did not last. By 750, a family called the **Abbasids** had wrested power from the Umayyad dynasty. An Umayyad named Abd al-Rahman fled to Spain. There he established a rival caliphate, or government, that made Cordoba one of the leading cities in the world. In the 9th and 10th centuries, Muslim dynasties rose up in Egypt, North Africa, and elsewhere.

Despite this loss of political unity, Islamic civilization flourished. Muslim rulers built great cities where scholars and artists made advances in many fields.

One of the most important cities was Baghdad, in present-day Iraq. In 762, the Abbasids made Baghdad their capital. From a small village, Baghdad grew into one of the world's largest cities. It became a major center of learning where Persian influences combined with the Arabic heritage of Islam.

In the 10th century, the **Fatimid dynasty** in Egypt built a capital city, Cairo, that rivaled Baghdad. Its university became the most advanced in the Muslim world. In Spain, the Muslim capital of Cordoba became one of the largest and wealthiest cities in the world. Jews, Christians, and Muslims worked and studied together in this thriving cultural center.

Muslims learned from other cultures, and they helped spread cultural elements to other places. Ideas as well as goods traveled along the Muslim trade routes that connected Asia, Europe, and Africa. For example, Muslims learned paper making from the Chinese, and they passed this knowledge on to Europeans. Furthermore, Muslims produced new scientific, medical, and philosophical texts based on earlier Greek works. Many of these texts were translated into Latin in the 12th century and became available to western Europeans for the first time.

As you read this chapter, keep in mind the great diversity of the Islamic world. Only a minority of Muslims were from Arabia. Persians, Egyptians, North Africans, Turks, and others all contributed to the great cultural blending we call Islamic civilization.

10.3 City Building and Architecture

Many large cities developed in Muslim lands. The growth of cities encouraged new kinds of architecture. Thousands of workers labored to build palaces, schools, orphanages, hospitals, mosques, and other buildings.

The City of Baghdad   One of the most glorious Muslim cities was the Abbasid capital of Baghdad. After the Abbasids rose to power, Caliph al-Mansur decided to move his capital east from Damascus to a site that was more central to his far-flung empire. The site he chose was Baghdad, a village between the Tigris and Euphrates Rivers. This location was a crossroads of trade routes connecting distant parts of the empire.

It took 100,000 architects, workers, and crafts-people four years to build the new capital. Because of its shape, people called the capital complex the "round city." At its center were the caliph's palace and the grand mosque. Around them were offices and the houses of court officials and army officers. A double wall with four heavily guarded gates surrounded the inner city.

Shops, markets, and residences grew up outside the wall. Soon Baghdad was one of the world's largest cities. Bridges, palaces, and gardens all added to its splendor. One Arab historian of the 11th century called Baghdad "a city with no equal in the world."

The Mosque   Muslims created distinctive forms of architecture. A particularly important type of building was the mosque, the Muslim house of worship.

Mosques usually had a minaret (tower) with a small balcony where the muezzin chanted the call to prayer. In the walled courtyard stood a fountain for washing before prayers.

Inside the mosque was the prayer room. Worshipers sat on mats and carpets on the floor. The imam, or prayer leader, gave his sermon from a raised pulpit called the *minbar*. Next to the minbar was the *mihrab,* the niche that indicated the direction of Makkah.

Many design styles and materials went into the building of mosques, reflecting the great diversity of Muslim lands. Like the cathedrals of Europe, mosques expressed the religious faith and the artistic heritage of their builders.

The minaret of the Great Mosque of Samarra has a spiral design. Muezzins follow spiral steps around the outside of the tower to the balcony at the top.

10.4 Scholarship and Learning

Scholarship and learning were highly valued in Islamic culture. Muhammad himself declared, "The ink of scholars is more precious than the blood of martyrs."

Students in Muslim schools discussed and debated philosophical ideas with their teachers.

Acceptance of the Arabic language helped promote learning. Beginning in the 8th century, Arabic became the language of scholarship and science throughout Muslim lands. A shared language and love of learning allowed scholars in Europe, North Africa, and the Middle East to exchange ideas and build on one another's work.

Muslim rulers built schools, colleges, libraries, and other centers of learning. In Baghdad, Caliph al-Ma'mun founded the House of Wisdom in 830. Scholars from many lands came together there to do research and to translate texts from Greece, Persia, India, and China.

Other cities also became great centers of learning. In Cairo, the Hall of Wisdom opened in the 10th century. Scholars and ordinary people could visit its library to read books. The huge library in Cordoba, Spain, held as many as 400,000 volumes. Buyers traveled far and wide to purchase books for its shelves.

Among the texts studied by Muslim scholars were the works of ancient Greek thinkers, such as the philosophers Plato and Aristotle. Following the example of the Greeks, Muslim philosophers used reason and logic to try to prove important truths.

Like Christian thinkers in Europe, Muslims sometimes wondered how to make reason and logical proof agree with their religious faith. Al-Kindi, an Arab philosopher of the 9th century, tried to resolve this issue. Humans, he said, had two sources of knowledge: reason, and revelation by God. People could use reason to better understand the teachings of faith. Some truths, however, could be known only through God's word. For example, no one could prove that there would be a resurrection, or rising from the dead, on the day of judgment.

Ibn Sina, a Persian, became Islam's most famous philosopher. Called Avicenna in Europe, Ibn Sina wrote in the early 11th century. He believed that all knowledge came from God and that truth could be known through both revelation and reason. For example, he presented a logical proof (argument) that the soul was **immortal**. His writings were widely translated and influenced many thinkers in medieval Europe.

immortal able to live forever

10.5 Science and Technology

Muslims showed an endless curiosity about the world God had made. In fact, the Qur'an instructed them to learn more:

Have they not looked at the camel—how it was created?
And at the sky—how it was raised up?

As a result of their interest in the natural world, Muslims made many advances in science and technology. Let's look at a few of their accomplishments.

Zoology   A number of Muslim scholars became interested in **zoology,** the scientific study of animals. Some wrote books describing the structure of animals' bodies. Others explained how to make medicines from animals. In the 800s, a scholar named al-Jahiz even presented theories about the **evolution** of animals. Muslims also established zoological gardens, or zoos, where exotic animals were displayed.

Astronomy   Muslim scholars made great advances in **astronomy,** the study of objects in the universe. Astronomy had many practical uses for Muslims. For example, compasses and **astrolabes** could be used to locate the direction of Makkah. These instruments allowed worshipers far from the holy city to pray facing the right direction. Astronomers also figured out exact times for prayer and the length of the month of Ramadan.

Beyond such practical matters, Muslim astronomers simply wanted to learn about the universe. Some of them realized that Earth rotated, or turned, like a spinning top. Many questioned the accepted idea that Earth was the center of the universe, with the sun and stars traveling around it. As later work showed, in reality Earth travels around the sun.

Irrigation and Underground Wells   Muslims made technological advances that helped them make the most of scarce water resources. Much of the land under Muslim rule was hot and dry. Muslims restored old irrigation systems and designed new ones. They built dams and aqueducts to provide water for households, mills, and fields. They improved existing systems of canals and underground wells. Some wells reached down 50 feet into the ground. Muslims also used water wheels to bring water up from canals and reservoirs.

zoology the scientific study of animals

evolution the process by which different kinds of animals and other living things develop

astronomy the science of the stars, planets, and other objects in the universe

astrolabe an instrument used to observe and measure the position of the sun and other heavenly bodies

The town of Hama, Syria, has 17 wooden waterwheels from medieval Muslim times. These waterwheels scooped water from the Orontes River into aqueducts, bringing it to homes and farms.

This copper astrolabe is from the ninth century.

10.6 Geography and Navigation

Another subject of study for Muslim scholars was geography. Muslim geographers examined plants and animals in different regions. They also divided the world into climate zones. Most educated people in medieval times believed that the Earth was round, but they disagreed about the Earth's size. Muslim scientists calculated the Earth's **circumference** within nine miles of its correct value.

Some Muslims studied geography simply out of curiosity. But geography had practical uses, too. For example, Muslims created extremely accurate maps. A scholar in Muslim Spain produced a world atlas with dozens of maps of lands in Europe, Africa, and Asia. A work called *The Book of Roads and Provinces* provided maps and descriptions of the main Muslim trade routes. *The Book of Countries* listed useful facts about the lands under Muslim rule. From this book, travelers could get information such as a region's physical features and water resources.

Travelers were another source of knowledge. Some travelers wrote guidebooks to help pilgrims make the journey to Makkah. Others explored and described foreign lands, like China and Scandinavia. One traveler wrote a 30-volume encyclopedia about all the places he had seen.

To aid in their travels, Muslims used navigational instruments. Muslim scientists adapted and perfected the compass and the astrolabe. Muslims probably learned about the compass from the Chinese. Compasses allowed people to identify the direction in which they were traveling. The astrolabe was probably invented by the Greeks. With this instrument, sailors at sea could use the position of objects in the sky to pinpoint their location.

circumference the distance around a circle or sphere

10.7 Mathematics

Muslims greatly advanced the study of mathematics. They based their work in part on ideas from India and classical Greece. For example, scholars in Baghdad's House of Wisdom translated the works of the Greek mathematician Euclid. They also translated important texts from India. Then they adapted what they learned and added their own contributions.

One of these scholars was the astronomer and mathematician al-Khwarizmi, who worked in the House of Wisdom in the 9th century. Al-Khwarizmi is best known as "the father of algebra." In fact, the word **algebra** comes from the title of one of his books.

Algebra is used to solve problems involving unknown numbers. An example is the equation "$7x + 4 = 25$." Using algebra, we can figure out that in this equation, x represents 3.

Al-Khwarizmi's famous book on algebra was translated into Latin in the 12th century. It became the most important mathematics text in European universities.

The translation of another of Al-Khwarizmi's books helped to popularize Arabic numerals in Europe. Actually, Muslims learned this way of writing numbers, along with fractions and decimals, from Indian scholars. Arabic numerals were a big help to business and trade. Compared to earlier systems, they made it easier for people to do calculations and check their work. We still use Arabic numerals today.

Muslims also spread the Indian concept of zero. In fact, the word *zero* comes from an Arabic word meaning "something empty." Ancient peoples used written symbols for numbers long before anyone thought of using a symbol for zero. Yet zero is very important in calculations. (Try subtracting 2 from 2. Without using zero, how would you express the answer?) Zero also made it easier to write large numbers. For example, zero allows people to distinguish between 123 and 1,230.

algebra a branch of mathematics that solves problems involving unknown numbers

The geometric designs in Muslim art and architecture are based on knowledge about advanced mathematical principles.

وقة الجناس الاسوي... منطقة وصل السقل... نعته من الطوبات الترك الصور... واذا سقرمية ورس... العسل في الثلاث اسهل موسانم... اعلم... ومره صفراوبط...

Muslim doctors treated patients with herbal remedies as well as drugs, diet, and exercise. This illustration of a lily plant is from an Arabic herbal encyclopedia of the 10th century.

pharmacist a person who prepares medications for use in healing

10.8 Medicine

Muslims made some of their most important contributions in the field of medicine. They learned a great deal from the work of ancient Greeks, Mesopotamians, and Egyptians. Then, as in other fields of study, they improved upon this earlier knowledge.

Muslim doctors established the world's first hospitals. By the 10th century, Baghdad had at least five hospitals. Most cities and towns also had one or two. Many hospitals served as teaching centers for doctors in training. Anyone who needed treatment could get it, because the government paid all medical expenses. There were even hospital caravans that brought medical care to people in remote villages.

Muslim hospitals had separate wards for men and women, surgical patients, and people with diseases that others could catch. Doctors treated ailments through drugs, diet, and exercise. They gave patients remedies made from herbs, plants, animals, and minerals. **Pharmacists** made hundreds of medications. Some drugs dulled patients' pain. Antiseptics (medications that fight infection) were used to clean wounds. Ointments helped the wounds to heal.

For some problems, surgeons performed delicate operations as a last resort. Drugs such as opium and hemlock put patients to sleep before operations. Muslim surgeons amputated (cut off) limbs, took out tumors, and removed cataracts (cloudy spots) from the eye. After surgery, doctors used animal gut to stitch up wounds.

Muslim doctors made many discoveries and helped spread medical knowledge. For example, al-Razi, a Persian doctor, realized that infections were caused by bacteria. He also studied smallpox and measles. His work helped other doctors diagnose and treat these deadly diseases.

The Persian philosopher Ibn Sina (Avicenna), whom you met earlier in this chapter, was also a great doctor. In fact, he has been called "the prince of physicians." His most important medical work, *The Canon of Medicine,* explored the treatment of diseases. It is one of the classics in the history of medicine.

Europeans later translated Ibn Sina's book and many other Muslim works into Latin. Medical schools then used these texts to teach their students. In this way, Muslim doctors had a major impact on European medicine.

10.9 Bookmaking and Literature

In the 8th century, Muslims learned the art of making paper from the Chinese. Soon they were creating bound books. Bookmaking, in turn, encouraged the growth of Muslim literature.

Craftspeople turned bookmaking into an art form. Bookmakers gathered sheets of paper into leather bindings. They illuminated the bindings and pages with designs in gold as well as with miniature paintings.

Books become a big business in the Muslim world. In Baghdad, more than 100 bookshops lined Papersellers' Street. In addition to copies of the Qur'an, many volumes of poetry and prose were sold.

Arabs had a rich heritage of storytelling and poetry. Arab poetry often honored love, praised rulers, or celebrated wit. Persians introduced epic poems, or long poems that tell a story. Prose eventually replaced poetry for recording history, events, and traditions. Writers also composed stories in prose.

One famous collection of stories was called *A Thousand and One Nights.* Also known as *Arabian Nights,* this book gathered stories that originally came from many places, including India and Persia as well as the Middle East. In the book, a wife tells her husband a new tale each night. The stories take place in Muslim cities and in places like China, Egypt, and India. A European translator later added tales that were not part of the medieval Arabic collection. Among these added tales are those about Aladdin's magic lamp, Ali Baba, and Sinbad the Sailor, which remain well known today.

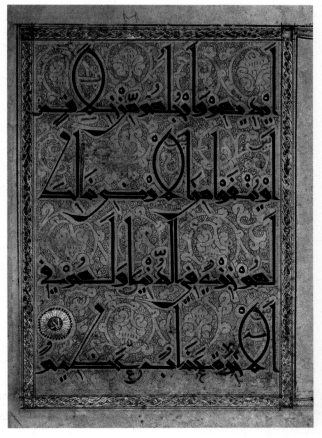

Bookmaking was an art in the Muslim world. Copies of the Qur'an were written with elaborate letters and decorated in gold.

Muslim literature was enriched by Sufism, or Islamic **mysticism**. This type of religious practice involves intense personal experiences of God rather than routine performance of rituals. Sufis longed to draw close to God in their everyday lives. One way to express their love and devotion was through poetry filled with vivid images and beautiful language. Rabi'a, a poet of the 8th century, shared her feelings in this verse:

> *But your door is open to those who call upon you.*
> *My Lord, each lover is now alone with his beloved.*
> *And I am alone with Thee.*

A 13th-century Sufi poet, Rumi, had an enormous influence on Islamic mysticism. Rumi wrote a long religious poem in Persian that filled six volumes. Pilgrims still travel to his tomb in Konya, Turkey.

mysticism a form of religious belief and practice involving sudden insight and intense experiences of God

10.10 Art and Music

Muslims created many forms of art and music. In this section, you'll look at four types of artistic expression in the medieval Islamic world.

Geometric and Floral Design   Muslims earned fame for their decorative art. Early in the history of Islam, Muslims rejected the use of images of humans or animals in their visual art, especially religious art. Only God, they said, can create something that is alive. Instead, artists turned to shapes and patterns found in nature and geometry to create marvelous designs and decorations.

Art sometimes was religious, as in the beautiful illuminated manuscripts of the Qur'an. But artists and craftspeople also applied their talents to everyday items like plates, candlesticks, glassware, and clothing. They decorated the walls of mosques and palaces with intricate designs.

A type of design called *arabesque* took its beauty from the natural world. Artists crafted stems, leaves, flowers, and tendrils (long, thread-like parts of plants) into elegant patterns that were repeated over and over. They carved, painted, and wove arabesque designs into objects both large and small. Metal boxes, ceramic bowls, tiles, carpets, and even entire walls displayed intricate arabesque designs.

Artists also used geometric shapes in their designs. Circles, triangles, squares, and hexagons had special meaning to Muslims. Artists used simple tools—rulers and compasses—to create abstract designs from these shapes. This basic design was then repeated and combined to create a complex pattern.

calligraphy the art of beautiful handwriting

Arabic calligraphy is featured in the decoration on the inside of this architectural dome.

Calligraphy   For Muslims, the highest form of decorative art was **calligraphy,** the art of beautiful handwriting. When Muslims began copying the Qur'an, they felt that only calligraphy was worthy to record the words of God. For this reason, they honored calligraphers above other artists.

Calligraphers used sharpened reeds or bamboo dipped in ink to write on parchment and paper. Some forms of calligraphy had letters with angles. Most featured round letters and cursive writing, in which the script flows and letters within words are connected.

In addition to copying the Qur'an, artists used calligraphy to decorate everyday items. They put elegantly written lines of poetry on pottery, tiles, and swords. Bands of calligraphy trimmed the bottoms of pieces of cloth. Calligraphy even adorned coins, which often featured verses from the Qur'an.

Verses of the Qur'an were also used to decorate mosques. Sometimes the holy verses were engraved along the tops of the outside walls or circled the inside dome of the mosque.

Textiles Manufactured cloths, or textiles, had long been important to the Arab people as practical items and as trade goods. Muslims in medieval times brought great artistry to the making of textiles. Weavers wove wool, linen, silk, and cotton into cloth, which then might be dyed with vivid colors. Valuable cloths sometimes featured long bands of inscriptions or designs showing important events. Fabrics were also embroidered, sometimes with gold thread.

Clothes showed rank and served as status symbols in the Muslim world. The caliph and his court wore robes made of the most valuable materials. Fine textiles served as awnings and carpets in the royal palace during festivals or when distinguished guests visited.

The lute, or oud, is a popular instrument in Muslim music.

Music in Muslim Spain There were several centers of music in the Islamic world, including Baghdad and Damascus. Persian musical styles were very influential in the cities of the east. But in Cordoba, Spain, a unique style developed that blended elements of Arab and native Spanish cultures.

A key figure in this cultural innovation was Ziryab, a talented musician and singer from Baghdad. Ziryab settled in Cordoba in 822. There he established Europe's first **conservatory,** or music school. Musicians from Asia and Africa came to Cordoba to learn from the great Ziryab. Many were then hired as entertainers at royal courts in other parts of the world.

Singing was an essential part of Muslim Spain's musical culture. Musicians and poets worked together to create songs about love, nature, and the glory of the empire. Vocalists performed the songs accompanied by such instruments as drums, flutes, and lutes. Although this music is lost today, it undoubtedly influenced later musical forms in Europe and North Africa.

conservatory an advanced school of music

10.11 Recreation

Fun was also part of Islamic culture. Two favorite pastimes that Muslims helped popularize were polo and chess.

Polo   Muslims first learned about the game of polo from the Persians. Polo is a sport in which teams on horseback use mallets (wooden sticks) to strike a ball through a goal. Muslims looked at horses as status symbols, and polo quickly became popular among the wealthy. Even Abbasid rulers began to raise champion Arabian horses to play polo. (Polo is often called the "sport of kings.")

Muslims adapted and refined the game of polo. Today the game is enjoyed all over the world.

Chess   The game of chess was probably invented in India. Persians introduced the game to the Muslim world in the mid 600s. It quickly became popular at all levels of society. Caliphs invited chess champions, including women and slaves, to their palaces to play in matches. Players enjoyed the intellectual challenge that chess presented.

Chess is a battle of wits in which players move pieces on a board according to complex rules. Each player commands a small army of pieces, one of which is the king. The goal is to checkmate the opponent's king. *Checkmate* means that the king cannot move without being captured.

As with polo, Muslims adapted and improved the game of chess. They spread it across Muslim lands and introduced it to Europe. Chess remains one of the world's most popular games.

This illustration of two men playing chess is from a 13th-century book of games. The exaggerated size and position of the chessboard indicates the popularity of the game at the time.

10.12 Chapter Summary

In this chapter, you learned about many of the contributions Muslims have made to world civilization. In a dazzling variety of fields, Islamic culture has left a lasting mark on the world.

In the 7th and 8th centuries, Arab conquests created a vast Muslim empire. Although the empire did not last as a political unit, Islamic civilization thrived.

Muslim rulers built great cities and centers of learning and scholarship. Muslim scholars learned from other cultures and helped to spread knowledge to other parts of the world.

Muslims made a number of advances in city building, architecture, technology, and the sciences. Muslim mathematicians built on the work of Indians and Greeks. Doctors, too, improved on ancient knowledge. Many of these advances had a major influence on Europe.

Having learned paper making from the Chinese, Muslims created beautiful books. Writers composed works of both poetry and prose. The religious poetry of Sufis celebrated the love of God.

Muslim artists and craftspeople created distinctive forms of decorative art. In Spain, a unique style of music developed that combined Arabic and Spanish influences. Two of medieval Muslims' favorite pastimes, polo and chess, are still enjoyed around the world.

As you have seen, Europeans owed a great debt to Islamic civilization. But by the 11th century, much of Christian Europe saw Islam as an enemy. In the next chapter, you will learn about the series of wars between Christians and Muslims, the Crusades.

Muslims greatly influenced the course of history as they traveled from place to place, trading cultural influences as well as goods.

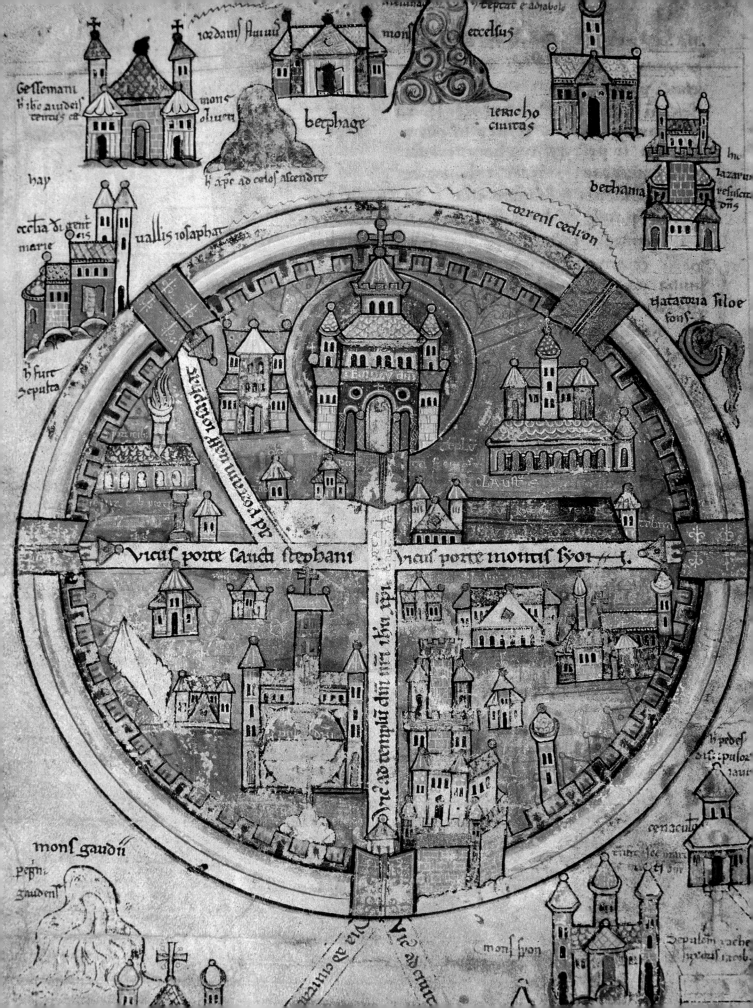

CHAPTER 11

◀ ◀ ◀ Christians, Muslims, and Jews fought for control over the sacred city of Jerusalem.

From the Crusades to New Muslim Empires

11.1 Introduction

In Chapter 10, you learned about Muslim contributions to world civilization. In this chapter, you will learn about the **crusades,** a series of religious wars launched against Muslims by European Christians.

Christians mounted a number of crusades between 1096 and 1291. A major purpose of the crusades was to gain control of Palestine. This area between Egypt and Syria was the ancient homeland of Jews and the place where Jesus had lived. Christians called it the **Holy Land**. The spiritual heart of Palestine was the city of Jerusalem. As you will learn, the city was sacred to Jews, Christians, and Muslims alike.

In the 11th century, Palestine came under the rule of a rising Muslim power, the Seljuk Turks. The Seljuks were building a huge empire. Their growing strength alarmed the Byzantine emperor in Constantinople. In 1095, the emperor asked Pope Urban II for help. The pope called on Christians to go on a crusade, or religious war, to turn back the Seljuks and win control of the Holy Land.

The next year, armies of crusaders set out from Europe. A series of wars began in which Christians fought with Muslims over Palestine and nearby lands.

Muslims were not the only targets of these religious wars. Crusaders also mounted violent campaigns against Jews and against Christians who were considered heretics. Crusades were waged in Europe and North Africa as well as the Middle East.

In this chapter, you will read the story of the crusades. You will explore the impact of these wars on Christians, Muslims, and Jews. You'll also learn how new Muslim empires arose after the crusades and how Islam continued to spread to new parts of the world.

Use this map as a graphic organizer to help you learn about the crusades.

sultan the sovereign ruler of a Muslim state

Anatolia a large peninsula at the western edge of Asia; also called Asia Minor

11.2 Events Leading Up to the Crusades

Why did European Christians begin going on crusades at the end of the 11th century? To answer this question, we need to look at what was happening in Muslim lands at this time.

During the 11th century, the Seljuk Turks established a new Muslim dynasty. The Turks were a Central Asian people who had been migrating into Muslim lands for centuries. The Seljuks were named for a Turkish chieftain who converted to Islam in the mid-10th century. In 1055, his descendants took control of the Abbasid capital of Baghdad. A Seljuk **sultan** now ruled the old Abbasid Empire.

The Seljuks were eager to expand their territory. Moving westward, they took Syria and Palestine from the Fatimid dynasty. They also over-ran much of **Anatolia** (Asia Minor), which was part of the Byzantine Empire. In 1071, they defeated a large Byzantine army at Manzikert in present-day Turkey.

The Seljuk advance alarmed Christians in Europe. They feared for the safety and property of Christians living in the east. The Seljuks' growing power seemed to threaten the Byzantine Empire itself. Christians also worried about the fate of the Holy Land, especially the city of Jerusalem.

Jerusalem was a sacred city to Jews, Christians, and Muslims. It was the spiritual capital of the Jews, where their great temple had once stood. For Christians, it was the city where Jesus was crucified and rose from the dead. For Muslims, it was the place where Muhammad rose to heaven during his Night Journey.

Jerusalem and the rest of Palestine first came under Muslim rule during the Arab conquests of the seventh century. Muslims built a shrine in Jerusalem, called the Dome of the Rock, to mark the spot where they believed Muhammad rose to heaven. Under Muslim rule, Jews, Christians, and Muslims usually lived together peacefully. People of all three faiths made pilgrimages to Jerusalem and built houses of worship there. Depending on the policies of various Muslim rulers, however, non-Muslims' rights and freedoms varied from time to time. Some Muslim rulers allowed the destruction of important Christian churches.

After the Seljuks took control of Palestine, political turmoil made travel unsafe for a time. Tales began reaching Europe of highway robbers attacking and even killing Christian pilgrims. Christians feared they would no longer be able to visit Jerusalem and other sacred sites in the Holy Land. Together with concern over the Seljuk threat to Christian lands, this fear helped pave the way for the crusades.

Two important shrines stand near each other in Jerusalem. The Dome of the Rock is where Muslims believe Muhammad rose to heaven. The Western Wall, what remains of the ancient Jewish Temple, is where Jews have gathered to pray throughout history. It is the holiest place in the world for Jews.

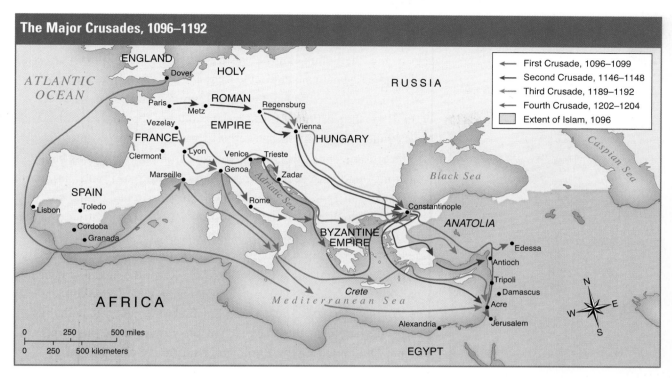

The Major Crusades, 1096–1192

Legend:
- First Crusade, 1096–1099
- Second Crusade, 1146–1148
- Third Crusade, 1189–1192
- Fourth Crusade, 1202–1204
- Extent of Islam, 1096

11.3 The Story of the Crusades

The crusades began as a response to the threat posed by the Seljuks. By 1095, the Seljuks had advanced to within 100 miles of the Byzantine capital of Constantinople. The emperor appealed to Pope Urban II for help.

The pope called nobles and church leaders to a council in Clermont, France. There he called for a crusade to drive the Muslims back and reclaim Jerusalem. He promised entry to heaven to all who joined the fight.

French-speaking nobles quickly organized armies to fight in the Holy Land. In addition to trained knights, thousands of townspeople, craftsmen, and peasants joined the crusade.

Throughout the crusades, Christian faith inspired many to put on the red cross worn by crusaders. But people joined the crusades for other reasons as well. Merchants saw the chance to earn money through trade. Younger sons of nobles hoped to gain estates in the Holy Land.

The First Crusade (1096–1099)   Four nobles led the First Crusade. Close to 30,000 crusaders fought their way through Anatolia and headed south toward Palestine. In June 1098, the crusaders laid siege to the city of Antioch in Syria. After nine months, a traitor let them through a opening in the city walls. Antioch fell to the Christians.

The next June, the crusaders surrounded Jerusalem and scaled the city walls. In July 1099, the city surrendered. The victorious crusaders massacred Muslims and Jews throughout the city. The survivors were sold into slavery. With Jerusalem taken, most of the crusaders went home. Some, however, stayed behind. They established four crusader kingdoms in Palestine, Syria, and modern-day Lebanon and Turkey.

The Second Crusade (1146–1148) The crusaders owed their early victories in part to a lack of unity among Muslims. When the crusades began, the Seljuk Empire was already crumbling into a number of smaller states. Muslims had trouble joining together to fight the invaders.

As Muslims started to band together, they fought back more effectively. In 1144, they captured Edessa, the capital of the northernmost crusader kingdom. Christians answered by mounting the Second Crusade.

The crusade ended in failure. An army from Germany was badly beaten in Anatolia. A second army, led by the king of France, arrived in Jerusalem in 1148. About 50,000 crusaders marched on the city of Damascus, which was on the way to Edessa. Muslims from Edessa came to the city's aid and beat back the crusaders. Soon after this defeat, the French army went home, ending the Second Crusade.

The Third Crusade (1189–1192) Over the next few decades, Muslims in the Middle East increasingly came under common leadership. By the 1180s, the great sultan Salah al-Din, called Saladin by Europeans, had formed the largest Muslim empire since the Seljuks. Salah al-Din united Egypt, Syria, and lands to the east. He led a renewed fight against the crusaders in the Holy Land.

Salah al-Din quickly took back most of Palestine. In 1187, his armies captured Jerusalem. Salah al-Din did not kill his prisoners, as the crusaders had done. Instead, he freed many captives or sold them for **ransom**. Others were sold into slavery.

The loss of Jerusalem shocked Europeans and sparked the Third Crusade. King Richard I of England, known as Richard the Lionheart, led the fight against Salah al-Din.

In 1191, Richard's army forced the surrender of the Palestinian town of Acre. Afterward, arrangements were made between the two sides to exchange prisoners. After waiting for a time, Richard felt that Salah al-Din was taking too long to meet his end of the bargain. Growing impatient, he ordered his men to kill all 2,700 of his Muslim prisoners.

Richard then fought his way toward Jerusalem, but his army was not strong enough to attack the city. Salah al-Din's forces had also grown weaker. In September 1192, the two leaders signed a peace treaty. The crusaders kept a chain of cities along the coast of Palestine. Muslims agreed to let Christian pilgrims enter Jerusalem.

Later Crusades The crusades to the Middle East continued for another 100 years. Some crusades were popular movements of poor people rather than organized military campaigns. In 1212, for example, tens of thousands of peasant children from France and Germany marched in a "Children's Crusade." Few, if any, ever reached the Holy Land. Some made it as far as European port cities, only to be sold into slavery by merchants. Some returned home. Many disappeared without a trace.

Richard the Lionheart of England led the Third Crusade to try to regain Christian control of Jerusalem from the Muslims.

ransom money paid in exchange for the release of prisoners

None of the later crusades succeeded in recapturing Jerusalem. Muslims, meanwhile, were gaining back the land they had lost. In 1291, they took Acre, the last crusader city. This victory ended some 200 years of Christian kingdoms in the Holy Land.

The Reconquista   Crusaders warred against Muslims in Europe and North Africa as well as the Middle East. One important series of wars was called the Reconquista (reconquest). Christians launched these wars to retake the **Iberian Peninsula** (modern-day Spain and Portugal) from Muslims.

As you have learned, the Umayyads established a Muslim dynasty in Spain in the eighth century. A unique culture flourished in cities like Cordoba and Toledo, where Muslims, Jews, and Christians lived together in peace. However, non-Muslims had to pay a special tax.

Over time, Christian rulers in northern Iberia chipped away at Muslim lands. The pace of reconquest quickened after the Umayyad caliphate in Cordoba broke up into rival kingdoms in 1002. Christians tried to take advantage of the Muslims' weakness. In 1085, they scored a key victory by capturing Toledo, in central Spain.

Muslims gradually gave up more and more territory, and new Muslim dynasties were not tolerant of Jews and Christians. In 1139, Portugal became an independent Christian kingdom. By 1248, only the small kingdom of Granada, along the southern coast of Spain, remained in Muslim hands.

Many Jews and Muslims remained in areas ruled by Christians. In the late 1400s, Queen Isabella and King Ferdinand wanted to unite Spain as a Catholic country. They used the **Inquisition,** a church court, against Muslims and Jews who had converted to Christianity. The Spanish Inquisition was extremely harsh. Judges, called *inquisitors,* sometimes used torture to find out whether supposed converts were practicing their old religion. Thousands of people were burned at the stake.

Isabella and Ferdinand also sent armies against Granada. In 1492, the city fell, and Muslims lost their last stronghold in Spain. In that same year, Jews were told to become Catholics or leave the country. More than 170,000 Jews left their homes forever. Muslims remained in Spain, but many were forced to accept baptism as Catholics. Spain expelled its remaining Muslims beginning in 1609. The **expulsion** of Muslims and Jews ended centuries of cooperation between these groups and Christians in Spain.

Iberian Peninsula a peninsula in southwestern Europe that today is divided between Spain and Portugal
Inquisition a judicial body established by the Catholic Church to combat heresy and other forms of religious error
expulsion removal by force

Later crusades, such as the Children's Crusade, were unsuccessful movements by poor people rather than the military.

11.4 Christians and the Crusades

For crusaders, the religious wars were a costly ordeal. But European Christians also reaped many benefits from the crusades.

New foods and fabrics from Arabian seaports were introduced to Christians through the travels and trading of crusaders.

Impact on Christians as a Group

Crusaders suffered all the terrible effects of war. Many were wounded or killed in battle. Others died from disease and the hardships of travel.

The impact of the crusades reached far beyond those who fought in the wars. The crusades brought many economic changes to Europe. Crusaders needed a way to pay for supplies. Their need increased the use of money in Europe. Some knights began performing banking functions, such as making loans or investments. Kings started tax systems to raise funds for crusades.

The crusades changed society as well. Monarchs grew more powerful as nobles and knights left home to fight in the Middle East. The increasing power of monarchs helped to end feudalism.

Contact with eastern cultures had a major impact on Christians' way of life. In the Holy Land, Christians learned about new foods and other goods. They dressed in clothing made of muslin, a cotton fabric from Persia. They developed a taste for melons, apricots, sesame seeds, and carob beans. They used spices like pepper. After crusaders returned home, European merchants earned enormous profits by trading for these goods.

The Experiences of Individuals

You have already learned how Richard I of England led the Third Crusade. Richard was devoted to the Christian cause and to knightly ideals of courage and honor. To pay for his armies, he taxed his people heavily. Both ruthless and brave, Richard spent most of his reign on the crusades.

Anna Comnena, the daughter of a Byzantine emperor, wrote about her experiences during the First Crusade. She expressed mixed feelings about the crusaders. She respected them as Christians, but she also realized that many were dangerous. She questioned whether all of the crusaders were truly fighting for God. She thought that some sought wealth, land, or glory in battle. Her suspicions proved to be justified. During the Fourth Crusade, a force of crusaders sacked and looted Constantinople.

11.5 Muslims and the Crusades

The crusades brought fewer benefits to Muslims than they did to Christians. Muslims did drive the crusaders from the Middle East, but they lost their lands in Iberia. In addition, the contact between cultures benefitted Muslims less than Christians. Muslim society was more advanced, so Muslims had less to gain.

Impact on Muslims as a Group The crusades were a terrible ordeal for many Muslims. An unknown number of Muslims lost their lives in battles and massacres. Crusaders also destroyed Muslim property.

Muslims did gain exposure to some new weapons and military ideas during the crusades. Like Europeans, they began to adopt a standing (permanent) army. Muslim merchants, especially in Syria and Egypt, earned riches from trade with Europe. This money helped to fund projects such as new mosques and religious schools. The crusades also brought political changes as Muslims banded together to fight their common foe. The Ayyubid dynasty founded by Salah al-Din ruled Egypt and parts of Syria and Arabia until 1250.

Christian crusaders took the city of Jerusalem during the First Crusade, murdering both Muslims and Jews in their victory.

The Experiences of Individuals Salah al-Din was the greatest Muslim leader during the crusades. His experiences taught him many valuable lessons. As a boy in Damascus during the Second Crusade, he saw that Muslims needed to defend themselves and Islam. As a soldier, he realized that Muslims had to be organized and to cooperate with one another. He unified Muslim groups under his fair and strong leadership.

Salah al-Din was famed for his courtesy as well as his military skill. Unlike the crusaders, he ransomed or freed most prisoners he took.

Usamah ibn-Munqidh also grew up during the crusades. Believing it was the will of God, Usamah fought fearlessly against crusaders. At the same time, he respected both Christians and Jews because of their faith in one God. This attitude served him well when he negotiated with crusaders.

Usamah wrote a valuable account of the crusades from a Muslim point of view. He told how Muslims and Christians observed and sometimes admired each other. He also described how the Muslims were willing to give their lives to protect their families, lands, and property from the crusaders.

11.6 Jews and the Crusades

The violence unleashed by the crusades caused great suffering for Jews. Crusaders in the Holy Land slaughtered Jews as well as Muslims. Other Jews became slaves. The crusades also dramatically worsened the lives of Jews in Europe.

Impact on Jews as a Group   During the First Crusade, European Jews suffered a series of violent persecutions. As crusaders crossed northern France and Germany, some of them murdered whole communities of Jews. They destroyed **synagogues** and holy books. They looted homes and businesses. Some crusaders tortured Jews to make them accept Christianity.

Anti-Semitism, or prejudice against Jews, spread among non-crusaders as well. Religious prejudice combined with envy of Jews who had become prosperous bankers and traders. Riots and massacres broke out in a number of cities in Europe.

By the end of the crusades, Jews' place in society had worsened. Jews could not hold public office. Christians took over trading businesses that had been run by Jews. In 1290, England expelled all Jews. France did the same in 1394. Many Jews relocated to eastern Europe.

Segregation of Jews spread throughout Europe during the 14th and 15th centuries. Jews were forced to live in crowded neighborhoods called *ghettos*. Typically, walls and gates separated the ghettos from the rest of the town or city.

The Experiences of Individuals   A German Jew named Eliezer ben Nathan experienced some of the horrors that took place in Europe during the First Crusade. Later, Eliezer wrote about the violent destruction of his community. He described Jews who killed their children and themselves rather than give up their religion. Eliezer admired the devotion of these people. He wondered how God could let so many Jews die. He also expressed his hatred for the crusaders.

Eleazar ben Judah, a Jewish scholar, also lived in Germany. During the Second Crusade, he and other Jews were forced to flee their town. They had to leave behind their belongings, including their holy books.

Several years later, two crusaders attacked Eleazar's home. The men killed his wife and three children. Eleazar survived the attack, although he was badly injured. This horrible event led him to wonder if his people would survive in Europe. Despite his suffering, he continued to preach love for all humanity as a Jewish leader in the city of Worms.

synagogue a Jewish house of worship

anti-Semitism prejudice toward Jews

segregation the forced separation of one group from the rest of a community

Crusaders rampaged through Jewish communities across Europe, killing and looting and destroying sacred buildings and books.

11.7 The Mongol Invasion

As you have learned, Muslims succeeded in driving the crusaders from the Holy Land. Even as the crusades were taking place, other changes were happening in Muslim lands. By the mid 1200s, Muslims faced a greater threat than European crusaders—the Mongols.

The Mongols were a nomadic people whose homeland was to the north of China. In the 13th century, Mongols began wars of conquest under their leader, Genghis Khan. After attacking northern China, Genghis Khan turned his eyes west. The Mongols swept across central Asia, destroying cities and farmland. Hundreds of thousands of Muslims were slaughtered. Many were carried off to Mongolia as slaves.

Under Genghis Khan's successors, the Mongols built an empire that stretched across much of Asia. They defeated the Seljuk Turks in Anatolia and seized parts of Persia. In 1258, they destroyed Baghdad and killed the caliph, ending the Abbasid dynasty.

In the west, Muslims were able to stop the Mongol advance. The Muslim resistance was led by the Mamluks, whose capital was in Cairo. The Mamluks were Muslims of Turkish descent. In the mid 1200s, they had overthrown the dynasty begun by Salah al-Din. In 1260, they defeated the Mongols in an important battle in Palestine. The Mamluks continued to rule Palestine, Egypt, Syria, Arabia, and parts of Anatolia until 1517.

Mongol leader Genghis Khan is shown in a ceremony in this 14th-century illustration.

The Mongols still ruled a huge empire in Asia, including China. Toward the end of the 1200s, they began converting to Islam. The adoption of Islam helped bring unity to their empire. The Mongols made Persian the language of government. They rebuilt the cities they had destroyed and encouraged learning, the arts, and trade.

The Mongol Empire was one of the largest the world had ever seen. It suffered, however, from fighting among rivals. Local rulers controlled different regions. By the mid 1300s, the empire was badly weakened. In the next section, you will learn about new empires that arose in Muslim lands during the next few centuries.

Mongol leader
Timur Lang kept
the Ottomans from
advancing, but they
regained control after
his death.

11.8 New Muslim Empires and the Expansion of Islam

New empires grew up in Muslim lands after the decline of the Mongols. Islam also continued its spread to new lands.

The Ottoman Empire   In the early 1300s, a Turk named Osman I started the Ottoman dynasty in northern Anatolia. The Ottomans quickly conquered new lands in Anatolia and southeastern Europe.

The Ottomans' advance was stopped for a time by a new enemy, Timur Lang. Timur came from a Mongol tribe in central Asia. He claimed descent from Genghis Khan.

Timur began building his own empire in the late 1300s. His armies overran much of central Asia, including present-day Iraq. They then invaded India, Syria, and Anatolia. In 1402, Timur defeated an Ottoman army at Ankara in Anatolia. The Ottomans were on the brink of collapse. But after Timur's death in 1405, they regained control of their lands.

Turning back toward Europe, the Ottomans set out to expand their empire. In 1453, they captured Constantinople, bringing an end to the Byzantine Empire. The city was renamed Istanbul. It became the Ottoman capital.

In the 1500s, the Ottomans destroyed the Mamluk Empire. They conquered Syria, Palestine, Egypt, and Arabia. At its height, their empire also took in parts of southeastern Europe, North Africa, and Persia, as well as Turkey.

The Ottomans allowed their subjects considerable freedom. Jews, Christians, and Muslims had their own local communities, called *millets*. Millets were allowed to govern themselves. A ruling class collected taxes and protected the sultan and the empire. In the empire's European provinces, some young Christian men were drafted and then raised in the sultan's palace. After most of them converted to Islam, they became elite soldiers and government officials.

The Ottoman Empire slowly declined after about 1700. It finally came to an end in the 20th century.

The Safavid Empire   Ottoman expansion to the east was stopped by another Muslim power. In 1501, Muslims in Persia founded the Safavid dynasty. Their **shahs,** or rulers, soon controlled parts of Iraq as well as Persia. Unlike the Ottomans, who were Sunni Muslims, the Safavids were Shi'a. The two groups fought a number of wars.

The Safavids became a great power. They promoted trade, the arts, and learning. Their dynasty lasted until the mid 1700s.

The Mughal Empire   A third Muslim empire was founded by Babur, a descendant of both Genghis Khan and Timur. In 1526, Babur

shah a ruler in certain Middle East lands, especially Persia (modern-day Iran)

invaded India and founded the Mughal Empire. The word Mughal is Arabic for "Mongol." Mughal emperors ruled most of India until sometime after 1700. Muslims still make up a significant minority of India's population today.

The Further Spread of Islam Muslim dynasties grew up in other places as well. Muslims in North Africa carried Islam south to West Africa. Pilgrims and merchants also spread Islam among peoples living around the Sahara Desert.

Traders brought Islam across the Indian Ocean to southeast Asia. By the late 1200s, there were Muslim kingdoms on the islands of Indonesia. Today, Indonesia has more Muslims than any other country in the world.

11.9 Chapter Summary

In this chapter, you read about the crusades. You also learned about events in Muslim lands after the crusades.

European Christians began the crusades to repel the Seljuk Turks and take the Holy Land away from them. Between 1096 and 1291, a number of crusades were fought in the Middle East. Crusaders won control of Jerusalem and set up four Christian kingdoms in the Middle East. In 1187, Muslims won back Jerusalem. By 1291, Muslims had recaptured all the crusader cities.

Crusaders also waged campaigns in North Africa and Europe. During the Reconquista, Christians drove Muslims from the Iberian Peninsula.

The crusades had long-lasting effects on Christians, Muslims, and Jews. In Europe, Jews suffered great hardship. Many were killed. Others lost their homes and property.

Islam survived both the crusades and the Mongol invasion. The Ottomans built a great Muslim empire in the Middle East and eastern Europe. The Safavid Empire arose in Persia and Iraq. The Mughal Empire brought Muslim rule to most of India. Islam also spread to West Africa and Indonesia.

This chapter concludes your study of the rise of Islam. In the next unit, you will explore the kingdoms of West Africa in medieval times.

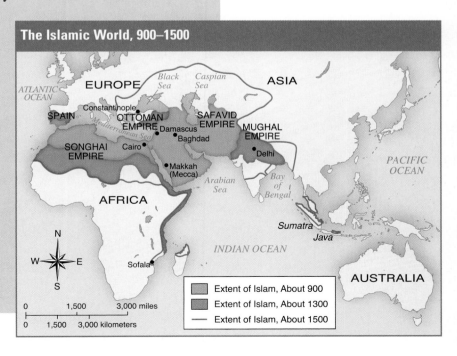

The Islamic World, 900–1500

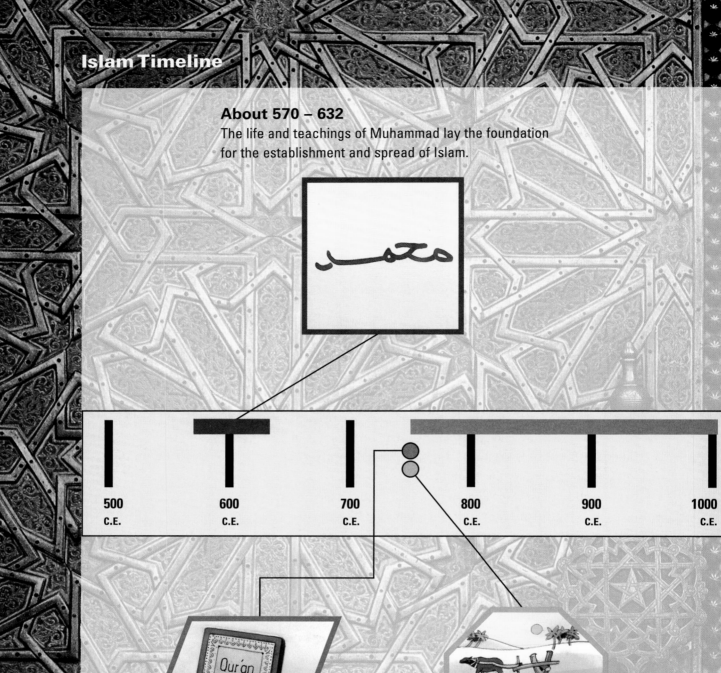

About 570 – 632
The life and teachings of Muhammad lay the foundation for the establishment and spread of Islam.

500	**600**	**700**	**800**	**900**	**1000**
C.E.	C.E.	C.E.	C.E.	C.E.	C.E.

About 750
Muslim bookmakers begin printing the Qur'an and volumes of poetry and prose. Islam and the Arabic language spread dramatically.

About 750
Muslims begin using water power for making paper, and constructing canals for transportation and irrigation.

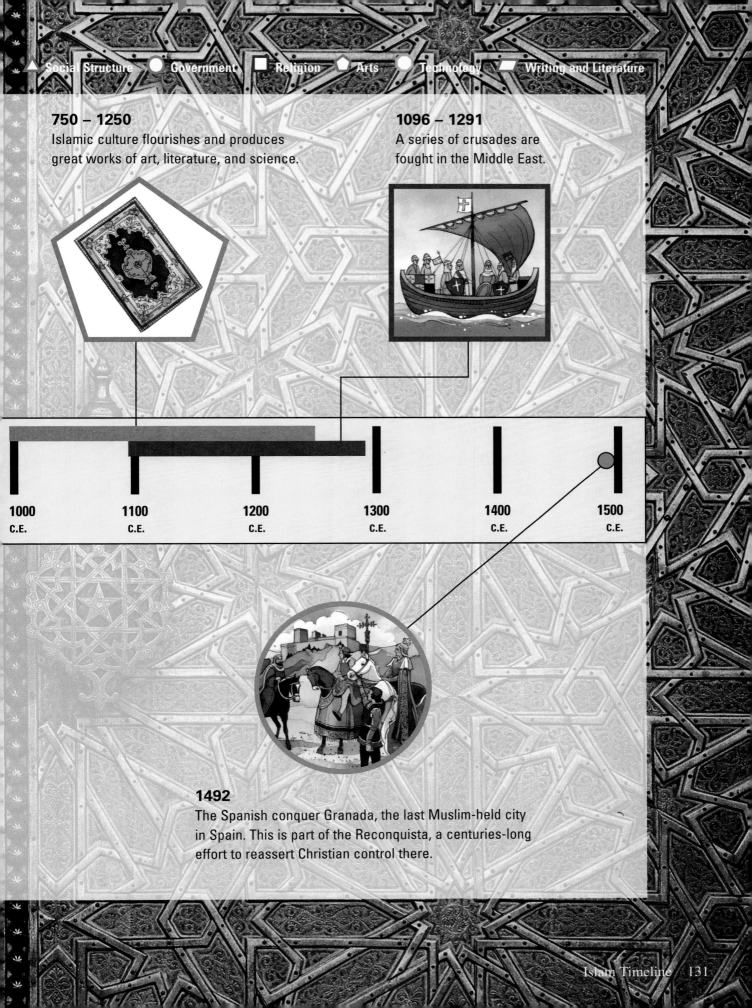

750 – 1250
Islamic culture flourishes and produces
great works of art, literature, and science.

1096 – 1291
A series of crusades are
fought in the Middle East.

1000 C.E.	**1100** C.E.	**1200** C.E.	**1300** C.E.	**1400** C.E.	**1500** C.E.

1492
The Spanish conquer Granada, the last Muslim-held city
in Spain. This is part of the Reconquista, a centuries-long
effort to reassert Christian control there.

The Culture and Kingdoms of West Africa

Setting the Stage

The Culture and Kingdoms of West Africa

In the last unit, you learned about the rise of Islam. In this unit, you will explore the history and culture of West Africa between about 500 and 1600 C.E.

Africa is south of Europe, between the Atlantic and Indian Oceans. To the north is the Mediterranean Sea.

Africa is the second largest continent on Earth, after Asia. It can be divided into four main regions: West Africa, North Africa, Central and South Africa, and East Africa.

Several vegetation zones form belts across Africa (see the second map on the opposite page). Four types of zones are especially important for our study of West Africa because of their effect on life there. Deserts are sandy, hot, and dry. A semidesert is a somewhat less dry zone of grasses and shrubs. In West Africa, this zone is called the Sahel. A savanna consists of grassland with tall grasses and scattered trees. Forest zones have the most abundant vegetation.

In ancient times, farming communities developed in the region south of the Sahara Desert. Rivers such as the Senegal and the Niger helped make the

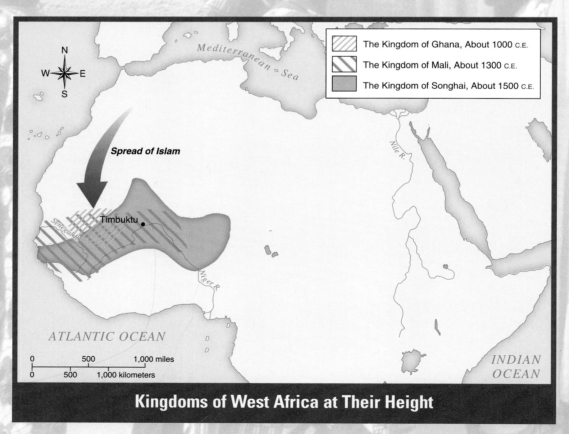

Kingdoms of West Africa at Their Height

land fertile. The rivers also provided fish and served as trade routes within the region.

For centuries, West Africa had limited contact with lands to the north because travel across the vast Sahara Desert was very difficult. By the late 700s C.E., however, an increasing number of Arab Muslim traders from North Africa were crossing the Sahara. Trans-Saharan trade played a key role in the growth of the three great medieval kingdoms of West Africa: Ghana, Mali, and Songhai.

Trade brought cultural change as well as goods to West Africa. In the 700s C.E., traders from North Africa brought Islam to the region. Islam had a deep impact on West African culture. The trading city of Timbuktu, on the Niger River, was a vital center of Islamic learning under both Mali and Songhai rule.

In this unit, you'll learn about the kingdoms and culture of West Africa. Let's begin our exploration by taking a closer look at how early societies developed in this region.

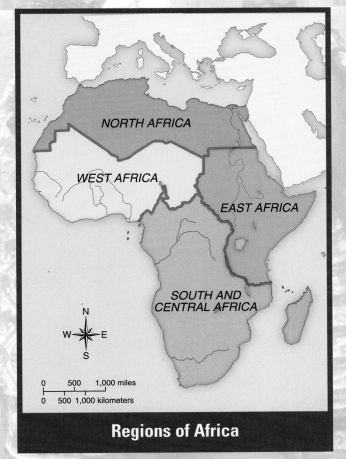

Regions of Africa

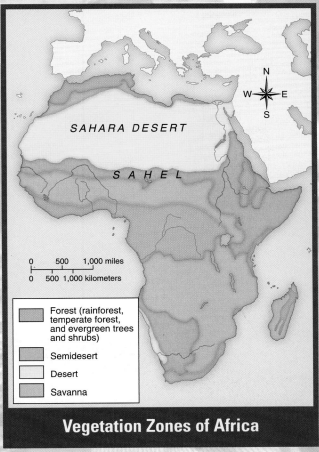

Forest (rainforest, temperate forest, and evergreen trees and shrubs)

Semidesert

Desert

Savanna

Vegetation Zones of Africa

CHAPTER 12

Early Societies in West Africa

12.1 Introduction

In this unit, you will learn about West African culture between about 500 and 1600 C.E. During this period, three **kingdoms** arose south of the Sahara Desert: Ghana, Songhai, and Mali. In this chapter, you will explore how these kingdoms developed out of early societies in West Africa.

People have lived in West Africa for hundreds of thousands of years. For most of this time, historians do not have written records to study. Muslim scholars first began writing about the kingdom of Ghana in the 800s. By then, Ghana was perhaps 300 years old, and possibly much older. How did the first kingdoms come to be? Why did they develop where they did?

To answer questions like these, historians and archeologists study many kinds of clues. For example, they look closely at geography. Natural features like rivers and vegetation help explain where people chose to settle and what kind of life they created for themselves. Scholars also try to understand evidence from ancient settlements. How were villages and towns laid out? What can this tell us about life there?

Artifacts also provide helpful clues. Iron tools, for example, show that farming methods improved in West Africa. Scholars have worked to understand how more efficient farming affected the growth of towns and cities. Gradually, scholars have pieced together a picture of how societies developed in West Africa.

In this chapter, you will explore current thinking about the origins of West African kingdoms. You will discover how early **family-based communities** developed into **villages** and how some villages grew into **towns** and **cities**. You will see how some cities became great kingdoms.

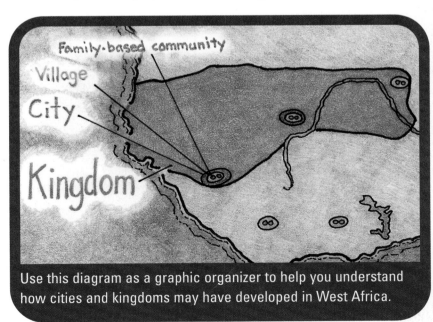

Use this diagram as a graphic organizer to help you understand how cities and kingdoms may have developed in West Africa.

Even today, people use canoes to travel along the Niger River.

12.2 Geography and Trade

Geography offers many clues about why people settle where they do and how they live. It also helps to explain patterns of trade. As you will see throughout this chapter, trade played a key role in the growth of West African societies. Let's take a look at the geography of West Africa and its influence on trade.

Geography   In the north, West Africa begins in the sands of the Sahara Desert. To the west and south it is bordered by the Atlantic Ocean, and to the east by the mountains of present-day Cameroon. This region includes the vegetation zones of desert, semidesert, savanna, and forest.

The Sahara Desert spreads across approximately 3,500,000 square miles in North Africa and the northern part of West Africa. Sand dunes cover one quarter of the Sahara, but this desert also has bare, rocky plains and even mountains. The Sahara is very dry except for some scattered oases. As you can imagine, it was not a suitable place for large settlements.

South of the Sahara is a zone of semidesert called the Sahel. The Sahel is not as dry as the Sahara. It has enough water for short grasses and some small bushes and trees to survive.

The southern part of the Sahel merges into the savanna, an area of tall grasses and scattered trees. The savanna has a long rainy season. Because of the rain, grains such as millet, sorghum, and rice can be grown there. Grasses provide food for cattle, camels, goats, and sheep. Rivers like the long Niger River help make nearby land fertile and also provide fish for eating.

The Niger River extends into the forest zone in the southern part of West Africa. This zone is wetter than the savanna. Its northern part is a **woodland forest** of trees and shrubs. Oil palms, yams, and kola trees grow here. The southern part of the zone is lush **rainforest,** where

woodland forest an area of abundant trees and shrubs
rainforest an area of lush vegetation and year-round rainfall

rain falls year-round. In the rainforest, tall trees such as mahogany and teak grow above swamps and lagoons.

Trade   The geography of West Africa influenced the patterns of trade that developed there. Different resources are found in each of the vegetation zones. As a result, people living in different zones had to trade to get items they could not provide for themselves. For example, people in the savanna may have traded grains in return for yams or mahogany from the forests.

Several major rivers served as trading routes in West Africa. The Niger is the region's longest river. It became a kind of trading highway. People in ancient times traveled the Niger and other rivers by canoe to trade goods. Some traders also crossed the desert from North Africa, but most early trade was between West African settlements.

12.3 Early Communities and Villages

By about 4000 B.C.E., some people had settled to farm south of the Sahara Desert. The earliest farming communities were made up of **extended families**. An extended family includes close relatives such as grandparents as well as aunts, uncles, and their children.

An extended-family community might have had about 15 to 20 members. Each community produced most of the things it needed. Family members worked together to clear the fields, plant seeds, and harvest crops. These small communities traded with one another for additional goods. Very likely, one of the male elders made decisions for the family community.

Over time, family communities joined together to form villages. A village might contain 100 to 200 people. The village leader was probably chosen for his wisdom.

Extended families usually banded together in villages to get needed help. For example, people might need to work together to control a flooding river or to mine for iron or gold. They may also have come together for protection. Archeologists have discovered ruins of high walls and gates at the ancient West African village of Dhar Tichitt. These structures suggest that the villagers united to protect themselves from attacks by outsiders.

extended family an immediate family (parents and their children) plus other close relatives, such as grandparents, aunts, uncles, and cousins

Early villages might have had homes built close together for protection.

12.4 The Development of Towns and Cities

Some West African villages gradually developed into towns and cities. Ancient cities in West Africa were not as large as modern cities, but some had thousands of residents.

Why did villages grow into cities in West Africa? Two important reasons were the growth of ironworking and the expansion of trade.

Ironworking and Trade   The Hittites of present-day Turkey mastered ironworking as long ago as 1500 B.C.E. Gradually, knowledge of ironworking spread. Eventually it reached West Africa, perhaps by way of traders who crossed the Sahara Desert. Some scholars think that ironworking developed independently among people in the northern part of West Africa.

By the 500s B.C.E., a people called the Nok were making iron tools. The Nok lived in what is now central Nigeria. Archeologists have found some of their iron tools and iron-smelting furnaces.

Smelting is the process of heating and melting ore in order to get iron or other metals from it. The Nok used enormous amounts of charcoal to fuel their iron-smelting furnaces. The red-hot iron was then hammered and bent into useful shapes by skilled workers called *blacksmiths*. Nok blacksmiths made axes, hoes, and weapons such as spears.

The craft of ironworking spread rapidly throughout West Africa. The ability to make tools out of iron brought major changes. With iron tools, farmers could clear land and grow crops more efficiently than with stone tools. The greater abundance of food supported larger villages where more people were free to work at other trades, such as weaving, metalworking, and pottery making.

More and more, villages produced surplus (extra) food and handmade goods. They could then trade their surplus for goods they could not produce themselves.

As goods traveled across West Africa, villages located along rivers or other easily traveled routes became trading sites. Villages that controlled trade routes became market centers and grew richer by charging for trading activity. They drew many people to work at new jobs, such as supervising trade and helping construct public buildings. Some of the villages grew into sizable towns and cities. Other large settlements grew up around natural resources, such as iron ore and good farmland.

Iron tools made farming more efficient. This allowed people to devote more time to weaving and other trades.

The Ancient City of Jenne-jeno In 1977, archeologists began **excavating** the ancient West African city of Jenne-jeno. Built in the third century B.C.E., Jenne-jeno existed for more than 1,600 years. Before it was rediscovered, historians thought that cities did not exist in West Africa until outsiders arrived and helped local people build them. The discovery of Jenne-jeno proved this theory wrong.

Jenne-jeno was built where the Niger River meets the Bani River. This was an ideal location for farming, fishing, and trade. The people of Jenne-jeno traded their surplus goods—such as catfish, fish oil, onions, and rice—for salt, iron ore, copper, and gold. The iron ore came from 50 miles away and the copper from 600 miles away.

Jenne-jeno grew into a busy city of about 20,000 people. It was surrounded by a circular wall 10 feet wide and 13 feet high. The wall may have been built to give the city more status and to make it easier to control the comings and goings of traders.

The people of Jenne-jeno lived in circular houses. At first the houses were made from bent poles and woven mats. Later they were built from mud blocks.

The ancient city of Jenne-jeno was built on this floodplain on the Niger River, less than two miles from the modern city of Jenne.

The city's people worked at many crafts. Besides farmers and fishermen, there were potters, metalsmiths, weavers, leatherworkers, bead makers, and ivory carvers.

The most respected people in Jenne-jeno were the blacksmiths. The people of West Africa prized iron even more than gold. They were amazed by the blacksmiths' ability to make useful tools from iron. People thought the blacksmiths had supernatural (magical or godlike) powers. For this reason, they gave blacksmiths many responsibilities. Blacksmiths acted as political leaders, judges, and doctors. Some were charged with predicting the future.

In recent years, scientists have studied the sites of other ancient cities in West Africa. They have found evidence of trade, craftsmanship, and wealth.

excavate in archeology, to carefully dig out an ancient site

12.5 The Rise of Kingdoms and Empires

Trade was a major factor in the rise of kingdoms in West Africa. Ghana, Mali, and Songhai were all trading powers that ruled over large areas. Historians often refer to them as empires as well as kingdoms.

How did the first kingdoms develop? The rulers of some trading cities in West Africa became wealthy by collecting taxes from the goods that were bought and sold. With their wealth, they could afford to raise large armies. These armies could conquer other trading areas nearby. Then the ruler could take over the trade of those areas and became even wealthier.

Rulers also collected **tribute** from the people they conquered. The payment of tribute was a sign that the ruler accepted the king's authority. Tribute could also pay for protection from outside attackers.

West African kings were both the political and the religious leaders of their kingdoms. They were believed to have special powers given to them by the gods. They performed religious ceremonies to please the gods.

As a king conquered more territory, the kingdom grew into an empire. Sometimes a

These modern horsemen from West Africa are a reminder of the armies that rulers were able to raise with the wealth they received from trade.

king sent a governor to rule a conquered area. Sometimes he allowed conquered people to rule themselves.

Becoming part of a kingdom or an empire had disadvantages. One was the obligation to pay tribute. Another was that men had to serve in the king's army. But there were advantages as well. Kings provided protection for the conquered territory. Armies made sure trade routes were safe, and they kept out raiders and foreign armies. Wars between small cities ended. Kings collected luxury goods from their subjects and passed them out fairly throughout the kingdom. They also gave expensive presents to their governors.

Three West African Kingdoms

0   500 miles
0   500 kilometers

GHANA   SONGHAI

Senegal R.

MALI   Niger R.

N
W   E
S

The great kingdoms of West Africa did not rely on only local trade. By the time Ghana became an important power, trans-Saharan trade was bringing new wealth to West Africa. Control of trade, particularly in West African gold, was also a key to the power of Mali. Songhai, too, relied on trade with distant lands. You'll learn more about the importance of trans-Saharan trade in the next chapter.

12.6 Chapter Summary

In this chapter, you learned how kingdoms and empires grew out of early societies in West Africa. Geography was a major factor in the development of these societies. Settled communities grew up below the Sahara Desert, where the land permitted farming. Geography also influenced trading patterns. Communities traded with one another for items they could not produce locally. Rivers such as the Niger served as trade routes.

The earliest societies in West Africa were family-based communities. Some of these communities joined together to form villages. Banding together in villages allowed people to take advantage of natural resources and protect themselves from attack.

Iron making and trade helped some villages grow into sizable towns and cities. Iron tools allowed farmers grow food more efficiently. As a result, more people could engage in other crafts. Villages traded with one another for their surplus goods. Some villages became important trading sites and grew into cities. Other large settlements developed around farmland or other natural resources.

Trade brought some cities great wealth. The wealthiest cities conquered neighboring areas, leading to the rise of kingdoms and empires. Rulers gained even more wealth through tribute as well as control of trade. In the next chapter, you will learn more about the importance of trade as you study the ancient kingdom of Ghana.

Ancient kingdoms developed because they controlled trading centers. This modern trading center of Mopti is on the Niger River.

Early Societies in West Africa   143

◀ Camel caravans transport salt from the desert mines and supplies to the miners.

Ghana: A West African Trading Empire

13.1 Introduction

In the last chapter, you learned how West African societies developed into kingdoms and empires. Ghana, Mali, and Songhai all created empires that gained much of their wealth from trade. In this chapter, you will learn more about the role of trade as you explore Ghana, the first of West Africa's empires.

The kingdom of Ghana lasted from sometime before 500 c.e. until its final collapse in the 1200s. It arose in the semidry Sahel and eventually spread over the valley between the Senegal and Niger Rivers. To the south was forest. To the north lay the Sahara Desert. Today this region is part of the nations of Mauritania and Mali. (The modern country of Ghana takes its name from the old kingdom, but it is located far to the south.)

The earliest writings about the kingdom of Ghana come from Arab scholars. These scholars recorded information they had gathered from travelers to Ghana. By the time they began writing about Ghana in the ninth century, it was already a flourishing empire.

We don't know for certain how Ghana developed into an empire. Possibly a group of warriors used iron weapons to defeat their neighbors. In fact, the word *ghana* means "war chief." We do know that control of trade, particularly in gold, made the king of Ghana and his people very wealthy. West Africans still sing songs about the majesty of ancient Ghana.

In this chapter, you will first learn about Ghana's **government** and **military**. Then you'll learn how Ghana's people acquired wealth by serving as **middlemen** in **trans-Saharan trade**. You'll look at how traders did business with one another. Finally, you'll find out how Ghana declined and a new empire, Mali, arose in West Africa.

Use this illustration as a graphic organizer to help you understand how trade enabled the West African kingdom of Ghana to become powerful and wealthy.

The king of Ghana usually wore beautiful clothes and fine jewelry when he held court.

13.2 Ghana's Government and Military

Arab scholars described Ghana as a fabled "land of gold." Their accounts paint a picture of a rich kingdom with a strong government and a large and powerful army.

The King and His Government Ghana was ruled by a powerful king. The king was the head of the army and had the final say in matters of justice. He also led the people in religious worship.

Ghana's king acquired great wealth through control of the gold trade. Gold was especially plentiful in areas to the south of Ghana. As you will see, Ghana collected taxes on gold that passed through the kingdom.

To preserve his wealth, the king tightly controlled the supply of gold. All of the gold nuggets, or chunks, found in the kingdom had to be given to the king. Other people could have only gold dust. One of the king's gold nuggets is said to have weighed almost 40 pounds. According to legend, another was large enough to be used as a hitching post for his horse.

Each day, the king held court with his people. The king arrived at court to the beating of royal drums. He was splendidly dressed in colorful robes, gold jewelry, and a cap decorated with gold. His people showed their respect for him by kneeling and throwing dust on their heads as he approached.

Once at court, the king conducted the business of his empire and heard the people's concerns. One Arab historian described the scene at the court like this:

Behind the king stand ten pages [young servants] *holding shields and swords decorated with gold and on his right are the sons of the vassal kings of his empire wearing splendid garments and their hair plaited [braided] with gold. The governor of the city sits on the ground before the king and around are ministers seated likewise. At the door...are dogs of excellent pedigree [ancestry] who hardly ever leave the place where the king is, guarding him. Round their necks, they wear collars of gold and silver.*

A large group of officials were paid from the kingdom's wealth to help the king govern. These officials were probably in charge of different parts of Ghana's society, such as the armed forces, industry, taxes, and foreigners. The king appointed governors to rule some parts of his empire, such as the capital city and some conquered areas.

When the king died, his son did not inherit the throne. The royal inheritance was **matrilineal,** which means that it was traced through women's bloodlines rather than men's. In Ghana, the son of the king's sister took over the throne.

Ghana's Military   Ghana's military included a regular army, reserve forces, and elite soldiers. The regular army was made up of several thousand career soldiers. They kept the borders secure, put down minor revolts, and maintained peace and order. These soldiers wore knee-length cotton pants, sleeveless tunics (long shirts), sandals, and **headdresses** decorated with feathers. The color of a soldier's tunic and the number of feathers in his headdress indicated his rank. The soldiers used weapons such as spears, daggers, swords, battle clubs, and bows and arrows. They were well paid and well respected.

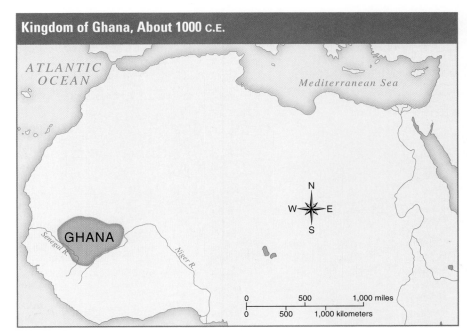

Kingdom of Ghana, About 1000 C.E.

ATLANTIC OCEAN

Mediterranean Sea

GHANA

Senegal R.

Niger R.

N W E S

0   500   1,000 miles
0   500   1,000 kilometers

During wartime, the king called up additional reserve forces and the troops of other governors under his rule. Every man in the empire was required to complete military training so that he would be ready to serve when called. Stories tell of a king who could call up an army of 200,000 warriors. This number no doubt grew as stories were passed on, but the king certainly could summon a sizable army.

An elite group of soldiers were selected for their courage, honesty, and intelligence. These soldiers served the king as bodyguards, escorts, and military advisors.

Ghana: A West African Trading Empire

13.3 Trade: The Source of Ghana's Wealth

Ghana was located between two areas that wanted to trade—North Africa and the southern forests of West Africa. Traders from the north crossed the Sahara with salt, copper, and cowrie shells (the shells were used as money). They traded these and other goods for kola nuts, hides, leather goods, ivory, slaves, and gold from the southern forests. Then they returned to North Africa, bringing the goods from the south to merchants there.

Ghana's location allowed it to control this trans-Saharan trade. Traders going to and from the south had to pass through Ghana. Each time, they paid heavy taxes on their goods. These taxes helped make Ghana rich.

The History of Trans-Saharan Trade Trans-Saharan trade has a long history. Archeologists have found evidence that North Africans brought back gold from the southern forests as long ago as 400 to 500 B.C.E. Travel across the Sahara, however, was very difficult.

Centuries later, two factors spurred the growth of trans-Saharan trade. The first was the introduction of the camel to the Sahara. The second was the spread of Islam.

Camels were first brought to the Sahara around 300 C.E. These animals are well suited for desert travel. A camel can drink up to 25 gallons of water at a time. As a result, it can travel several days in the desert without stopping. Also, camels have double rows of eyelashes and hairy ear openings that help keep out blowing sand.

The introduction of camels allowed traders to establish caravan routes across the Sahara. By the fourth century, large amounts of gold were being minted into Roman coins in North Africa. It is likely that the gold came from West Africa.

Trade expanded even more because of the spread of Islam. In the seventh century, Muslims invaded Ghana's empire. Besides wanting to convert West Africans to Islam, Muslims hoped to control trade in West Africa.

Camels were especially suited to transport goods across the Sahara.

Ghana turned back the invaders, but many Muslims settled in West African towns and became merchants.

Control of the trans-Saharan trade made Ghana wealthy and powerful. By the year 1000, Ghana's empire dominated the trade routes between North and West Africa.

The Journey South

The traders who traveled to West Africa faced a long, difficult journey. The trans-Saharan caravan routes began in North Africa along the northwestern border of the Sahara. From there they stretched across the desert, crossed through Ghana, and continued south to the Gulf of Guinea and east to present-day Chad.

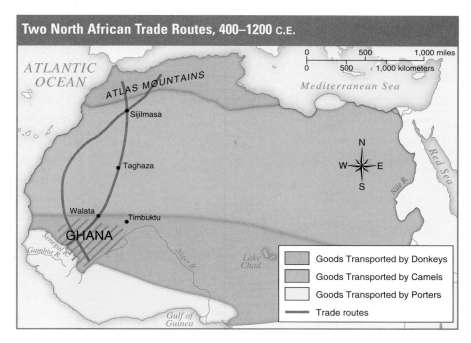

Two North African Trade Routes, 400–1200 C.E.

Goods Transported by Donkeys
Goods Transported by Camels
Goods Transported by Porters
Trade routes

In 1352, a Muslim historian and traveler named Ibn Battuta crossed the Sahara with a trade caravan. Battuta's account of his trip shows what the traders' journeys were like.

Battuta's caravan began at the oasis city of Sijilmasa, on the northern edge of the Sahara in the foothills of the Atlas Mountains. Donkeys carried goods from Europe, Arabia, and Egypt to Sijilmasa from the Mediterranean coast. Then camel caravans took the goods south.

Battuta and his caravan stayed in Sijilmasa for a few months, waiting for the rainy season to end. When the watering places were full and there was grass for the animals to eat, the traders set out. The caravan traveled from oasis to oasis. Each day, the traders walked until the afternoon, when the sun was high in the sky. Then they rested until the sun went down.

Walking across the Sahara was difficult and dangerous. Caravans sometimes lost their way, and some traders died in the desert. During one stretch of Battuta's trip, the travelers could not find water, so they slaughtered some of their camels and drank the water stored in the animals' stomachs.

On its way through the desert, the caravan stopped at Taghaza, a village where salt mines were located. There it took on a load of salt. When the traders reached the town of Walata at the edge of the desert, they transferred their salt and other goods from the camels to donkeys and **porters**. Then they continued south, passing through Ghana on their way to markets on the Gulf of Guinea, near the southern forests. The entire journey took about two months.

porter a person who is hired to carry loads

People in Italy and in Muslim lands used West African gold to make coins.

13.4 The Gold-Salt Trade

Many items were traded between North Africa and the southern forests, but the two that were most in demand were gold and salt. The North Africans wanted gold, which came from the forest region south of Ghana. The people in the forests wanted salt, which came from the Sahara. Ghana made most of its money from the taxes it charged on the gold-salt trade that passed through its lands.

Wangara: The Secret Source of Gold Gold has long been a symbol of wealth in much of the world. In the time of Ghana's empire, people in Muslim lands and Italy made coins from gold. Muslims also needed gold to purchase silk and porcelain from China, which would accept only gold in exchange.

In an area known as Wangara, gold was plentiful. Wangara was located near the forests south of Ghana, but no one except the people of Wangara knew exactly where. The Wangarans kept the locations of their gold mines secret. According to ancient stories, merchants occasionally captured a gold miner and tried to force him to reveal the location of Wangara. The miners would give up their lives rather than reveal the secret.

In one story, after the capture of a miner, the Wangarans stopped trading for three years. They wanted to make sure no one had discovered where Wangara was. To this day, no one knows for certain exactly where Wangara's mines were located.

Taghaza: A Village Built with Salt To West Africans, salt was more precious than gold. Their culture had little use for gold, except as an item for trade. But they craved salt, and for good reason. Salt is an important part of a person's diet. When people and animals perspire (sweat), they lose salt in their perspiration. People who live in areas with hot climates, like West Africa, perspire a lot and must replace the salt they lose. West Africans also needed salt to keep their food from spoiling and to give to their cattle. In addition, they liked the taste.

West Africans had no local source of salt. They had to obtain it from Taghaza and other places in the Sahara Desert.

deposit a layer or mass of a material found in rock or in the ground

Salt was produced in two ways in the Sahara. One method was through evaporation. Water was poured into holes in the salty earth. The water slowly drew out the salt and then evaporated in the sun. The salt that remained was scooped out and packed into blocks. The second way to get salt was through mining. At Taghaza, salt **deposits** were found about three feet below the surface of the earth. Miners, who were slaves owned by Arab merchants, reached the salt by digging trenches and tunnels. Then they dug it out in large blocks.

If it weren't for salt, Taghaza would not have existed. It was a dismal place, without crops or vegetation. People lived there for one purpose: to mine and sell salt. Even the houses and mosque were built with salt blocks. Trade caravans passed through Taghaza on their way through the Sahara. There they picked up salt to sell in Ghana and the southern forests. Because no food was produced in Taghaza, the miners had to rely on caravans to bring food, such as millet, camel steaks, and dates. If the caravans didn't come, the miners starved.

Ghana's System of Taxes   Traders paid taxes to Ghana on all the goods they carried through the empire. Goods were taxed both when traders entered Ghana and when they left. Ghana charged one-sixth of an ounce of gold for each load of salt that came into the kingdom from the north. It then charged one-third of an ounce of gold for each load the traders took out of the kingdom to the south. The traders also paid taxes for carrying other types of goods. For every load of copper, they were charged five-eighths of an ounce of gold. They paid a little more than one ounce of gold per load of general merchandise.

The taxes enriched Ghana's treasury. They also helped pay for armies that protected the kingdom and allowed the king to conquer other territories. Traders benefited as well because Ghana protected the trade routes from bandits who might rob the caravans.

In West Africa, salt is made by the evaporation of water in areas called *salt flats*. The salt is mined by digging it out in large blocks.

Even today, salt is an important trade item in West Africa.

13.5 The Exchange of Goods

When trade caravans entered Ghana, they brought their goods to the great marketplace in the capital city of Kumbi. From there, they headed to the southern forests to trade with the Wangarans.

Kumbi had the busiest market in West Africa. Many local craftspeople sold their goods there. Ironsmiths sold weapons and tools. Goldsmiths and coppersmiths sold jewelry. Weavers sold cloth, and leatherworkers sold leather goods. There were blue blouses from Spain and robes from Morocco. People could also buy cattle, sheep, honey, wheat, raisins, dried fruit, ivory, pearls, and slaves. All goods, including slaves, were paid for with gold dust.

Kumbi had one of the largest slave markets in West Africa. The slaves came from the southern border of Ghana. They were captured by raiders and brought to Kumbi to be sold. Many were bought by Arab merchants, who took them across the Sahara and sold them to North Africans or Europeans.

Trade with the Wangarans took place along a river in the southern forests. The traders carried out their business using a system of silent barter, or trade. The caravans arrived bringing wool, silk, cotton, dates, figs, grains, leather, and salt. They spread out their goods along the river. The traders beat on a drum to announce that they were making an offer to trade. Then they walked several miles away from the site.

When the Wangarans heard the drum, they traveled to the site by boat. They put some gold dust next to the goods, beat a drum, and left. Later, the traders returned. If the amount of gold dust was acceptable, they took it and left. If not, they went away again and waited for the Wangarans to return and leave more gold dust. The groups bargained back and forth this way without ever meeting in person until the trade was complete.

This system of silent barter had two advantages. First, it allowed people who spoke different languages to conduct trades. Second, it allowed the Wangarans to guard the secret of where their gold mines were located.

13.6 The Decline of Ghana and the Rise of Mali

Ghana's empire reached its height around 1000 C.E. War and the loss of natural resources led to its downfall.

In the second half of the 11th century, Muslim warriors called Almoravids began attacking Ghana's empire. In 1076, they captured the capital city of Kumbi. Ghana's king regained power in 1087, but the old empire had broken apart.

The loss of natural resources further weakened Ghana. A growing population had put great stress on scarce resources like trees and water. Trees were cut down to provide charcoal for iron-smelting furnaces. Water became so scarce that farmers could no longer grow crops. People were forced to leave in search of better conditions. The empire came to an end in 1203 when a rival kingdom took over Kumbi.

The disappearance of Ghana opened the way to the rise of a new power, Mali. Around 1240, a group of West Africans called the Mande conquered Kumbi. Their homeland of Mali was south of Kumbi, closer to the Niger River. The Mande built an empire that reached from the Atlantic Ocean to beyond the Niger River, and from the southern forest to the salt and copper mines of the Sahara.

Like Ghana, Mali gained much of its wealth from the control of trade, particularly in gold. Its leaders had accepted Islam, and under their rule the Muslim faith became even more influential in West Africa. You will learn more about the impact of Islam on West African culture in the next chapter.

Natural resources such as water and trees are scarce in areas like the Sahel.

13.7 Chapter Summary

Trade played a key role in the growth of kingdoms and empires in West Africa. The first of these was Ghana.

Ghana had a powerful government and a strong army. It was ideally located to control the trans-Saharan trade between North Africa and the southern forests of West Africa.

Ghana became wealthy by charging taxes on the goods that passed through its lands, especially gold and salt. Years of war and the loss of natural resources led to Ghana's downfall in the 13th century.

The next great West African empire, Mali, also built its wealth on trade. In the next chapter, you will learn about the impact of Islam on Mali and the rest of West Africa.

◀ ◀ The Grande Mosque in Mopti, Mali,
was built of bricks and mud.

CHAPTER 14

The Influence of Islam on West Africa

14.1 Introduction

In the last chapter, you learned about the role of trade in the rise of Ghana and other West African kingdoms. Now you will explore how the Islamic faith influenced West African culture.

During the seventh century, Islam spread quickly through the Middle East and North Africa. In the eighth century, trans-Saharan trade brought Muslim merchants and traders to West Africa. Over the next few hundred years, Islam spread among West Africans. As you will see, both Mali and Songhai eventually accepted Islam. The new faith left a lasting mark on the culture of West Africa.

West Africans often blended Islamic culture with their own traditions. For example, West Africans who became Muslims began praying to God in Arabic. They built mosques as places of worship. Yet they also continued to pray to the spirits of their ancestors, as they had done for centuries.

Islamic beliefs and customs affected many areas of life besides religious faith. In this chapter, you will learn about the spread of Islam in West Africa. Then you will look at Islam's influence on several aspects of West African culture. You'll explore changes in **religious practices, government** and **law, education, language, architecture,** and **decorative arts**. You can still see the effects of these changes in West Africa today.

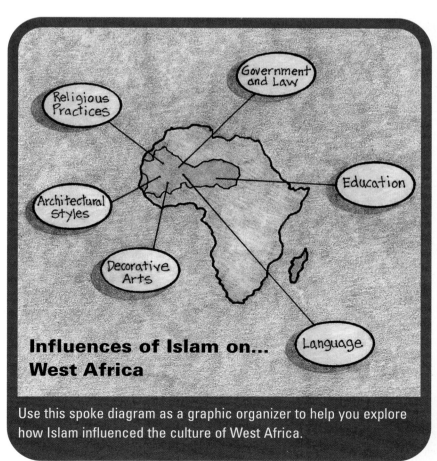

**Influences of Islam on...
West Africa**

Use this spoke diagram as a graphic organizer to help you explore how Islam influenced the culture of West Africa.

Traders and the missionaries who accompanied them spread Islam to Ghana.

14.2 The Spread of Islam in West Africa

Trans-Saharan trade brought Islam to West Africa in the eighth century. At first, Muslim traders and merchants lived side by side with the non-Muslims of West Africa. Over time, however, Islam played a growing role in West African society.

Traders Bring Islam to Ghana   Between 639 and 708 C.E., Arab Muslims conquered North Africa. Before long, they wanted to bring West Africa into the Islamic world. But sending armies to conquer Ghana was not practical. Ghana was too far away, and it was protected by the Sahara Desert.

Islam first reached Ghana through Muslim traders and missionaries. The king of Ghana did not convert to Islam. Nor did the majority of the people. But the king did allow Muslims to build settlements within his empire.

Many Muslim merchants and traders settled in Kumbi, the great marketplace of Ghana. Over time, a thriving Muslim community developed around the trans-Saharan trade with North Africa. The Muslims in Kumbi had 12 mosques and their own imam (spiritual leader). Scholars studied the Qur'an.

In the 11th century, Muslims from the north called the Almoravids waged jihad (holy war) in West Africa. In 1076, they captured Kumbi. The Almoravids did not stay in power long, but under their rule Islam became more widespread in Ghana.

Islam in Mali   To the south of Ghana, the Mande also accepted Islam. The tolerance shown by Muslims toward traditional religious practices helped Islam to spread. For example, West Africans continued to pray to the spirits of their ancestors.

In about 1240, the Mande conquered Kumbi. They took control of the trade routes to North Africa and built the empire of Mali.

The early leaders of Mali accepted Islam, but they did not follow all of its teachings. In 1312, a new leader, Mansa Musa, took over in Mali. He became the first West African ruler to practice Islam devoutly.

Under his rule, Mali became a major crossroad of the Islamic world. Muslim merchants, traders, and scholars from Egypt and North Africa came to Mali to do business or to settle.

Like other Muslims, Musa made a hajj, or pilgrimage, to the sacred city of Makkah in Arabia. The hajj was an enormous undertaking. The trip would cover some 3,000 miles. Officials and servants started preparing for the trip months before Musa left. As many as 80,000 people may have accompanied Musa on the hajj.

Musa reached Cairo, Egypt, in July 1324, after eight months of travel. A writer from Cairo described Musa's caravan as "a lavish display of power, wealth, and unprecedented by its size and pageantry." Ahead of Musa arrived 500 slaves, each carrying a six-pound staff of gold. He was followed by a caravan of 200 camels carrying 30,000 pounds of gold along with food, clothing, and supplies.

In Cairo, Musa met the local sultan, or ruler. When he was asked to kneel before the sultan, Musa felt insulted. He was very proud of being the ruler of Mali. After Musa finally agreed to kneel, the sultan invited him to sit beside him as his equal.

After leaving Cairo, Musa traveled to Arabia to visit Makkah and Madinah. When word spread that the king of Mali was visiting, people lined the streets to see him. Musa's wealth impressed the people and rulers of Arabia. He paid in gold for all the goods and services he received. He also gave expensive gifts to his hosts.

Because of Musa's hajj, Mali gained acceptance as an important empire. By 1375, Mali appeared on a European map of West Africa.

Islam in Songhai   One of the groups within Mali's empire was the Songhai people. In the 1460s, the great warrior Sunni Ali became the new ruler of Songhai. He built a powerful army that enabled Songhai to break away from Mali and eventually conquer it.

The early rulers of Songhai did not seriously practice Islam. In the 1490s, Muslims in Songhai rebelled. They placed Askia Mohammed Toure, a devout Muslim, on the throne. Toure set up rigid controls to be sure Islam was practiced properly. He also led a series of wars to convert non-Muslims to Islam. Under his rule, Songhai's empire covered a territory as large as western Europe.

The pilgrimage of Mansa Musa to Makkah was so impressive that European mapmakers produced this map of West Africa with his image prominently displayed.

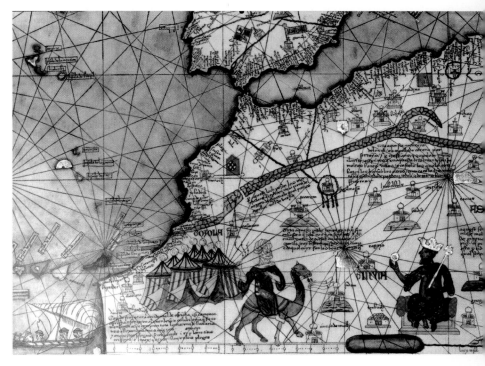

14.3 New Religious Practices

amulet a piece of jewelry or other object used as a charm to provide protection against bad luck, illness, injury, or evil

As Islam spread in West Africa, people adopted new religious practices and ethical values. African Muslims learned Islam's Five Pillars of Faith. They prayed in Arabic, fasted, worshiped in mosques, went on pilgrimages, and gave alms. They were taught to regard all Muslims as part of a single community.

West Africans also began to celebrate Muslim religious festivals. The festival of Eid al-Fitr marks the end of the holy month of Ramadan. Eid al-Adha commemorates a key event in the story of the prophet Abraham. As a test of faith, God asked Abraham to sacrifice his son. God spared the boy after Abraham proved his faith by being willing to offer his son to God.

Alongside these new customs, West Africans kept some of their old religious practices. Muslim leaders allowed them to continue religious traditions as long as they did not contradict the Five Pillars of Faith. So, for example, West African Muslims continued to show respect for the spirits of dead ancestors. They kept their belief in spirits who could help those who prayed to them or made sacrifices to them. They used **amulets,** or charms, that they believed helped people or protected them from harm.

With the introduction of Islam, West Africans began praying five times a day.

In the last chapter, you read about Ibn Battuta, an Arab who traveled to Mali in the 14th century. Battuta was upset by some local customs. For instance, women, including the daughters of rulers, went unclothed in public. Battuta also saw Muslims throwing dust over their heads when the king approached. These customs upset him because they went against the teachings of Islam.

Yet Battuta was also impressed by the devotion of West Africans to Islam. He wrote, "Anyone who is late at the mosque will find nowhere to pray, the crowd is so great. They zealously learn the Qur'an by heart. Those children who are neglectful in this are put in chains until they have memorized the Qur'an."

14.4 New Ideas About Government and Law

Muslims in the Middle East and North Africa developed Islamic forms of government and law. Muslim rulers in West Africa adopted some of these ideas.

One important change concerned the line of **succession,** or inheritance of the right to rule. In West Africa, succession to the throne had traditionally been matrilineal. That is, the right to rule was traced through a woman rather than a man. As you have learned, in Ghana the son of the king's sister inherited the throne.

With the coming of Islam, the power of the ruler became greater and local chiefs grew less important.

After the arrival of Islam, succession became **patrilineal**. Under this system, the right to rule passed from father to son.

A second change affected the structure of government. Muslims believed in a highly centralized government. After West African kings converted to Islam, they started to exercise more control of local rulers. Rulers also adopted titles used in Muslim lands. Often the head of a region was now called the *sultan* or the *amir* or *emir*. Amir and emir are shortened forms of Amir al-Muminin. This Arabic expression means "Commander of the Faithful."

A third major change was the adoption of shari'ah (Islamic law). In many towns and cities, shari'ah replaced traditional customary law. The customary law of West Africa was very different from shari'ah. Laws were not written, but everyone knew what they were and accepted them. A chief or king usually enforced customary law but did not give physical punishments. Instead, the guilty party paid the injured party with gifts or services. The family or clan of the guilty person could also be punished.

One example of customary law was "trial by wood." Suppose a man was accused of not paying debts or of injuring another person. The accused man was forced to drink water that had been poured over sour, bitter wood. If the man vomited, he was believed to be innocent.

Unlike customary law, shari'ah is written law. Muslims believed that shari'ah came from God. As you learned in Unit 2, shari'ah was administered by judges called *qadis*. The qadis heard cases in a court. They listened to witnesses and ruled on the basis of the law and the evidence presented to them.

succession inheritance of the right to rule
patrilineal based on a man's family line

14.5 A New Emphasis on Education

Muslims greatly value learning. In West Africa, Muslims encouraged people to become educated. They built many schools and centers of learning.

One key center was the trading city of Timbuktu, on the Niger River. Under Mali and Songhai rule, Timbuktu became famous for its community of Islamic scholars. It remained an important center of learning until Songhai was conquered by Morocco in the late 1500s.

Several universities were built in Timbuktu. The most famous was the University of Sankore. It became one of the world's great universities.

Sankore was made up of several

The influence of Muslims, who greatly value education, made the city of Timbuktu a center for learning. Several universities were established there.

small, independent schools. Each school was run by an imam, or scholar. The imams at Sankore were respected throughout the Islamic world.

Students at Sankore studied under a single imam. The basic course of learning included the Qur'an, Islamic studies, law, and literature. After mastering these subjects, students could go on to study a particular field. Many kinds of courses were available. Students could learn medicine and surgery. They could study astronomy, mathematics, physics, or chemistry. Or they could take up philosophy, geography, art, or history.

The highest degree at Sankore required about 10 years of study. During graduation, students wore a cloth headdress called a *turban*. The turban was a symbol of divine light, wisdom, knowledge, and excellent moral character.

When travelers and traders passed through Timbuktu, they were encouraged to study at one of the universities. Trade associations also set up their own colleges. Students in these colleges learned about the profession of trading in addition to Islam.

Muslims also set up schools to educate children in the Qur'an. Timbuktu had 150 or more Qur'anic schools where children learned to read and interpret Islam's holy book.

With their love of education, Muslims treasured books. Muslims did not have printing presses, so books had to be copied by hand. Mosques and universities in West Africa built up large libraries of these precious volumes. Some individuals also created sizable collections. One Islamic scholar's private library contained 700 volumes. Many of his books were among the rarest in the world.

14.6 A New Language

In Unit 2, you learned that Islam is rooted in Arabic culture. As Islam spread, so did the Arabic language.

In West Africa, Arabic became the language of religion, learning, commerce, and government. West Africans continued to use their native languages in everyday speech.

For Muslims, Arabic was the language of religion. The Qur'an, of course, was written in Arabic. All Muslims were expected to read the Qur'an and memorize parts of it. As West Africans converted to Islam, more and more of them learned Arabic.

Arabic also became the language of learning. The scholars who came to West Africa were mainly Arabic-speaking Muslims. Some of their students became scholars themselves. Like their teachers, they wrote in Arabic.

Scholars used Arabic to write about the history and culture of West Africa. They wrote about a wide variety of topics. They described how people used animals, plants, and minerals to cure diseases. They discussed ethical behavior for business and government. They told how to use the stars to determine the seasons. They recorded the history of Songhai. They also wrote about Islamic law. These writings are an invaluable source of knowledge about West Africa.

Finally, Arabic became the language of trade and government. Arabic allowed West African traders who spoke different languages to communicate more easily. Arabic also allowed rulers to keep records and to write to rulers in other countries.

Arabic, the language in which the Qur'an is written, became the language of learning, government, and trade.

Islamic architects built flat-roofed houses made of sun-dried bricks.

14.7 New Architectural Styles

The influence of Islam brought new styles of architecture to West Africa. People designed mosques for worship. They also created a new design for homes.

Traditionally, West Africans had built small shrines to the forces of nature. As they converted to Islam, they began to build mosques. The materials that were most available in the savanna were mud and wood. Using these materials, West Africans built mosques that blended Islamic architectural styles with their own traditional religious art. For example, the minaret (tower) of one mosque was designed to look like the symbol of a Songhai ancestor.

After his pilgrimage to Makkah, the Mali ruler Mansa Musa wanted to build more mosques. He convinced al-Saheli, an architect from Spain, to return to Mali with him. Al-Saheli built several structures in Mali. One of them is the most famous mosque in West Africa, Djingareyber. (See the photograph on page 154.) Located in Timbuktu, Djingareyber was built out of limestone and earth mixed with straw and wood. The walls of the mosque have beams projecting out of them. Workers used the beams as **scaffolding** when the building needed to be repaired.

Al-Saheli also introduced a new design for houses. Most traditional houses in West Africa were round with a cone-shaped, thatched roof. Al-Saheli built rectangular houses out of brick and with flat roofs. The outside walls were very plain and had no windows. Only a single wooden door decorated with a geometric design interrupted the rows of bricks.

Al-Saheli introduced another feature to houses that made life easier during the rainy season. To help prevent damage from rainwater, he built clay drain pipes.

scaffolding a framework used to support workers and materials during the construction or repair of a building

14.8 New Styles in Decorative Arts

In Unit 2, you learned how Muslims used calligraphy (artistic writing) and geometric patterns in their decorative arts. West Africans adopted these designs for their own art and **textiles**.

Muslims used calligraphy to decorate objects with words or verses from the Qur'an. West Africans adopted this practice. They began using the Arabic word for God to decorate costumes, fans, and even weapons. They also wrote verses from the Qur'an in amulets.

Geometric patterns were an important element in Islamic art. Recall that Muslims used these patterns rather than drawing pictures of animals or people. Geometric designs were popular in traditional West African art as well. West Africans used them to decorate textiles for clothing and everyday objects such as stools and ceramic containers. The arrival of Islam reinforced this practice.

Muslims also influenced the way people dressed in West Africa. Arab Muslims commonly wore an Arabic robe as an outer layer of clothing. An Arabic robe has wide, long sleeves and a long skirt. Muslims used writing to identify and decorate their robes. West Africans adopted the Arabic robe. Like Arabs, they still wear it today.

Islam reinforced the West African tradition of using geometric designs in decorations.

textile a woven cloth

14.9 Chapter Summary

In this chapter, you learned about the influence of Islam in West Africa. Islam left a deep mark on West African culture.

Traders and missionaries first brought Islam to Ghana in the eighth century. The influence of Islam grew under the rulers of Mali and Songhai.

Islam affected many areas of life in West Africa. It changed how people practiced religion. It brought new ideas about government and law. The royal succession became patrilineal. Government became more centralized. Shari'ah replaced customary law.

The Islamic love of learning brought a new emphasis on education to West Africa. People studied in Qur'anic schools and at Islamic universities. Timbuktu became a center of Islamic and academic study.

With the spread of Islam, Arabic became the language of religion, learning, commerce, and government. New styles of architecture developed as West Africans built mosques and changed the designs of their homes. They also adopted new styles in their decorative arts.

Traditional West African culture did not disappear with the arrival of Islam. In the next chapter, you will learn more about the cultural legacy of West Africa.

CHAPTER 15

◀ Kente cloth and hand-carved furniture are traditional arts in West African culture.

The Cultural Legacy of West Africa

15.1 Introduction

In the last chapter, you learned about the impact of Islam on West Africa. Now you will explore West Africa's rich cultural legacy.

West African culture is quite diverse. Many groups of people, each with their own language and ways of life, have lived in West Africa. From poems and stories to music and visual arts, their cultural achievements have left a lasting mark on the world.

One important part of West African culture is its **oral traditions**. Think for a moment of the oral traditions in your own culture. When you were younger, did you learn nursery rhymes from your family or friends? How about sayings such as "A penny saved is a penny earned"? Did you hear stories about your grandparents or more distant ancestors? You can probably think of many things that were passed down orally from one generation to the next.

Imagine now that your community depends on you to remember its oral traditions so they will never be forgotten. You memorize stories, sayings, and the history of your city or town. You know who the first people were to live there. You know how the community grew, and even which teams have won sports championships. On special occasions, you share your knowledge through stories and songs. You are a living library of your community's history and traditions.

In parts of West Africa, there are people who have this task. They are talented poet-musicians called *griots*. For many centuries, griots have helped to preserve West Africa's history and cultural legacy.

In this chapter, you'll learn about the role of both oral traditions and **written traditions** in West Africa. You'll also explore West African **music** and **visual arts**. Along the way, you'll see how the cultural achievements of West Africans continue to influence our world today.

Visual Arts

Music

Oral and Written Traditions

Use this illustration of a cultural center as a graphic organizer to help you explore how the cultural achievements of West Africans influence the world today.

Modern-day court musicians play traditional instruments in honor of the sultan of Cameroon.

15.2 West African Oral and Written Traditions

For centuries, the beliefs, values, and knowledge of West Africans were passed down orally from one generation to the next. In medieval times, written traditions also became important. In this section, we'll look at the oral and written traditions of West Africa.

Griots: Record Keepers of the People   A griot is a verbal artist of the Mande people. These poet-musicians tell stories, sing songs of praise, and recite poems, often while playing a drum or stringed instrument. They perform music, dance, and drama. But griots are much more than skilled entertainers. They also educate their audiences with historical accounts and **genealogies,** or histories of people's ancestry. In many ways, they are the record keepers of their people.

genealogy an account of the line of ancestry within a family

Long before the Mande had written histories, griots kept the memory of the past alive. Every village had its own griot. The griot memorized all the important events that occurred there. Griots could recite everything from births, deaths, and marriages to battles, hunts, and the coronations of kings. Some griots could tell the ancestry of every villager going back centuries. Griots were known to speak for hours, and sometimes even days.

This rich oral tradition passed from griot to griot. Rulers relied on griots as their trusted advisors. They used the griots' knowledge of history to shed light on their current problems.

The most cherished of griot history is the story of Sundjata Keita. Sundjata was the king who founded Mali's empire in the 13th century. The griot stories about him go back to his own day. Sundjata is still a hero to many people in West Africa.

The art of the griots remains alive today. Some of the most famous stars in West African popular music are griots. These artists have changed traditional oral works into modern music. Poets and storytellers make recordings and appear on radio broadcasts performing both old and new works.

Folktales   West Africa's oral tradition includes hundreds of **folktales**. West Africans used folktales to pass along their history and to teach young people morals and values.

Many traditional folktales were brought to the Americas by West Africans who were sold into slavery beginning in the 1500s. The tales were spread orally among Africans and their descendants. They became a part of the culture of North and South America and the West Indies.

One example comes from a type of folktale known as a "trickster" tale. These stories tell of a clever animal or human who outsmarts others. Trickster tales are popular in many cultures. In West Africa, one famous trickster was the hare. West Africans brought tales of the hare to America, where he became known as Brer Rabbit. In the 19th century, a writer named Joel Chandler Harris retold a number of African American stories about Brer Rabbit. These stories have since been woven into American culture.

Proverbs   West African oral tradition includes proverbs, or popular sayings. West African proverbs use images from everyday life to express ideas or give advice. They tell us a great deal about the wisdom and values of West Africans.

One proverb shows the value that Africans placed on stories. The proverb states, "A good story is like a garden carried in the pocket." Another shows the importance of oral tradition. "Every time an old man dies," the proverb says, "it is as if a library has burnt down." Enslaved West Africans brought proverbs like these to the Americas.

Written Tradition   After Islam spread to West Africa, written tradition became more important. As you learned in Chapter 14, Muslims published many works in Arabic. A number of these writings were preserved in mosques and Qur'anic schools. Today they are a key source of information about West African history, legends, and culture.

Modern writers in West Africa are adding to the literary legacy of the region. Some of them have turned ancient oral traditions into novels and other works.

folktale a story that is usually passed down orally and becomes part of a community's tradition

Griots, or storytellers, continue the oral traditions of the West African culture. They also represent the importance of elders in West African society.

15.3 West African Music

Music has always been an important part of life in West Africa. Music serves many functions in West African society. It communicates ideas, values, and feelings. It celebrates historic events and important occasions in people's lives. For instance, there are songs for weddings, funerals, and ceremonies honoring ancestors. Among the Yoruba of present-day Nigeria, mothers of twins have their own special songs. In Ghana, there are songs for celebrating the loss of a child's first tooth.

The musical traditions of West Africa continue to influence both African and world culture. Let's look at some key aspects of West African music.

Call and Response   A common style of music in West Africa is known as **call and response**. In call-and-response singing, a leader plays or sings a short phrase, known as a *call*. Then a group of people, the chorus, answer by playing or singing a short phrase, the *response*. The leader and chorus repeat this pattern over and over as they perform the song.

Enslaved Africans brought call-and-response songs to the Americas. Slaves used the songs to ease the burden of hard work, celebrate social occasions, and express outrage at their situation. This African tradition has influenced many American musical styles, including gospel, jazz, blues, rock and roll, and rap.

Musical Instruments   Traditional musical instruments in West Africa include three that have been used by griots for centuries. They are the *balafon*, the *ngoni*, and the *kora*.

The balafon probably was the original griot instrument. Like a xylophone or marimba, a balafon is made of wooden bars laid across a frame. The musician strikes the bars with a mallet, or hammer, to make melodies. The balafon is used today in popular music in modern Guinea.

The ngoni is a small stringed instrument. It is made of a hollowed-out piece of wood carved in the shape of a canoe. The strings are made of thin fishing line. The ngoni is the most popular traditional stringed instrument in Mali today.

The kora is a harplike instrument with 21 strings. The body of the kora is made of a gourd that has been cut in half and covered with cow skin. The kora's strings,

call and response a song style in which a singer or musician leads with a call and a group responds

Drumming is an important part of West African music. Drums of different sizes and shapes often have bells and rattles attached to them.

like those of the ngoni, are made of fishing line.

People around the world have been introduced to kora music by West African musicians. Some modern musicians in West Africa combine the sounds of the kora with electronic music.

Drumming Drums play an important role in West African culture. Drummers perform during parties, religious meetings, and ceremonies such as weddings and funerals.

West African drums are made of hollowed-out logs or pieces of wood. The drums are covered with animal skins.

Drummers in West Africa play in ensembles, or groups. The ensembles include different types and sizes of drums, along with bells and rattles. Drumming, singing, and dancing take place together in a circular formation. Sometimes drum ensembles use a call-and-response style.

The balafon is a traditional musical instrument of West Africa made of wooden bars attached to a horizontal frame. The bars are struck with a hammer much like a xylophone.

West African slaves brought their drumming traditions to the Americas. Over time, West African drum music evolved into new styles, particularly in Cuba. West African drum music and Afro-Cuban drumming are now popular elements of world music.

Dance In West Africa, dance is as much a part of life as singing and drumming are. Traditional West African dances are still performed in Africa and around the world.

West Africans perform dances for all kinds of occasions. They dance during rituals and during ceremonies that mark important events in people's lives. Dances can celebrate a success at work or help educate children. West Africans also perform dances to seek the help of spirits and to connect with dead ancestors.

Dance movements often reflect the conditions people live in. Among forest people, for example, dancers move as if they are finding their way through forest undergrowth.

Some dancers wear elaborate masks that represent the spirits of traditional West African religion. For example, to ask the spirits for abundance for their community, dancers may wear masks of wild animals and imitate their movements.

The Cultural Legacy of West Africa   169

15.4 West African Visual Arts

West African culture includes many forms of visual art. The traditional art of West Africa served a number of functions. Some art objects, like fabrics and baskets, satisfied everyday needs. Others, like masks and sculptures, were used in rituals and ceremonies, or to honor ancestors, spirits, or royalty.

The Yoruba people of Ife, Nigeria, made brass sculptures of their royalty. Notice the crown on this brass head.

Sculpture   West Africans of ancient and medieval times used religious sculptures to call upon the spirits to help them in every phase of life. They also used sculptures to honor their leaders.

A wealth of West African sculpture has been discovered in Nigeria. The oldest examples come from the Nok culture (500 B.C.E. to 200 C.E.). The Nok made **terra-cotta** sculptures of human figures. The sculptures tended to have long, narrow heads, unusual hair styles, and dramatic expressions. Scholars believe that they represented ancestors or mythical figures.

The Yoruba people of Ife, Nigeria, also made sculptures of terra-cotta. Later they used bronze and copper. By the 11th century C.E., they were making brass sculptures of royalty. Later, they taught their neighbors in Benin (founded in 1100 C.E.) how to make brass sculptures. Benin artists produced sculptures in honor of the royal court. By the 16th century, they were making elaborate plaques that showed the king's power and authority.

Masks   Wooden masks have been a part of West African life for centuries. Masks were worn during ceremonies, in performances, and in sacred rites. Like sculptures, they were used to bring the spirits of gods and ancestors into the present.

West African masks are detailed and expressive. They have inspired a number of artists around the world. Among these artists is Pablo Picasso, a world-famous Spanish painter of the 20th century.

terra-cotta a baked clay often used to make pottery and sculptures

Textiles   West Africans have a long tradition of making textiles that are both beautiful and symbolic. Three well-known types of West African textiles are stamped fabrics, story fabrics, and kente cloth.

West Africans make stamped fabric by drawing a grid of squares on a piece of cloth using a thick dye. They use stamps to fill in the squares with patterns. The stamps represent proverbs, historical figures, objects, plants, or animals.

Story fabrics depict events. For example, they might show kings performing great feats, like hunting lions. Some West Africans make story fabrics using a technique called **appliqué**. In appliqué, smaller pieces of fabric are attached to a larger, background piece to make designs or pictures.

The most famous West African textile is kente cloth. To make kente, people sew together narrow strips of silk or simple fabrics. The colors and designs of kente have symbolic meanings that reflect the makers' history, values and beliefs, or political or social circumstances.

The influence of West African textiles can be seen in quilts made by African American slaves. Today, commercially made kente cloth is worn around the world.

Everyday Objects   West African visual arts also include the design and decoration of everyday objects. Skilled artists turn practical objects into things of beauty. Some examples are ceramic storage containers, utensils, furniture, and baskets.

In many parts of West Africa, baskets are made by the coil method. The basket maker winds fibers into coils and then uses strips of fiber to bind the coils together. Some of these baskets are made so tightly that they can hold water.

Enslaved West Africans brought their basket-making tradition to America and taught it to their descendants. This art is still practiced in the American South.

appliqué a technique in which shaped pieces of fabric are attached to a background fabric to form a design or picture

This brass sculpture was made by the Yoruba people of Ife.

15.5 Chapter Summary

In this chapter, you explored the cultural legacy of West Africa. You learned about written and oral traditions, music, and visual arts. The cultural achievements of West Africans are still influential today.

Griots helped to preserve the history and culture of West Africa. Folktales and proverbs are also part of West Africa's oral tradition. In medieval times, Muslim scholars added a body of written tradition to this rich heritage.

Important elements of West African music include call and response, traditional instruments, drumming, and dance. Visual arts include sculptures, masks, textiles, and the design of everyday objects. Music and art played vital roles in West African life.

This chapter concludes your study of medieval West Africa. In the next unit, you will learn about imperial China.

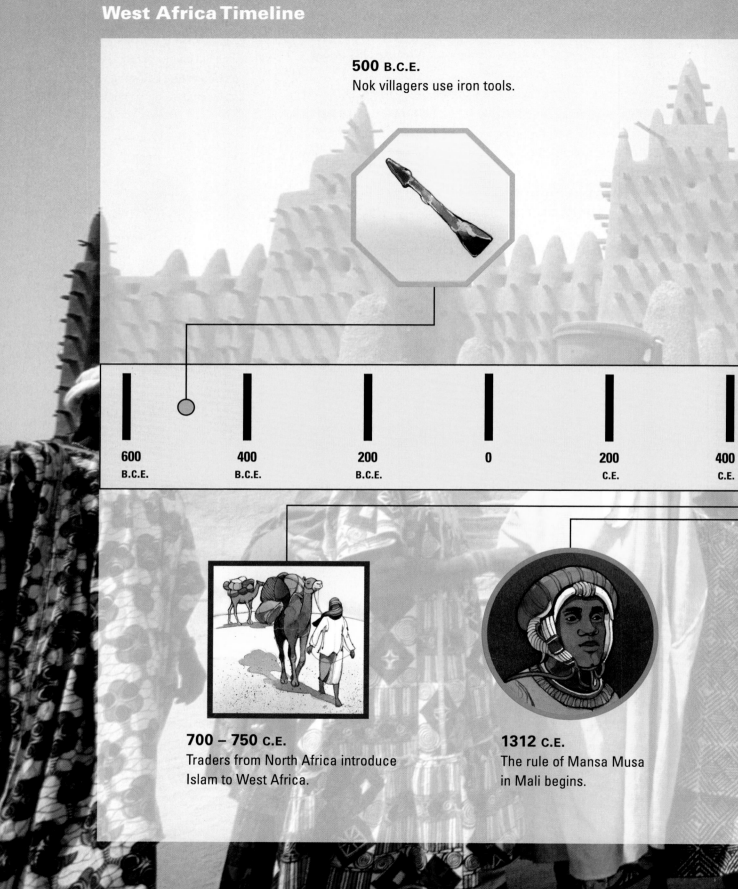

500 B.C.E.
Nok villagers use iron tools.

| 600 B.C.E. | 400 B.C.E. | 200 B.C.E. | 0 | 200 C.E. | 400 C.E. |

700 – 750 C.E.
Traders from North Africa introduce Islam to West Africa.

1312 C.E.
The rule of Mansa Musa in Mali begins.

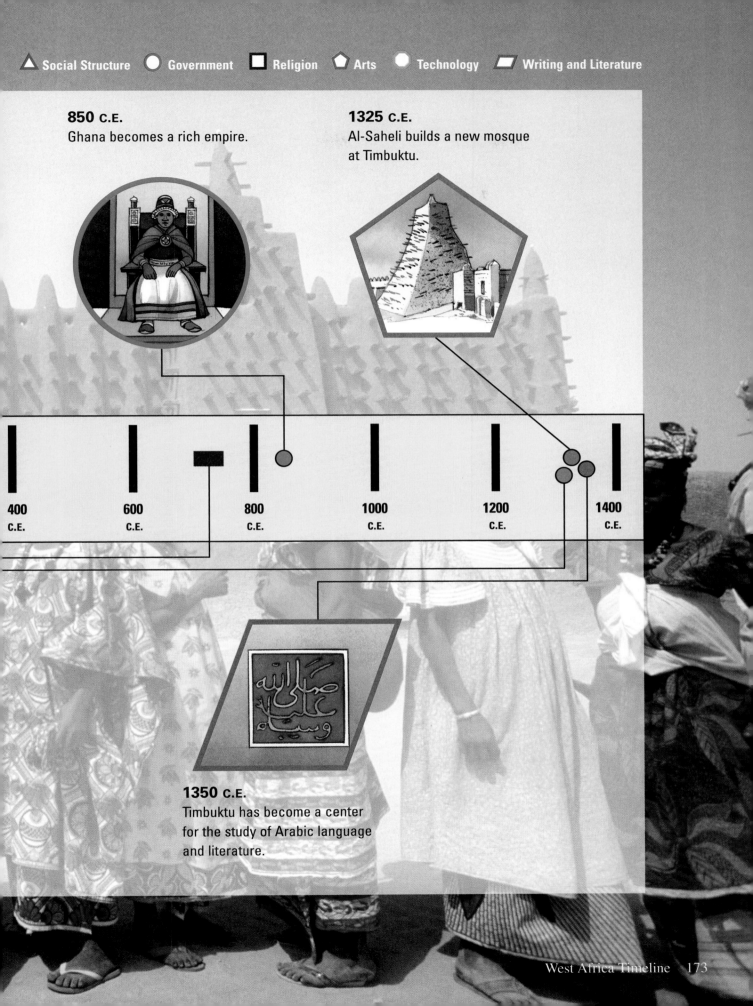

△ Social Structure ● Government □ Religion ⬠ Arts ● Technology ▱ Writing and Literature

850 C.E.
Ghana becomes a rich empire.

1325 C.E.
Al-Saheli builds a new mosque at Timbuktu.

400 C.E.   600 C.E.   800 C.E.   1000 C.E.   1200 C.E.   1400 C.E.

1350 C.E.
Timbuktu has become a center for the study of Arabic language and literature.

Imperial China

Setting the Stage

Imperial China

In the last unit, you learned about the kingdoms of West Africa. In this unit, you will explore imperial China during the period from 220 to 1644 C.E. (The word *imperial* means "ruled by an emperor.")

China, a huge country about the size of the United States, takes up most of the landmass of East Asia. China stretches from Siberia in the north to the tropical regions of the south. Mountains and deserts cover much of the land. Five large rivers run through it. One of the most important is the Chang Jiang, the third longest river in the world. Another is the Huang He, or Yellow River. The Huang is sometimes called "China's Sorrow" because its flooding causes so much damage. It is called "Yellow" because of the heavy amount of silt it carries.

China is a land of extremes. In some places it is bitterly cold; in others it is either hot and dry or hot and humid. China has some of the world's highest mountains. It also has deserts far below sea level. Each area of the country is different. The northwest has deserts, glaciers, and tall mountains. The northeast has mountains and forests. Southern China has fertile lowlands.

Chinese civilization developed on the North China Plain, around the Huang He, and spread southward to the Chang Jiang Basins. Most of the events you'll read about took place in this region. The area's rivers, fertile soil, and fairly warm and rainy climate made it easy for people to grow and transport food. As Chinese civilization developed, it expanded to include more territory, particularly in the north and the west. By the 1700s, all of these regions became part of a unified China.

Unifying and governing such a large and diverse country was a major challenge for China's rulers. The expansion of China was the work of a number of imperial dynasties, or ruling families. The Qin dynasty (221 to 206 B.C.E.) was the first to bring China under the rule of an emperor. The Han dynasty (206 B.C.E. to 220 C.E.) expanded the emperor's rule and created a "golden age" of stability and prosperity. In this unit, you will focus on Chinese history from the end of the Han dynasty to 1644 C.E. (the end of the Ming dynasty).

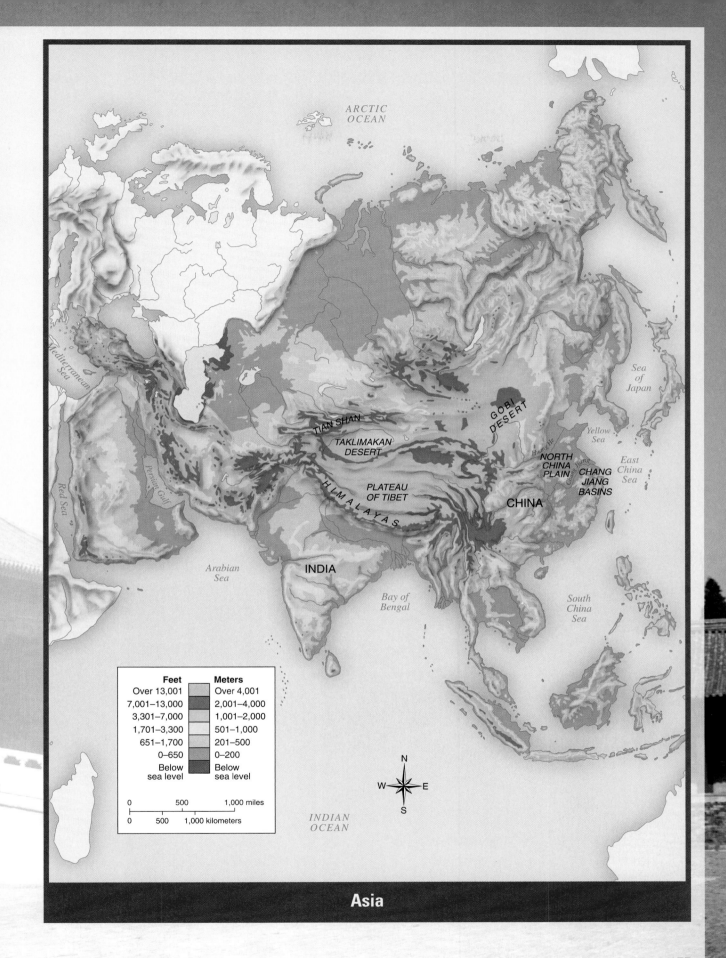

ARCTIC
OCEAN

Mediterranean
Sea

Red
Sea

Persian Gulf

Arabian
Sea

INDIA

Bay of
Bengal

TIAN SHAN

TAKLIMAKAN
DESERT

PLATEAU
OF TIBET

H I M A L A Y A S

GOBI
DESERT

NORTH
CHINA
PLAIN

CHANG
JIANG
BASINS

CHINA

Huang He

Chang Jiang

Sea of
Japan

Yellow
Sea

East
China
Sea

South
China
Sea

INDIAN
OCEAN

Feet	Meters
Over 13,001	Over 4,001
7,001–13,000	2,001–4,000
3,301–7,000	1,001–2,000
1,701–3,300	501–1,000
651–1,700	201–500
0–650	0–200
Below sea level	Below sea level

0   500   1,000 miles

0   500   1,000 kilometers

N
W E
S

Asia

CHAPTER 16

◀ ◀ Scholars took exams to become scholar-officials and help the emperor rule.

The Political Development of Imperial China

16.1 Introduction

Welcome to **imperial China**. Historians divide Chinese history into periods ruled by **dynasties,** or ruling families. In this chapter, you will learn about China's political development under several dynasties from 220 to 1644 C.E.

China was first unified under an emperor in the third century B.C.E. From the beginning, emperors needed help to rule their large country. Emperor Han Wu Di, for example, once sent out this announcement:

> *Heroes Wanted! A Proclamation*
> *Exceptional work demands exceptional men…. We therefore command the various district officials to search for men of brilliant and exceptional talents, to be our generals, our ministers, and our envoys to distant states.*

Over time, Chinese emperors tried several ways of finding qualified people to administer their government. One method was to rely on an **aristocracy** of wealthy landowners. Emperors like Han Wu Di, however, preferred to choose officials for their merit, or worth. During the Han dynasty, candidates for government jobs had to prove their knowledge and ability by passing strict tests. As a result, a class of scholar-officials evolved. Under later emperors, this system developed into a **meritocracy,** or rule by officials of proven merit.

In the 13th century C.E., a nomadic people called the Mongols build a great empire in Asia. Toward the end of the century, the Mongols took over China. Under Mongol emperors, government officials were foreigners. Under this **government by foreigners,** some officials were Mongol friends and relatives of the emperor. Others were trusted people from other lands.

How did these three approaches to government affect China? Which won out in the end? In this chapter, you'll explore these questions.

Use this illustration as a graphic organizer to understand how Chinese emperors chose people to help govern the country.

16.2 The Government of Imperial China

In 221 B.C.E., Prince Zheng, the head of the state of Qin, became the first Chinese ruler to claim the title of emperor. He took the name Qin Shihuangdi, which means "First Emperor of Qin." From that time on, China generally had an imperial government headed by an emperor or, sometimes, an empress.

China's Imperial Dynasties Chinese emperors named a relative—often a son—to become emperor after their deaths. In this way they established a dynasty, or line of rulers from the same family.

From ancient times, Chinese rulers based their right to govern on the Mandate of Heaven. According to this idea, Heaven had chosen a particular dynasty to rule. The Chinese believed that Heaven supported the dynasty for as long as an emperor ruled well. Natural disasters such as floods, famines, plagues, and earthquakes were taken as signs that Heaven was displeased. If an emperor ruled badly and lost the Mandate of Heaven, the people could overthrow him.

The table lists the imperial dynasties that ruled China between 221 B.C.E. and 1644 C.E. In this unit, you'll focus on the dynasties that followed the Han dynasty.

China's Imperial Dynasties		
Dynasty	**Time Period**	**Known For**
Qin dynasty	221 – 206 B.C.E.	unification of China under an emperor
Han dynasty	206 B.C.E. – 220 C.E.	a golden age for a united China
Six dynasties	220 – 581 C.E.	a period of chaos and division
Sui dynasty	589 – 618 C.E.	reunification of China
Tang dynasty	618 – 907 C.E.	economic development and growth; many inventions and discoveries
Five dynasties in the north Ten kingdoms in the south	907 – 960 C.E. 907 – 970 C.E.	a period of chaos and division
Song dynasty	960 – 1279 C.E.	economic development and growth; many inventions and discoveries
Yuan dynasty (the Mongols)	1279 – 1368 C.E.	control of China by foreigners
Ming dynasty	1368 – 1644 C.E.	opening up of China to foreign influences at the start of the dynasty, closing down of China by the end of the dynasty

China's Breakup and Reunification   The Han dynasty of ancient China held power for more than 400 years. This was a golden age of expansion and prosperity for China. In 220 C.E., however, the Han lost their grip on power. A long period of disunity followed. This period ended when the Sui and Tang dynasties reunified China.

China was divided into warring kingdoms from 220 to 589 C.E.

What happened to bring about the end of Han rule? Like earlier emperors, the Han governed China with the help of a large **bureaucracy** of government officials. As long as the bureaucracy was skilled, honest, and hard working, China prospered. By 220, however, corrupt (dishonest) relatives and servants of the emperor had seized control of the government.

The result was disastrous. High taxes ruined families. Workers were forced to labor for long periods of time on public projects. Bandits attacked the countryside. This led **warlords** to oppose the emperor and fight with one another. The government grew weak and could not protect farmers.

bureaucracy a highly organized body of workers with many levels of authority

warlord a military leader operating outside the control of the government

Small farmers also suffered because they had to pay taxes and give half of everything they produced to their landlords. As they fell into debt, they had to give up their land to large landowners and work for them.

At last the farmers rebelled. The Han dynasty had lost the Mandate of Heaven.

No new dynasty took over from the Han. Instead, China broke apart into separate kingdoms, just as Europe did after the fall of Rome. Nomadic invaders ruled the north. Several short-lived dynasties ruled the south.

In 589, the northern state of Sui conquered the south and reunified China. The Sui dynasty created a new central government and ruled for 29 years. By 617, however, heavy taxes led to unrest and a struggle for power.

In 618, a general named Li Yuan declared himself emperor and established the Tang dynasty. Tang rulers built on the accomplishments of the Sui dynasty. They strengthened the central government and increased Tang influence over outlying areas.

Under the Tang, a unified China enjoyed a period of wealth and power that lasted nearly 300 years. Let's look now at how Tang rulers approached problems of government.

16.3 Aristocracy: The Tang Dynasty

Like emperors before them, Tang rulers relied on a large bureaucracy. Officials collected taxes and oversaw building and irrigation projects. They provided for the army and made sure the laws were obeyed. But how could emperors make sure they chose the best people for these positions?

Earlier emperors answered this question in different ways. Before the Han dynasty, emperors chose aristocrats to help them govern. Aristocrats, or nobles, were wealthy and powerful landowners. But simply being wealthy did not make a person talented and knowledgeable.

To improve the bureaucracy, Han emperors created **civil service examinations**. Candidates took long tests to prove they were qualified to hold office. The tests had questions on Chinese classics, poetry, and legal and administrative issues. Mainly they were based on the works of Confucius, China's great philosopher and teacher. This was the beginning of a system in which a class of scholar-officials ran the government.

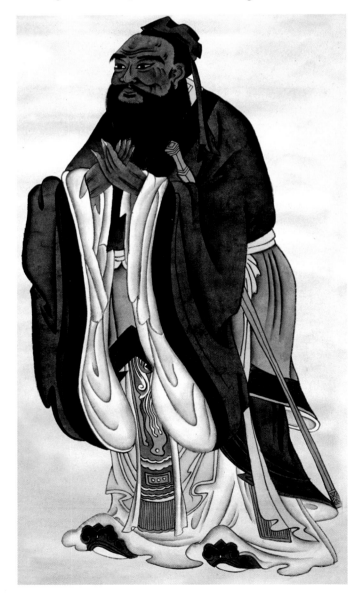

Civil service exams to choose government officials were based on the teachings of this man, Confucius.

Tang emperors also used civil service exams to fill some government positions. Early in the dynasty, however, emperors chose aristocrats for most high-level jobs. Some officials were hired because their fathers or grandfathers had held high government rank. Some were hired because of personal recommendations. Often, aristocrats gained positions by marrying into the imperial family.

Even the civil service exams favored aristocrats. The tests were supposedly open to all except for certain groups, such as merchants, actors, and beggars. In theory, any man could attend the university where students prepared for the exams. In reality, however, only the wealthy could afford tutors, books, and time to study. As a result, aristocrats held almost all offices in the early part of the dynasty.

Peasant rebellions and battles between generals ended the Tang dynasty in 907. Once again, China split apart. Five military dynasties followed one another to power in the north. The south broke up into independent kingdoms.

Beginning in 960, the Song dynasty rose to power. Gradually, Song emperors reunified the country. As you will see, they built on the civil service system to reform the way government officials were chosen.

16.4 Meritocracy: The Song Dynasty

Under Song emperors, the idea of scholar-officials reached its height. The Song relied on civil service exams and opened them up to far more candidates. In this way, they created a meritocracy: rule by officials chosen for their merit.

The exams were influenced by a new school of thought known as neo-Confucianism. This new teaching blended the teachings of Confucius with elements of Buddhism and Daoism (two traditional Chinese religions). A neo-Confucian scholar, Zhu Xi, selected and commented on classic Chinese writings. In 1190, his work was published as the *Four Books*. This work became the basis of study for all civil service exams.

During the Song dynasty, scholar-officials performed many tasks. Here scholars are arranging ancient manuscripts.

Confucius taught that people must act properly in five important relationships: ruler and subject, father and son, older sibling and younger sibling, husband and wife, and friend and friend. Except for friends, one person in each relationship is above the other. Those above should be kind to those below. Those below should respect and obey those above. In particular, subjects must be loyal to rulers. Song emperors and scholars believed that officials who had studied Confucius would be rational, moral, and able to maintain order.

Under the Song, people from lower classes gained the ability to become scholar-officials. They could attend the new state-supported local schools and go on to the university to become scholars. If they passed a local test, they could take the imperial exam in the capital. Here they wrote essays and poems in a certain style. They answered questions about political and social problems based on Confucian ideas.

The exams were set up to prevent cheating. Candidates were locked in a small room for several days. A second person copied each paper so that the examiners wouldn't know whose work they were reading.

Only a small proportion of candidates passed the difficult exams. Those who failed could take the tests again in the future. Those who passed had to wait a few years before their first appointment. When it came, it was for a job far from their hometown so that they couldn't play favorites among family and friends. At the end of three years, officials could move up in rank.

Despite the hardships, people were happy to get such respected jobs. As government officials, they also enjoyed certain privileges, such as being excused from taxes and military service.

16.5 Government by Foreigners: The Period of Mongol Rule

In the 13th century, the Mongols conquered almost all of Asia. In 1276, the Mongols captured China's imperial capital. Three years later, the last Song emperor died in flight.

The Mongol leader, Kublai Khan, took the title of emperor of China. He called his dynasty the Yuan dynasty. For nearly 100 years, from 1279 to 1368, China was under Mongol rule.

Under the Mongols, Chinese society was divided into four classes. The Mongols were at the top. Next came foreigners from outside China who were their friends. These people included Tibetans, Persians, Turks, and Central Asians. Many of them were Muslims. The third class was made up of the northern Chinese, who were more accustomed to the Mongols than the southerners were. The southern Chinese came last.

Even though scholars did not hold government jobs during the rule of the Mongols, they still enjoyed a comfortable life.

Kublai Khan ended the system of civil service exams. He did not believe that Confucian learning was needed for government jobs, and he did not want to rely on Chinese to run his government. To fill important positions, he chose other Mongols that he felt he could trust. Some of these people were his relatives.

But there weren't enough Mongols to fill every job. Besides, many were illiterate (unable to read and write). Kublai and later Mongol emperors needed people who could handle the paperwork of a complex government. They were forced to appoint trusted foreigners to government positions, even some Europeans. Chinese scholars were used only as teachers and minor officials. Other Chinese worked as clerks, and some of them rose to important positions.

Without the examination system, however, there was a shortage of capable administrators. In 1315, the Mongols restored the exam system. Even then, they set limits on who could take the exam, which favored Mongol and other non-Chinese candidates.

As time went on, fighting among Mongol leaders weakened the government. So did their greed. Officials were often corrupt, perhaps in part because they had not been taught Confucian ideals.

The Mongols had also made enemies of many native Chinese. In the 1350s and 1360s, rebels rose up to fight them. In 1368, the Mongol dynasty collapsed, and the Chinese reestablished their own government under the Ming dynasty. The Ming ruled China for nearly 300 years.

16.6 The Revival of the Civil Service System

Under Ming emperors, civil service exams were again used to fill government positions. This system lasted into the 20th century.

In many ways, the exam system served China well. It provided a well-organized government. The education of its scholar-officials emphasized moral behavior, justice, kindness, loyalty to the emperor, proper conduct, and the importance of family. These values helped to unify Chinese culture.

The civil service system gave poor men who were ambitious and hard working the chance to be government officials. At the same time, it ensured that officials were trained and talented, not merely rich or related to the emperor.

Yet China's civil service system may also have stood in the way of progress. The exams did not test understanding of science, mathematics, or engineering. People with such knowledge were therefore kept out of the government. Confucian scholars also had little respect for merchants, business, and trade. Confucians had often considered merchants to be the lowest class in society because they bought and sold things rather than producing useful items themselves. Under the Ming, this outlook dominated, and trade and business were not encouraged. In addition, the bureaucracy became set in its ways. Its inability to adapt contributed to the fall of the Ming in 1644.

Civil service exams lasted for several days. Candidates were locked in small cells like these during the tests.

16.7 Chapter Summary

In this chapter, you learned how China was governed between 220 and 1644 C.E. Chinese emperors relied on a bureaucracy to help them govern. At different times, they used various ways of choosing government officials.

Early emperors chose officials from the aristocracy. The Han tried to improve government by creating a civil service examination system. Candidates for government jobs had to pass tests based mostly on Confucian learning.

After the long period of division, the Sui and Tang dynasties reunified China. Civil service exams continued, but aristocrats filled most government jobs under the Tang.

The Song dynasty used civil service exams to create a meritocracy of scholar-officials. Mongol emperors, however, relied on family members, friends, and trusted foreigners. Under the Ming, the Chinese restored their civil service system.

Now that you have an overview of Chinese government, it's time to look at other aspects of Chinese history. In the next chapter, you'll learn about the growth of China's economy during the Song dynasty.

The Grand Canal provides a waterway between northern and southern China.

CHAPTER 17

China Develops a New Economy

17.1 Introduction

In the last chapter, you learned about changes in China's government. In this chapter, you will learn about the growth of China's **economy** during the Song dynasty, from about 960 to 1279 C.E.

The Song period was a time of great prosperity. Changes in **agriculture,** especially a boom in the production of rice, fed the growth of the economy. **Trade** and **commerce** flourished. These developments had started during the Tang dynasty. Under the Song, they would help make China one of the most advanced societies in the world.

Along with prosperity came **urbanization,** or the growth of cities. During this period, China's huge cities dwarfed the cities of medieval Europe.

An Italian traveler named Marco Polo first saw China toward the end of the Song dynasty. He marveled at China's crowded cities and bustling markets. Polo was especially impressed by the boat traffic on the Grand Canal. This great waterway linked northern China with the Chang Jiang (Yangtze) river valley in the south. Farmers and merchants used the canal to ship their crops and goods. Polo wrote, "It is indeed surprising to observe the multitude and the size of the vessels that are continually passing and repassing, laden [loaded] with merchandise of the greatest value."

In this chapter, you will learn how changes in agriculture, trade and commerce, and urbanization made China so prosperous. Let's begin by finding out how changes in agriculture helped to spur the growth of China's economy.

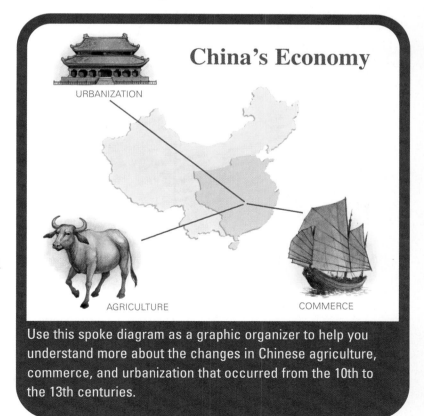

China's Economy

URBANIZATION

AGRICULTURE

COMMERCE

Use this spoke diagram as a graphic organizer to help you understand more about the changes in Chinese agriculture, commerce, and urbanization that occurred from the 10th to the 13th centuries.

Rice, grown in southern China, became the country's most important crop during the 13th century. Peasants worked hard during the growing season. Above, a peasant is preparing the rice paddy with a water buffalo (left) before rice seedlings are planted (right). Opposite, a chain pump provides water for the rice paddy (top), and peasants harvest the rice by hand (bottom).

harrow a farm tool used to break up and even out plowed ground

17.2 Changes in Agriculture

Changes in agriculture were a major reason for the growth of China's economy during the Song dynasty. This period saw a huge increase in the production of rice as well as new and better farming methods. Let's look at how and why these changes happened.

Reasons for Agricultural Changes There were several reasons for the changes in Chinese agriculture. The first was the movement of farmers to the fertile basins of the Chang Jiang river in southern China.

During the Tang dynasty, northern China was the wealthiest and most populous part of the country. But wars and attacks by people from Mongolia drove many landowners to move south. Under the Song, southern China continued to grow. By 1207, about 65 million people lived in the south, compared to 50 million in the north.

The move to the south changed what farmers grew. Northern farmers had cultivated wheat and millet. These crops grew well in the north's cold, dry climate. In contrast, the south's climate was warm and wet. Wetlands covered most of the Chang Jiang valley. These conditions were ideal for cultivating rice plants, which need a lot of water.

Rice farmers, though, had their own problems. Rice crops were frequently destroyed by drought (periods of dry weather) and violent storms called *typhoons*. Even if a crop survived, it took five months to mature from planting to harvest.

During the 11th century, a new kind of rice was brought to China from Southeast Asia. The new type of rice was resistant to drought, and it matured in two months instead of five. Now farmers could plant at least two crops of rice each year, and rice production boomed.

Production increased even more with new and better farming techniques and tools. An improved plow and **harrow** made it easier to prepare fields for planting. Farmers began using fertilizer to produce larger crops. A device called a **chain pump** helped farmers irrigate land at the edges of lakes, marshes, and rivers. To grow rice on hillsides, farmers created flat areas called terraces. More and more land was devoted to farming, and landowners became wealthier.

chain pump a pump with containers attached to a loop of chain to lift water and carry it where it is wanted

Characteristics of the New Agriculture Imagine visiting a farming area in southern China during the 13th century. Small farms cover every bit of suitable land. Terraced hillsides spread as far as the eye can see. Rice grows on the terraces in flooded fields called *paddies*. Elaborate irrigation systems crisscross the paddies, bringing water where it's needed.

Early in the growing season, you can see water buffaloes pulling a plow and harrow to level the fields and prepare them for planting. The seeds have been growing in seedbeds for a month. Now workers will transplant the young plants to the paddy.

Growing rice takes a lot of hard work done by many hands. In the fields, large numbers of workers walk backward as they transplant the rice plants in straight rows. Two months from now, the workers will harvest the rice by hand.

Before and during the growing season, the rice paddy has to be constantly watered and drained. Dams, dikes, gated channels, and chain pumps help to move water into and out of the paddies.

Although rice is the main crop, peasants also grow tea, cotton, and sugar. To feed silkworms, they grow mulberry trees. In the southern hill area, you see tea plants. The Chinese had once used tea only as medicine. But by the ninth century, tea was the national drink. Tea drinking became a social custom, and teahouses became popular. To meet the demand, farmers grew more tea.

Results of Agricultural Changes The shift to rice growing was an important development for China. First, it increased food production. The abundance of food helped support a larger population. For the first time, China's population grew to more than 100 million people.

With ample food, peasants could take time away from farming to make silk, cotton cloth, and other products to sell or trade. Rice farmers could also market their surplus rice. Landowners became rich enough from growing rice to buy luxury items. All these changes encouraged the growth of trade and commerce, which we will look at next.

17.3 The Growth of Trade and Commerce

Trade and commerce had already begun growing during the Tang dynasty. Tang emperors eased restrictions on merchants, and they actively promoted trade. Products like rice, silk, tea, jade, and porcelain traveled along trade routes to India, Arabia, and Europe. Under the Song, business activity blossomed even more.

Reasons for Growth in Trade and Commerce   One reason for the growth of trade and commerce was that wealthy landowners were eager to buy luxuries. The demand for luxuries encouraged traders as well as Chinese artisans, who made silk and other goods.

Commerce was also helped by water transportation. A vast network of rivers and canals connected different parts of China. Farmers in central China could ship their rice north along the Grand Canal. Busy boat owners had plenty of business, because it was cheaper and faster to move goods by water than by road. A **barge** could travel 45 miles a day, compared to 25 miles a day for an oxcart.

Improvements in navigation helped increase overseas trade. Navigational charts and diagrams, along with the magnetic compass (a Chinese invention), made it easier for sailors to find their way on long voyages.

With so much buying and selling going on, people needed more **currency**. During the 11th century, the government minted huge numbers of copper coins—so many that there was a copper shortage. Moneylenders began issuing paper money to merchants. The idea caught on, and the government printed paper money in large quantities. The increase in currency further spurred the growth of commerce.

Characteristics of China's Commercial Growth Let's take a trip on the waterways of China in the 13th century. Our first stop is at a market town along a canal. The canal is crowded with barges loaded with rice and other goods. The barges are sailed, rowed, or pushed along with the help of long poles. Oxcarts and pack animals trudge along the roads and over the bridges that cross the canal. Peasants are coming to town to sell their surplus crops and animals, as well as things they have made at home, such as silk, charcoal, and wine.

On the streets and bridges, merchants have set up small shops to attract customers who are visiting the city. Street peddlers sell goods from the packs they carry.

You also see "deposit shops" where merchants trade long strings of copper coins for paper money. Paper money is much easier to carry around, but unlike copper, it has no value in itself. If there is too much paper money in

barge a long boat with a flat bottom

currency the form of money used in a country

circulation, it loses its value. For this reason, the government controls the amount of paper money that is available. It also threatens to cut off the heads of counterfeiters (people who print fake money).

Let's continue our journey to a port city on the eastern coast. In the harbor, men are loading silk, ceramics, sugar, and rice wine into sailing vessels called *junks*. These ships are big enough to hold several hundred men. Notice their sails, which are made of bamboo matting. The junks will soon depart for Korea, Japan, Southeast Asia, India, the East Indies, and even Africa. They will return loaded with indigo, spices, silver, ivory, and coral.

Results of Growth in Trade and Commerce   The increase in trade and commerce had several effects. First, it resulted in the growth of the merchant class. Second, business activity brought increased prosperity, giving China the highest standard of living in the world. Third, many commercial centers grew into big cities. You'll learn about China's increasing urbanization in the next section.

Commerce greatly expanded in China under the Song dynasty. This scene shows commercial life in the northern Song city of Kai-Feng during the 13th century.

As population increased and commerce grew, huge cities like Kai-Feng developed. These two scenes are part of a 15-foot scroll called *Ch'ing Ming Festival on the River.*

17.4 Urbanization

Urbanization increased during the Song dynasty as cities sprouted up all over China. Chinese cities became the largest in the world. The city of Hangzhou had perhaps 2 million people within its walls. It's no wonder that Marco Polo was impressed with the cities he visited. European cities of this period had no more than 50,000 residents.

Reasons for Urbanization   Why did the growth of cities increase under the Song? One answer is that the growth of commerce encouraged people to move to cities and towns. There, people could make a living as merchants, traders, peddlers, and shopkeepers. In addition, landowners left their farms because they preferred the shops and social life of the cities. More people brought still more opportunities for business, and cities grew even larger.

Characteristics of Cities   China's cities at this time were crowded, exciting places. The crowds in Hangzhou astonished Marco Polo. He wrote, "Anyone seeing such a multitude would believe it impossible that food could be found to feed them all, and yet on every market day all the market squares are filled with people and with merchants who bring food on carts and boats."

Let's stroll through a typical 13th-century city. The streets are filled with rich landowners, merchants, traders, moneylenders, and visiting peasants eager to sell their surplus crops. Signs in the market area identify the goods sold in each shop—silk, silver, pearls, food items, fans, lacquerware, porcelain, and many more.

In the entertainment area musicians, jugglers, acrobats, and puppeteers perform outdoors. There are theaters, restaurants, wine shops, and teahouses. Food vendors carrying trays of food on their heads provide plenty to eat.

You might be surprised to see young girls whose feet are so tightly bound with cloth that their toes are bent under. The girls will grow up to have tiny feet, which the Chinese consider beautiful. But they will also have difficulty walking.

This custom of foot binding first became common during the Song dynasty. It marked a decline in the status of women. Some followers of neo-Confucianism taught that women were inferior to men. In addition, women in cities did not take part in farmwork. In the countryside, women enjoyed greater status because they did do farmwork.

Results of Urbanization   The growth of cities changed the way many ordinary Chinese lived. Cities were vibrant centers of activity, from buying and selling to hobbies and board games. Public works projects provided employment for many city dwellers. Urbanization also stimulated culture, giving artists an audience of wealthy, leisured people. Paintings produced during the Song period are considered some of the finest in the world.

17.5 Chapter Summary

In this chapter, you learned about changes in agriculture, trade and commerce, and urbanization during the Song dynasty. During this time, the center of Chinese civilization shifted from the north to the south. The south's warm, wet climate was ideal for growing rice. Rice became China's most important crop.

A new kind of rice seed and improvements in farming methods greatly increased rice production. This helped support a larger population. It also gave landowners money for buying luxuries, which stimulated the growth of commerce.

Commerce was also helped by a network of rivers and canals. Improvements in navigation made overseas trade easier. Traders and merchants supplied the goods people wanted to buy. As China moved to a money economy, the increase in currency helped business grow.

Commercial activity contributed to the growth of cities. Merchants, peasants, peddlers, and traders sold all kinds of goods. China enjoyed the highest standard of living in the world.

Chinese scientists and inventors also contributed to China's prosperity. Next you'll learn about some of their inventions and discoveries.

CHAPTER 18

The first mechanical clock used a water wheel to create sounds every quarter hour.

Chinese Discoveries and Inventions

18.1 Introduction

In Chapter 17, you learned about economic changes in China during the Song dynasty. In this chapter, you will explore **discoveries** and **inventions** made by the Chinese between about 200 and 1400 C.E. Many of these advances came during the Tang and Song dynasties.

Over the centuries, Chinese scholars and scientists studied engineering, mathematics, science, and medicine, among other subjects. Their studies led to impressive scientific and technological progress that was often far ahead of European advances.

To understand the importance of one Chinese invention, imagine that you are a trader in the 10th century. You are far out at sea on a Chinese junk loaded with goods you are bringing to Korea. Without any landmarks to guide you, how do you know which direction you're headed? Normally you might steer by the sun or the stars. But what if clouds cover the sky? Can you still figure out which way to travel?

In the past, you might have been lost. But thanks to the magnetic compass, you can find your way. Your compass is a magnetized needle that aligns itself with the Earth's magnetic poles so that one end points north and the other south. By the Song dynasty, the Chinese were using this type of compass to help them navigate on long voyages. People still use the same kind of device today.

Like the compass, other Chinese inventions and discoveries allowed people to do things they had never done before. In this chapter, you will learn about Chinese advances in **exploration** and **travel, industry, military technology, everyday objects,** and **disease prevention**. As you'll see, the influence of many Chinese ideas reached far beyond China.

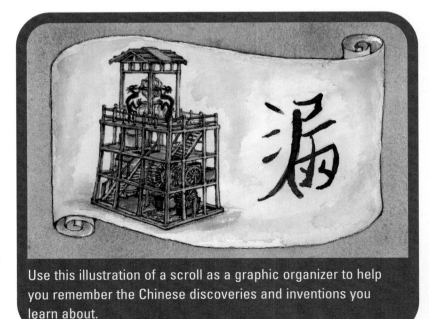

Use this illustration of a scroll as a graphic organizer to help you remember the Chinese discoveries and inventions you learn about.

18.2 Exploration and Travel

Several Chinese inventions made exploration and travel safer and faster. Some innovations benefited traders and other voyagers who ventured out to sea. Others improved travel on rivers, lakes, canals, and bridges inside China.

Paddlewheel boats were easily maneuvered, which made them effective warships.

Improving Travel by Sea

The Chinese developed the first compass as early as the third century B.C.E. The first Chinese compasses were pieces of a magnetic mineral called *lodestone*. The Earth itself is like a giant magnet with north and south poles. Because lodestone is magnetic, it is influenced by Earth's magnetic poles. If you put a piece of lodestone on wood and float it in a bowl of water, the lodestone will turn until it points in a north-south direction.

The Chinese eventually replaced the lodestone with a steel needle. They had learned that rubbing a needle with lodestone made the needle magnetic. A needle used as a compass gave a more accurate reading than a piece of lodestone.

By the Song dynasty, the Chinese were using magnetic compasses for navigation at sea. Compasses made long sea voyages possible because sailors could figure out directions even without a landmark or a point in the sky to steer by. The compass remains an important navigational tool today.

The Chinese also made sea travel safer by improving boat construction. By the second century C.E., they discovered how to build ships with watertight compartments. Builders divided the ships into sections and sealed each section with caulk, a sealant that keeps out water. If there was a leak, it would be isolated in one compartment. The other compartments would stay dry, keeping the ship afloat. Modern shipbuilders still use this technique.

Improving Travel on Rivers, Lakes, Canals, and Bridges

Within China, people often traveled by boat on rivers or across lakes. An invention called the *paddlewheel boat* speeded up this type of travel.

Have you ever paddled a canoe or other small boat? As you push your paddle through the water, the boat moves forward. In the fifth century, the Chinese adapted this idea by arranging a series of paddles in a wheel. As the paddlewheel turned, the paddles moved continuously through the water, causing the boat to move forward.

Paddlewheel boats allowed the Chinese to travel much faster on rivers and lakes. We still use this type of boat for pleasure trips today.

Another innovation, the **canal lock,** was invented in the 10th century, during the Song dynasty. As you've learned, the Chinese used canals extensively. As the surrounding land sloped up, parts of canals were at different levels. Before canal locks were invented, the Chinese had to drag their boats up stone ramps to reach water at a higher level. Sometimes the boats would be seriously damaged.

Canal locks solved this problem. When a boat entered the lock, a gate was lowered to hold in water. The water was then allowed to rise until it reached the level of the water up ahead. Then the boat floated on. To go "downhill," water was let out of the lock until it fell to the level of the water down below.

The invention of locks made canal travel much easier. Locks could raise boats as much as 100 feet above sea level. They are used today on rivers and canals around the world, including the famous Panama Canal.

The Chinese also found ways to improve bridges. For example, in 610 C.E., a Chinese engineer invented a new type of arched bridge. In Europe, Roman-designed bridges rested on arches that were half-circles. The new Chinese bridge used arches that were a smaller part, or segment, of a circle. This made the bridges broader and flatter than semicircular arches. Called a **segmental arch bridge,** the new bridge took less material to build, and it was stronger as well.

The segmental arch bridge is one of China's most prized technological achievements. Today bridges with this design stretch over expressways around the world.

canal lock a gated chamber in a canal used to raise or lower the water level

segmental arch bridge a bridge supported by arches that are shallow segments (parts) of a circle

The Great Stone Bridge spanning the river Chiao Shui was the world's first segmental arch bridge. It has a span of 123 feet.

The scene on the woodblock below (center) was carved with the engraving tools shown. It was then covered with ink, and paper was pressed onto it to create the print at the bottom. Notice that the printed scene is a mirror image of the carved scene on the woodblock.

18.3 Industry

Some of the advances made by the Chinese led to new industries. In this section, you'll learn about China's paper, printing, porcelain, and steel industries.

Paper The Chinese invented the art of papermaking by the second century C.E. The earliest Chinese paper was probably made out of the bark of the mulberry tree. Later, rags were used.

Papermaking became an important industry in China. For more than 500 years, the Chinese were the only people in the world who knew the secret of making paper. From China, knowledge of papermaking traveled to Japan and across Central Asia. Europeans probably first learned about this art after 1100. Considering how important paper is for recording and transmitting information, it's hard to think of an invention that touches our daily lives more today.

Printing The invention of paper made another key development possible—printing. In about the seventh century, the Chinese invented a technique called *woodblock printing*. The printer first drew characters (symbols) on paper. He then glued the paper to a wooden block. When the glue was dry, the printer carved out the wood around the characters, leaving the characters raised on the wood.

To print from the block, the printer covered the characters with black ink. Then he spread paper over the block and smoothed the paper with a brush. Some artists still use block printing today to create fine art prints.

By the 8th century, there was an entire woodblock printing industry in China. Printers turned out religious and other works on scrolls. In the 10th century, the Chinese started printing modern-style books with pages.

In the 11th century, during the Song dynasty, the Chinese invented **movable type**. Movable type consists of separate blocks for each character. Printers made their type by carving characters out of clay and baking them. To print, they selected the characters they needed and placed them in an iron frame in the order they would appear on the page. When the printing job was done, the type could be removed from the frame and used again.

With the invention of movable type, printers no longer had to create a new set of woodblocks for each item they printed. This dramatically lowered the cost of printing. By making written materials more widely available, advances in printing helped spread learning throughout China.

Europe first developed movable type in the 1400s. Until recently, all newspapers, books, and magazines were printed using movable type.

Porcelain A famous Chinese invention is the type of fine pottery called **porcelain**. Some historians think the first porcelain was made as early as the first century C.E.

Porcelain is made by combining clay with the rocks quartz and feldspar. The mixture is baked in a kiln, or oven, at very high temperatures. The resulting pottery is white, hard, and waterproof. Light can pass through it, which makes it look quite delicate and beautiful.

By the 10th century, the Chinese were making porcelain of great beauty. Craftspeople learned how to paint pictures on porcelain pieces. They also made colored glazes to decorate their porcelain.

Porcelain making became a major industry in China. Hundreds of thousands of people worked to **mass-produce** dishes, bowls, and vases. Some washed the clay. Others applied the glaze or operated the kiln.

Chinese porcelain became a prized item for trade. The Europeans did not learn how to make fine porcelain until the 18th century.

Many people think that medieval Chinese porcelain is the finest in the world. People today still refer to fine dinnerware as "china."

Steel The Chinese first made steel, a very useful metal, before 200 B.C.E. Steel is made from iron, but it is less brittle than iron and easier to bend into different shapes.

The earliest Chinese steel was made from cast iron. The Chinese were the first to learn how to make cast iron by melting and molding crude iron. Later they learned that blowing air onto molten (melted) cast iron causes a chemical reaction that creates steel.

In the fifth century, the Chinese learned to mix cast iron with wrought iron. Wrought iron is softer than cast iron. Combining these two forms of iron under high heat changes them into steel.

These discoveries eventually made it possible to produce large amounts of steel cheaply. In the 1800s, the mass production of steel was crucial to the European Industrial Revolution. Today, iron and steel making are among China's most important industries.

The art of making porcelain was invented in China and became a major industry there.

porcelain a hard, white pottery; also called *china*

mass-produce to make similar items in quantity by using standardized designs and dividing labor among workers

18.4 Military Technology

During the Song and Mongol periods, the Chinese developed powerful weapons. The invention of **gunpowder** made these weapons possible.

The Chinese who first made gunpowder were alchemists, people who practiced a blend of science and magic known as **alchemy**. Alchemists experimented with mixtures of natural ingredients, trying to find a substance that might allow people to live forever. They also searched for a way to make gold out of cheaper metals.

Chinese alchemists experimented with a salty, white mineral called *saltpeter*. They may have believed that saltpeter could extend life.

Perhaps by accident, they discovered that it could be used to make an explosive powder. In 850 C.E., during the Tang dynasty, alchemists recorded a formula for gunpowder. They warned others to avoid it because it was dangerous.

In the 10th century, the Chinese made the first weapon that used gunpowder: the flamethrower. Early flamethrowers contained gunpowder mixed with oil. The Chinese used them to spray enemies with a stream of fire.

Between the 11th and 14th centuries, the Chinese created many other weapons using gunpowder. Artillery shells, for example, exploded after being hurled at enemies by a **catapult**. The sound of the exploding shells confused the enemy and terrified their horses. Small bombs called *grenades* were lit and thrown by hand.

In the 13th century, the Chinese used large bombs that were as explosive as modern bombs. Around the same time, they developed weapons much like today's rifles and cannons.

Travelers brought knowledge of gunpowder to Europe by the early 1300s. Gunpowder changed the way war was waged in Europe and around the world forever. Weapons like crossbows and spears gave way to guns and artillery.

Rocket technology was developed in China during the Song dynasty. Rockets used a black powder made of saltpeter, charcoal, and sulfur. At first rockets were used only in fireworks. Later the Chinese used them as weapons. They even made a two-stage rocket for their armies. The first stage propelled the rocket through the air. The second stage dropped arrows on the enemy.

By 1300, rockets had spread through much of Asia and into Europe. The rockets that we use to explore space today are based on principles discovered by the Chinese.

This model of a 14th-century bees' nest rocket launcher was re-created based on a medieval drawing and written descriptions.

gunpowder an explosive powder made of saltpeter and other materials

alchemy a combination of science, magic, and philosophy that was practiced in medieval times

catapult a slingshot-like war machine used for shooting rocks, shells, and other objects

18.5 Everyday Objects

Do you ever play games with a deck of cards? If so, you're using a Chinese invention. The Chinese invented a number of the everyday objects we take for granted today, including playing cards, paper money, and mechanical clocks. All these inventions came during the Tang dynasty.

Playing cards were invented in China in about the ninth century. Printers used woodblock printing to make the cards from thick paper. Famous artists drew the designs that appeared on the backs of the cards.

Europeans were introduced to playing cards by around 1300. Today, card games are played throughout the world.

Paper money was invented by the Chinese in the late eighth or early ninth century. Before that time, coins were the only form of currency.

Like playing cards, paper money was printed with wood blocks. By 1107, Song printers were using multiple wood blocks to print each bill. A single bill would have many colors. Paper money is the most common form of currency in the world today.

The Chinese developed the first mechanical clock in about the eighth century. The new clock was more accurate than earlier time-keeping devices such as sundials and hourglasses. The Chinese devised a wheel that made one complete turn every 24 hours. Dripping water made the wheel turn. Every quarter hour drums would beat, and every hour a bell would chime. The sounds let people know what time it was.

The Chinese improved the mechanical clock in 1092, during the Song dynasty. The new clock worked on the same principles as the first one, but it was much more complex and accurate.

Europeans first developed mechanical clocks in the late 1200s. As with Chinese clocks, a bell rang to indicate the hour. Later, dials and hands were added. Modern-day mechanical clocks are based on the same fundamental principles as early Chinese clocks.

Playing cards were invented in about the ninth century in China. A typical pack had 30 cards, and many different games were played with them.

Doctors and patients in China during the Middle Ages benefitted from new knowledge of medicine and treatment of diseases.

18.6 Disease Prevention

Chinese knowledge of medicine and disease prevention dates to ancient times. Before the first century C.E., the Chinese developed a way of fighting infectious diseases. (An infectious disease is one that can spread from person to person.) When someone died of an infectious disease, the Chinese burned a chemical that gave off a poisonous smoke. They believed that the smoke would destroy whatever was causing the disease.

Today we know that many diseases are caused by germs. We prevent the spread of disease by using disinfectants (substances such as bleach that kill germs). The poisonous smoke used by the Chinese was a type of disinfectant.

During the Song dynasty, the Chinese discovered another way to prevent the spread of disease. A Chinese monk recommended steaming the clothes of sick people. He believed that the steam would prevent others from becoming ill. The idea was sound, because hot temperatures kill many germs. Today we boil medical instruments to kill disease-causing germs.

Sometime around the 10th century, the Chinese discovered how to **inoculate** people against smallpox, a dreaded infectious disease. Inoculation is a way of stimulating a person's **immune system** to fight a particular disease. It works by exposing the person to a disease-carrying substance. To inoculate people against smallpox, Chinese physicians took a small part of a scab from an infected person and

inoculate to protect against disease by transmitting a disease-causing agent to a person, stimulating the body's defensive reactions

immune system the body's natural defense against disease

made it into a powder. Then they inserted the powder into the nose of the person they wanted to immunize (protect against the disease).

The Chinese knew that they had to take care when exposing people to smallpox. Sometimes the treatment itself caused people to become ill. To be as safe as possible, the Chinese took the infectious material from people who had already been inoculated.

Chinese knowledge about smallpox inoculation eventually led to the development of drugs called **vaccines**. We now have vaccines for many diseases, including smallpox and the flu.

vaccine a substance used to immunize people against a disease

We owe a debt to China for many of our modern advances. The invention of rockets, for instance, was the first step toward space exploration.

18.7 Chapter Summary

In this chapter, you learned about Chinese inventions and discoveries between about 200 and 1400 C.E. The influence of many of these advances spread far beyond China. Many Chinese inventions and discoveries continue to affect our lives today.

Several Chinese ideas improved travel and exploration. They include the compass, paddle-wheel boats, canal locks, and segmental arch bridges. Advances in papermaking and printing helped spread learning. Chinese porcelain became famous for its quality and beauty. The Chinese also discovered ways of making steel.

The Chinese revolutionized military technology. They discovered how to use gunpowder to make powerful weapons. They also developed the first rockets.

A number of Chinese inventions enriched people's everyday lives. Among them are playing cards, paper money, and mechanical clocks. The Chinese also made great strides in medicine and disease prevention. They developed the first disinfectants and discovered how to inoculate people against smallpox.

These scientific and technological advances were often far ahead of those made in Europe. Several, such as paper and gunpowder, eventually made their way to the western world. But the Chinese generally had little contact with other cultures. In the next chapter, you will learn more about the relationship between China and the outside world.

Chinese Discoveries and Inventions   203

CHAPTER 19

◀ ◀ Gates in China's walled Forbidden City
have been opened to welcome visitors.

China's Contacts with the Outside World

19.1 Introduction

In the last chapter, you learned about Chinese scientific and technological advances. In this chapter, you will learn about China's **foreign contacts**. You'll focus on three dynasties: the Tang dynasty (618–907), the Mongol or Yuan dynasty (1279–1368), and the Ming dynasty (1368–1644).

At times, the Chinese welcomed foreign contacts. Great **cultural exchange** resulted as new ideas and products flowed into and out of China.

In the seventh century, for example, a Chinese monk named Xuan Zang traveled to India. He brought back thousands of Buddhist scriptures. The Chinese honored him for making Buddhism widely known. Although it was foreign in origin, Buddhism became very popular in China.

Many Chinese, however, resented foreign influence. Less than two centuries after Xuan Zang's trip to India, one scholar-official harshly criticized Buddhism. "Buddha," he said, "was a man of the barbarians who did not speak the language of China and wore clothes of a different fashion. His sayings did not concern the ways of our ancient kings, nor did his manner of dress conform to their laws." At times, such feelings led rulers to try to limit the influence of foreigners.

In this chapter, you will learn how the Chinese both welcomed and rejected foreign contacts. You'll find out how cultural exchange affected China. You will also discover how later Ming emperors tried to close China's doors to foreign influence.

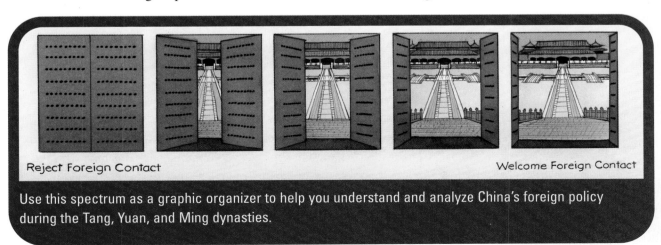

Reject Foreign Contact   Welcome Foreign Contact

Use this spectrum as a graphic organizer to help you understand and analyze China's foreign policy during the Tang, Yuan, and Ming dynasties.

19.2 Foreign Contacts Under the Tang Dynasty

During the Tang dynasty (618–907), China welcomed contact with foreigners. Traders and visitors brought new ideas, goods, fashions, and religions to China.

The Influence of Traders and Visitors Beginning in the Han dynasty, traders and visitors came to China by a network of trade routes across Central Asia. From Chang'an, China's capital, camel caravans crossed the deserts of Central Asia through oases. The routes followed by the caravans are called the Silk Road, though many goods besides silk were traded.

For a time, travel along the Silk Road became unsafe because of fighting in Central Asia. The Tang made travel safe again by taking control of much of Central Asia. As a result, trade flourished with Central Asian kingdoms, Persia (modern-day Iran), and the Byzantine Empire. Traders also traveled by sea between China and Korea, Japan, Indonesia, and India.

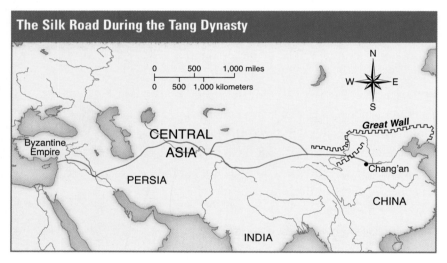

The Silk Road During the Tang Dynasty

Merchants, missionaries, and other visitors also came to China. Thousands of Arabs, Turks, Persians, Tibetans, Indians, Jews, Koreans, Japanese, and other people lived in seaports and in Chang'an.

All these foreign contacts brought much cultural exchange. Chinese sent their silk, porcelain, paper, iron, and jade along the trade routes. In return, they received ivory, cotton, perfumes, spices, and horses. From India the Chinese learned to make sugar from sugarcane and wine from grapes. New medicines also came from India.

The Tang Chinese, especially the upper classes, welcomed new products and ideas from foreign cultures. They wore rubies, pearls, and other jewels. They drank from goblets made of glass, a material that had been unknown in China. They ate new foods, such as spinach, garlic, mustard, and peas. They used cloves to treat toothaches. Sitting in chairs from Central Asia instead of on floor cushions became a status symbol. Polo, a Persian sport played on horseback, became the rage among upper-class women and men.

Chinese music was greatly influenced by melodies and musical instruments from India, Persia, and Central Asia. Artists and artisans also copied new foreign styles. Silversmiths, for example, began using

Persian designs. Not all Chinese, however, were happy about this imitation of foreigners.

New religions also entered China. The Tang tolerated foreign religions. Jews, Christians, and Muslims built houses of worship in Chang'an. They could even preach, although they converted few Chinese.

The Indian religion of Buddhism had come to China hundreds of years earlier. Under the Tang, it became a major part of Chinese life. Many Chinese became Buddhists. Buddhist monks came to teach in China, and Chinese pilgrims went to India to study. Buddhist monks and nuns paid no taxes. They ran schools, public baths, hospitals, and lodgings for travelers. Monasteries accumulated great wealth. Buddhism influenced Chinese art by providing new subjects for painting and sculpture. Buddhist festivals became popular holidays.

Changing Attitudes   Toward the end of the Tang dynasty, foreigners and their beliefs became less welcome in China. The government placed restrictions on foreigners when a people called the Uighurs began attacking China from across the border. In cities, violence broke out against foreign merchants. Many Chinese resented their prosperity.

The wealth of Buddhist monasteries also brought resentment. Some people, it was said, became monks just to avoid paying taxes. In addition,

Foreign visitors, such as those from the west and Korea, were always welcomed in the court.

influential Chinese began attacking Buddhism as a foreign religion.

In 843, the Tang government, which needed money, began seizing Buddhist property. Thousands of Buddhist monks and nuns were forced to give up their way of life. Monasteries, shrines, and temples were destroyed. Precious metals from statues were melted down and turned over to the treasury. The persecution of Buddhists lasted only a few years, but it greatly weakened the power of the monasteries.

Despite this distrust of foreigners, the Chinese continued to trade with other lands. By the end of the Tang dynasty, trade was shifting from the Silk Road. A flourishing sea trade developed between China, India, and the coasts of Southeast Asia. Thanks to the compass and improved shipbuilding techniques, overseas trade continued to thrive during the Song dynasty (960–1279).

19.3 Foreign Contacts Under the Mongols

As you learned in Chapter 16, the Song dynasty came to an end when the Mongols conquered China. Recall that the Mongol leader Kublai Khan became emperor of China in 1279. He called his dynasty the Yuan dynasty. Under the Mongols, foreigners ruled China for nearly 100 years.

The vast Mongol empire stretched clear across Asia. Travel along the Silk Road became very safe, since the entire region was now under one government's control. The Mongols also developed a far-reaching **maritime** trade. Travel and trade expanded as never before, and more and more foreigners came to China.

Thriving Trade and Cultural Exchange   By welcoming traders and other foreigners, the Mongols encouraged cultural exchange. The Mongols respected merchants and actively promoted trade. They set up stations along the Silk Road every 20 miles, where traders could find food and a place to sleep. Muslim merchant associations managed the Silk Road trade. They traded Chinese silk and porcelain for medicines, perfumes, and ivory.

Some of the foreign visitors who traveled the Silk Road from Europe to China were Christian missionaries. They wanted to convert the Chinese to Christianity. They also wanted Kublai Khan to form an alliance between Europeans and Mongols against the Muslims. Both goals failed. Still, Christian missionaries did make some converts, and they helped bring new ideas to China.

Sea trade also flourished under the Mongols. Ships from India brought diamonds and pearls. Ginger, cotton, and muslin came from Ceylon. From Java came black pepper, white walnuts, and cloves.

Many foreigners who came to China brought special skills. Muslim architects, for example, built the Mongol capital of Dadu, today's Beijing. Persians brought their advanced knowledge of astronomy, mathematics, medicine, and water management. Jamal al-Din, a Persian astronomer, introduced new and better astronomical

maritime relating to the sea

Kublai Khan and other Mongol officials enjoyed hunting.

instruments. He also helped to develop a new calendar and set up an **observatory**. Muslim and Persian doctors established new hospitals.

Foreign contacts also allowed skills and information from China to spread to other parts of the world. Europeans, for example, learned about the Chinese inventions of gunpowder and printing.

The Role of Foreigners in China Foreigners enjoyed high status under the Mongols. Foreign merchants were given special privileges. Unlike Chinese merchants, they could travel freely and didn't have to pay taxes. They also spoke foreign languages, which the Chinese were forbidden to learn.

Kublai Khan appointed many visiting foreigners to official positions in his government. The most famous was Marco Polo, the young Italian you met in Chapter 17.

Polo first traveled to China as a teenager with his father and uncle, who were merchants from Venice. Their route took them across Persia and along the southern branch of the Silk Road. All along the way, Marco Polo paid attention to the interesting new things he saw.

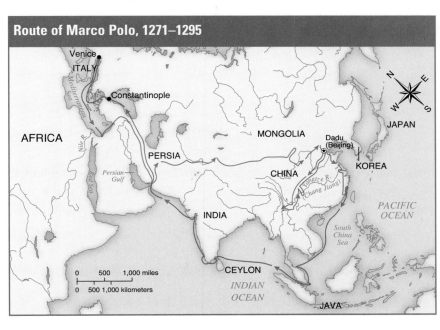

Marco Polo followed a land route to reach China. He returned home by sea.

After three and a half years and over 5,000 miles, the Polos reached the court of Kublai Khan. The khan liked Marco and enjoyed his accounts of his travels. As emperor of China, he sent Marco on inspection tours around China.

Although Marco Polo didn't read or write Chinese, he observed carefully. He traveled around China for about 17 years before beginning his journey home. When he returned to Italy, he dictated an account of his experiences to a writer who wrote a book about him. The tale of Polo's travels gave Europeans firsthand knowledge of China and further stimulated interest in trade.

Under Kublai Khan, life was more pleasant for Mongols and foreigners like Marco Polo than it was for the native Chinese. The Chinese were at the bottom of the social order. They resented the restrictions placed on them. They also disliked being ruled by foreigners, especially since a few foreign government officials were harsh and dishonest. The Chinese hated a Muslim finance minister named Ahmed so much that they assassinated him. The resentment that built up under Mongol rule helped make the Chinese suspicious of further contact with foreigners.

19.4 Foreign Contacts Under the Ming Dynasty

The Chinese eventually rebelled against the Mongols. From 1368 to 1644, the Ming dynasty ruled China. Although foreign contacts continued, later Ming rulers tried to isolate China from foreign influences.

Tributaries and Maritime Expeditions The Ming saw China as the oldest, largest, most civilized, and most important country in the world. Other nations, they felt, should acknowledge China's superiority by paying tribute.

Under the Ming, many other countries were China's **tributaries**. The Chinese emperors acknowledged their rulers, provided military help, and allowed them to trade with China. When ambassadors from the tributaries visited China, they had to *kowtow* before the emperor. This meant they had to kneel three times and touch their heads to the floor three times each time they knelt.

In return for bringing tribute, the ambassadors were given valuable gifts. They were also allowed to buy and sell goods at official markets. These exchanges benefited the foreigners even more than the Chinese.

Emperor Chengzu, who came into power in 1402, wanted more tributaries. He gave a trusted adviser, Zheng He, the title "Admiral of the Western Seas" and told him to sail to "the countries beyond the horizon…all the way to the end of the earth." Zheng He was to parade China's power, give gifts, and collect tribute.

In 1405, Zheng He set off with a fleet of more than 300 ships. The fleet was the greatest in the world. It carried more than 27,000 men. They included sailors, soldiers, officials, translators, merchants, and doctors. To feed this enormous force, ships carried huge loads of rice and other food. They had tubs of earth for growing vegetables and fruit on board. Large watertight compartments were converted into aquariums that held fresh fish for the crew.

The largest ships had 4 decks, 9 masts with 12 sails, and 12 watertight compartments. Cabins were provided so that merchants on long trading voyages could bring their wives.

Zheng He made seven expeditions between 1405 and 1433. At first, he traveled only as far as India. Later he reached the Persian Gulf and even sailed to ports along the east coast of Africa. Thirty or more of the places he visited became tributaries of China.

tributary a ruler or country that pays tribute to a conqueror

The Chinese had never seen a giraffe before Zheng He brought one back to China.

The admiral's ships returned laden with precious gifts. From India they brought sashes made of gold thread and decorated with pearls and gems. They also brought back medicinal herbs, dyes, spices, gems, pearls, and ivory. There were even exotic animals such as zebras, ostriches, lions, leopards, and giraffes.

Turning Inward When Zheng He died, in about 1434, a new emperor was on the throne. The government needed money to fight off attempted Mongol invasions. Scholar-officials persuaded the emperor to stop the expensive expeditions.

From that time on, the dynasty turned inward. Ming rulers wanted to protect their people from foreign influences, so they forbade travel outside China. All contact with foreigners had to be approved by the government.

The Ming and its scholar-officials wanted a strongly unified state based on a single ruler and traditional values. The huge and complex government bureaucracy was staffed by scholar-officials chosen by examinations. The outlook of the scholars dominated Chinese thought and government into the 20th century.

The Ming desire for uniformity made it difficult for the government to change in response to new conditions. In the end, the government became too rigid to adapt. Peasant rebellions helped to bring down the government in 1644, ending the Ming dynasty.

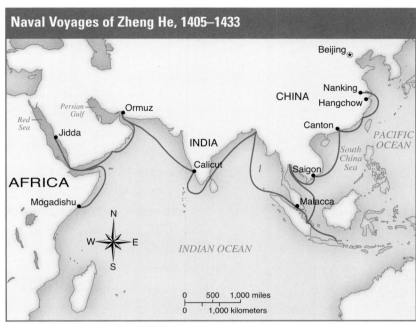

Zheng He made seven voyages of exploration. He eventually reached Africa.

19.5 Chapter Summary

At various times, China welcomed or rejected foreign contacts. During the Tang dynasty, ideas and goods from other places flowed into China. Buddhism became very popular. Eventually, however, many Chinese turned against Buddhism and other foreign influences.

China's Mongol rulers promoted trade and gave foreigners important positions in the government. Cultural exchange flourished. At the same time, the Chinese resented their foreign rulers. Their distrust lasted long after Mongol rule ended.

Under the early Ming, China collected tribute from other lands and undertook great maritime expeditions. Later Ming emperors, however, tried to close off China from foreign influence.

This chapter concludes your study of China. In the next unit, you will learn about China's neighbor to the east, Japan.

Imperial China Timeline

About 850
Tang dynasty records a
formula for gunpowder.

500	600	700	800	900	1000
C.E.	C.E.	C.E.	C.E.	C.E.	C.E.

618 – 907
Buddhist religion expands under
the Tang dynasty.

920
First written record of foot binding,
which reduces the status of women.

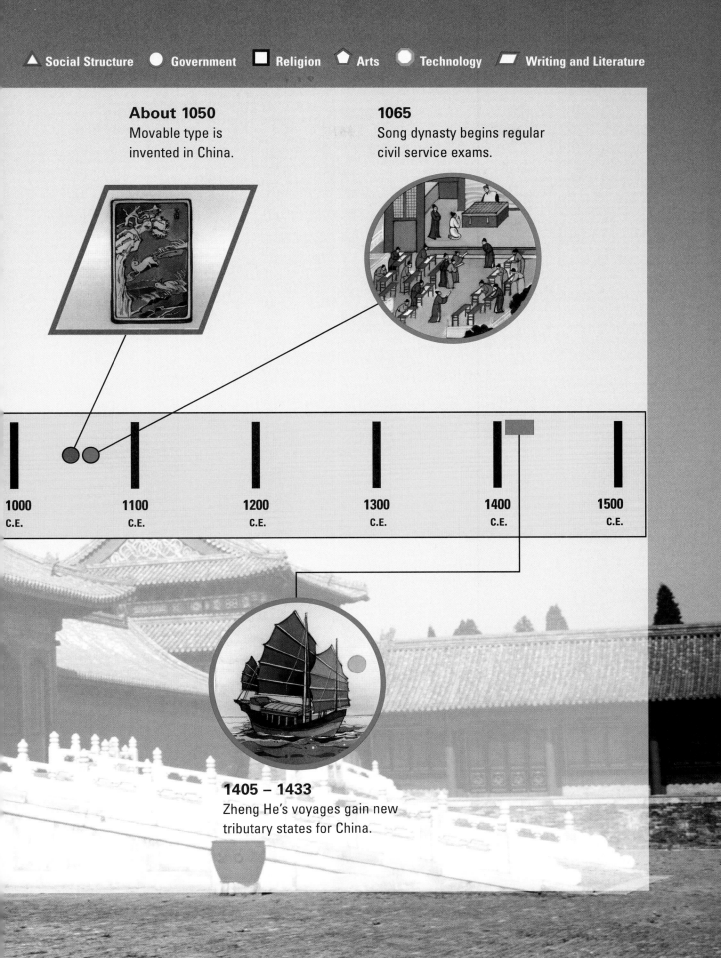

▲ Social Structure ● Government ■ Religion ⬠ Arts ◉ Technology ▱ Writing and Literature

About 1050
Movable type is
invented in China.

1065
Song dynasty begins regular
civil service exams.

1000	1100	1200	1300	1400	1500
C.E.	C.E.	C.E.	C.E.	C.E.	C.E.

1405 – 1433
Zheng He's voyages gain new
tributary states for China.

UNIT 5

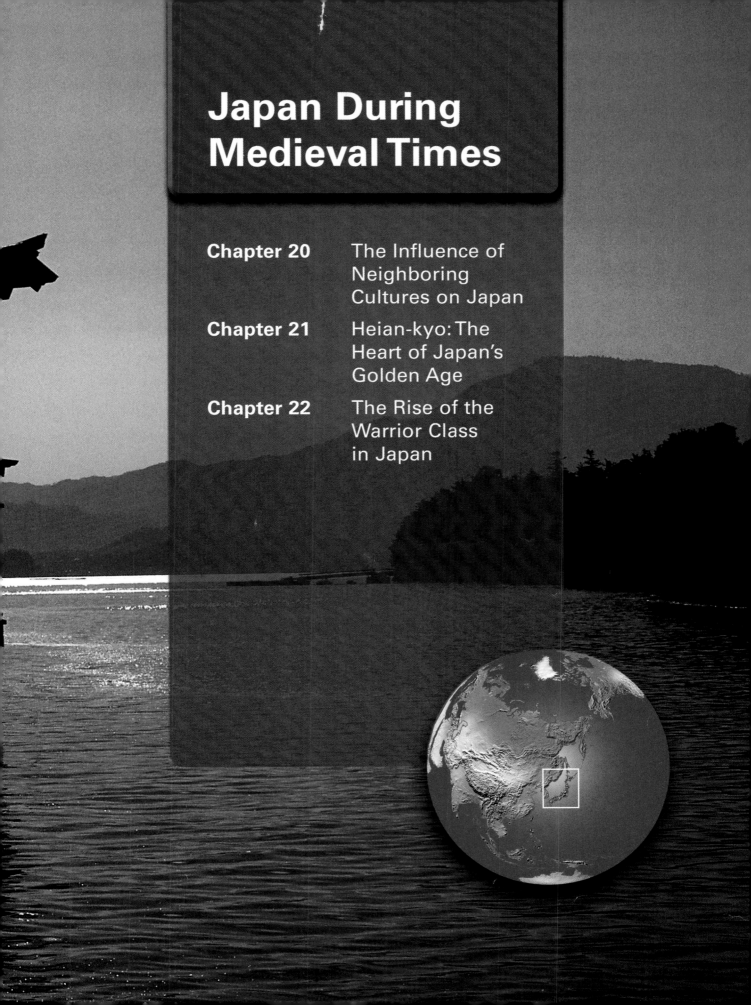

Japan During Medieval Times

Setting the Stage

Japan During Medieval Times

In the last unit, you learned about imperial China. In this unit, you will explore the civilization of Japan from 500 to 1700 C.E.

One ancient legend says Japan was created by a god who reached down from the sky and dipped a spear into the ocean. As he drew the spear back up, drops of water fell from the sky and became the islands of Japan. When you look at a map, it is easy to see how such a story could have been told. Japan is a series of islands in the Pacific Ocean, off the northeast coast of Asia. There are four large islands and 3,900 smaller ones. The large islands—Hokkaido, Honshu (the largest), Shikoku, and Kyushu—form the shape of half-moon.

Natural disasters are common on the islands of Japan. Typhoons begin

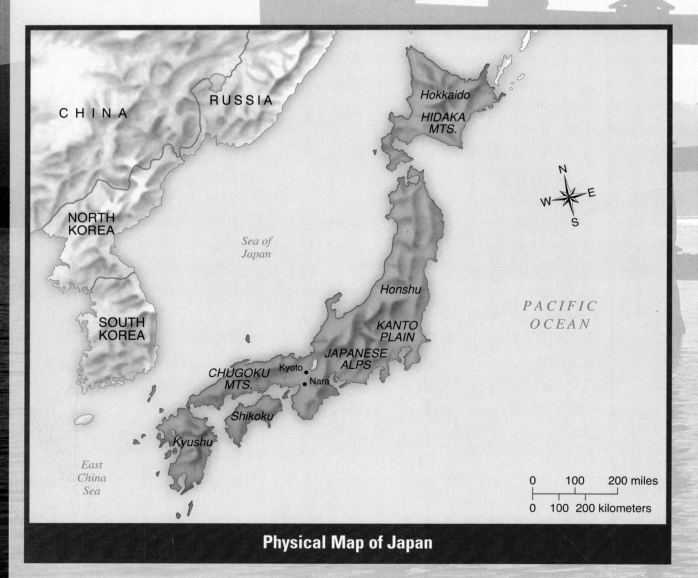

Physical Map of Japan

over the ocean and then hit the land. There are many active volcanoes on the islands. And earthquakes occur frequently.

There is not a lot of land for growing crops in Japan. Mountains cover three fourths of the land, and lush forests grow on their slopes. But the land between the mountains is fertile plain. Rain falls frequently. It is a good environment for growing crops that need a lot of water, such as rice.

Japan's culture is very old. Scholars can trace Japanese history back to about 10,000 B.C.E. This unit focuses on the period from around 500 C.E., when Japan began to develop a unified civilization, through the 1600s, when warriors known as samurai lived in castles.

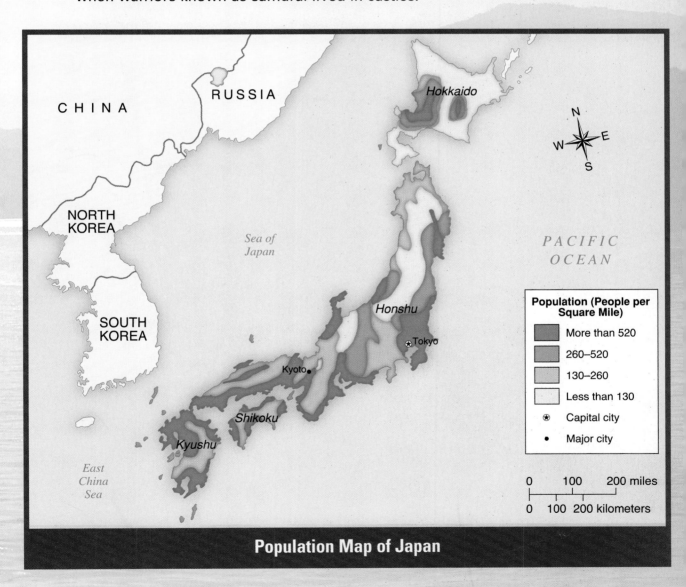

Population Map of Japan

◀ ◁ This scroll illustrates the exchange of products and ideas between China and Japan.

The Influence of Neighboring Cultures on Japan

20.1 Introduction

The island country of Japan lies just off the eastern coast of the Asian mainland. Japan's culture has been enriched by borrowing from other places in Asia. In this chapter, you will explore how Japan's neighbors influenced Japanese culture from the sixth to the ninth centuries C.E.

Many cultural ideas traveled to Japan by way of the Korean Peninsula. Some of these ideas had originally come from China and India. For example, Japan learned about Confucianism from a Chinese scholar who came to Japan from a Korean kingdom. In the mid 500s, Buddhist priests from Korea visited Japan. In this way, Japan was introduced to Buddhism, a religion that had begun in India 1,000 years earlier.

In 593, a young man named Prince Shotoku came to power in Japan. The prince admired Chinese and Korean culture, and he encouraged contact with the mainland. In 607, he sent an official representative to the Chinese court. Upper-class Japanese began traveling to China, where they learned about Chinese literature, art, philosophy, and government.

Over the next 300 years, Japan eagerly absorbed **elements of culture**—objects, ideas, and customs—from the Asian mainland. The spread of cultural elements from one society to another is called **cultural diffusion**. In this chapter, you will learn how cultural diffusion helped to shape Japanese culture. You'll also discover how Japan blended ideas from other cultures into its own unique civilization.

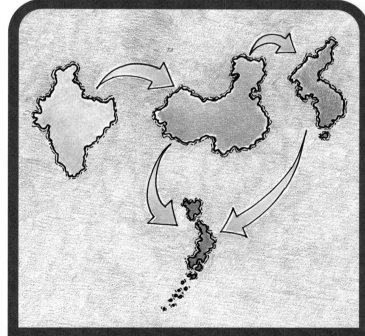

Use this graphic organizer to help you learn more about the neighboring cultures that influenced Japan.

The Influence of Neighboring Cultures on Japan **219**

20.2 Cultural Influences of India, China, and Korea on Japan

By the time Prince Shotoku came to power in 593, cultural influences from the Asian mainland had been reaching Japan for hundreds of years. For example, craftspeople from the Korean Peninsula had brought knowledge of bronze casting and advanced ironworking to Japan. Visitors from Korea had also introduced Japan to Confucianism and Buddhism. But as Shotoku and later rulers sought out contact with the mainland, the pace of cultural diffusion quickened.

The Japan of Prince Shotoku's day was an agricultural society. People grew rice and other crops. The upper classes owned slaves and lived in houses with wooden floors and roofs of wood or thatch. The common people lived in huts with dirt floors and thatched roofs. Family life centered on the mother, who raised the children. Fathers often lived apart from their families. Compared to later eras, women enjoyed relatively high status.

Japan at this time was far from being a unified country. Power was divided among the chiefs of a number of clans called *uji*. But one ruling family in the region of Yamato, on the island of Honshu, had grown powerful enough to loosely control much of Japan. Prince Shotoku, who ruled as **regent** under the Empress Suiko, came from this line of rulers.

Countries That Influenced Japanese Culture

| 0 | 750 | 1,500 miles |

| 0 | 750 | 1,500 kilometers |

CHINA

KOREA

JAPAN

INDIA

N W E S

regent one who rules in the name of another

Under Shotoku and later rulers, Japan took an active interest in Korean and Chinese culture. Sometimes knowledge of mainland culture came from Japanese who traveled to China. Sometimes it came in the form of gifts, such as books and objects of art, sent from the mainland to Japan. Sometimes it came from Korean workers who settled in Japan, bringing their knowledge and skills with them.

During the next three centuries, Japan sent thousands of people—officials, students, translators, and monks—on flimsy ships across the sea to China. Often these people stayed in China for years. When they returned home, they brought with them what they had learned. They also brought many examples of mainland culture, including paintings, religious statues, and musical instruments. As a result of these contacts, the Japanese acquired new ideas in government, the arts, architecture, and writing.

The Japanese didn't just change their old ways for new ways. Instead, they blended new ideas with their own traditions to create a unique culture. Let's look at several areas in which this happened, beginning with government.

20.3 Government: Imitating the Chinese System

Starting with Prince Shotoku, Japanese rulers adopted new ideas about government from China. China's form of government was both like and unlike Japan's. For example, the emperors in China and Japan had quite different powers. In China, the emperor was the sole ruler. In Japan, the emperor had only loose control over semi-independent clans, the uji. Each uji controlled its own land. The uji leaders struggled among themselves for the right to select the emperor and influence his decisions.

While Japanese emperors depended on local leaders, the Chinese emperor ruled with the help of a bureaucracy of government officials. At least in theory, appointments to government jobs were based on merit. Any man who did well on an examination could become an official.

During the seventh and eighth centuries, Japanese rulers adopted a Chinese style of government. Japanese tradition credits Prince Shotoku with starting this development. Borrowing Confucian ideas, the prince created a set of ranks for government officials. In 604, he issued a set of guidelines called the Seventeen Article Constitution. The guidelines stated that the emperor was the country's supreme ruler: "In a country there are not two lords; the people have not two masters. The sovereign is the master of the people of the whole country."

Later rulers went much further in bringing Chinese-style changes to Japan. In 645, the future emperor Tenchi created the Taika Reforms. A major purpose of the reforms was to strengthen the central government. Control of the land was taken away from clan leaders and given to the emperor. The emperor then redistributed the land to all free men and women. In return, people paid heavy taxes to support the **imperial** government.

By the 700s, Japan's imperial government looked much like China's. It was strongly centralized and supported by a large bureaucracy. Over time, however, one key difference emerged. Prince Shotoku had called for government officials to be chosen on the basis of their ability, as in China. But during the ninth century, a powerful **aristocracy** developed in Japan. As a result, members of noble families held all the high positions in the government.

Prince Shotoku was the first Japanese ruler to borrow ideas about government from China. Shotoku is shown here with his two sons.

imperial belonging or related to an emperor

aristocracy a ruling class of noble families

The Horyuji Temple in Nara contains Japan's oldest existing wooden structures.

20.4 City Design: Adapting Chinese Ideas for a Magnificent City

With a stronger central government and a large bureaucracy, Japan needed a new capital city. In 710, the imperial government built a Chinese-style capital on the site of the modern city of Nara.

The new city was a smaller version of Chang'an, China's capital. Chang'an had an area of 35 square miles and a population of 2 million people. Nara, with about 8 square miles, had no more than 200,000 people. As in Chang'an, Nara's streets were laid out in an orderly checkerboard pattern. A wide boulevard ran down the center. In the northern section, Buddhist temples and monasteries clustered near the imperial palace buildings.

There was one major difference between the two capitals. Chang'an was surrounded by a wall as protection against enemies. Nara did not have a wall.

20.5 Religion: Buddhism Comes to Japan by Way of China and Korea

Nara's Buddhist temples were another result of cultural diffusion. Buddhism began in India in the 500s B.C.E. About 1,000 years later, it came to Japan from China by way of Korea.

Japan's original religion was Shinto. This religion expresses the love and respect of the Japanese for nature. Its followers worship spirits called *kami*. Impressive natural objects are kami, such as wind, lightning, rivers, mountains, waterfalls, large trees, and unusual stones. So are the emperor and other special people.

Instead of emphasizing a code of morality, Shinto stresses purifying whatever is unclean, such as dirt, wounds, and disease. Touching the dead also makes one unclean. Most of all, however, Shintoists celebrate life and the beauty of nature.

In contrast, Buddhists see life as full of pain and suffering. The founder of Buddhism, Siddhartha

Gautama, taught that life is an endless cycle of birth, death, and rebirth. To escape this painful cycle, one must follow a moral code called the Eightfold Path. Buddhism's moral code emphasizes showing respect for others, acting rightly, and achieving wisdom through **meditation**. Following the path leads to enlightenment, or seeing the world as it really is. Those who achieve enlightenment can enter nirvana, a state of perfect peace. They will never be born again into a life of suffering.

By finding the path to enlightenment, Siddhartha became the Buddha, or "enlightened one." As Buddhism spread through India, a new form arose, called Mahayana, or "Greater Vehicle." This name symbolizes a core teaching of Mahayana: that all people can reach nirvana. Its followers believe in *bodhisattvas,* buddhas who can enter nirvana but choose instead to help others reach enlightenment. These godlike spirits live in different paradises. Worshipers pray to them in hopes of being reborn into one of these paradises themselves. It is this form of Buddhism that spread along trade routes to China. The influence of Chinese culture brought Buddhism to Korea.

Mahayana arrived in Japan in 552 when a Korean king sent the Japanese emperor a statue of the Buddha and a recommendation for the new religion. The statue arrived at the emperor's court surrounded by chanting monks, books of prayer, gongs, and banners. The emperor was not quite sure what to make of it. "The countenance [expression] of this Buddha," he said, "is of a severe dignity such as we have never at all seen before. Ought it to be worshiped or not?"

After a fierce controversy, the emperor and his court adopted the new religion. They admired its wisdom and rituals, and they considered the Buddha a magical protector of families and the nation. Later rulers, such as Prince Shotoku, learned more about Buddhism through contact with China.

Buddhism did not replace Shinto. Instead, both religions thrived and even blended together. Buddhists built shrines to kami, and Shintoists enshrined bodhisattvas. Even today, ceremonies to celebrate birth and marriage often come from Shinto, the joyful religion. Funeral ceremonies are Buddhist, the religion that acknowledges suffering and pain.

meditation a spiritual discipline that involves deep relaxation and an emptying of distracting thoughts from the mind

In this painted scroll from Nara, people sit in meditation or prayer near a Buddhist temple.

Kana was used by many women writers. This scroll is called "Questions of a Virtuous Woman."

syllable a unit of sound in a word; for example, *unit* has two syllables, "u" and "nit"

20.6 Writing: Applying Chinese Characters to the Japanese Language

Ancient Japanese was only a spoken language. The Japanese had no writing system of their own. Written documents were in Chinese, a language the Japanese had learned from Korean scholars. Over time, however, the Japanese adapted Chinese characters (symbols) to write their own language.

First, Japanese scholars began using *kanji*, or "Chinese writing," to write Japanese words. Kanji enabled the Japanese to keep records, record legends, and develop their own literature. But using Chinese characters to read and write Japanese was difficult. The two languages have different grammar, sounds, and pronunciations.

By 900, the Japanese invented *kana* ("borrowed letters"). This way of writing used simplified Chinese characters to stand for **syllables** in Japanese words. Kana allowed the Japanese to spell out the sounds of their own language. As a result, they were able to write freely in Japanese. Both kanji and kana are still part of written Japanese today.

20.7 Literature: Adapting Chinese Poetic Form

The earliest literary works in Japan are poems that date from the seventh and eighth centuries. Using Chinese characters, Japanese poets developed a form of poetry called *tanka*. This poetic form was modeled after Chinese poetry.

Tanka is based on having a set number of syllables in each line of a poem. Each short poem had 31 syllables, divided into five lines of 5, 7, 5, 7, and 7 syllables. The poems are often devoted to love and to the beauty of nature.

Try to count the syllables in this Japanese tanka. On the right is an English translation. Has the translator kept to the tanka form?

Haru tateba	*When spring comes*
Kiyuru koori no	*The melting ice*
Nokori naku	*Leaves no trace;*
Kimi ga kokoro mo	*Would that your heart too*
Ware ni tokenan	*Melted thus toward me.*

20.8 Sculpture: Carving Techniques Travel to Japan from China and Korea

Like Buddhism, new techniques and subjects of sculpture came to Japan from Korea and China. And like Buddhism, these sculptural ideas began their journey in India.

Archeologists have found examples of early Japanese sculpture around burial mounds that date to the fourth and fifth centuries. The sculptures are clay figures of armored warriors, saddled horses, robed ladies, and objects like houses and boats. They were probably meant to accompany or protect the dead.

Meanwhile, Buddhism was inspiring new subjects for sculpture on the Asian mainland. As these ideas moved east, sculptors' techniques and materials gradually changed. You can see this in the work of three different artists—one Chinese, one Korean, and one Japanese—shown here.

At the top, from China, is a stone image of the Buddha. The Chinese began carving images like these on cave walls near the end of the fifth century. Notice the faint smile, the way the hand touches the face, and the waterfall pattern of the folds in the clothing. The figure's position and gestures identify him as the Buddha of the future, whose arrival will begin a golden age.

The second statue was fashioned by a Korean artist. This time the Buddha has been cast in bronze and covered in gold leaf. How is this statue similar to the stone carving from China? In what ways is it different?

From the middle of the sixth century to the middle of the seventh century, Chinese and Korean immigrants created most of Japan's religious art. Japanese artists learned new techniques from them.

The third statue is located near Horyuji Temple in Nara. It was carved by a Japanese artist in the seventh century. Although the Japanese understood bronze working, sculptors in Japan preferred to work in wood. As in the other statues, the Buddha's clothing falls into a waterfall pattern. But the Japanese artist has added original touches, like the sweetness of the Buddha's smile and the gentle, graceful way he touches his chin.

These three statues of the Buddha were created by Chinese (top), Korean (center), and Japanese artists. What similarities and differences can you see in the statues?

20.9 Architecture: Adapting Temple Designs with Roots in India and China

New forms of temple design came to Japan from India by way of China. Like sculpture, temple architecture evolved as it moved east. In India, Buddhist monasteries featured shrines called *stupas* with roofs shaped like bells or upside-down bowls. The Chinese replaced the bell shape with a series of stories and curved roofs, creating structures called **pagodas**. These towerlike buildings always had three, five, seven, or nine roofs.

When Buddhism arrived in Japan, the Japanese adopted the pagoda design. For Buddhist worship, Prince Shotoku founded the Horyuji, a magnificent temple in Nara. Its wooden buildings included a hall for worship and a pagoda. Lofty pagodas were soon built all over the capital. They were intended to contain relics of the Buddha and bodhisattvas.

Buddhist pagodas may have inspired Shinto priests to build their own permanent shrines. Shinto shrines reflected Japan's agricultural society and the Japanese love of nature. Based on the idea of the raised storehouse, a symbol of plenty, they had raised floors and thatched roofs. Unpainted and undecorated, they blended in with their natural surroundings.

This five-storied pagoda, part of Horyuji Temple, is over 100 feet tall.

pagoda a tower-shaped structure with several stories and roofs

20.10 Music: Adopting New Music and Instruments from China

Japan's native music consisted of chanted poems, war songs, folk songs, and Shinto prayers. All were recited, using just a few notes. Sculpted clay figures from early Japan show musicians playing the cither (a stringed instrument), flutes, and percussion instruments.

As contacts with the Asian mainland increased, the Japanese imported music from the rest of Asia, especially China. *Gagaku,* a form of Chinese court music, arrived in Japan in the sixth century. Gagaku is still sometimes played in Japan, much as it was in China 1,500 years ago.

New kinds of music required new musical instruments. One of the most interesting was a wind instrument the Chinese called a *sheng.* The Japanese pronounced the name *sho*. The sho was a type of mouth organ. It was designed to look like a phoenix, a mythical bird. Its sound was said to imitate the call of the phoenix.

This modern-day quartet is playing some of the traditional musical instruments of gagaku.

20.11 Chapter Summary

From the sixth to the ninth centuries, the Japanese acquired and adapted elements of other Asian cultures. Objects, ideas, and customs came to Japan from India, China, and Korea.

From China, the Japanese borrowed the idea of a strong central government supported by a bureaucracy. To house the imperial government, they built a new capital modeled after China's capital city.

Buddhism, which began in India, came to Japan from China by way of Korea. Buddhism strongly influenced Japanese religion, art, and architecture.

Koreans introduced the Japanese to Chinese writing. The Japanese invented kanji and kana to write Japanese words and sounds with Chinese characters. Poets used Chinese characters to write tanka, a type of poetry based on Chinese models.

Like Buddhism, ideas about sculpture traveled from India to Korea and China, and then to Japan. Similarly, India's stupas inspired Chinese pagodas. Japan then adapted this architectural style. Finally, new kinds of music and instruments came to Japan from China.

All of these cultural elements blended into Japan's unique civilization. In the next chapter, you will learn about the Golden Age of Japanese culture.

This scroll from the 12th century illustrates a Japanese minister's trip to China.

CHAPTER 21

◀ ◀ This scene from *The Tale of Genji* illustrates the luxurious lifestyle of the Heian period.

Heian-kyo: The Heart of Japan's Golden Age

21.1 Introduction

In Chapter 20, you learned that other Asian cultures influenced Japan. Now you'll see how a uniquely Japanese culture flowered from the 9th to the 12th centuries.

As you have learned, Japan is close enough to the mainland of Asia to be affected by cultural ideas from the continent. At the same time, the waters separating Japan from the mainland helped protect the Japanese from conquest by other Asian peoples. As a result, Japan remained politically independent and had the chance to develop its own civilization.

For most of the 8th century, the city of Nara was Japan's imperial capital. During this time, contacts with China brought many new cultural ideas to Japan. Then, in 794, the emperor Kammu moved the capital to Heian-kyo. (*Kyo* means city in Japanese.) This event marks the start of the **Heian period,** which lasted until 1185.

The Heian period is often called Japan's **Golden Age**. During this time, aristocrats led a great flourishing of Japanese culture. The aristocrats prized beauty, elegance, and correct manners. Over time, they developed new forms of literature and art. Poets wrote delicately about feelings and the fragile beauties of nature. Court women composed diaries and other types of nonfiction. Painters and sculptors invented new styles of art. Performers entertained the court with new kinds of music, dance, and drama.

The brilliant culture of the Heian period still influences Japanese art and life today. In this chapter, you will learn more about Japan's Golden Age. You'll look at how Heian aristocrats lived and how they created new kinds of Japanese art and literature.

Use this illustration as a graphic organizer to help remember what life was like for a Japanese noble during Japan's Golden Age.

Phoenix Hall was once part of a grand temple near Heian-kyo.

21.2 A New Capital

During the 8th century, the Buddhist priests of Nara gained a great deal of influence over the Japanese court. In 784, the emperor Kammu decided to move his capital away from Nara, in part because he thought the priests' power was damaging to the government. The emperor also wanted a larger, grander city for his capital.

The first site Kammu chose was Nagaoka, about 30 miles from Nara. But the move was troubled from early on. As money poured in to build the new city, rumors of **corruption** flew. People said the land had been acquired through a deal with a rich Chinese family. The site also seemed to be unlucky, because the emperor's family suffered illnesses at this time. In 794, the emperor stopped work on the city. Once again he ordered that the capital be moved.

This time Kammu chose a village on the Yodo River. The site was both lovelier than Nagaoka and easier to protect from attacks. Kammu began building a new city he called Heian-kyo, "The Capital of Peace and Tranquility."

Heian-kyo became the first truly Japanese city. Today it is called Kyoto. Like Nara, Heian-kyo was laid out in a checkerboard pattern like the Chinese city of Chang'an. Built on a grand scale, the walled city was lovely and elegant. It was set in forested hills, amid streams, waterfalls, and lakes. It had wide, tree-lined streets. Shrines and temples blended with the area's natural beauty.

Heian-kyo's crisscrossing streets were modeled after those of Chang'an, but the city's architecture was Japanese. In the center of the city were palaces and government offices. Wealthy Heian families lived in mansions surrounded by beautiful gardens with artificial lakes. The grounds of each home covered three to four acres and were enclosed by a white stone wall.

Inside the mansions, large rooms were divided by screens or curtains and connected with open-air covered hallways. Simplicity was considered beautiful, so there were few objects on the wood floors other than straw mats and cushions. The Japanese did not use chairs.

Daily life was very formal, and correct manners were extremely important. For example, a Heian lady sat behind a portable screen. The screen hid her from view while she talked and took part in life around the house. An unmarried lady would permit her suitor to see past the screen only after a romance had become serious.

corruption dishonest or illegal practices, especially involving money

21.3 The Rise of the Fujiwara Family

During much of the Heian period, aristocrats were the political and cultural leaders of Japan. By the mid-9th century, the real power in the imperial court shifted from the emperor to aristocratic families. The most important of these noble families were the Fujiwara, who controlled Japan for nearly 300 years.

The Fujiwara were never actually rulers. The Japanese believed that the emperor's family was descended from Japan's sun goddess. This gave the royal family a special right to govern. But the Fujiwara had other ways of exercising power.

First, beginning in 858, the Fujiwara married many of their young daughters into the royal family. They also made sure that sons of Fujiwara royal wives were chosen to be emperors. Second, the Fujiwara acted as advisors to the emperor. In reality they had more power than the rulers they guided. They often coaxed older emperors to retire so that a child or youth could take the throne. Then the Fujiwara ruled as regents in the young emperor's name.

The most successful Fujiwara leader was Fujiwara Michinaga, who led Japan from 995 to 1028. He never had an official role in the government. However, this smart, ambitious man had the respect of all around him. He was the father-in-law of four emperors and the grandfather of three more. He lived in great wealth and luxury. Michinaga rightly said, "This world, I think, is indeed my world."

Michinaga is one of the best-known people in Japan's history. During his time in power, the Fujiwara family became even richer. They built palaces, mansions, and temples. After Michinaga's death, his son built a famous temple that came to be called Phoenix Hall. It likely earned this name because it was shaped like a bird in flight. Part of the temple still stands today as a beautiful reminder of Japan's Golden Age.

The Fujiwara family used their power to better their own lives. However, they also kept peace in Japan for nearly three centuries. This peace helped Japanese culture blossom during the Heian period.

Fujiwara Michinaga, one of the most powerful leaders during Japan's Golden Age, was very wealthy. In this page from the diary of Lady Murasaki, Michinaga is entertained by boats on a large pond at his home.

21.4 Social Position in the Heian Court

Rank was highly important during the Heian period. A person's rank was determined almost completely by what family he or she came from. Being born into a high-ranking family mattered more than personal qualities or skills.

There were nine main ranks in the Heian court hierarchy. High court nobles filled the top three ranks. These nobles were appointed by the emperor, and they dealt directly with him. Less important officials filled the fourth and fifth ranks. Nobles in all these ranks received profits from rice farms throughout the countryside. They also received money from taxes paid by peasant farmers. The sixth through the ninth ranks were filled by minor officials, clerks, and experts in such fields as law and medicine.

The nine main ranks were divided into classes such as senior and junior, upper and lower. In all, there were some 30 subranks. Each rank brought with it specific privileges and detailed rules about conduct. Members of different ranks had different types of houses and carriages. Rank determined the number of servants people had and even the number of folds in the fans they carried. Men of the first, second, and third ranks carried fans with 25 folds. Men of the fourth and fifth ranks used fans with 23 folds. The fans of those in lower ranks had 12 folds.

This precise ranking system also determined such matters as what color clothing a noble could wear and the height of the gatepost in front of his family's home. In addition, if a person was found guilty of a crime, rank determined how harsh the sentence would be.

Noble women in higher ranks had servants to help them with their personal needs from morning to night.

21.5 Beauty and Fashion During the Heian Period

Heian society prized beauty, elegance, and fashion. To be described as *yoki* (good), people had to come from an important family. They also had to look nice and be sensitive to beauty in nature, poetry, and art. Individuals were judged by how good their taste was. The ability to recognize beauty was valued over qualities like generosity and honesty.

Both men and women groomed themselves with great care. Small, pointed beards were considered attractive on male **courtiers**. For women, long hair was an important beauty feature. Ideally, a woman's hair would grow longer than she was tall.

The Japanese of this time considered white teeth unattractive, so both men and women carefully blackened their teeth. They used a dye made from iron and other ingredients soaked in tea or vinegar. How one smelled was also very significant, so both men and women wore scents. Perfume competitions were frequent and popular. People guarded their scent recipes carefully.

For women, makeup was also important. Women used white face powder to make themselves look very pale. Over the chalky powder, a Heian woman put touches of red on her cheeks. Then she painted on a small red mouth. She also plucked out her eyebrows and painted on a set in just the right spot on her forehead.

A woman's clothing needed to be beautiful. An aristocratic woman might wear as many as 12 silk under-robes at a time. When she rode in a carriage, she might dangle a wrist so that people could see the lovely layers of colored silk.

The love of beauty also showed in Heian architecture, calligraph, poetry, and artwork. Concern with form and beauty was so great that courtiers sometimes performed stylized dances as part of their official duties.

Long hair, eyebrows painted high on the forehead, and bright red lips were signs of beauty during the Heian period.

courtier a member of a ruler's court

Noblemen, dressed in silk robes and court hats, enjoy a game of *kemari*. The object of the game was to keep the ball in the air as long as possible.

21.6 Entertainment at the Heian Court

Heian-kyo's aristocrats had plenty of leisure time for sporting events, games, and contests. Men enjoyed watching horse races, archery contests, and sumo wrestling. In sumo wrestling, young men of great weight try to throw each other to the ground or out of the ring. When the weather was warm, men and women alike enjoyed watching boat races along the river that ran through the city.

Groups of courtiers played a game called *kemari*, in which they kicked a leather ball back and forth, keeping it in the air for as long as possible. They played in the same elegant robes they wore at court. Women used the stone pieces of the popular board game *go* to play a game called *rango*. The object was to balance as many stones as possible on one finger.

Each of the many festivals and celebrations on the Heian calendar had its own customs. Many involved contests that tested athletic, poetic, or artistic skill. For example, in the Festival of the Snake, cups of wine were floated in a stream. Guests took a cup and drank from it. Then they had to think up and recite a poem. Other special days featured contests that judged the best-decorated fans, the most fragrant perfumes, the loveliest artwork, or the most graceful dancing.

Dancing was an important skill for Heian-kyo's nobles, since dance was part of nearly every festival. *Bugaku* performances were a popular form of entertainment. Bugaku combined dance with music and drama. Bugaku dancers wore masks and acted out a simple story using memorized movements.

21.7 Sculpture and Painting During the Heian Period

During the Heian period, artists continued to be influenced by Chinese art. Gradually, however, sculptors and painters created their own Japanese styles.

Early Heian sculptors commonly made an entire work from one piece of wood. Later in this period, sculptors made statues by carving separate pieces from carefully selected wood and then joining them. With the help of assistants, sculptors could make the separate parts in large quantities. As a result, they could create a group of similar statues quickly and precisely. Jocho, an artist who worked for Fujiwara Michinaga, probably developed this technique.

Jocho made perhaps the greatest masterpiece of Heian sculpture, the Amida Buddha. This Buddha, "The Lord of Boundless Light," was the subject of much popular worship in Japan. Jocho's beautifully carved statue expresses a sense of deep peace and strength.

In painting, Heian artists consciously developed a Japanese style. To distinguish it from Chinese-style art, they called it *yamato-e,* or "Japanese painting." Painters drew their scenes with thin lines and then filled them in with bright colors. Lines were made quickly to suggest movement. In a restful scene, lines were drawn more deliberately.

At first artists used the new style to paint Buddhist subjects. But over time they focused on nonreligious scenes. There were four main types of yamato-e: landscapes showing the four seasons, places of natural beauty, people doing seasonal tasks, and scenes from literature (called "story paintings").

The new style of painting was used to decorate walls, screens, and the sliding doors of houses and temples. Some of the most famous examples of yamato-e, however, are scroll paintings. A scroll painting shows a series of scenes from right to left, so that viewers see events in time order as they unroll the scroll. Scroll painting had been invented in China, but Heian painters added their own distinctive touches. For example, they often showed scenes inside buildings from above, as if the viewer were peering though an invisible roof.

This statue is made of joined pieces of wood. The peg at the shoulder would have fit into the arm piece.

21.8 Writing and Literature During the Heian Period

Writing was the most valued form of expression in Heian Japan. Everyone was expected to show skill in using words well. Early Heian writers composed artful poems in Chinese. As time went on, distinctly Japanese ways of writing developed, both in daily life and in the creation of works of literature.

Writing in Daily Life Poetry was part of daily life in Heian-kyo. People were expected to make up poetry in public. If they could not think up a few clever lines to fit an occasion, others noticed the failure. Men and women carefully created poems to charm each other. When someone received a poem from a friend, family member, or acquaintance, he or she was expected to write a response. The reply poem was supposed to have the same style, mood, and **imagery** as the original.

In the last chapter, you learned how the Japanese used kana to write the syllables of their language with simplified Chinese characters. In Heian times, there were two ways of writing syllables, much like two separate alphabets. One, *katakana,* was more formal. Men used katakana when they wrote anything important. The second way of writing syllables was *hiragana*. Characters in hiragana are formed with simple strokes that make writing and reading easier and faster. Hiragana was mostly seen as "women's writing." Court women favored hiragana for personal writing, and some of them used it to create lasting works of literature. Over time, hiragana took its place alongside katakana as part of Japan's written language.

Heian writers took care to present their work in a beautiful manner. Calligraphy skills were as important as the ability to create poetry. People believed that handwriting revealed their character and goodness better than the words they used. Calligraphy was often displayed on colorful, handmade paper. Sometimes the paper was even perfumed.

Women Become Japan's Leading Writers The female companions to the courtiers of Heian-kyo were usually selected for their intelligence. They often took a great interest in literature. As a result, women led the flowering of a golden age of Japanese literature in the 10th and 11th centuries.

imagery descriptive or imaginative language, especially when used to inspire mental "pictures"

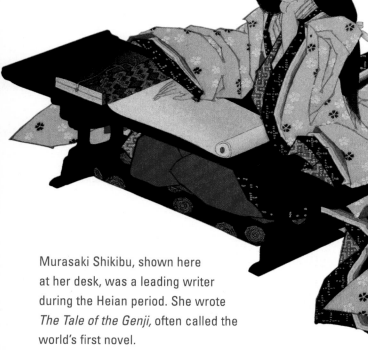

Murasaki Shikibu, shown here at her desk, was a leading writer during the Heian period. She wrote *The Tale of the Genji,* often called the world's first novel.

The best-known Heian writer was Murasaki Shikibu. Born into the Fujiwara family, she served as a lady-in-waiting to one of the daughters of Michinaga Fujiwara. Her novel, *The Tale of Genji,* is a Heian masterpiece. Today it is regarded as one of the great works in world literature.

The Tale of Genji is often called the world's first novel. The book follows the love life of Genji, a fictional prince. It paints a vivid picture of life in the Heian court. Much of the book focuses on the thoughts and feelings of the characters, particularly the women. As a result, *The Tale of Genji* has served as a model for the modern romance novel.

Shikibu also kept a diary about her life in the court. Like her novel, her diary offers historians a close look at court life in the 10th and 11th centuries.

The other leading writer of the time was Sei Shonagon. Like *The Tale of Genji,* Shonagon's *Pillow Book* presents a detailed picture of life in Heian-kyo. *Pillow Book* is a collection of clever stories, character sketches, conversations, descriptions of art and nature, and various lists. Here is Shonagon's list of "Things That Should Be Short":

A piece of thread when one wants to sew something in a hurry.
A lamp stand.
The hair of a woman of the lower classes should be neat and short.
The speech of a young girl.

Like Sei Shonagon, many Heian women wrote their thoughts and experiences in diaries. A book called *The Gossamer Years* is the earliest existing example. This diary by an unknown noblewoman describes her unhappy life as companion to a Fujiwara leader. Writers often included artwork, poems, and letters in their diary entries.

The Tale of Genji describes the life of Japanese nobles during the Heian period. The painting on this detail of a six-panel screen is an illustration of a scene from the novel.

Heian-kyo: The Heart of Japan's Golden Age   237

21.9 The End of the Heian Period

The Heian period is known as Japan's Golden Age of peace. But despite the glittering imperial court, problems were brewing that would bring an end to the Heian period.

Aristocrats in Heian-kyo lived very well, but in Japan's rural areas most people were quite poor. The peasants' farming and other work supported Heian-kyo's rich. Even so, the wealthy looked down on the poor and ignored their problems.

While the rich focused on culture in Heian-kyo, events in the countryside began to weaken the Heian court. The practice of giving large estates to top nobles slowly reduced the emperors' power. Those who owned these estates paid no taxes. After a time, tax-free land was quite common. The government could no longer collect enough taxes to support the emperor.

Japan's rulers began to lose control. Bandits roamed the countryside. People of different religions began to band together to attack and rob each other. The government was now too weak to supply law enforcement. Estate owners created their own police and armies to protect their lands. The profits from landowners' estates went to paying the warriors instead of supporting the emperor.

By the 12th century, the power of some local lords rivaled that of the weakened imperial government. Fighting broke out over control of the land. Meanwhile, various clans struggled for power in the capital. By 1180, there was civil war in Japan.

In 1185, Minamoto Yoritomo, the head of a military family, seized power. A new era began in which military leaders controlled Japan. You will read more about this era in the next chapter.

The wealthy nobles during the Heian period ignored the problems of poor people in Japan's rural areas.

21.10 The Effect of the Heian Period on Japan Today

As you have learned, the Heian period saw the birth of a uniquely Japanese culture. The effects of this flowering of culture are still felt today. In fact, much of Japan's culture has remained quite constant since the Heian period. This can be seen most clearly in Japan's literature and drama.

Heian authors influenced many later Japanese writers. *The Tale of Genji* by Murasaki Shikibu and *Pillow Book* by Sei Shonagon are classics. They are as basic to Japan as Shakespeare's works are to English speakers.

The success of these writers had a major effect on Japan's written language. The Japanese people today write with the same characters used in *The Tale of Genji*.

Heian influence can also be seen in modern poetry. The short poems called *tanka* were very popular in Heian times. Tanka poetry is still a vibrant part of Japanese literature today.

This painting is another illustrated scene from *The Tale of Genji*.

Modern Japanese drama also shows Heian influences. As you may recall, the bugaku performances of Heian times blended dance and drama. Bugaku led to Japan's unique **Noh theater**. In Noh dramas, a chorus sings a heroic story as performers dance and act it out. Noh theater is centuries old, but it is still a popular form of entertainment in Japan.

Noh theater a classic form of Japanese drama involving heroic themes, a chorus, and dance

21.11 Chapter Summary

In this chapter, you learned about the Golden Age of Japanese culture. During the Heian period, aristocrats—especially the Fujiwara family—dominated the imperial court. They created a culture that was uniquely Japanese.

The aristocrats of Heian-kyo lived in great luxury. They prized beauty, elegance, and correct manners. Heian artists created new Japanese forms of sculpture and painting. Court women wrote classic works of Japanese literature.

The Heian period ended in civil war and the rise of new military leaders. In the next chapter, you will learn how these leaders created a warrior culture in Japan.

CHAPTER 22

◀ Samurai wore colorful armor made of metal, silk, and leather.

The Rise of the Warrior Class in Japan

22.1 Introduction

In the last chapter, you read about the court culture of Heian-kyo. Now you will learn about the rise of a powerful warrior class in Japan: the **samurai**.

As you learned in Chapter 21, in 1185 Minamoto Yoritomo came to power in Japan. In 1192, he took the title of shogun, or commander-in-chief. Yoritomo did not take the place of the emperor. Instead, he set up a military government with its own capital in the city of Kamakura. While the imperial court remained in Heian-kyo, emperors played a less and less important role in governing Japan.

The start of the Kamakura government marked the beginning of a new era in Japanese history. Increasingly, professional warriors—samurai—became Japan's ruling class. The era of the samurai lasted for 700 years, until the emperor was restored to power in 1868.

Samurai were famed for their courage and skill. One young samurai told of being shot in the left eye with an arrow. Plucking out the arrow, he used it to shoot down the enemy marksman.

Over time, an elaborate **culture** and **code of conduct** grew up around the samurai. A samurai was expected to be honest, brave, and intensely loyal to his lord. In fact, the word *samurai* means "those who serve." The samurai code was very strict. Samurai often killed themselves with their own swords rather than "lose face" or personal honor.

The samurai were more than fearless fighters. They were educated in art, writing, and literature. Many were devout Buddhists. Their religion helped them prepare for their duties and face death bravely.

In this chapter, you will meet Japan's samurai. You will learn about their code of conduct and the lasting mark they left on Japanese culture.

Use this illustration of a samurai as a graphic organizer to help you learn more about the samurai's unique military skills and why the samurai are important in Japan's history.

Minamoto Yoritomo, Japan's first shogun, liked to release wild cranes on the beach near his castle.

22.2 The Rise of the Samurai

The military government established by Minamoto Yoritomo was led by a **shogun,** or commander-in-chief. Although emperors continued to rule in name, the real power shifted to the shoguns.

Samurai Under the Shoguns   Yoritomo and his successors rewarded warriors, or samurai, with appointments to office and grants of land. In return, the samurai pledged to serve and protect the shogun.

The rise of the samurai brought a new emphasis on military values in Japanese culture. All samurai trained in the arts of war, especially archery. During this period, women as well as men could be samurai. Girls and boys alike were trained to harden their feelings and to use weapons. One samurai wrote,

> *Of what use is it to allow the mind to concentrate on the moon and flowers, compose poems, and learn how to play musical instruments?... Members of my household, including women, must learn to ride wild horses, and shoot powerful bows and arrows.*

Shifting Loyalties   By the 14th century, Japan's warrior society resembled the lord-vassal system of medieval Europe. The shogun now ruled with the help of warrior-lords called **daimyos**. In turn, the daimyos were supported by large numbers of samurai. The daimyos expected to be rewarded for their obedience and loyalty with land, money, or administrative office. The samurai expected the same from the daimyos they served.

Over time, the position of the shogun weakened as daimyos became increasingly powerful. Daimyos began treating their lands like independent kingdoms. Samurai now allied themselves with their daimyo lords.

In the late 15th century, Japan fell into chaos. Daimyos warred with one another for land and power. Samurai fought fierce battles on behalf of their lords.

After a century of bloody warfare, a series of skilled generals defeated their rival daimyos and reestablished a strong military government. In 1603, the last of these leaders, Tokugawa Ieyasu, became shogun. Ieyasu established a new capital in Edo (present-day Tokyo).

For the next 250 years, Japan was at peace. Samurai served under shoguns and administered the government. It was during this time that the samurai ideal came to full flower. Let's look now at what the samurai way of life was like.

22.3 The Samurai's Armor and Weapons

A samurai was, first and foremost, a warrior. Let's look at what a samurai wore in battle and the weapons he used.

Armor A samurai went into battle dressed in heavy armor. Under the armor he wore a colorful robe called a *kimono* and baggy trousers. Shinguards made of leather or cloth protected his legs.

Samurai armor was unique. It was made of rows of small metal plates coated with lacquer and laced together with colorful silk cords. This type of armor was strong, yet flexible enough for the samurai to move freely.

Boxlike panels of armor covered the samurai's chest and back. Metal sleeves covered his arms. Broad shoulder guards and panels that hung over his hips provided additional protection. Some samurai wore thigh guards as well.

After dressing in his body armor, the samurai put on a ferocious-looking iron mask that was meant to frighten his opponents as well as protect his face. Last came his helmet. Before putting on the helmet, he burned incense in it. That way, his head would smell sweet if it were cut off in battle.

Weapons Samurai fought with bows and arrows, spears, and swords. A samurai's wooden bow could be up to eight feet long. Such long bows took great strength to use. In battle, sharpshooters on horseback rode toward each other, pulling arrows from the quivers on their backs and firing them at the enemy.

In hand-to-hand combat, some foot soldiers used spears to knock riders off their horses and to kill an enemy on foot with a powerful thrust.

The samurai's most prized weapon, however, was his sword. Japanese sword makers were excellent craftsmen, and samurai swords were the finest in the world. They were flexible enough not to break, but hard enough to be razor sharp. Samurai carried two types of swords. To fight, they used a long sword with a curved blade. A shorter sword was used for cutting off heads.

Wearing a sword was the privilege and right of the samurai. Swords were passed down through generations of warrior families and given as prizes to loyal warriors. Even after peace was established in the 17th century, samurai proudly wore their swords as a sign of their rank.

Samurai wore elaborate suits of armor with many layers. The layers allowed the samurai to be protected while moving freely.

This series of drawings shows a samurai putting on a suit of armor.

22.4 Military Training and Fighting

The way the first samurai trained and fought was called "The Way of the Horse and the Bow." Later, the art of swordsmanship became more important than archery.

Military Training Learning the skills of a samurai required extensive training. Young samurai were apprenticed to archery masters who taught them mental and physical techniques. Samurai practiced until they could shoot accurately without thinking. They also learned to breathe properly and to shoot at their enemies while riding on the back of a galloping horse.

The art of fencing, or swordsmanship, was just as demanding. A samurai had to learn how to force an enemy to make the first move, how to stay out of range of an enemy sword, and how to fight in tight spaces or against more than one opponent. He practiced continually until he could fence well without thinking about it.

Sometimes in battle a samurai might lose or break his sword. Samurai learned to continue the fight by using other objects as weapons, such as metal fans or wooden staffs. They also learned how to fight without weapons by using **martial arts**. This type of fighting often involves using an opponent's strength against him.

Battle According to ancient texts, the samurai had a unique style of battle. First, messengers from opposing sides met to decide the time and place of combat. Then the two armies faced each other a few hundred yards apart. Samurai on both sides shouted out their names, ancestors, heroic deeds, and reason for fighting. Only then did the armies charge, with mounted samurai firing arrows as they urged their horses forward.

As the two armies clashed, samurai fought savagely in hand-to-hand combat. Enemies fought a series of one-on-one duels. Each samurai found an opponent who matched him in rank. He would try to knock his opponent off his horse, wrestle him to the ground, and slit his throat.

martial arts styles of fighting or self-defense, such as modern-day judo and karate, that mostly began in Asia

Samurai classes in the art of swordmanship, or fencing, taught samurais essential skills for battle.

After the battle, the winning side cut off the heads of opponents they had killed. The heads were cleaned and mounted on boards. The samurai presented the heads for inspection to the warlord in charge to prove they had really killed their foes. After this ceremony, the victorious lord rewarded his samurai with swords, horses, armor, or land.

22.5 Mental Training

A samurai's education in the art of war included mental training. Samurai had to learn self-control so they could overcome emotions that might interfere with fighting, especially the fear of death. They also learned to be always alert and prepared to fight.

Training in Self-Control To learn how to endure pain and suffering, young samurai went for days without eating, marched barefoot in snow on long journeys, and held stiff postures for hours without complaining. To overcome the fear of death, they were told to think of themselves as already dead. Here is what some samurai were told:

Samurai learned to control their emotions and to always be prepared.

Meditation on inevitable death should be performed daily. Every day when one's body and mind are at peace, one should meditate upon being ripped apart by arrows, rifles, spears and swords, being carried away by surging waves, being thrown into the midst of a great fire, being struck by lightning, being shaken to death by a great earthquake, falling from thousand-foot cliffs, dying of disease or committing seppuku [suicide] at the death of one's master.

Training in Preparedness Samurai could never relax. An attack could come when it was least expected, even when a samurai was playing music or dancing. For this reason, samurai had to develop a "sixth sense" about danger. This came from long and grueling training.

The experience of one young samurai illustrates this kind of training. The young man's fencing master used to whack him with a wooden sword throughout the day whenever he least expected it. These painful blows eventually taught the young man to always stay alert.

Teachers also told stories about being prepared. One story was about a samurai who was peacefully writing when a swordsman tried to attack him. Using his sixth sense, the samurai felt the attack coming. He flicked ink into his attacker's eyes and escaped. In another story, a samurai woman who was suddenly attacked thrust a piece of rolled-up paper into her attacker's eyes and gave a war shout. Her attacker ran away.

Samurai also were trained in the art of writing, or calligraphy.

22.6 Training in Writing and Literature

By the more peaceful 17th century, samurai were expected to be students of culture as well as fierce warriors. Two important aspects of culture were writing and literature.

Samurai practiced calligraphy, the art of beautiful writing. A calligrapher's main tools were a brush, a block of ink, and paper or silk. The calligrapher wet the ink block and rubbed it on an ink stone until the ink was the right consistency. Then he carefully drew each character with his brush.

Samurai also wrote poetry. One famous samurai poet was Matsuo Basho. He invented a new form of short poetry that was later called *haiku*. A haiku has three lines of 5, 7, and 5 syllables, making 17 syllables in all. A haiku poet uses images to suggest an idea or create a mood. Basho added to the beauty of haiku by choosing simple words. Here is his most famous haiku:

Furu ike ya	*An ancient pond*
Kawazu tobikumu	*A frog jumps in*
Mizu no oto	*The splash of water.*

22.7 Training for the Tea Ceremony

Another aspect of culture that samurai studied was the tea ceremony. The tea ceremony fostered a spirit of harmony, reverence, and calm. It also served as an important way to form political alliances among samurai.

Each step of the ceremony had to be performed a certain way. A tea master invited guests into a small room. They entered through a doorway so low they had to crawl.

The tearoom was very simple. The only decorations were a scroll painting or an artistic flower arrangement. Guests sat silently, watching the master make and serve the tea. They then engaged in sophisticated discussions as they admired the utensils and the beautiful way the tea master had combined them.

To make the tea, the master heated water in an iron urn over a charcoal fire. Then he scooped powdered green tea from a container called a *tea caddy* into a small bowl. He ladled hot water into the bowl with a wooden dipper and then whipped the water and tea with a bamboo whisk. Each guest in turn took the bowl, bowed to the others, took three sips, and cleaned the rim with a tissue. Then he passed the bowl back to the master to prepare tea for the next guest.

22.8 Training in Spiritual Strength

Most samurai were Buddhists. Two forms of Buddhism that became popular in Japan were Amida and Zen. Samurai were drawn to both kinds of Buddhism, but especially Zen.

Amida Buddhism   In the 12th century, a monk named Honen founded a popular form of Amida Buddhism. These Buddhists believed that all people could reach paradise. Honen taught that believers could reach paradise by relying on the mercy of Amida Buddha.

Amida had been an Indian prince. When he became a Buddha, it was said, he set up a western paradise called the Pure Land. Honen said that believers could enter the Pure Land by prayerfully repeating Amida's name over and over— up to 70,000 times a day. Then, when a believer died, Amida Buddha and a group of bodhisattvas would be waiting to escort the believer into the Pure Land.

Honen's disciple Shinran made this "Pure Land Buddhism" even more popular. He taught that believers could reach the western paradise by sincerely saying Amida's name only once.

Many samurai believed in Amida Buddha, depicted in this statue.

Zen Buddhism   Another form of Buddhism, Zen, appealed to many samurai because of its emphasis on effort and discipline. Unlike Amida, Zen stressed self-reliance and achieving enlightenment through meditation. To reach enlightenment, Zen Buddhists meditated for hours, sitting erect and cross-legged without moving.

Samurai who believed in Zen Buddhism used simple gardens like this one to help them meditate.

According to Zen Buddhism, becoming enlightened required giving up everyday, logical thinking. To jolt the mind into enlightenment, masters posed puzzling questions called *koans*. Probably the most famous koan is, "What is the sound of one hand clapping?"

Zen masters created gardens to aid in meditation. These artfully arranged gardens were often simple and stark. They symbolized nature instead of imitating it. Rocks in sand, for example, might represent islands in the sea.

Zen Buddhism was a good match for the samurai way of life. Zen helped samurai learn discipline, focus their minds, and overcome their fear of death.

22.9 The Code of Bushido and Samurai Values

The samurai code developed over several centuries. By the 17th century, it took final form in Bushido, "The Way of the Warrior."

The code of Bushido governed a samurai's life. It called on samurai to be honest, fair, and fearless in the face of death. Samurai were expected to value loyalty and personal honor even more than their lives.

Loyalty and Personal Honor

A samurai's supreme duty was to be so loyal to his lord that he would gladly die for him. If his lord was murdered, a samurai might avenge his death. A samurai poem says,

*Though a time come
when mountains crack
and seas go dry,
never to my lord
will I be found double-hearted!*

Samurai were also expected to guard their personal honor. The least insult on the street could lead to a duel. One samurai, for example, accidentally knocked his umbrella against another samurai's umbrella. This quickly turned into a quarrel and then a sword fight, resulting in the first samurai's death.

Samurai were fair, honest, and loyal to their lords above all else. They would fight deadly duels to avenge an insult or their lord's death.

Ritual Suicide The price for failing to live up to the code of Bushido was *seppuku*, or ritual suicide. There were many reasons for seppuku, including preserving personal honor and avoiding capture in battle. Samurai might also perform seppuku to atone for a crime, a shameful deed, or an insult to a person of higher rank. Some samurai killed themselves when their lord died, as a form of protest against a wrong or an injustice, or to shame their lord into behaving better. Finally, a samurai might be ordered to perform seppuku as punishment for a crime.

Seppuku became an elaborate ceremony. Guests were invited. The samurai prepared by taking a bath, unbinding his long hair, and putting on the white clothes used for dressing a corpse. He was served his favorite foods. When he finished eating, a sword was placed on the tray. He took the sword and plunged it into and across his stomach, trying to make a complete circle. A swordsman standing behind him quickly cut off his head to end his agony.

22.10 Women in Samurai Society

The position of women in samurai society declined over time. In the 12th century, the women of the warrior class enjoyed honor and respect. By the 17th century, samurai women were treated as inferior to their husbands.

Samurai Women in the Twelfth Century   In the 12th century, samurai women enjoyed considerable status. A samurai's wife helped manage the household and promote the family's interests. When her husband died, she could inherit his property and perform the duties of a vassal. Though women rarely fought, they were expected to be as loyal and brave as men.

Some women, like Tomoe Gozen, did take part in battles alongside men. Fighting one-on-one, she killed several enemies in a battle. Then she fenced with the enemy leader, who tried to drag her from her horse. When he tore off her sleeve, she angrily spun her horse around and cut off his head.

A woman named Koman is another famous warrior. During a battle on a lake, she saved her clan's banner by swimming to shore under a shower of arrows with the banner in her teeth.

Samurai Women in the Seventeenth Century   As the warrior culture developed, women's position weakened. By the 17th century, samurai men were the unquestioned lords of their households. According to one saying, when young, women should obey their fathers; when grown, their husbands; and when old, their sons.

Girls did not even choose their own husbands. Instead, families arranged marriages for their daughters to increase their position and wealth. Wives were expected to bear sons and look after their husbands. Sometimes they were even expected to kill themselves when their husbands died.

A popular book of the time told women how to behave. They were to get up early and go to bed late. During the day they must weave, sew, spin, and take care of their households. They must stick to simple food and clothes and stay away from plays, singing, and other entertainment.

Not all Japanese women were treated the same way. Peasant women had some respect and independence because they worked alongside their husbands. But in samurai families, women were completely under men's control.

In the 12th century, women as well as men were taught the military skills needed to be a samurai.

22.11 Comparing Japan and Europe in the Middle Ages

The Japan of the samurai was both like and unlike Europe during the Middle Ages. In both societies, ties of loyalty and obligation bound lords and vassals. Both had rulers who rose to power as military chiefs. But in Europe, a military leader like William the Conqueror ruled as king. In Japan, the shogun ruled in the name of the emperor.

The daimyos of Japan were like the landholding lords of Europe. Both types of lords built castles and held estates that were worked by peasants.

Both the samurai of Japan and the knights of Europe were warriors who wore armor, rode horses, and owned land. Just as European knights had a code of chivalry, the samurai had the code of Bushido. The samurai code, however, was much more strict, since it demanded that a samurai kill himself to maintain his honor.

22.12 The Influence of Samurai Values and Traditions in Modern Times

Japan's warrior society lasted until 1868, when political upheavals restored the power of the emperor. Modern Japan still feels the influence of the long era of the samurai.

In the 1940s, the Japanese who fought in World War II stayed true to the warrior code. Many soldiers killed themselves rather than surrender. Suicide pilots crashed planes loaded with explosives into enemy battleships. These pilots were called *kamikazes* ("divine winds") after the storms that helped destroy an invading fleet in the 13th century.

The martial arts of the samurai are studied in Japan and around the world. Sports like judo and fighting with bamboo swords reflect samurai discipline and skill.

Other elements of samurai culture persist today. People in Japan continue to write haiku and practice calligraphy. Zen gardens and the tea ceremony remain popular. And the samurai ideals of loyalty to family and respect for rank are still alive in modern Japan.

Today instructors teach samurai fighting techniques to students wearing traditional padded armor.

22.13 Chapter Summary

At the end of the 12th century, a class of warriors rose to prominence in Japan. Called *samurai,* these fierce warriors dominated Japan for nearly 700 years.

Samurai served shoguns (military leaders of Japan) and daimyos (local warlords). Over time, an elaborate samurai culture developed. Samurai wore flexible armor, rode horses, and fought with bows, spears, and swords. They were well trained as fearless fighters. They also studied literature and the arts. Many were Buddhists. The discipline of Zen Buddhism especially appealed to samurai.

Samurai were expected to live by a strict code that came to be called Bushido. This code prized honor, loyalty, and fearlessness in the face of death.

Women enjoyed high status in early samurai society, and some women fought as warriors. Over time, however, the status of samurai women declined.

In some ways, Japan's samurai society resembled Europe in the Middle Ages. In both Europe and Japan, a lord-vassal system developed. The samurai can be compared with European knights. Samurai values and traditions continue to influence Japan today.

This chapter concludes our study of Japan. In the next unit, you will learn about three great native cultures of the Americas.

Samurai fought individual battles with samurai of equal rank.

Japan Timeline

552
Buddhism is introduced
to Japan.

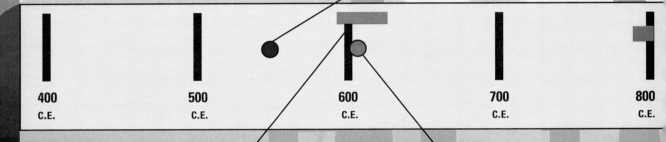

400
C.E.

500
C.E.

600
C.E.

700
C.E.

800
C.E.

593 – 628
Prince Shotoku rules Japan.

607
Construction of the oldest surviving
five-storied pagoda begins.

Social Structure ▲ **Government** ● **Religion** ■ **Arts** ⬠ **Technology** ⬡ **Writing and Literature** ▱

800 – 900
Hiragana writing develops.

あ
か
さ

1192
The first shogun is appointed.

| 800 | 900 | 1000 | 1100 | 1200 |
| C.E. | C.E. | C.E. | C.E. | C.E. |

794 – 1185
Aristocrats lead a golden age of culture during the Heian period.

UNIT 6

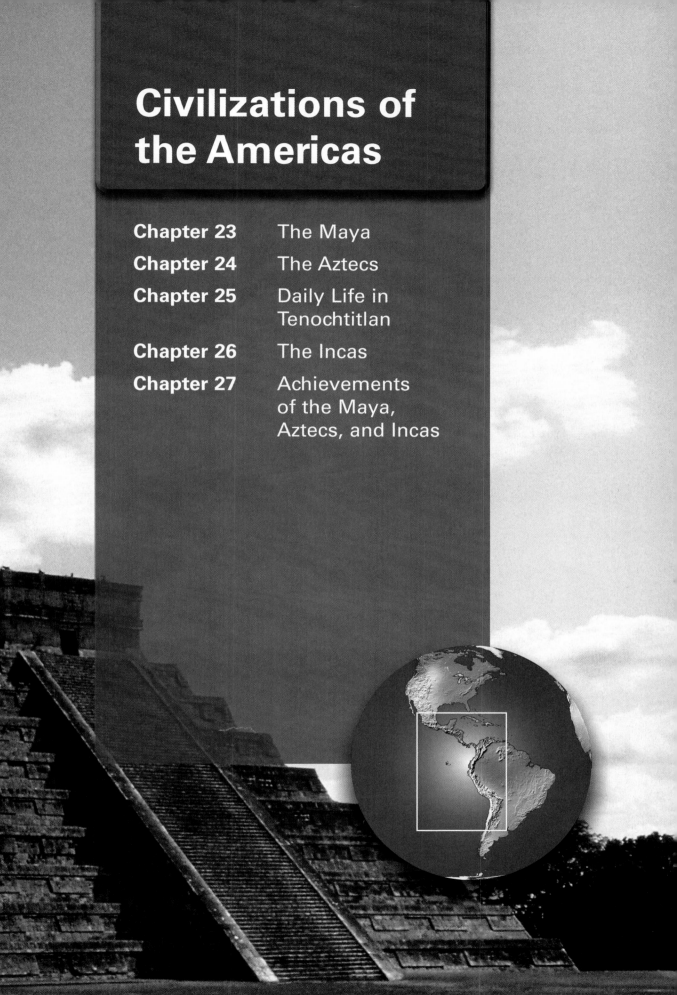

Civilizations of the Americas

Setting the Stage

Civilizations of the Americas

In the last unit, you learned about Japan. In this unit, you will explore three great civilizations of the Americas: the Maya, the Aztecs, and the Incas.

These civilizations flourished in Central and South America. Although the region extended into the deserts of southern Mexico, most of the area was covered with dense vegetation. Pine forests covered the mountain highlands. Thick rain forests and jungles, broad grasslands, and swamps spread across the warmer, wetter lowlands.

ATLANTIC OCEAN

Chichen Itza

Tenochtitlan

Palenque Tikal

Copan

PACIFIC OCEAN

Cuzco

N
W E
S

| 0 | 500 | 1,000 miles |
| 0 | 500 | 1,000 kilometers |

Mayan civilization
Inca civilization
Aztec civilization

The Mayan, Aztec, and Inca Civilizations

More than 10,000 years ago, bands of hunter-gatherers crossed a land bridge that once linked Asia and North America. By 7000 B.C.E., Mesoamerica was home to many hunter-gather settlements.

Over time, people settled in small villages and began farming. They grew corn, beans, squash and other foods. As the population increased, different cultures, languages, and religions arose. People exchanged goods and ideas. Some settlements grew from centers of trade or religion into massive city-states.

In this unit, we'll focus primarily on the period from 300 C.E., when the Mayan civilization first reached its height, to the early 1500s C.E., at the end of the Aztec and Inca Empires.

The three civilizations we'll explore in this unit were different in many respects. But all three had a stable food supply; technology; a social structure with different jobs and status levels; a system of government; a religious system; and a highly developed culture that included architecture, art, and music.

Let's start our exploration of the Americas with the Maya.

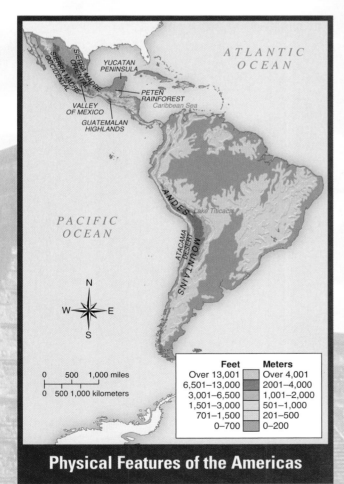

Physical Features of the Americas

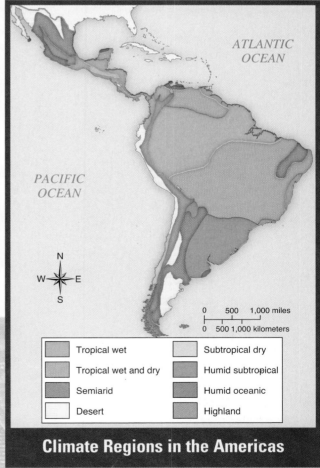

Climate Regions in the Americas

CHAPTER 23

◀ The Maya built entire cities of stone. The ruins of the ancient city of Tikal still stand.

The Maya

23.1 Introduction

Our journey through the Americas begins with an exploration of the **Mayan civilization**. This great civilization lasted 3,500 years, from about 2000 B.C.E. to 1500 C.E. At its peak, it included present-day southern Mexico and large portions of Central America. In this chapter, you will learn about some of the most important achievements of the Mayan civilization.

You can still see the ruins of some amazing stone cities built by the Maya. The ruins of the ancient city of Tikal (shown on the opposite page) lie deep in the Guatemalan jungle.

Imagine standing at the heart of this city in the year 750 C.E. You are in a large, open plaza surrounded by eight soaring temple-pyramids. They reach into the sky like mountains. On the ground, as far as you can see, are structures on raised platforms. The structures are painted in bright colors. Nearby, in the center of the city, you see large palaces made of hand-cut limestone blocks. These palaces are the homes of the ruler, priests, and nobles. Farther out are the stone houses of the merchants and artisans. At the very edge of the city, you glimpse thousands of small, thatched-roof house-mounds where the peasants live.

Tikal was only one of more than 40 Mayan cities. How did the Maya create such great cities and such an advanced civilization? In this chapter, you will trace the development of Mayan civilization. Then you will take a closer look at several aspects of Mayan **culture,** including **class structure, family life, religious beliefs and practices,** and **agricultural techniques**.

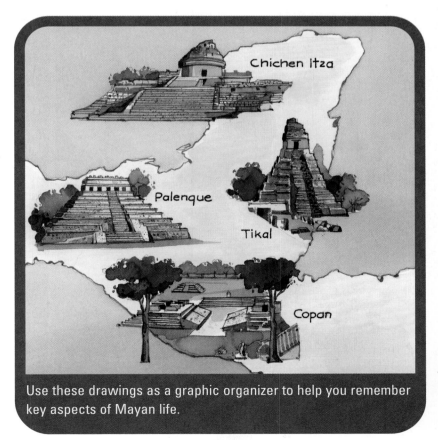

Use these drawings as a graphic organizer to help you remember key aspects of Mayan life.

23.2 The Development of Mayan Civilization

While the Roman Empire was declining in western Europe, the Maya were creating an advanced civilization in the Americas. Mayan civilization reached its height between 300 and 900 C.E. During this time, Mayan culture spread over much of **Mesoamerica**, including part of present-day southern Mexico, Belize, most of Guatemala, and parts of Honduras and El Salvador.

The landscape in which the Maya lived varied greatly. In the south, pine forests covered the mountain highlands. In the northern and central regions were rainforests, grasslands, and swamps. These areas are known as the lowlands. Thick jungle covered the southern part of the lowlands. This is where Mayan civilization reached its highest development. Today this area is called the Peten region of Guatemala.

Mesoamerica "Middle America," the region extending from modern-day Mexico through Central America

The Origins of Mayan Civilization

The Maya built their civilization in part on ideas they inherited from a people called the Olmec. The Olmec lived in the jungle areas on the east coast of Mexico. Their civilization reached its peak between 1200 and 500 B.C.E.

Like early civilizations in other parts of the world, the Olmec civilization was based on agriculture. By 2000 B.C.E., people in parts of Mexico had turned from hunting and gathering to farming as their main source of food. A particularly important crop was maize, or corn.

Farming allowed the Olmec to create permanent settlements. The Olmec established farming villages throughout the region. They also created trade routes that stretched for hundreds of miles.

By 1400 B.C.E., the Olmec had a capital city that boasted palaces, temples, and monuments. They were the first Mesoamericans to develop large religious and ceremonial centers. They were also the first to use a solar (sun) calendar. The Maya would build on all these achievements.

One of the most extraordinary achievements of the Olmec was their monumental stone heads, believed to be portraits of their leaders. More than 30 such heads have been discovered. They stand over 8 feet high and weigh about 10 tons. The massive heads were sculpted without the use of metal tools.

Three Periods of Mayan Civilization Mayan civilization began to arise in eastern and southern Mexico around 2000 B.C.E. Historians divide the history of Mayan civilization into three main periods: Pre-Classic, Classic, and Post-Classic.

The long Pre-Classic period lasted from about 2000 B.C.E. to 300 C.E. During this time, the Maya farmed the land and lived in simple houses and compounds, or groups of buildings.

Gradually, Mayan culture became more complex. As the Mayan population grew, settlements became larger. The Maya began constructing public buildings for governmental and religious purposes. About 50 B.C.E., they began to adapt the writing system of the Olmec and develop their own system of **hieroglyphic** writing. Mayan civilization reached its peak during the Classic period, from around 300 to 900 C.E. The achievements you will study in this chapter date from this time.

During the Classic Period, the Maya adapted and developed ideas they had learned from the Olmec. For example, they improved on Olmec building techniques. Even though the Maya lacked metal tools and had not discovered the wheel, they built enormous stone cities that boasted elaborate and highly decorated temple-pyramids and palaces. The Maya also built observatories for studying the heavens. They charted the movements of the moon, stars, and planets. They used their knowledge of astronomy and mathematics to create complex and highly accurate calendars.

Mayan society during the Classic period consisted of many independent states. Each state had farming communities and one or more cities. At its height, the Mayan Empire included over 40 cities, including Tikal, Copan, Chichen Itza, and Palenque.

Around 900 C.E., the Classic civilization collapsed. The Maya abandoned their cities in the southern lowland area, and the great cities fell into ruin in the jungle. No one knows for certain why this happened. At the end of this chapter, we will look at some theories that may explain the mystery.

hieroglyphic writing that uses pictures as symbols

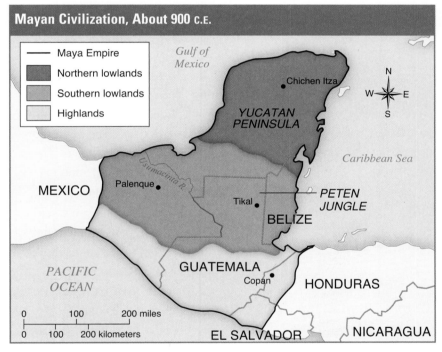

Mayan Civilization, About 900 C.E.

- —— Maya Empire
- Northern lowlands
- Southern lowlands
- Highlands

Gulf of Mexico
Chichen Itza
YUCATAN PENINSULA
Caribbean Sea
Usumacinta R.
Palenque
MEXICO
Tikal
PETEN JUNGLE
BELIZE
PACIFIC OCEAN
GUATEMALA
Copan
HONDURAS
EL SALVADOR
NICARAGUA

0   100   200 miles
0   100   200 kilometers

To the north, on the Yucatan Peninsula, Mayan cities continued to prosper during the Post-Classic period. This period lasted from about 900 C.E. to 1500 C.E. During this time, the Maya continued their warfare and empire building, but they had fewer great artistic and cultural achievements.

Even at the height of their empire, the Maya were not one unified nation. Instead they lived in many city-states with separate governments. What united them as Maya was their common culture: their social system, languages, calendar, religion, and way of life. Let's take a closer look at some aspects of Mayan culture, starting with class structure.

The social pyramid of the Mayan civilization shows the ruler of each city-state at the top with the rest of Mayan society below him. Each layer of the pyramid represents a different group of people and their level of importance in the society. Notice that there are many more people at the bottom of the pyramid than at the top.

social pyramid a social structure in the shape of a pyramid, with layers representing social classes of different rank or status

23.3 Class Structure

During the Classic period, the Maya lived in independent city-states, like Tikal. Within each state, Mayan society was structured like a pyramid. The ruler of each city-state was at the top of the **social pyramid**. The rest of Mayan society was organized in a series of layers below him.

The Ruler The highest authority in the state was the *halach uinic*, a Mayan word that means "true man." He ruled the state with the help of his advisors. He decided when and where to go to war.

The Mayan ruler was considered a god-king. During religious ceremonies, he wore a headdress that was as tall as a person. When he died, a son or other close male relative succeeded him. Mayan rulers were almost always men, but scholars believe that women had considerable influence, probably through family relationships.

Nobles and Priests The next layer in the social pyramid was made up of nobles and priests. They were the only members of Mayan society who knew how to read and write.

The nobles served as officials, and oversaw the administration of the states. They gathered taxes, supplies, and labor for projects like the construction of temples. Nobles led peasant armies in times of war. During battles, they wore elaborate costumes, including gold jewelry and animal robes made from the skin of jaguars.

Priests were important because they maintained favor with the gods. Like nobles, they inherited their position from their fathers. Priests led rituals, offered sacrifices, and foretold the future. They were consulted to determine the best days for going into battle. In addition to their religious duties, priests were often mathematicians, astronomers, and healers.

Merchants and Artisans   Although the Mayan economy was based mostly on farming, trade and crafts were also important. These functions were carried out by merchants and artisans.

The Maya were accomplished traders. They traveled by sea, river, and well-constructed roads to trade with other city-states. Merchants in the lowlands imported valuable products from the highlands. These products included stones such as obsidian and jade; *copal,* a tree sap that the Maya used as incense during religious ceremonies; and *quetzals,* birds with shiny green feathers used in headdresses.

Mayan artisans made a wide variety of objects, many of them designed to pay tribute to the gods. They painted books on paper made from the bark of fig trees. Artists painted murals, or wall paintings, of Mayan life and important battles. They created sculptures for temples and decorative designs on palace walls. The Maya were also skilled weavers and potters.

Peasants   The peasants were the backbone of Mayan society. They worked hard on the land, growing maize, squash, beans, and other crops to feed the population. During the growing season, men spent most of the day in the fields, farming with wooden hoes. Women usually stayed closer to home, preparing food, weaving, and sewing.

When they were not working on the land, peasants spent time building pyramids and temples. In exchange for their work, they sometimes attended royal weddings and religious events. Peasants also served as soldiers during wars.

Slaves   At the bottom of the social pyramid were the slaves. Slaves performed manual labor for their owners. Some were born into slavery, but free people sometimes became slaves. Some children became slaves when their parents sold them for money to feed the rest of the family. War prisoners of humble origin were made slaves. (Those of higher rank were sacrificed to the gods.) And some people were made slaves as a punishment for serious crimes.

In general, slaves were not treated badly. Sometimes they actually had easier lives than peasants, depending on what job they did and where their masters lived. But slaves were not free to come and go as they pleased. Often they were sacrificed when their masters died.

Now that we've looked at the Mayan class structure, let's take a look at what daily life was like for the majority of Maya: the peasants.

Slaves in Mayan society performed a variety of tasks for their masters.

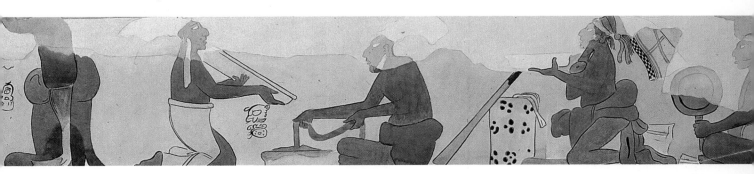

Mayan families had many daily tasks, including weaving, cooking, washing clothes, fishing, and working the land.

ritual a set of actions that is always performed the same way as part of a religious ceremony

23.4 Family Life

In city-states like Copan (in present-day Honduras), Mayan peasants lived in one-room huts built of interwoven poles covered with dried mud. Several family houses were often grouped around a courtyard. A house containing the kitchen was often placed directly behind the main house. Peasant families worked hard, but ceremonies and **rituals** provided a break from work and a chance to honor important events.

Duties of Family Members   Life for Mayan peasant families was not easy. Mayan women rose before dawn to get the fire burning in the fireplace. With the help of her daughters, a Mayan woman cleaned the corn that had been boiled and left to soak and soften overnight. Then she set to work at the grinding stone, pounding corn into meal. She patted the meal into *tortillas* (a Spanish word meaning "little breads") or *tamales* and cooked them over the fire. These might serve as the morning meal, or they might be saved for dinner. On special days, they might also have hot chocolate, a drink the Maya made from cacao beans.

During the day, women and older girls cared for small children and for the family's few animals, like ducks and turkeys. They swept their homes, and they gathered, spun, and wove cotton into cloth.

Mayan fathers and sons ate their morning meal quickly before leaving to work the fields. When they weren't busy with the crops, men and boys hunted and trapped animals. They also helped construct large buildings such as palaces and temples. In times of war, peasant men served as soldiers.

Special Occasions   Although Mayan families worked hard, they also took time to celebrate the important events in their lives. The birth of a child was a time of rejoicing. As soon as possible after the birth, the family called in a priest to perform a ceremony much like baptism. The priest forecast the baby's future and gave advice to help guide the parents in raising the child.

At three months of age, girls went through another ceremony. The number 3 was special to Mayan women because it represented the three stones of the fireplace. In the three-month ceremony, the baby girl was introduced to the tools she would use throughout her life. Small items were placed in the baby's hands, such as tools for spinning and weaving, carrying water and cooking, and soaking and grinding maize.

A similar ceremony was held for boys at four months of age. The number 4 was special to Mayan men. It represented the four sides of the plot of land where a boy would spend his life. The baby boy was given farmer's tools, such as axes and planting sticks, and the spears, knives, and traps of a hunter.

Another important ceremony in every Mayan child's life was the **coming-of-age ceremony**. Girls went through this ceremony at the age of 12, boys at 14. The long ceremony involved confessions, cleansing with water, and reciting the rules of behavior. Finally, the priest cut a white bead from the boys' hair and removed a string of red shells from around the girls' waists. Boys and girls had worn these symbols of innocence since they were quite young.

Marriage Customs   The next big event for a Mayan youth was marriage. Men usually married around the age of 20. Girls married when they were as young as 14.

The bride and groom did not choose each other. Instead, marriages were negotiated by the village *atanzahab,* or matchmaker. These negotiations were not simple. Families had to agree on how much food and clothing would be given to the bride's family. They also had to agree on the number of years a young man would work for his new wife's family.

Once the details of a marriage were worked out, the villagers built a hut for the couple behind the home of the bride's parents. When the home was ready, the bride and groom put on clothing woven for the occasion. After a priest blessed the marriage, the villagers celebrated.

Clearly, rituals and ceremonies were an important part of daily life to the Maya. Let's look more closely at Mayan religious beliefs and practices.

coming-of-age ceremony
a ceremony that celebrates the end of childhood and acceptance into the adult community

The marriage ceremony was an important event in the life of a young Mayan man or woman.

23.5 Religious Beliefs and Practices

Religion was very important to the Maya. The Maya built their cities around ceremonial and religious centers. Their magnificent temple-pyramids rose high above the jungle canopy, like mountains reaching into the sky. Temple plazas provided gathering places for people to attend rituals and ceremonies.

Scholars have learned about the Mayan religion from studying present-day Mayan practices, ancient artifacts, and documents written during the Post-Classic period. Here are some of the things they have discovered.

Beliefs and Rituals   The Mayan religion was polytheistic, which means it included many gods. In fact, the Maya believed in more than 160 gods. The primary Mayan gods were forces or objects in nature that affected people's daily lives, like the god of rain, the god of corn, and the god of death. Many gods had animal characteristics. The jaguar was especially important to the Maya.

The Maya believed that the gods had created the world and could influence or even destroy it. The same god that sent life-giving rain could also ruin the crops with hailstones. So, it was extremely important to honor the gods.

According to Mayan beliefs, only priests could explain signs and lead people through rituals aimed at pleasing the gods. Priests performed **sacrifices** and conducted ceremonies. They consulted sacred books, read omens, interpreted signs, and predicted the future. No decision was made without seeking the gods' advice. No action was taken without first honoring the gods.

The Maya honored their gods with offerings such as plants, food, flowers, feathers, jade, and shells. The Maya believed that blood gave the gods strength, so they also made blood offerings by sacrificing animals and, sometimes, humans. The people who were sacrificed were usually orphans, slaves, and nobles captured during war.

In the ancient city of Chichen Itza, on the Yucatan Peninsula, humans were sacrificed by being

In this reproduction of a Mayan painting, a richly dressed priest is being served by slaves during a Mayan religious ceremony.

thrown into a sacred well whose water level was 60 feet below the ground. Any victims who survived the fall were pulled from the water and asked what message they had brought back from the gods.

Human sacrifice played a role in an ancient Mayan game called **pok-a-tok**. Every Mayan city had at least one ball court where the game was played. Scholars believe that there were two teams of nobles. Players tried to hit a solid rubber ball through a stone ring by using their leather-padded elbows, wrists, and hips. People from all levels of Mayan society watched and placed bets on the outcome of the game. Slaves, land, and homes could be won and lost during a game. Surviving art from the ball courts shows members of the losing team being sacrificed and the captain of the defeated team being beheaded.

pok-a-tok a Mayan ball game that had religious significance

The Sacred Calendar The Maya used their knowledge of mathematics and astronomy to develop a complex calendar system. Two main calendars were used for religious and other purposes. The first was a daily calendar, based on the solar (sun) year. It divided the year into 18 months of 20 days each, plus 5 "unlucky" days. This totaled 365 days, as in our calendar.

The second calendar was the sacred or ritual calendar. It was called the *tzolkin,* or Sacred Round. The Sacred Round was based on 13 months of 20 days each, making 260 days in all. It had two cycles that worked together to identify a particular day. One cycle was made up of the numbers 1 to 13. The other cycle was a set of 20 day names. Each of the day names represented a particular god. Every 260 days, a given combination of numbers and day names, such as 1 Ik, would occur.

This is the ball court at the ancient Mayan city of Chichen Itza. Notice the height of the stone rings embedded in the walls.

Only priests could "read" the hidden meaning of the Sacred Round. Priests used the sacred calendar to determine the best days to plant, hunt, cure, do battle, and perform religious ceremonies. To this day, there are calendar priests in southern Mexico who use the 260-day calendar in this way.

Like Mayan art and architecture, the calendar system reflects a highly advanced civilization. This civilization was made possible by the ability of the Maya to create a stable food supply. Next you'll learn about the agricultural techniques the Maya used to ensure that they had sufficient food.

23.6 Agricultural Techniques

The Maya were creative, skillful farmers. They used their knowledge of calendars and seasonal change to help them become even better at growing food. But Mayan farmers faced many challenges. In the end, crop failure may have played a key role in the collapse of the Classic Mayan civilization.

Cutting and burning plants and trees is an easy way to clear land for farming, and the ash from the fire helps fertilize crops. However, this slash-and-burn technique uses up the soil quickly and can be dangerous, as fires sometimes get out of control.

slash-and-burn agriculture
a farming technique in which vegetation is cut away and burned to clear land for growing crops

Challenges Facing Mayan Farmers The primary Mayan food was maize, or corn. Other typical Mayan crops were beans, squash, and chili peppers. Fortunately, beans and squash, when eaten with corn, supply people with a naturally healthful and balanced diet.

One of the most difficult challenges the Maya faced was how to grow enough food to feed their growing population. Farming was not easy in the regions where they lived. Their land included dense forests, little surface water (such as lakes or streams), and poor soil.

The Maya responded to this challenge by developing different agricultural techniques for the various environments in which they lived. In the mountainous highlands, they built terraces, or earth steps, into the hills to create more flat land for planting. In the swampy lowlands, the Maya constructed raised-earth platforms surrounded by canals that drained off extra water. This technique helped them to grow more food without having to increase the amount of land they used.

A different technique was used in the densely forested lowland areas. In city-states like Palenque (in present-day Mexico), the Maya used **slash-and-burn agriculture**. First they cleared the land by cutting and burning plants and trees. Then they planted their crops. Unfortunately, this kind of farming wears out the soil. Lowland soil was not very rich to begin with, so land that was planted for 2 to 4 years had to be left to rest for 2 to 10 years. Slash-and-burn farmers had to have a lot of land, since each year some areas were planted while others were recovering.

The Mayan agricultural system worked as long as settlements were spread out and not too large. As populations increased, the Maya had trouble raising enough food to feed everyone. In the constant quest for land, they drained swamps and cleared hillsides. They also used household gardens in the cities to increase the amount of land available for growing food.

The End of the Classic Period Creative agricultural techniques were not enough to save the Classic Mayan civilization. For about 600 years, the great cities of the southern lowlands thrived. Then, in the space of 50 to 100 years, the civilization that supported these centers fell apart. By 900 C.E., the Maya had abandoned their cities to the jungle.

The collapse of the Classic Mayan civilization is one of the great mysteries of Mesoamerican history. Many theories have been proposed to explain what happened. Some historians believe that the populations of the cities grew faster than the Mayan farming systems could sustain them. Scholars have also proposed that long periods of drought, or dry weather, caused massive crop failure.

Another possible cause of the Maya's downfall was uncontrolled warfare. In the centuries after 300 C.E., the skirmishes that were common among city-states escalated into full-fledged wars. A final possibility is that invaders from central Mexico helped to destroy the Mayan city-states.

Perhaps a combination of factors brought an end to the Classic period. What we do know is that the great cities disappeared. The Maya migrated away from the old Mayan heartland and returned to village life. Stone by stone, the jungle reclaimed the great pyramids and plazas.

Although the great Mayan cities are ruins today, Mayan culture lives on. About 2 million Maya still live in the southern Mexican state of Chiapas. Millions more are spread throughout the Yucatan Peninsula and the cities and rural farm communities of Belize, Guatemala, Honduras, and El Salvador.

The walls of Mayan tombs were painted with scenes of important events and daily life. This tomb painting is of warriors in battle.

23.7 Chapter Summary

In this chapter, you read about the rise of the Mayan civilization. This great civilization was developed in three main periods: Pre-Classic, Classic, and Post-Classic.

The Maya's greatest cultural achievements came during the Classic period. In studying this period, you explored the Maya's complex social structure and their family life, religion, and farming techniques. In the next chapter, you will learn about the next great civilization that arose in Mesoamerica: the Aztec Empire.

A. Thevet cosmographe du Roy
numero de años .LI.
tenochtitlan
colhuacan. pueblo.
tenayucan. pueblo

◀ ◀ These drawings were created in Mexico around 1540 to show details of Aztec life.

The Aztecs

24.1 Introduction

In Chapter 23, you read about the Mayan civilization of southern Mexico and Central America. In this chapter, you will learn about the **Aztecs,** a Mesoamerican people who built a vast empire in central Mexico. The Aztec Empire flourished from 1428 to 1519 C.E., when it was destroyed by invaders from Spain.

The Aztecs had a colorful **legend** about the beginnings of their empire. Originally a wandering group of hunter-gatherers, the Aztecs had a belief that one day they would receive a sign from the gods. They would see an eagle perched on a great cactus with "his wings stretched toward the rays of the sun." In its beak, the eagle would hold a long snake. When they saw this eagle, the Aztecs would know they had found the place where they would build a great city.

In the mid 1200s C.E., the Aztecs entered the high Valley of Mexico, a fertile basin in central Mexico. Several times other groups in the valley pushed the Aztecs away from their lands. In 1325, the Aztecs took refuge on an island in Lake Texcoco. There Aztec priests saw the eagle, just as the gods had promised. And so the Aztecs set about building a city they called **Tenochtitlan,** which means "the place of the fruit of the prickly pear cactus." In time, the island city became the center of the Aztec Empire.

In this chapter, you will learn more about where the Aztecs came from and how they built their magnificent capital city. You'll also discover how this humble band of nomads rose to become the masters of a great **empire**.

Use this drawing of the Mexican flag as a graphic organizer to help you understand the three stages in the development of the Aztec civilization.

24.2 The Aztecs in the Valley of Mexico

The Aztec Empire arose in the Valley of Mexico, a fertile area nearly 8,000 feet above sea level. By the time the Aztecs arrived in the mid 1200s C.E., the valley had been a center of civilization for more than a thousand years. Two groups in particular had built civilizations there that strongly influenced the Aztecs. Let's take a brief look at these civilizations. Then we'll see how the Aztecs came to the valley and gradually rose to power.

Teotihuacan, the "City of the Gods," was an expansive city of plazas, pyramids, and avenues. The Pyramid of the Sun, shown above, was constructed of volcanic rock and limestone.

Civilization in the Valley of Mexico   From about 100 to 650 C.E., the Valley of Mexico was dominated by the Teotihuacans. These people built an enormous capital city, Teotihuacan. One of the city's buildings, the Pyramid of the Sun, was more than 200 feet high.

After Teotihuacan's collapse around the 700s, a group from the north, the Toltecs, migrated into the valley. Toltec civilization reached its height in the 10th and 11th centuries. The Toltecs built a number of cities. Their capital, Tollan, boasted large pyramids topped with temples.

During the 1100s, new groups invaded the valley. They took over Toltec cities and established new city-states. But the influence of the Toltecs and the Teotihuacans continued to be felt in the culture that was developing in the valley.

The Arrival of the Aztecs   Sometime around 1250 C.E., a new group arrived in the Valley of Mexico. A nomadic band of hunter-gatherers, they called themselves the Mexica. We know them today as the Aztecs.

The name Aztec comes from Aztlan, the Mexicas' legendary homeland. According to Aztec tradition, Aztlan was an island in a lake to the northwest of the Valley of Mexico. The Aztecs had left the island around 1100 C.E. They wandered through the deserts of northern Mexico for many years before coming to the Valley of Mexico.

When the Aztecs came to the heart of the valley, they found lakes dotted with marshy islands. Thriving city-states controlled the land around the lakes.

The Aztecs had a difficult time establishing themselves in the valley. The people living in the city-states thought the Aztecs were crude barbarians. But the Aztecs were fierce warriors, and the city-states were willing to employ them as **mercenaries**.

mercenary a soldier who is paid to fight for another country or group

After settling in the valley, the Aztecs began to be influenced by the legacy of the Teotihuacans and the Toltecs. They made pilgrimages to the ancient ruins of Teotihuacan. They adopted Quetzalcoatl, the Teotihuacans' feathered serpent god, as one of their own gods.

The Aztecs viewed the Toltecs even more highly, as rulers of a Golden Age. Aztec rulers married into the surviving Toltec royal line. The Aztecs even began to claim the Toltecs as their own ancestors.

In 1319, stronger groups forced the Aztecs to move away from Chapultepec, a rocky hill where they had made their home. The Aztecs fled to the south, where they became mercenaries for the city-state of Colhuacan. But trouble came again when the Aztecs sacrificed the daughter of the Colhua chief. This led to a war with the Colhuas, who drove the Aztecs onto an island in the shallow waters of Lake Texcoco.

It was here, the Aztecs said, that they spotted an eagle perched atop a cactus with a long snake in its beak. Grateful for the sign they had been waiting for, the Aztecs set to work building the city they called Tenochtitlan.

The island turned out to be a good site for the Aztecs' city. The lake provided fish and water birds for food, and the island was easy to defend. Over time, the Aztecs' new home would grow into one of the great cities of the world.

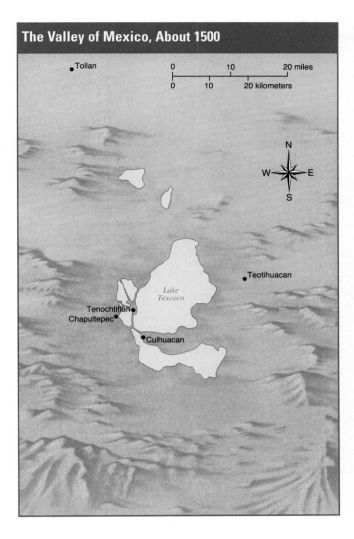

The Valley of Mexico, About 1500

From Mercenaries to Empire Builders The Aztecs started building Tenochtitlan in 1325 C.E. For the next 100 years, they served as mercenaries for a powerful group called the Tepanecs. Through this **alliance** the Aztecs gained land, trading connections, and wealth.

Eventually, however, the Aztecs rebelled against the heavy-handed rule of the Tepanecs. Under the Aztec leader Itzcoatl, Tenochtitlan joined with two other city-states in the Triple Alliance. In 1428, the alliance fought and defeated the Tepanecs. Together the allies began a series of conquests that laid the foundation for the Aztec Empire.

As Tenochtitlan became a great power, Itzcoatl set out to reshape Aztec history. He burned records that referred to his people's humble origins. Instead, he connected the Aztecs to the distinguished Toltecs.

With their growing power and a glorious (though legendary) past, the Aztecs were ready for their new role as empire builders. Let's look now at the great city that would become the center of their empire.

alliance a group of countries, city-states, or other entities who agree to work together, often to fight common enemies

The Aztecs   273

The Aztecs of Tenochtitlan farmed on chinampas, small floating islands they constructed from mud and plants.

24.3 Tenochtitlan: A City of Wonders

As the Aztecs' power grew, their capital city of Tenochtitlan developed into one of the largest cities in the world. When Spanish explorers first glimpsed Tenochtitlan in 1519, they were amazed to see a majestic city crisscrossed by canals and boasting impressive temples and palaces. With a population of between 200,000 and 300,000 people, Tenochtitlan was larger than London, Paris, or Venice.

How did the Aztecs turn an unwanted island into such a great city? First they reclaimed land from the lake by sinking timbers into the water to serve as walls and filling in the area between the timbers with mud, boulders, and reeds. In this way they created small islands called *chinampas,* or "floating gardens." Eventually the Aztecs expanded the city's land surface until it covered over five square miles. They even merged Tlatelolco, originally a separate island, with Tenochtitlan.

Gradually, Tenochtitlan grew into the magnificent city that so amazed the Spanish. At the center of the city—both physically and spiritually—lay a large ceremonial **plaza**. Here the Aztecs gathered for religious rituals, feasts, and festivals. A wall about eight feet tall enclosed this area. The wall, which was called the Coatepantli ("snake wall"), was studded with sculptures of serpents. The palaces and homes of nobles lined the outside of the wall.

Inside the plaza, a stone pyramid called the Great Temple loomed 150 feet into the sky. People could see the pyramid, which was decorated with bright sculptures and murals, from several miles away. It had two steep stairways leading to double shrines. One shrine was dedicated to the chief god, Huitzilopochtli. The other was dedicated to Tlaloc, the rain god. In front of the shrines stood the stone where priests performed human sacrifices. An altar called the *tzompantli* ("skull rack") displayed the skulls of thousands of people who had been sacrificed. (You will learn more about the role of human sacrifice in the Aztec religion in the next chapter.) Other structures in the plaza included

plaza a public square or other open area in a city where people can gather

more shrines and temples, the ritual ball court, military storehouses, and guest rooms for important visitors.

Just outside the plaza stood the royal palace. The two-story palace seemed like a small town. The palace was the home of the Aztec ruler, but it also had government offices, shrines, courts, storerooms, gardens, and courtyards. At the royal **aviary,** trained staff plucked the valuable feathers of parrots and quetzals. Wild animals captured throughout the empire, like pumas and jaguars, prowled cages in the royal zoo.

The city's main marketplace was located in the northern section, in Tlatelolco. Each day as many as 60,000 people came from all corners of the Aztec Empire to sell their wares. Goods ranged from luxury items like jade and feathers to necessities like food and rope sandals. Merchants also sold gold, silver, turquoise, animal skins, clothing, pottery, chocolate and vanilla, tools, and slaves.

Although Tenochtitlan spread over five square miles, people had an easy time getting around. Four wide avenues met at the foot of the Great Temple. A thousand workers swept and washed down the streets each day, keeping them cleaner than streets in European cities. At night, pine torches lit the way. People also traveled by foot on smaller walkways or by canoe on the canals that crossed the city. Many of the canals were lined with stone and had bridges.

Three **causeways** linked the island to the mainland. The longest of them stretched five miles. The causeways were 25 to 30 feet wide. They all had wooden bridges that could be raised to let boats through or to protect the city in an enemy attack.

The city boasted other technological marvels, like the aqueduct that carried fresh water for irrigation. Twin pipes ran from the Chapultepec springs, three miles away. While one pipe was being cleaned or repaired, the other could transport water. A **dike** 10 miles long ran along the east side of the city to hold back floodwaters.

Thousands of people visited Tenochtitlan each year. Some came to do business. Others came as pilgrims. Still others came simply to gaze in wonder at the capital of the Aztec world.

aviary an enclosed space or cage for keeping birds
causeway a raised road built across water or low ground
dike a wall or dam built to hold back water and prevent flooding

Temples dedicated to various gods rose along the streets and canals of the city of Tenochtitlan.

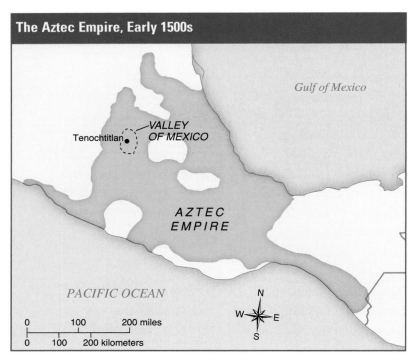

The Aztec Empire, Early 1500s

Gulf of Mexico

VALLEY OF MEXICO

Tenochtitlan

AZTEC EMPIRE

PACIFIC OCEAN

0   100   200 miles
0   100   200 kilometers

N
W   E
S

24.4 The Aztec Empire

Tenochtitlan began as simply the Aztecs' home city. After the Aztecs and their allies defeated the Tepanecs in 1428 C.E., the city became the capital of a growing empire. Under Moctezuma I in the mid 1400s, the Aztecs extended their empire to faraway regions.

By the early 1500s, the Aztec Empire stretched from the Gulf of Mexico to the Pacific Ocean. It covered much of Central Mexico and reached as far south as the current border with Guatemala. At its height, the empire included more than five million people.

An Empire Based on Tribute

Unlike other empire builders, the Aztecs did not start colonies. Nor did they force conquered peoples to adopt their ways. Instead, the Aztec Empire was a loose union of hundreds of city-states that were forced to pay tribute to the Aztecs.

Collecting tribute was the empire's most important business. The Aztecs relied on tribute to support Tenochtitlan's huge population. Tribute took the form of whatever valuable items a city could provide. Cities might pay in food, cacao, gems and stones, cotton, cloth, animals, animal skins, shells, building materials, or even soldiers. Tax collectors stationed around the empire made sure that cities paid regularly.

Each year, huge amounts of goods flowed into Tenochtitlan. An average year brought 7,000 tons of maize; 4,000 tons each of beans, seed, and grain; and at least 2 million cotton cloaks. Warriors, priests, officials, servants, and other workers all received payment in tribute goods.

Warfare   The demands of the empire made war the center of Aztec life. Successful battles allow the Aztecs to increase their sources of tribute. They also gained more territory, laborers, and sacrificial victims. As you will learn in the next chapter, the Aztecs believed that their chief god, Huitzilopochtli, required human blood for survival, so in war they took as many prisoners as possible to use in sacrifices. They also used the threat of human sacrifice to frighten city-states into paying tribute.

Every male Aztec was trained to be a soldier. In battle, the Aztecs used weapons such as bows and arrows, spears, clubs, and wooden swords with sharp stone blades. Warrior knights carried shields decorated with figures of animals such as the jaguar and eagle. The figures represented different strengths that the Aztecs believed they received from these animals.

An Aztec declaration of war followed a ritualized pattern. First, the Aztecs asked a city to join the empire as an ally. The city had 60 days to agree. If the ruler refused, the Aztecs declared war.

The battle began when thousands of Aztec warriors descended upon the city. As the armies faced each other, a general gave the signal to attack. Aztec warriors excelled at hand-to-hand fighting. Most wars ended after one battle, usually with an Aztec victory.

After the city had fallen, the Aztecs brought their captives to Tenochtitlan. Some became slaves, but most were sacrificed to Huitzilopochtli.

The Aztecs made only a few demands on the defeated city. The people had to pay tribute, honor the god Huitzilopochtli, and promise obedience to the Aztec ruler. Otherwise, conquered cities remained independent. They kept their religion, customs, and language. They usually even kept their leaders.

These lenient conditions made it easy for the Aztecs to rule. But most of the conquered people never thought of themselves as true Aztecs. They wanted their freedom. These feelings led to a lack of unity in the Aztec Empire. Eventually, the Spanish would take advantage of that weakness by making allies of the Aztecs' enemies when they invaded Mexico in 1519. You will learn more about the Spanish conquest of the Aztecs in Unit 7.

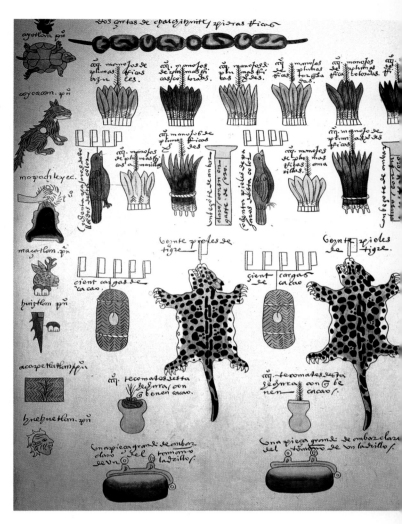

These modern drawings of Aztec life show some of the forms of tribute paid to the Aztecs, such as feathers, jade, and tiger skins.

24.5 Chapter Summary

In this chapter, you learned about the rise of the Aztecs from a band of nomads to the masters of a great empire. The Aztecs arrived in the Valley of Mexico in the mid 1200s C.E. In 1325, they began building their capital city of Tenochtitlan. But the Aztec Empire only began to emerge in 1428, when the Aztecs and their allies rebelled against the Tepanecs.

Over the next 100 years, the Aztecs expanded their empire through warfare and alliances. Eventually the empire included hundreds of cities and millions of people. In the next chapter, you will learn about the daily life of the Aztecs at the height of their empire.

CHAPTER 25

◀ ◀ The Great Market in the city of Tenochtitlan was a center of daily life for the Aztecs.

Daily Life in Tenochtitlan

25.1 Introduction

In Chapter 24, you learned how the Aztecs built their empire in central Mexico. Now you will explore what life was like in the Aztecs' capital city of Tenochtitlan.

Imagine that you are an Aztec child living outside Tenochtitlan in the 1400s C.E. One morning your father, a chili pepper farmer, takes you to the great market at Tenochtitlan. Your father finds the vegetable section, where he spreads out his mat and displays his peppers. Then he begins to shout out prices. He gladly trades with a noblewoman, exchanging peppers for precious cacao beans. Later he trades his remaining peppers for a handmade clay cooking pot for your mother.

After all the peppers are gone, your father takes you on a long stroll around the city. You see the Great Temple where priests perform sacrifices and the ball court where nobles play a game called *tlachtli*. You gaze in wonder at the beautiful houses where noble families live and the splendid palace of the Aztec ruler. After the long walk home, you hungrily eat a simple mush made of maize before going to sleep.

This imaginary trip to Tenochtitlan suggests many aspects of **daily life** for Aztecs in the 1400s. In this chapter, you'll learn more about how the people of Tenochtitlan lived. You'll explore Aztec **class structure, marriage, family life, food, markets, religious practices,** and **recreation**.

Use this drawing as a graphic organizer to help you collect information about Aztec daily life.

25.2 Class Structure

Aztec society was divided into five main social classes. At the top of the class structure were the ruler and his family. Next came a noble class of government officials, priests, and high-ranking warriors. The third and largest class was made up of commoners, citizens who were not of noble rank. Below the commoners were the peasants, who were neither slaves nor citizens. At the bottom of the class structure were the slaves.

Each class had its own privileges and responsibilities. However, an Aztec's status was not fixed. Commoners could move up in social class by performing brave deeds in war or by studying to be priests. And a noble could fall in rank if he failed to live up to his responsibilities. Let's look at the role of each class, beginning with the ruler and his family.

The Ruler   The Aztec ruler, or emperor, was considered **semidivine**. Called *tlatoani,* or "he who speaks," the emperor maintained the empire and decided when to wage war.

The position of ruler was not **hereditary,** as it was in many other societies. When an emperor died, his son did not automatically become ruler. Instead, a group of advisors chose the new ruler from the emperor's family. Each new ruler was expected to acquire new possessions of his own. This was an important motive for constant warfare.

Government Officials, Priests, and Military Leaders
The emperor was supported by a noble class of government officials, priests, and military leaders. Officials in Tenochtitlan counseled the emperor, worked as judges, and governed the city's four districts. Other nobles throughout the empire ruled cities, collected tribute (payments), or erected public buildings and roads.

The emperor appointed government officials for life. Noble status was not hereditary, but most sons of nobles earned high offices themselves.

Priests conducted all religious rites and served individual gods. Some priests ran the schools that trained boys for government jobs and the priesthood. Other priests studied the skies and made predictions about the future. Generally only nobles became priests, but sometimes an Aztec from lower classes rose this high. Girls could become priestesses.

semidivine more than human but not fully a god
hereditary passed on from parent to child; inherited

This artwork shows people from various classes of Aztec society. Use the information from the text and visual clues in the image to try to identify which group in the Aztec class structure each figure represents.

Commoners could also rise to become military leaders. All Aztec men were trained to be soldiers, and a common soldier could become a leader by capturing enemies in battle. Military leaders commanded groups of soldiers and took part in war councils.

Commoners   The broad class of commoners included several smaller classes. The highest-ranking commoners were professional traders called *pochteca*. The pochteca led caravans to distant lands to acquire exotic goods. Some also served as spies for the emperor, reporting what type of tribute a city could provide.

Aztec painters created beautiful murals for emperors and other high-ranking Aztec officials.

The pochteca had their own god and lived in a separate section of Tenochtitlan. They paid taxes with rare goods. They enjoyed many privileges. For example, they could own land and send their children to the nobles' schools. Unlike noble status, membership in this class was hereditary.

Below the pochteca came craftspeople and artisans, like potters, jewelers, and painters. Some worked in their homes and traded their goods at the market. Others worked in the royal palace and made items specially for the emperor.

Most commoners worked as farmers, fishers, laborers, and servants. Instead of owning land, they were loaned plots of land for homes and farms by their *calpulli,* or **ward**. All commoners paid tribute to the nobility in the form of crops, labor, or manufactured goods.

Peasants   About 30 percent of the Aztec people were peasants. Unlike slaves, people in this class were free, but they were considered inferior to commoners. Peasants did not belong to a calpulli and were not loaned land to farm. Instead, they hired out their services to nobles.

Slaves   At the bottom of Aztec society were the slaves. Prisoners of war, lawbreakers, or debtors might be forced into slavery. Unlike slaves in many societies, Aztec slaves had a number of rights. They could own property, goods, and even other slaves. In addition, slaves did not pass their status on to their children, who were born free. In fact, the mother of the emperor Itzcoatl was a slave. Many slaves gained their own freedom after working off a debt, upon completing their term of punishment for a crime, or when their masters died.

Now let's look at what daily life was like for the Aztecs of Tenochtitlan, beginning with marriage customs. We'll focus mostly on the majority of Aztecs, the commoners.

ward a neighborhood that is a political unit within a city

25.3 Marriage

Marriage and family life were important to Aztecs of all social classes. Marriage marked an Aztec child's entry into adulthood. Most men married around the age of 20, while young women tended to marry around 16.

Marriages were arranged by the families of the bride and groom. The young man's family chose the bride. They then engaged the services of a matchmaker, an older woman who approached the bride's family. It was customary for the bride's family to refuse at first. The matchmaker then returned a few days later. This time the bride's family usually accepted the union and set the **dowry**.

Even among commoners, an Aztec wedding was as elaborate as the families could afford. The festivities began at the bride's house. Relatives, friends, the groom's teachers, and the important people of the calpulli enjoyed a banquet with the bride and gave her presents.

That evening, the guests marched to the groom's home for the wedding ceremony. An old woman, usually the matchmaker, carried the bride on her back. To symbolize the bond of marriage, during the ceremony the matchmaker tied the groom's cloak to the bride's blouse.

After the ceremony, the young couple retired to the bridal chamber to pray for four days, while their guests celebrated. On the fifth day, the couple emerged and attended another grand banquet. Then they settled down on a piece of land in the groom's calpulli.

The Aztecs permitted men to practice **polygamy,** or to marry more than one wife. An Aztec man could take as many wives as he could afford. However, only one of the wives was considered the "primary" wife, and only marriage to the primary wife was celebrated with special rites and ceremonies.

If a marriage was unhappy, either spouse could ask for a divorce. A man could divorce his wife if she neglected her duties at home, had a poor temper, or did not bear children. A woman could divorce her husband if he beat her, deserted her, or failed to support her and her children. Aztec society encouraged divorced women to remarry.

dowry a gift of money or goods presented to a man or a woman upon marriage

polygamy marriage in which a man or a woman has more than one spouse

This page from the Codex Mendoza shows a young couple's marriage festivities. Can you identify the bride, the groom, and the matchmaker?

25.4 Family Life

Men had higher status than women in Aztec society, and within the family the father was the master of the house. Aztec women, however, had their own rights and responsibilities. Married woman could own property and sell goods. Some older women also practiced a profession, such as matchmaking or midwifery.

Among commoners, the skills of both men and women were necessary to care for the household and the family. Men built the house and worked as farmers or at a craft. Women fixed meals, tended the garden, and looked after livestock. Many Aztec women wove beautiful clothes of many colors. Some made cloaks in patterns of sun designs or with images of shells, fish, cacti, snakes, or butterflies. Women traded these cloaks for other goods at the market.

One of a woman's most important jobs was to bear and care for children. The Aztecs believed that the purpose of marriage was to bring children into the world, so they honored a woman's role in giving birth as much as they did a man's role in fighting wars.

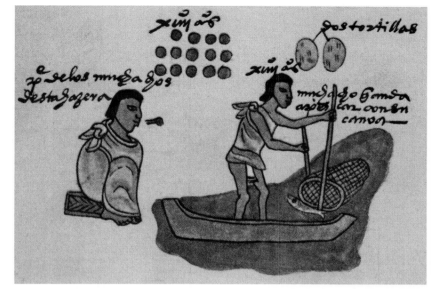

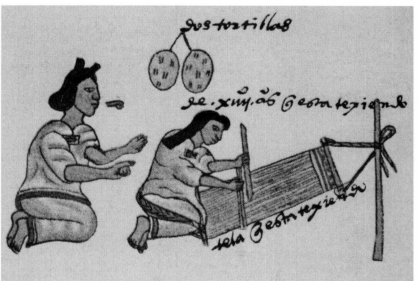

Parents taught their sons and daughters important skills, such as fishing, canoeing, weaving, and cooking.

Aztec parents began training their children at a young age. All children of commoners helped out around the house. Little boys fetched water and wood, while older boys learned how to fish and handle a canoe. Eventually boys accompanied their fathers to work or to the market. Girls' tasks centered on running a home and included cleaning house and grinding maize. When they were about seven years old, girls began learning to weave from their mothers.

In addition to working, all boys attended school. Commoners probably started school around the age of six, but they only attended part-time. At the *telpochcalli,* or "house of youth," boys mostly trained to be soldiers. The sons of nobles went to the *calmecac* instead. There they learned the skills of being priests, government officials, or military commanders.

25.5 Food

The Aztecs of Tenochtitlan ate both homegrown foods and foods that were imported from distant places. The mainstay of the Aztec diet, however, was maize. The Aztecs found maize so useful because it could be dried and then stored for a long time. Women boiled and skinned maize kernels and ground them into flour. Then they baked fresh tortillas for each meal on clay griddles. They also made tamales by wrapping maize in husks and steaming it.

The preparation of tortillas and other foods was a daily task for Aztec women.

The daily routine of Aztec commoners shows the importance of maize. After working for several hours, commoners ate a simple meal in the late morning. The meal usually consisted of a maize porridge called *atole*. The porridge was often seasoned with peppers or sweetened with honey. At midday, commoners ate their main meal of tortillas, maize cakes, boiled beans, or tamales. Pepper or tomato sauce sometimes spiced up these dishes. Most families had only two meals. But some people ate a thin porridge, usually made of maize, just before going to bed.

Aztec commoners had occasional variety in their meals. To provide meat for special occasions, families might raise a few turkeys or a hairless breed of dog. Or they might hunt wild game, such as rabbits and pigeons.

Aztec farmers also grew such crops as red peppers, tomatoes, sage, squash, green beans, sweet potatoes, and avocados. When crops were bad, the Aztecs turned to other sources of food. They caught water creatures, such as frogs and shrimp, and collected insect eggs. They even skimmed algae, a type of plant, off the surface of the lake and formed it into small cakes.

The wealthy ate quite a different diet, both on a daily basis and at the feasts they attended. They prized delicacies like winged ants and a lizardlike creature called an *axolotl*. The upper classes also ate exotic imported foods. They enjoyed cocoa with their morning meal and pineapples, oysters, and crabs at their banquets.

25.6 Markets

Markets were an important part of the Aztec economy. Each city in the empire had its own market, usually located in the square in front of the town's temple. Large towns held markets every day, while small villages held them about every five days. Some towns had their own specialties. The people of Tenochtitlan might travel to nearby Texcoco for fine cloth and to faraway Acolman to buy dogs for meat.

At Tlatelolco, the bustling market in Tenochtitlan, people bought and sold everything from food and utensils to warrior costumes, quetzal feathers, and slaves. Instead of using money, Aztecs used a barter system, trading one kind of good for another. Some expensive goods had an agreed-upon value. For instance, a warrior's costume and shield were worth about 60 cotton cloaks.

Many individuals brought their wares to market. Farmers brought extra crops they had grown, while craftspeople brought handmade goods. The pochteca had a special place in the markets, since they brought exotic goods from faraway places. They supplied fine green jade and quetzal feathers. They also provided raw materials that were unavailable around Tenochtitlan. For example, they sold metals like gold and silver, as well as tortoiseshells for making spoons.

Guards watched over the market to make sure sellers acted honestly. When a problem arose—for example, a person accusing a seller of cheating—the guards took the parties to a court located at one end of the market. There three judges sat, waiting to hear the story and render their verdict.

The market also had a social purpose. People came there to meet friends, gossip, and hear the news of the day. Some people simply enjoyed strolling up and down the aisles, buying snacks and seeing all the wonderful things the sellers had to offer.

People bartered, or traded, in the marketplace for the things they needed.

25.7 Religious Practices

Religion was central to Aztec life and society. The Aztecs believed that humans needed the gods to survive. It was the gods who granted a good harvest or, if they were displeased, sent earthquakes and floods. Consequently, it was important to please the gods through elaborate rituals and ceremonies. Priests presented the gods with flowers, ears of maize, clothing, or images made of wood, while the people sang and danced.

The Aztecs adopted some of their gods from other Mesoamerican groups. For example, Tlaloc, the rain god, was an ancient Meso-american god. Quetzalcoatl ("feathered serpent") had been worshiped by the Teotihuacans. But the Aztecs' own chief god was Huitzilopochtli, the sun god and the god of war. In fact, the Aztecs called themselves the "people of the sun."

The Aztecs saw the sun as a warrior who fought each night against the forces of darkness. In Aztec belief, the survival of the universe depended upon the sun winning these battles. And the way to keep the sun strong was to offer him nourishment in the form of blood.

For this reason, most Aztec rituals included some form of blood sacrifice. Every morning Aztec priests sacrificed hundreds of birds to Huitzilopochtli. Priests also pierced their skin with cactus spikes to offer their own blood.

The richest form of sacrifice, however, was that of humans. The Aztecs particularly valued the sacrifice of warriors captured in battle, because they believed that the blood of strong warriors was especially nourishing. Scholars think the Aztecs also used human sacrifice to frighten other cities into accepting their rule.

In Tenochtitlan, up to several thousand people may have gone to sacrificial deaths each year. Four priests pinned the victim to the stone in front of Huitzilopochtli's temple, while another cut out the living heart. Some victims may have died willingly in the belief that they would accompany the sun god in his daily battle across the sky.

The Aztecs also made sacrifices to other gods. They threw the sacrificial victims of the fire god into a great blaze. To honor the goddess of corn, they cut off women's heads. Overall, the Aztecs practiced human sacrifice on a much larger scale than any other Mesoamerican group.

This illustration from the 1500s shows Aztecs making a human sacrifice to the sun god.

25.8 Recreation

While work, warfare, and rituals were all important to the Aztecs, they also had some time for recreation. They enjoyed music and dancing, and nobles liked to go on hunts.

Another entertainment was *patolli*, a game played on a cross-shaped board divided into 52 squares. The board symbolized the 260-day calendar, which the Aztecs shared with the Maya and other Mesoamerican peoples. Five times around the board equaled 260 days. To move around the board, players threw several white beans marked with holes. The holes told them how many spaces to move the colored stones that served as game pieces. The first person around the board five times was the winner.

Patolli was a popular game among Aztecs and other Mesoamerican peoples. White beans marked with holes were thrown like modern dice to tell players how many spaces they could move on the cross-shaped board.

All social classes played patolli, but it's likely that only members of the nobility played the ball game *tlachtli*. Similar to Mayan ball games, tlachtli was played on a long, narrow court shaped like the letter I and surrounded by high walls. A small ring projected over the court from each side wall. Two teams faced each other across a line that ran between the rings. The object of the game was to get a rubber ball through the ring on the other's team side of the court. Players could not touch the ball with their hands or feet, so they threw themselves on the ground to hit the ball with their elbows, knees, and hips.

Hundreds of spectators gathered to watch each game. They often risked clothes, feathers, and gold by betting on which team would win. Some people lost all their wealth in such bets and had to sell themselves into slavery.

Tlachtli had religious meaning as well. The Aztecs believed that the tlachtli court represented the world and the ball represented a heavenly body. Because of these religious ties, the Aztecs built their tlachtli courts near the most important temples, like the Great Temple in Tenochtitlan.

25.9 Chapter Summary

In this chapter, you learned about daily life in the Aztecs' capital city of Tenochtitlan. You read about the structure of Aztec society and the customs governing marriage and family life. You discovered what the Aztecs ate, how they traded goods in their markets, and how they worshiped and played. In the next chapter, you will travel to South America to learn about another people who built an empire in the Americas: the Incas.

CHAPTER 26

The city of Machu Picchu was a religious center of the Inca Empire.

The Incas

26.1 Introduction

In Chapter 25, you learned about daily life in the Aztec Empire of Mexico. Now you will learn about the **Inca Empire,** a great society that developed in the Andes Mountains of South America. The Inca Empire arose in the 1400s C.E. It lasted until 1532, when the Incas were conquered by Spanish explorers.

From north to south, the Inca Empire stretched more than 2,500 miles. To communicate across this vast distance, the Incas used runners called *chasquis* to relay messages from one place to another.

Imagine that you are a young chasqui. From your messenger station along the Royal Road, you see another chasqui racing toward you. You know he carries an important message from the emperor. You dart out of the messenger station and run alongside the other runner while he hands you a set of strings called a *quipu*. Knots tied at different places in the strings stand for numbers. They will help you remember the message. The other chasqui also gives you a verbal message. Once he is certain that you have both parts of the message, he stops running. His work is over. Now it is up to you to get the message to the next station as quickly as possible.

This remarkable relay system helped the Incas manage their far-flung empire. In this chapter, you will explore how the Inca Empire was built and maintained. You'll also learn about the Incas' **class structure, family life, religion,** and **relations with other peoples**.

Use this illustration as a graphic organizer to help you understand more about the Inca Empire.

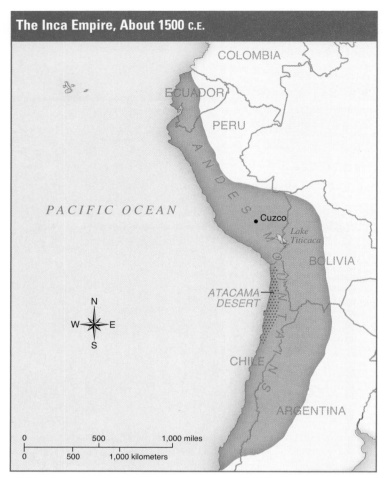

The Inca Empire, About 1500 C.E.

COLOMBIA
ECUADOR
PERU
PACIFIC OCEAN
Cuzco
Lake Titicaca
BOLIVIA
ATACAMA DESERT
CHILE
ARGENTINA

ANDES MOUNTAINS

N
W — E
S

0   500   1,000 miles
0   500   1,000 kilometers

26.2 The Rise of the Inca Empire

At the height of their power in the early 1500s C.E., the Incas ruled over a vast, well-organized empire. From north to south, the Inca Empire stretched almost the length of the Andes mountain range, a distance of 2,500 miles. It reached from the Pacific Coast in the west to the Amazon River Basin in the east. Today this territory includes most of Peru and Ecuador, as well as parts of Bolivia, Chile, and Argentina. Perhaps 10 million people lived under Inca rule.

How did the Incas build and manage such a huge empire? In part, the Incas adopted ideas and institutions that had been pioneered by earlier cultures. Two peoples who had an especially strong influence on the Incas were the Moche and the Chimu.

The Moche lived along the northern coast of Peru from about 100 B.C.E. to 700 C.E. They built cities, dug irrigation canals, and developed special classes of workers.

The Chimu kingdom in northern Peru flourished during the 1300s and 1400s. Like the Moche, the Chimu built well-planned cities and used elaborate irrigation methods. They preserved the artistic traditions of the Moche and passed them on to the Incas. They also built good roads and created a message system using runners. The Incas adopted and improved upon all of these achievements.

The Beginnings of the Empire   The center of the Inca Empire was the capital city of Cuzco, which was located in a valley high in the mountains of southern Peru. The Incas first settled in this area around 1200 C.E. Apart from this fact, their early history is cloaked in myth.

According to one Inca legend, the people were descended from Inti, the sun god. Inti commanded his son, Manco Capac, to rise out of the waters of Lake Titicaca. Manco Capac then founded the Inca tribe.

In another legend, Inti appeared before a later Inca ruler. He said the Incas must become a great power and educate the people they met. But for more than 200 years, the Incas increased their territory by only about a dozen miles around Cuzco.

The Incas began expanding their empire in 1438, when they were attacked by the neighboring Chancas. The Inca emperor and many citizens fled Cuzco. But one of his sons, Yupanqui, stayed behind and led his army against the Chancas. Inca legend says that the stones on the battlefield turned into powerful warriors. Yupanqui's victory made his people the strongest group in the area.

After driving off the Chancas, Yupanqui took the name Pachacuti, which means "earthshaker." He also seized the throne. Pachacuti and his son Topa Inca then launched a series of conquests against nearby tribes. With each victory, the Inca army became larger and more skilled.

Soon the Incas subdued almost every major group in the central Andes. In 1470, they conquered the Chimu. By the 1500s, their empire covered about 350,000 square miles.

Roads and Messengers   To manage their far-flung holdings, Inca leaders came to rely on a system of roads. The two main routes were the coastal road and the inland road, which was called the Royal Road. Smaller roads connected them.

Some historians have said that the Incas' system of roads was as impressive as that of ancient Rome. About 15,000 miles of road linked all corners of the empire. The roads crossed tropical jungles, high mountains, and raging rivers. Inca officials used the roads to travel throughout the empire. Shelters were placed every 15 to 30 miles to give travelers places to rest.

The roads also allowed the emperor at Cuzco to communicate with officials in distant places. The Incas sent messages by an elaborate relay system. They built messenger stations every couple of miles along the main roads. Chasquis, or messengers, carried the messages from one station to the next. Using this system, messages could travel more than 250 miles a day.

A message consisted of memorized words, and sets of strings called *quipus*. The quipus served as memory aids. Knots tied at various places and on strings of different colors stood for numbers. The Incas had no system of writing, but the quipus helped them keep track of populations, troops, and tribute, as well as information about their legends and achievements. The oral comments that accompanied a quipu helped a trained expert decipher the message. For the Inca government, quipus proved to be an effective substitute for written language.

Chasquis counted the knots and strings on quipus to relay messages about various things, such as the number of people in a military troop or the amount of goods given in tribute to an Inca leader.

26.3 Class Structure

Inca society was based on a strictly organized class structure. There were three broad classes: the emperor and his immediate family, nobles, and commoners. Throughout Inca society, people who were "Inca by blood"—those whose families were originally from Cuzco—held higher status than non-Incas.

As the Inca Empire grew, its class structure became more complex. Let's look at the roles and responsibilities of each social class in the empire.

The Emperor   At the top of Inca society was the emperor, called the Sapa Inca. The Incas believed that the Sapa Inca was descended from Inti, the sun god. For this reason, the Sapa Inca ruled with complete authority.

Everything in the empire belonged to the Sapa Inca. He lived in great splendor. When the Spanish came to Cuzco in the 1500s, they were dazzled to see fine gardens, golden statues, and jars made of gold and silver studded with emeralds. Servants carried the Sapa Inca everywhere on a golden **litter**. His subjects dared not look him directly in the eye.

The Sapa Inca could have many wives and hundreds of children. But he had one "primary" wife, who was called the Coya. Traditionally, to ensure the purity of the royal blood, the Coya was the Sapa Inca's full sister. The Sapa Inca chose his heir from their children.

Nobles   Below the Sapa Inca were the nobles. The Inca nobility was made up of leaders who helped administer the vast empire.

All nobles enjoyed certain privileges. They received gifts of land, servants, llamas, and fine clothing. They did not pay taxes, and men had the right to marry more than one wife. However, nobles were not all of equal rank. There were three main classes of nobles: Capac Incas, who were considered relatives of the emperor; Hahua Incas, who did not share the royal blood; and *curacas,* who were leaders of people conquered by the Incas.

litter a seat or chair on which a person is carried; a kind of carriage for high-ranking people

The highest-ranking nobles were the Capac Incas. Like the emperor himself, they were believed to be descended from Manco Capac, the legendary founder of the Inca dynasty.

Capac Incas controlled the empire's land as well as its valuable resources, such as llamas, coca leaves, and gold. They held the most important posts in the government, army, and priesthood. The *apus,* or governors, of the four quarters of the empire came from this group.

As the empire grew, the Incas needed more nobles to staff the government's complex bureaucracy. As a result, some people who were not true Incas also gained entry into the noble class. Called Hahua Incas, they were considered "Incas by privilege." Often leaders from around Cuzco became Hahua Incas. Sometimes people of common birth gained this status as well.

Additional conquests created a need for the third class of nobles, the curacas. The curacas were local leaders of conquered peoples. Curacas carried out various jobs. Many collected taxes. Others worked as inspectors, making sure everyone followed Inca laws and customs, such as wearing proper clothing and keeping clean homes. Curacas were required to spend time in Cuzco learning these laws and customs. They were allowed to rule their people only if they followed Inca ways.

Commoners   Most of the people in the Inca Empire were commoners who worked as farmers and herders. The Incas did not practice slavery in the usual sense of the word. However, they did require commoners to support the government, both through the products of their labor and by working on government-sponsored projects. Men did jobs like building roads, while women might weave cloth.

In this illustration, dating from about 1565, Inca farmers harvest potatoes.

Inca farmers grew a variety of crops, including squash, peppers, beans, peanuts, more than 20 types of corn, and more than 200 types of potato. The most important crop was the potato, which could survive heavy frosts at altitudes as high as 15,000 feet above sea level. Corn could be grown at altitudes nearly as high. The Incas enjoyed corn fresh, fried, and popped.

Inca farmers were required to give most of their crops to the government. The government placed the crops it collected in storehouses throughout the empire. The food was then distributed to warriors, temple priests, and people in need. For example, the government gave food to people who could no longer work, particularly the aged, the sick, and the disabled.

ayllu an Inca clan (group of related families), the basic unit of Inca society

communal shared by a community or group

In this Inca coming-of-age ceremony, a boy receives the weapons of an Inca warrior.

26.4 Family Life

Families in the Inca Empire belonged to larger clans called **ayllus**. The ayllu was the basis of Inca society. Everyone was born into an ayllu, and most people lived their entire lives within the borders of its land. So to understand family life in the Inca Empire, we need to begin with the ayllu.

Life in the Ayllu Groups of families made up the ayllus, which ranged in size from small villages to large towns. Each ayllu had its own farming land and homes, but the ayllu did not own the land. As you have read, everything in the empire belonged to the emperor. The government loaned land to the ayllus for living and for farming. The people of an ayllu then worked this **communal** land cooperatively to grow crops and produce goods.

Everyone had responsibilities to the ayllu and to the government. All members of the ayllu had to work, except for the very young and the very old. The leaders of the ayllu made sure all the work got done. For instance, a leader might assign some men to clear the fields and others to dig irrigation ditches.

The households of the ayllu came under the authority of a series of curacas. One head of household ruled every 10 households. Fifty of these heads of household came under the supervision of a higher-level curaca. At still higher levels, curacas managed groupings of 100, 500, 1,000, 5,000, and 10,000 households.

One of the functions of the curacas was to make sure ayllus paid their taxes. The Incas had no currency, so taxes were paid in the form of goods and labor. The Sapa Inca claimed one third of everything an ayllu produced. Another third supported the Inca temple system. Commoners kept the remaining third for themselves.

In addition, men had to pay the *mit'a,* or public duty tax. Men paid the mit'a by contributing labor to government projects each year. In response to the government's need, the leaders of an ayllu assigned work to its members. For example, men might repair roads, build storehouses, or work in the mines.

Childhood Most Incas were born into ayllus of hardworking commoners. The children of commoners learned about their responsibilities early in life. Young children performed simple tasks around the home. As they grew older, girls took care of the babies, fetched water, cooked, made clothing, and learned to weave. Boys looked after the animals and helped in the fields.

The children of most commoners did not receive any formal education. Instead, they learned the skills they needed, as well as Inca customs, from their elders. Some especially talented boys were trained in crafts or record keeping so they could serve the emperor.

Unlike boys from commoner families, the sons of nobles had special *amautas,* or tutors. Amautas taught religion, geometry, history, military strategy, public speaking, and physical training.

Around the age of 15, all boys received a loincloth, a strip of cloth worn around the waist. The sons of nobles underwent a much more elaborate ritual. These boys had to pass month-long tests of courage, strength, and discipline. After passing these tests, the boys swore loyalty to the Sapa Inca and received the weapons of an Inca warrior.

Inca couples agreed to marry by holding hands and exchanging sandals.

Marriage Young men and women remained at home until they married. Unlike the emperor and the nobility, male commoners married only one wife. Young men married in their early 20s, while girls could marry at 16.

People usually married within their ayllu. Some marriages were arranged by families or by the young people themselves. In some cases, the local curaca chose a wife for a young man who was not yet married. Every year, the curaca also held a "marriage market" where young men chose brides. When a couple agreed to marry, they held hands and exchanged sandals.

Once they were married, couples established their own homes. Commoners typically lived in one-room houses made of adobe brick or stone. Noble families had fancier houses with several rooms. While nobles enjoyed the help of servants, commoners worked hard to produce their own food and clothing and to fulfill their responsibilities to the ayllu.

26.5 Religion

Religion was an important part of Inca life. Like other groups in the Americas, the Incas believed that the gods influenced their daily lives. Consequently, they showed their devotion to the gods through a number of practices. Let's look first at the Incas' basic beliefs about the gods, and then at their rituals and other religious practices.

Religious Beliefs The Incas believed in many gods who controlled various aspects of nature. For example, Illapu was the weather god and rain giver. Paca Mama was the Earth Mother, and Mama Cocha was the goddess of the sea. The Incas believed that all these gods had received their power from a supreme god, Viracocha, the creator of the world.

But to the Incas, the most important god was Inti, the sun god. Inti was important for two reasons. First, Incas believed that the emperor's family was descended from Inti. Second, Inti was also the god of agriculture, which was the basis of Inca life.

The Incas also believed that spirits dwelled in certain sacred objects and places, called *huacas*. Huacas included temples, charms, and places in nature such as springs and rocks. Because the Incas believed in an afterlife, the tombs and bodies of the dead were also considered huacas. People often prayed and made offerings to all these huacas.

Religious Practices The Inca religion was highly formal and required a large number of priests to conduct rituals and ceremonies. Priests worked at temples and shrines devoted to the gods. The most important temples were those dedicated to Inti. The high priest, a close relative of the Sapa Inca, presided over the Sun Temple in Cuzco. Priests who worked in the sun temples in the countryside came from the families of curacas.

Like the Maya and the Aztecs, the Incas offered sacrifices to the gods. Some sacrifices took place

In this Inca festival held in honor of the sun god, Inti, men in traditional dress carry skeletons on platforms.

regularly. For example, each day priests threw corn on a fire to encourage the sun to appear. "Eat this, Lord Sun," the priests said, "so that you will know we are your children." In many rituals, the Incas sacrificed live animals, usually llamas or guinea pigs.

The Incas also practiced human sacrifice, but only on the most sacred occasions or in times of a natural disaster. At such times children might be sacrificed, because the Incas believed that their purity honored the gods.

In addition to performing rituals and sacrifices, priests practiced **divination** to try to predict the future. Divination helped the Incas decide what course of action to take. For example, a priest might ask an **oracle** when the army should attack another tribe.

Chosen Women   A unique aspect of Inca religion was the role played by the Chosen Women. Each year, government officials visited all the towns in the empire to search for the most beautiful, graceful, and talented girls between the ages of 8 and 10. Selected girls were honored as Chosen Women and taken to live in convents. There they studied Inca religion, learned how to prepare special food and drink for religious ceremonies, and wove garments for the Sapa Inca and the Coya.

Around the age of 15, many Chosen Women left their convents. Some went to work in temples or shrines. Others became convent teachers, called *mamaconas*. Still others went to Cuzco and became wives of nobles or secondary wives of the Sapa Inca himself.

A few Chosen Women were sacrificed at important religious ceremonies. The rest spent almost their whole lives either serving Inti or fulfilling their roles as wives of nobles or the emperor. Only in old age were they sometimes allowed to return to the homes and families they had left so many years earlier.

The Chosen Women in Inca society were honored as servants of Inti.

divination the art of telling the future or finding hidden knowledge through religious means
oracle a person through whom a god or spirit is believed to speak

26.6 Relations with Other Peoples

The Incas had several methods of bringing other groups of people into the empire. They did not immediately resort to war. Instead, the Sapa Inca generally sent a delegate to meet with a tribe. The delegate explained that the tribe could join the Inca Empire and enjoy peace and prosperity. Everyone understood that the alternative was war against the strong Inca army.

When faced with these options, many tribes chose to join the empire. Their leaders were then allowed to retain some local power. In this way, the Incas expanded their empire without always having to fight.

If a tribe resisted, however, the two sides met in battle. The Incas used a variety of weapons, including spears, axes, and clubs. They were especially skilled at hurling stones with a sling. The fighting often cost the enemy tribe many of its men. Usually the Incas won.

Sometimes the Incas moved a defeated tribe to other parts of the empire, so that its people lost their native lands as well.

Becoming part of the empire meant adopting the ways of the Incas. The leaders of a conquered tribe had to build a sun temple. While the tribe could go on worshiping its own gods, it had to accept the Inca gods as the most powerful. Local leaders and their sons were brought to Cuzco to study Inca laws as well as Quechua, the official language. Then they returned to their people as curacas.

As the new territory accepted Inca ways, teachers arrived to create Inca-style villages. When necessary, they organized ayllus and taught the people how to build storehouses, irrigation systems, and terraced farming fields.

Meanwhile, the Incas took an important religious object belonging to the tribe and kept it in Cuzco. The Incas claimed they acted out of respect for the local religion. In reality, the object was held "hostage" in the capital. If the tribe ever rebelled, the government could destroy the sacred object.

As the Inca expanded their empire, foreign tribes could choose to join the empire or face Inca warriors in battle.

Despite these efforts, sometimes the Incas failed to bring a tribe fully into their empire. In such cases they might remove—and usually kill—the local leader. Some rebellious tribes were forced to move far away. The government then settled loyal members of the empire in their place. In this way, the Incas reduced the chance of resistance to their rule.

Many historians have wondered what drove the Incas to conquer such a huge empire. Part of the answer may lie in a unique Inca belief. The Incas thought that even after death, the Sapa Inca continued to rule the lands he had conquered. In order for the new emperor to establish his own source of power and wealth, he had to take new lands. Only then would he have land that belonged to him alone.

Inca soldiers lead captive people away from their homelands to be resettled elsewhere in the empire.

26.7 Chapter Summary

In this chapter, you learned about life in the Inca Empire. In the 1400s, the Incas began rapidly expanding their power from their base in Cuzco. Eventually they created a huge empire that extended almost the length of the Andes Mountains. An impressive system of roads and messengers helped the emperor manage his vast holdings.

The strict Inca class structure had three main levels: the emperor and his family, the nobility, and the commoners. All Incas belong to ayllus, which provided the empire with crops, goods, and labor. Like other peoples in the Americas, the Incas engaged in many religious practices to maintain a proper relationship with their gods. As empire builders, they used a variety of means to bring other groups under their control.

You have now learned about three great empires in the Americas: those of the Maya, the Aztecs, and the Incas. In the next chapter, you'll explore the achievements of these three peoples in greater depth.

CHAPTER 27

◄ These artworks are from the Aztec (upper),
Inca (lower left), and Mayan civilizations.

Achievements of the Maya, Aztecs, and Incas

27.1 Introduction

In Chapter 26, you learned about the Inca Empire of South America. You have now studied three great peoples of the Americas: the Maya, the Aztecs, and the Incas. In this chapter, you will revisit the cultures of these peoples and explore their unique **achievements**.

The history of these cultures stretches from very ancient times to just a few centuries ago. Mayan civilization dates back to 2000 B.C.E. It reached its height in the Classic Period from about 300 to 900 C.E. The Aztecs and the Incas built their empires in the two centuries before the Spanish arrived in the 1500s.

Scholars have learned about these cultures in a variety of ways. They have studied artifacts found at the sites of old settlements. They have read accounts left by Spanish soldiers and priests. And they have observed traditions that can still be found today among the descendants of the Maya, Aztecs, and Incas.

The more we learn about these cultures, the more we can appreciate what was special about each of them. The Maya, for example, made striking advances in writing, astronomy, and architecture. Both the Maya and the Aztecs created highly accurate calendars. The Aztecs adapted earlier pyramid designs to build massive stone temples. The Incas showed great skill in engineering and in managing their huge empire.

In this chapter, you will study these and other accomplishments of the Maya, the Aztecs, and the Incas. You will focus on three main areas: **science** and **technology, arts** and **architecture,** and **language** and **writing**.

Use this illustration as a graphic organizer to help you explore the achievements of the Maya, the Aztecs, and the Incas.

solar year the time it takes Earth to travel once around the sun

stele a stone slab or pillar with carvings or inscriptions

Mayan priests still use sacred calendars. This priest is at a ceremony on February 24, 2000, to celebrate the end of the Mayan solar year 5,115. He prays for peace and prosperity in the coming year of 5,116, which began February 25.

27.2 Achievements of the Maya

Many of the greatest achievements of the Maya date from the Classic Period (about 300 to 900 C.E.). Hundreds of years later, their ideas and practices continued to influence other Mesoamerican groups, including the Aztecs.

Science and Technology The Maya made important breakthroughs in astronomy and mathematics. Throughout Mayan lands, priests studied the sky from observatories. They relied on simple methods, such as looking through a forked stick. Still, they were able to track the movements of stars and planets with striking accuracy.

The Maya used their observations to calculate the **solar year**. The Mayan figure of 365.2420 days was amazingly precise.

These calculations allowed the Maya to create their solar calendar of 365 days. Recall that they also had a sacred 260-day calendar. Every 52 years, the first date in both calendars fell on the same day. This gave the Maya a longer unit of time that they called a Calendar Round. For the Maya, this 52-year period was something like what a century is to us today.

Mayan astronomy and calendar making depended on a good understanding of mathematics. In some ways, the Mayan number system was like ours. The Maya used place values for numbers, just as we do. However, instead of being based on the number 10, their system was based on 20. So instead of place values for 1s, 10s, and 100s, the Maya had place values for 1s, 20s, 400s (20 times 20), and so on.

The Maya also recognized the need for zero—a discovery made by few other civilizations. In the Mayan system for writing numbers, a dot stood for one, a bar for five, and a shell for zero. To add and subtract, people lined up two numbers and then combined or took away dots and bars.

Arts and Architecture The Maya were equally gifted in arts. They painted using colors mixed from minerals and plants. We can see the artistry of Mayan painters in the Bonampak murals, which were found in Chiapas, Mexico. The murals show nobles and priests, as well as battle scenes, ceremonies, and a human sacrifice. These pictures have helped scholars learn about Mayan life.

The Maya also constructed upright stone slabs called **steles,** which they often placed in front of temples. Most steles stood between 5 and 12 feet tall, although some rose as high as 30 feet. Steles

usually had three-dimensional carvings of gods and rulers. Sometimes the Maya inscribed them with dates and hieroglyphics in honor of significant events.

Weaving is a traditional Mayan art passed down through generations of women.

Another important art was weaving. We know from steles and paintings that the Maya wove colorful cloths in complex patterns. Women made embroidered tunics called *huipiles* and fashioned lengths of cloth for trade. Mayan women use similar techniques today. They still make their huipiles in traditional designs. People from different towns can be distinguished by the colors and patterns of their garments.

In architecture, the Maya built temple-pyramids from hand-cut limestone bricks. An unusual feature of Mayan buildings was a type of arch called a *corbel vault*. Builders stacked stones so that they gradually angled in toward each other to form a triangular archway. At the top of the arch, where the stones almost touched, one stone joined the two sides. The archway always had nine stone layers, representing the nine layers of the underworld (the place where souls were thought to go after death).

Language and Writing   The Maya developed the most complex system of writing in the Americas. They used hieroglyphics to represent sounds, words, and ideas. Hieroglyphic inscriptions have been found on stoneware and other artifacts dating from as early as 50 B.C.E.

Over time, the Maya created hundreds of **glyphs**. Eventually, scribes could write down anything in the spoken language. They often wrote about rulers, history, myths and gods, and astronomy.

Not all Mayan groups shared the same language. Instead, they spoke related **dialects**. Today, about four million Mesoamericans still speak one of 30 or so Mayan languages.

glyph a symbol or character in a hieroglyphic system of writing
dialect a regional variety of a language

The people of the Valley of Mexico have use chinampas, or artificial islands, for centuries. The land bordering these canals in the famous Xochimilco Floating Gardens in Mexico City was created with chinampas.

27.3 Achievements of the Aztecs

The Aztecs adapted many ideas from earlier groups, including their calendars and temple-pyramids. But the Aztecs improved on these ideas and made them their own.

Science and Technology   One of the Aztecs' most remarkable technological achievements was the building of their island city, Tenochtitlan. As you read in Chapter 24, the Aztecs enlarged the area of the city by creating artificial islands called *chinampas*. To make a chinampa, they first formed a bed of soil by piling boulders and mud on a mat made of reeds. They tied the mat to wooden posts and drove the posts into the lake. Trees and willows planted around the posts anchored the soil beds.

Today, flower farmers in Xochimilco, near Mexico City, still use chinampas. Tourists enjoy taking boat trips to see these "floating gardens."

Just as impressive as the chinampas were the three causeways that connected Tenochtitlan to the mainland. The causeways were often filled with people traveling to and from the capital. During the rainy season, when the lake waters rose, the causeways also served as dikes.

For tracking time, the Aztecs adapted the Mayan solar and sacred calendars. The 365-day solar calendar was especially useful for farming, since it tracked the seasons. Priests used the sacred 260-day calendar to predict events and to determine "lucky" days for such things as planting crops and going to war.

One of the most famous Aztec artifacts is a calendar called the Sun Stone. Dedicated to the god of the sun, this beautifully carved stone is nearly 12 feet wide and weighs almost 25 tons. The center shows the face of the sun god. Today the Sun Stone is a well-known symbol of Mexico.

Arts and Architecture   The Aztecs practiced a number of arts, including poetry, music, dance, and sculpture. Poets wrote verses to sing the praises of the gods, to tell stories, and to celebrate the natural world. Poetry was highly valued, as you can see in this short poem:

> *I, the singer, I make a poem*
> *That shines like an emerald*
> *A brilliant, precious, and splendid emerald*

Aztec poets sung their poems or recited them to music. Sometimes actors performed them, creating a dramatic show with dialogue and costumes.

Music and dance were important parts of Aztec ceremonies and holidays. People dressed up for these special occasions. Women wore beautiful blouses over their skirts. Men painted their faces, greased their hair, and wore feathered headdresses. The dancers formed large circles and moved to the beat of drums and the sound of rattle bells. The dances had religious meaning, and the dancers had to perform every step correctly. Sometimes thousands of people danced at one time. Even the emperor occasionally joined in.

The Aztecs were also gifted painters and sculptors. Painters used brilliant colors to create scenes showing gods and religious ceremonies. Sculptors fashioned stone statues and relief sculptures on temple walls. They also carved small, lifelike figures of people and animals from rock and semiprecious stones such as jade. In technical craft and beauty, their work surpassed that of earlier Mesoamerican cultures.

In architecture, the Aztecs are remembered most today for their massive stone temples. The Aztecs were unique in building double stairways, like those of the Great Temple in Tenochtitlan. You may remember that the staircases led to two temples, one for the sun god and one for the god of rain. Smaller pyramids nearby had their own temples where sacrificial fires burned before huge statues of the gods.

Language and Writing   Spoken language was raised to an art form in Aztec society. Almost any occasion called for dramatic and often flowery speeches. The rich vocabulary of the Aztec language, Nahuatl, allowed speakers to create new words and describe abstract concepts.

The Aztec system of writing used both glyphs and pictographs. A **pictograph** is a drawing that stands for an idea. For example, the Aztec pictograph for war was a symbol of a shield and a club.

The Aztecs did not have enough pictographs and glyphs to express everything that could be spoken in their language. Instead, scribes used writing to list data or to outline events. Priests used these writings to spark their memories when relating stories from the past.

In the spectacular Aztec pole dance, dancers tie their feet to long cords wound around a tall pole. They jump from the top of the pole, and the cords unwind as the dancers fly around the pole until they reach the ground.

pictograph a written symbol that represents an idea or object

This Inca suspension bridge, over the Apurimac River near Cuzco, is still in use today.

27.4 Achievements of the Incas

Like the Aztecs, the Incas often borrowed and improved upon ideas from other cultures. But the Incas faced a unique challenge in managing the largest empire in the Americas. Maintaining tight control over such a huge area was one of their most impressive accomplishments.

As you read in Chapter 26, the Incas created a large bureaucracy with many layers of authority. The various levels of officials were in charge of larger and larger units within the empire. As more groups were brought into the empire, local leaders were trained in Inca laws and customs.

Through this system, the Incas not only unified their empire but also spread Inca culture throughout their lands. Let's look at some of the Incas' unique cultural achievements.

Science and Technology   The Incas' greatest technological skill was engineering. The best example is their amazing system of roads.

As you learned in Chapter 26, the Incas built roads across the length and width of their empire. To create routes through steep mountain ranges, they carved staircases and gouged tunnels out of rock. They also built **suspension bridges** over rivers. Thick rope cables were anchored at stone towers on either side of the river. Two cables served as rails, while three others held a walkway.

In agriculture, the Incas showed their technological skill by vastly enlarging the system of terraces used by farmers in the Andes. The Incas anchored their steplike terraces with stones and improved the drainage systems in the fields. On some terraces, they planted different crops at elevations where the plants would grow best.

To irrigate the crops, the Incas built canals that brought water to the top of the terrace. From there, the water ran down, level by level. People in South America still grow crops on some Inca terraces.

The Incas also made remarkable advances in medicine. Inca priests, who were in charge of healing, practiced a type of surgery called **trephination**. Usually the patient was an injured warrior. Priests cut into the patient's skull to remove bone fragments that were pressing against the brain. As drastic as this sounds, many people survived the operation.

Arts and Architecture   One of the most important Inca arts was the making of textiles for clothing. The quality and design of a person's clothes were a sign of status. The delicate cloth worn by Inca nobles often featured bright colors and bold geometric patterns. Inca women also made fine feather tunics, or shirts, weaving feathers from jungle birds right into the cloth.

Another important art was the fashioning of objects out of gold. The Incas prized gold, which they called the "sweat of the sun." Gold covered almost every inch inside the Temple of the Sun in the capital city of Cuzco. Goldsmiths also fashioned masks, sculptures, knives, and jewelry.

Music was a major part of Inca life. The Incas played flutes, seashell horns, rattles, drums, and panpipes. Scholars believe that the modern music of the Andes mountain region preserves elements of Inca music.

In architecture, the Incas are known for their huge, durable stone buildings. The massive stones of Inca structures fit together so tightly that a knife blade could not be slipped between them. Inca buildings were sturdy, too—many remain standing today.

Language and Writing The Incas made their language, Quechua, the official language of the empire. As a result, Quechua spread far and wide. About 10 million people in South America still speak it today.

The Incas did not have a written language. As you have learned, they had an ingenious substitute: the knotted sets of strings called *quipus*. The Incas used quipus as memory aids in sending messages and recording information.

Peruvian musicians today use instruments similar to some of those used by the Incas, such as these panpipes and drums.

27.5 Chapter Summary

In this chapter, you explored the cultural achievements of the Maya, Aztecs, and Incas. All three peoples had unique accomplishments in science and technology, arts and architecture, and language and writing.

Some of these achievements are especially noteworthy. The Maya are admired today for their writing system, their calendar, their knowledge of astronomy, and their architecture. The Aztecs are noted for their calendar and their massive temples. The Incas showed great skill in managing their huge empire and in engineering.

In the next unit, you will return to Europe. You will pick up where you left off at the end of Unit 1 to discover what happened in Europe after the Middle Ages.

Civilizations of the Americas Timeline

About 50 B.C.E.
The Maya begin to create
a system of hieroglyphs.

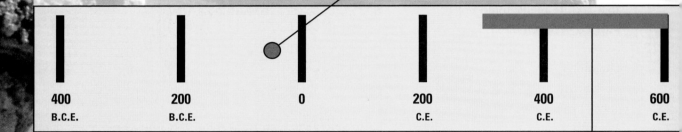

400	200	0	200	400	600
B.C.E.	B.C.E.		C.E.	C.E.	C.E.

About 300 – 900 C.E.
During the Classic period, Mayan social structure is
headed by the halach uinic and includes nobles and
priests, merchants and artisans, peasants, and slaves.

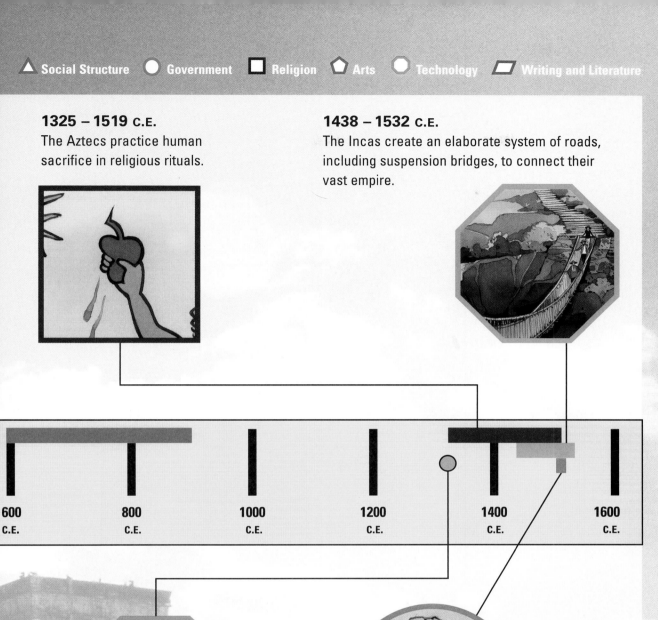

1325 – 1519 C.E.

The Aztecs practice human sacrifice in religious rituals.

1438 – 1532 C.E.

The Incas create an elaborate system of roads, including suspension bridges, to connect their vast empire.

| 600 C.E. | 800 C.E. | 1000 C.E. | 1200 C.E. | 1400 C.E. | 1600 C.E. |

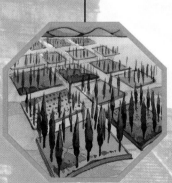

1325 C.E.

The Aztecs begin building their capital, Tenochtitlan, using chinampas.

Early 1500s C.E.

The Incas rule an empire with perhaps 10 million people and stretching over 2,500 miles.

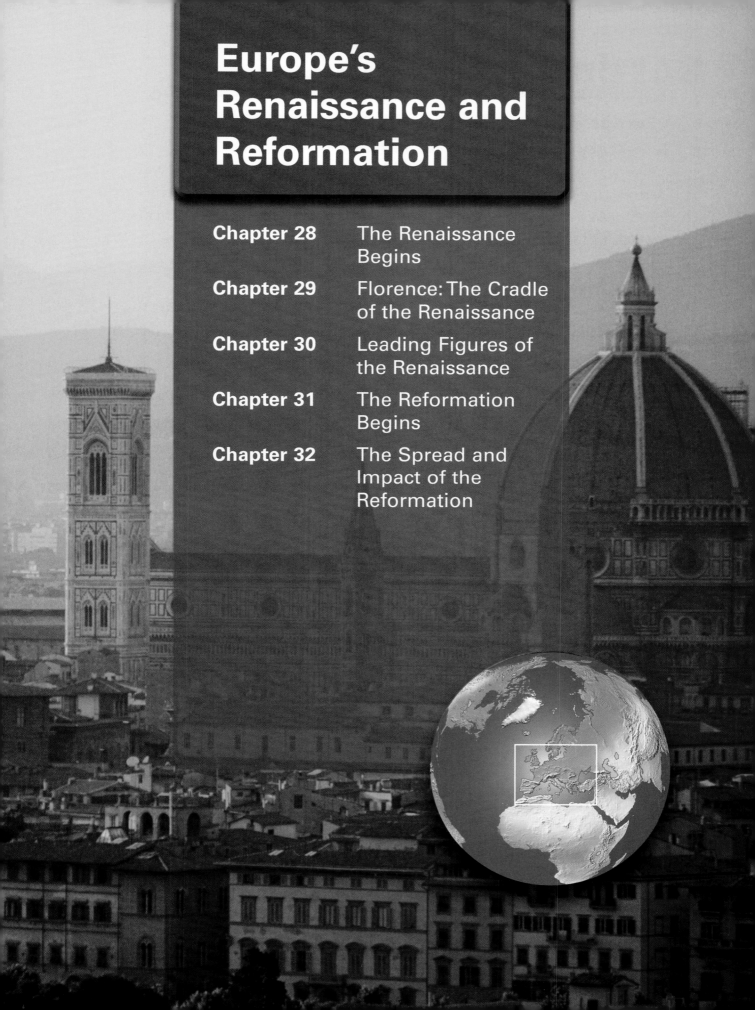

Europe's Renaissance and Reformation

Setting the Stage

Europe's Renaissance and Reformation

In the last unit, you learned about three ancient civilizations in the Americas. Now you'll return to the continent of Europe and learn how western Europe developed after the Middle Ages. You'll explore two important European periods: the Renaissance (1300s to 1600s C.E.) and the Reformation (1500s to 1600s C.E.). Notice that the two periods overlapped during the 1500s and 1600s.

The Renaissance   The word *renaissance* means "rebirth." During Europe's Renaissance, there was a rebirth of interest in art and learning from classical times. People rediscovered the great Greek and Latin writers and read them closely. The ideas in these works inspired artists and scholars to start questioning old ideas and think differently about the world around them.

The Renaissance began in towns and cities in Italy and then spread across Europe. One of the causes of the Renaissance was an increase in trade with the East. In the Late Middle Ages, returning crusaders brought back new goods and ideas from Asia. Trade routes were soon established. Traders brought luxury goods such as silk, spices, and porcelain from Asia and Africa to Europe. Merchants then made these goods available throughout Europe. As trade and commerce expanded, towns and cities grew more important. They became the centers of Renaissance life.

The Reformation   As you learned in your study of the Middle Ages, the Roman Catholic Church was the one Christian church in western Europe in medieval times. In the early 1500s, the ideas of the Renaissance and the new spirit of questioning caused people to start questioning the practices and teachings of the Catholic Church. Eventually, a group of reformers broke away from the church. Called Protestants, they set up new Christian churches throughout northern Europe. This movement became known as the Reformation. The Reformation began in Germany, far from the base of the Catholic Church in Rome, and then spread to other parts of northern Europe.

The Renaissance and Reformation were both periods of sweeping change. Let's start our exploration of these periods with a look at how the Renaissance began.

Europe in the Fifteenth Century

CHAPTER 28

◄ ◄ Raphael painted this Renaissance mural,
The School of Athens, around 1510 C.E.

The Renaissance Begins

28.1 Introduction

Toward the end of the Middle Ages, a great flowering of culture called the **Renaissance** began in Italy and spread throughout Europe. In this chapter, you will learn what the Renaissance was and how it began.

Renaissance is a French word that means "rebirth." The Renaissance got its name from a rebirth in interest in **classical art** and **learning** that took place from the 1300s through the 1500s C.E. (*Classical* refers to the cultures of ancient Greek and Rome.) Although there was no sudden break with the Middle Ages, the Renaissance changed many aspects of people's lives over time.

You may recall from Unit 1 that medieval European society was based on feudalism. Most people lived on feudal manors in the countryside. The Roman Catholic Church encouraged people to think more about life after death than about daily life on Earth. Except for the clergy, few people were educated.

By the Late Middle Ages, changes were occurring that helped pave the way for the Renaissance. Trade and commerce increased, and cities grew larger and wealthier. Newly wealthy merchants and bankers supported the growth of the arts and learning. A renewed interest in classical culture started a flood of new ideas. Greek and Roman examples inspired new styles of architecture, new approaches to the arts, and new ways of thinking.

Beginning in Italy, a philosophy called **humanism** developed. Humanists believed in the worth and potential of all individuals. They tried to balance religious faith with belief in the power of the human mind. Humanists took a fresh interest in human society and the natural world. This way of thinking contributed to the burst of creativity during the Renaissance.

In this chapter, you'll explore how the Renaissance differed from the Middle Ages and classical times. Then you'll look at some changes in European life that led to the Renaissance.

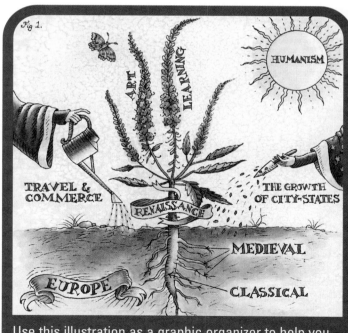

Use this illustration as a graphic organizer to help you think about the Renaissance as a flowering plant that was fed by trade and commerce, the growth of city-states, and the ideas of humanism.

28.2 What Was the Renaissance?

The Renaissance began in Italy in the mid 1300s and spread to other parts of Europe in the 1400s and 1500s. Let's look more closely at this "great rebirth" of interest in classical art and learning. Then we'll use art to explore the link between the Renaissance and the classical world.

Renewed Interest in the Classical World The Renaissance began with the rediscovery of the classical world of ancient Greece and Rome. After the fall of Rome in the fifth century C.E., classical culture was never entirely forgotten. The Roman Catholic Church helped keep knowledge of ancient times alive by copying documents that survived from the classical period. Still, this knowledge reached relatively few people during most of the Middle Ages.

In the Late Middle Ages, merchants and crusaders brought back goods and ideas from the East, including classical learning that had been preserved in the Byzantine Empire. Europeans also read classical works that came to them by way of Muslim scholars.

This flow of ideas led to a rediscovery of Greek and Roman culture. Scholars started collecting and reading ancient manuscripts from monasteries. Artists and architects studied classical statues and buildings. The renewed interest in classical culture led to the great flowering of art and learning that we call the Renaissance.

Exploring the Rebirth of Classical Ideas Through Art
We can trace the link between the classical world and the Renaissance by looking at art. Let's explore some of the characteristics of art from classical, medieval, and Renaissance times.

Classical Art The classical period lasted from about 500 B.C.E. to 500 C.E. The classical artists of Greece and Rome created sculptures, pottery, murals, and mosaics. The purpose of much of their art was to show the importance of people and leaders, as well as gods and goddesses. Here are additional characteristics of classical art:

- Artists valued balance and harmony.
- Figures were lifelike but often idealized (more perfect than in real life).
- Figures were nude or draped in togas (robes).
- Bodies looked active, and motion was believable.
- Faces were calm and without emotion.
- Scenes showed either heroic figures or real people doing tasks from daily life.
- In paintings, there was little background or sense of **perspective** (for example, showing people and objects bigger or smaller to make them look closer or farther away).

perspective the appearance of distance or depth on a flat surface, as in a painting

This example of classical art was created in 450 B.C.E. A Roman statue of a discus thrower, it celebrates the classical ideals of balance and power.

Medieval Art   The medieval period lasted from about 500 to 1300 C.E. Medieval artists created stained glass windows, sculptures, illuminated manuscripts, paintings, and tapestries. The purpose of much medieval art was to teach religion to people who could not read or write. Here are additional characteristics of medieval art:

- Most art was religious, showing Jesus, saints, people from the Bible, and so on.
- Important figures in paintings were shown as larger than others around them.
- Figures looked stiff, with little sense of movement.
- Figures were fully dressed in stiff-looking clothing.
- Faces were serious and showed little feeling.
- Painted figures were two-dimensional, or flat.
- Paint colors were bright.
- Backgrounds were mostly one color, often gold.

This example of medieval art was created for a church in France in 110 C.E. The sculpture shows Jesus sending his apostles out to preach.

Renaissance Art   The Renaissance lasted from the 1300s to the early 1600s. Renaissance artists created sculptures, murals, drawings, and paintings. The aim of much Renaissance art was to show the importance of people and nature, not just religion. Here are additional characteristics of Renaissance art:

- Artists showed religious and nonreligious scenes.
- Art reflected a great interest in nature.
- Figures were lifelike and three-dimensional, reflecting an increasing knowledge of anatomy.
- Bodies looked active and were shown moving.
- Figures were either nude or clothed.
- Scenes showed real people doing everyday tasks.
- Faces expressed what people were thinking.
- Colors were shown responding to light.
- Paintings were often symmetrical (balanced, with the right and left sides having similar or identical elements).
- Full backgrounds showed perspective.

This example of Renaissance art is a mural titled *The School of Athens*. It was painted by Raphael around 1510. Ancient Greek philosophers, such as Plato and Aristotle, are shown surrounded by some of the Renaissance artists they inspired centuries later.

If you compare these lists, you can see that Renaissance artists were inspired more by classical art than medieval art. Like classical artists, Renaissance painters and sculptors depicted subjects that were not always religious. They tried to show people as lifelike and engaged in everyday activities. They also tried to capture the way things look in the real world.

Renaissance art reflects a rebirth of interest in the classical world. What changes brought about this revival of classical culture? Let's find out.

28.3 The Growth of Trade and Commerce

One reason for the flowering of culture during the Renaissance was the growth of trade and commerce. Trade brought new ideas as well as goods into Europe. A bustling economy created prosperous cities and new classes of people who had the wealth to support art and learning.

Starting in the 11th century, the Crusades strengthened contacts between western Europe and Byzantine and Muslim cultures. Traders brought goods and ideas from the East that helped to reawaken interest in classical culture. In the 13th century, the Mongol conquests in Asia made it safer for traders to travel along the Silk Road to China. The tales of the Italian traveler Marco Polo sparked even greater interest in the East. Food, art, and such luxury goods as silk and spices moved along the trade routes linking Europe to Africa and Asia.

Italian cities like Venice and Genoa were centrally located on the trade routes that linked the rest of western Europe with the East. They became bustling trading centers that attracted traders, merchants, and customers. So did cities in the north like Bruges and Brussels. Trading ships carried goods to England, Scandinavia, and present-day Russia by way of the English Channel and the Baltic and North Seas. Towns along the routes connecting southern and northern

This 15th-century French illustration shows the exchange of goods and money in a Renaissance town.

Europe, such as Cologne and Mainz in Germany, provided inns and other services for traveling merchants.

The increase in trade led to a new kind of economy. During the Middle Ages, people bartered, or traded goods for other goods. During the Renaissance, people began using coins to buy goods, creating a money economy. Coins came from many places, so moneychangers were needed to convert one type of currency into another.

As a result of all this activity, craftspeople, merchants, and bankers became more important in society. Craftspeople produced goods that merchants traded all over Europe. Bankers exchanged currency, loaned money to merchants and rulers, and financed their own businesses.

Some merchants and bankers grew very rich. With their abundant wealth, they could afford to make their cities more beautiful. Wealthy **patrons** commissioned (ordered and paid for) new buildings and art. They also helped to found (start) universities. Prosperous Renaissance cities grew into flourishing educational and cultural centers.

patron a person who supports the arts or other activities by supplying money for them

28.4 The Influence of Italian City-States

The Renaissance began in northern and central Italy. One reason it began there was the prosperity of Italian **city-states**.

In the Late Middle Ages, most of western Europe was made up of fiefs ruled by nobles. Above the nobles were monarchs. In Italy, however, growing towns demanded self-rule and developed into independent city-states. Each city-state consisted of a powerful city and the surrounding towns and countryside.

The Italian city-states conducted their own trade, collected their own taxes, and made their own laws. Some city-states, such as Florence, were **republics** that were governed by elected councils. Council members included commoners as well as nobles.

In theory, the power in republics belonged to the people. In fact, it often lay in the hands of rich merchants. During the Middle Ages, guilds of craftspeople and merchants became very powerful. During the Renaissance, groups of guild members (called *boards*) often ruled Italian city-states. Boards were supposed to change members often. However, wealthy families often gained long-term control. As a result, some city-states were ruled by a single family, like the fabulously rich Medicis in Florence.

Trade made the Italian city-states wealthy. Italy's central Mediterranean location placed its cities in the middle of the trade routes that connected distant places with the rest of western Europe. People from all over Europe came to northern Italy to buy, sell, and do their banking.

Some Italian city-states developed specializations. Florence became a center for cloth making and banking. Milan produced metal goods and armor. The port city of Genoa was a trading center for ivory and gold from northern Africa. Venice, the most powerful city-state, had hundreds of ships that controlled the trade routes in the Mediterranean Sea. Silk, spices, and perfume from Asia flowed into Venice.

The city-states' wealth encouraged a boom in art and learning. Rich families paid for the creation of statues, paintings, beautiful buildings, and elegant avenues. They built new centers of learning, such as universities and hospitals. From the city-states of Italy, Renaissance ideas spread to the rest of Europe.

This is a late-15th-century map of Florence, one of Italy's most powerful city-states. Notice the man on a hill in the lower right corner; the artist drew himself looking over Florence.

city-state an independent state consisting of a city and its surrounding territory

republic a form of government in which people elect representatives to rule in their name

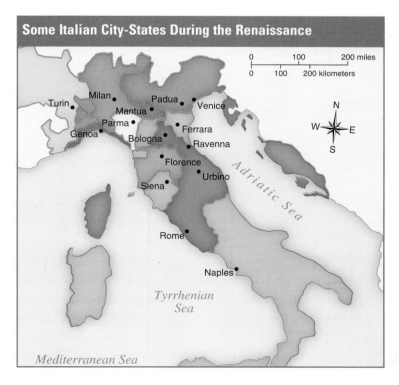

Some Italian City-States During the Renaissance

Humanist scholars in the 15th century spent time reading, studying, and writing about classical culture.

28.5 The Growth of Humanism

The interest in learning during the Renaissance was spurred by humanism. This way of thinking sought to balance religious faith with an emphasis on individual dignity and an interest in nature and human society.

Humanism first arose in Italy as a result of the renewed interest in classical culture. Many early humanists eagerly hunted for ancient Greek and Roman books, coins, and other artifacts that could help them learn about the classical world.

One of the first humanists was an Italian poet named Francesco Petrarch. Petrarch especially loved old books. He searched for them all over Europe and encouraged his friends to bring him any they found. Eventually, he created a large collection of ancient Latin and Greek writings, which he made available to other scholars.

Scholars from all over Europe traveled to Italy to learn about the new ideas inspired by classical culture. They studied such subjects as art, architecture, government, and language. They read classical history and poetry. They began to ask probing questions. What did classical artists find most beautiful about the human body? How did the Romans construct their buildings?

In their studies of classical culture, humanists discovered a new way of looking at life. They began to create a philosophy based on the importance and dignity of each individual. Humanists believed that all people had the ability to control their own lives and achieve greatness. In education, they stressed study of the **humanities**—a group of subjects that focused on human life and culture. These subjects included grammar, rhetoric (the study of persuasive language), history, poetry, and ethics (the study of moral values and behavior).

humanities areas of study that focus on human life and culture, such as history, literature, and ethics

Humanists tried to put ancient ideas into practice. Architects, for example, studied Greek and Roman ruins. Then they designed buildings with pillars, arches, and courtyards like those of classical buildings.

The humanists did not simply imitate the past. They also tried to improve on the work of the Greeks and Romans. In universities, scholars began to teach methods of observation and experimentation. Renaissance scientists proposed new ideas about stars and planets. Artists and students of medicine closely studied human anatomy. Poets wrote about religious subjects and everyday experiences such as love. Writers produced works of history and studies of politics.

The influence of classical ideals changed ideas about government. Humanists separated the state and its right to rule from the church. In doing so, they helped lay the foundation for modern thinking about politics and government.

Humanist ideals also affected people's thinking about social standing. In feudal times, people were born into a certain status in society. If someone was born a peasant, he or she would always have less status than a noble. Renaissance thinkers prized individual achievement more than a person's class or family. This emphasis on individualism was an enormous shift from medieval thinking.

The humanists' new ideas sometimes brought them into conflict with the Catholic Church. The church taught that laws were made by God and that those who broke them were sinful. It encouraged people to follow its teachings without question in order to save their souls. For the church, life after death was more important than life on Earth. In contrast, humanists believed that people should use their minds to question everything. Most tried to balance religious faith and its emphasis on the afterlife with an active interest in daily life. Some directly challenged teachings that were dear to the church. An Italian humanist, Giordano Bruno, paid for his ideas by being burned at the stake.

Francesco Petrarch is considered the founder of Italian Renaissance humanism. A well-known poet, he wears a laurel wreath in this portrait to symbolize his crowning as poet laureate in Rome in 1341.

28.6 Chapter Summary

In this chapter, you explored the beginnings of the Renaissance. The Renaissance was a flowering of art and learning that was inspired by a rediscovery of classical culture. It began in Italy and spread throughout Europe.

Several factors contributed to the Renaissance. The growth of trade and commerce created prosperous cities and classes of people with the wealth to support education and the arts. Italian city-states helped spread Renaissance ideas. The new philosophy of humanism spurred interest in learning and fresh ways of thinking. In the next chapter, you will explore some of the advances that came out of the Renaissance.

CHAPTER 29

Florence: The Cradle of the Renaissance

29.1 Introduction

In the last chapter, you learned that the Renaissance began in Italy. In this chapter, you will visit the Italian city of Florence to learn about a number of **advances** that were made during the Renaissance.

Florence is located on the Arno River, just north of the center of Italy. The city is often called the "cradle of the Renaissance." Between 1300 and 1600, it was home to some of the greatest artists and thinkers of the Renaissance.

Renaissance Florence was a beautiful city. One of its most notable buildings was the *duomo,* or cathedral, of Santa Maria del Fiore. The domed cathedral was the center of the city's religious life. Nearby was the Palazzo Vecchio (Old Palace). This building was the headquarters of the city government. The grand Palazzo Medici was the home of Florence's ruling family, the Medicis. A more humble house was the Casa di Dante (Dante's House). It was the home of Italy's most famous poet.

During Renaissance times, Florence was the banking center of Europe. People from around Europe came to the Mercato Nuovo (New Market) to trade their coins for florins, the gold coins of Florence. Another busy spot was the Ponte Vecchio (Old Bridge). This beautiful bridge spanned the Arno River and was lined with the shops of fine jewelers and goldsmiths.

Florence's wealth helped to make it a cultural leader during the Renaissance. In this chapter, you will visit several places in the city to learn about Renaissance advances in a number of fields. You'll explore Renaissance **architecture** and **engineering, painting, sculpture, literature,** and **science** and **mathematics**. You'll also find out about Florentine **politics** and **commerce** and **trade**.

Use this map as a graphic organizer to help you explore various aspects of Renaissance life and advances through sites in the city of Florence.

29.2 The City of Florence

Florence was Italy's leading cultural center during the Renaissance. The city was the birthplace of the great poet Dante Alighieri. The famed painter and sculptor Michelangelo grew up there. So did the brilliant thinker and artist Leonardo da Vinci. Other Florentines, such as the sculptor Donatello, also made their mark on the Renaissance.

What made Florence so special? One answer is its location. As you remember from the last chapter, in Renaissance times Italy was divided into city-states. Florence was one of these city-states. The city's location on the Arno River made it an important center for trade and commerce. Florence became the hub of woolen-cloth trading for all of Europe. About 100,000 residents lived inside the city walls.

Renaissance Florence was dominated by a single family, the Medicis. The Medicis acquired their wealth through Florence's major industry: banking. In the early 14th century, Florence became Europe's banking center.

The banking and wool trades created wealth that supported intense cultural activity in Florence. The city and its rich residents could afford to be patrons of talented artists and

The Palazzo Vecchio housed the government of Florence. Local authorities wanted to awe people with their power and also have a place of safety, so this building was made to look like a fortress or castle.

thinkers. The Medicis, for example, spent lavish sums on art. Their home was a gathering place for artists, philosophers, and poets. Michelangelo once lived for a time in the Medici household, where he mingled with other artists.

Over time, the work produced by Florentines inspired still more creative activity. People learned from one another, and they sometimes competed to produce even greater work. Florentines were also influenced by ideas from other places. The city drew travelers from many parts of the world. Some came to do business. Some came to study art with Florence's master artists. Others came to learn at the city's schools and libraries. These visitors brought new ideas, goods, and technologies that enlivened the city.

Florentines were also inspired by the freedom of ideas that was at the core of humanism. Recall that humanists prized the individual and tried to look with fresh eyes at nature and human society. You'll see the influence of humanism throughout this chapter as you study examples of Renaissance advances.

29.3 Advances in Architecture and Engineering

You have learned that the humanist scholars of the Renaissance were influenced by classical ideas. So too were architects and builders. Renaissance architects studied Greek and Roman ruins, and they modeled their own buildings on what they learned. They were particularly attracted to rounded arches, straight columns, and domed roofs.

Architects also added their own ideas to classical building styles. During the Renaissance, wealthy families built private townhouses known as *palazzi* (palaces). Many had shops on the ground floor and homes above. Most palazzi were built around a private courtyard, which might contain statues and other works of art.

Public spaces were often influenced by humanist ideals. For example, humanists valued good citizenship. Architects designed public buildings where citizens could interact in settings that were grand yet welcoming. They used Roman-inspired, roofed porches called *loggia* to join buildings and create outdoor plazas.

Advances in engineering made new kinds of architecture possible. For instance, one of the most impressive architectural feats of the Renaissance was the great cathedral, the Duomo di Santa Maria del Fiore. Florentines started building this eight-sided cathedral in 1296, but they had to leave an opening for the dome. At the time, they didn't know how to build a large enough dome that would not collapse. It took a Renaissance architect, Filippo Brunelleschi, to solve the problem.

The dome of the Duomo di Santa Maria del Fiore rises from the octagonal (eight sided) cathedral. Its design is one of the great engineering achievements of the Renaissance.

Brunelleschi had studied ancient ruins in Rome. He had also learned about the mathematics involved in creating buildings. The dome he designed and built for the cathedral took true engineering genius. It used no internal support beams or columns. Instead, eight huge stone arches met at the top of the dome and leaned against each other. Hoops of iron, wood, and brick wrapped around the arches, keeping them in place. Brunelleschi invented machines called **hoists** to raise building materials and food to workers at the top of the dome as they were building it.

The magnificent dome was finished in 1436. It stood more than 300 feet above the city. It still stands today, over 500 years later. From its top you can see most of the city of Florence.

hoist a mechanical device used to lift people or heavy objects

29.4 Advances in Painting

Wealthy patrons made Renaissance Florence a thriving center of art. The Medicis spent huge sums of money on fine palaces, paintings, and statues. The Palazzo Medici was filled with works of art that were commissioned by the family.

Patrons like the Medicis created opportunities for talented painters, who made a number of advances in style and technique. As you learned in the last chapter, Renaissance painters were influenced by the renewed interest in classical culture and the spread of humanism. They wanted to depict real people who were posed in lifelike ways and who showed feelings. They also wanted to include realistic backgrounds. The result was a very different style from the more flat, rigid painting of the Middle Ages.

Renaissance painters were the first to use techniques of perspective. This is Botticelli's *Adoration of the Magi*. Notice the sense of distance, or depth, in the painting.

One key advance made by Renaissance painters was the discovery of perspective. Painters use perspective to create the appearance of depth on a flat surface. Renaissance artists used several techniques to indicate depth. One was the size of objects. The smaller a painted object, the farther away it appears to be. The larger an object, the closer it appears to be. Painters also learned that a feeling of depth could be created by lines that came closer together as they receded into the distance. They discovered that careful shading could make figures and objects look three-dimensional. *Adoration of the Magi,* a famous painting by Sandro Botticelli, shows some of these techniques.

Science and mathematics helped artists make other advances. The Florentine artist Masaccio used geometry to figure out how to divide the space in a painting to make scenes appear more as they would in real life. Leonardo da Vinci and others studied anatomy. They observed bodies and how they moved. Their studies helped them to portray the human body more realistically.

Renaissance science also gave painters new materials, such as oil-based paints, to work with. Oil paint was made by mixing powdered pigments (colors) with linseed oil. This type of paint was thicker and dried more slowly than the older, egg-based paint. Oil paint also allowed artists to paint over previous work and to show details and texture in new ways.

29.5 Advances in Sculpture

Like painters, Renaissance sculptors were influenced by the humanist interest in realism. They were also inspired by ancient Roman statues dug up from ruins. Sculptors began carving figures that looked like real people and showed emotions.

For the first time since the days of ancient Greece and Rome, sculptors made freestanding statues that could be viewed in the round. This was very different from the relief sculptures of medieval times. The new statues caused quite a sensation. They seemed to symbolize the humanist ideals of independence and individuality.

Donatello, a Florentine, was one of the first sculptors to use the new, more lifelike style. His work expressed personality and mood. A good example is his statue of David, the young warrior in the Bible story of David and Goliath. In the 1500s, Giorgio Vasari, an architect and painter, wrote that Donatello's *David* is "so natural…it is almost impossible…to believe it was not molded on the living form." This statue is thought to be the first life-size nude statue since classical times.

Donatello's work influenced Florence's other great sculptor, Michelangelo. This famous artist is renowned both for his painting and his sculpture. He was also a talented poet and architect. Of all these arts, he preferred sculpture because it seemed to bring his subjects to life.

Michelangelo created his own majestic statue of David. It may be the world's most widely admired sculpture. Carved in white marble, Michelangelo's *David* stands about 17 feet tall. It is famed as an ideal of male beauty, yet it reflects humanist ideas. David's expression shows the concentration and tension of a real youth on the verge of battle.

Michelangelo's *David* was installed in the Piazza della Signoria, the plaza in front of the Palazzo Vecchio. It became the prized expression of Renaissance genius in Florence.

Michelangelo had an enormous influence on other artists. Giorgio Vasari was one of his followers. He wrote, "What a happy age we live in! And how fortunate are our craftsmen, who have been given light and vision by Michelangelo."

Moses (above) by Michelangelo sits at the tomb of Pope Julius II in Rome. Michelangelo's *David* is perhaps the most admired sculpture in the world.

29.6 Advances in Literature

Literature, like other Renaissance art forms, was changed by the rebirth of interest in classical ideas and the rise of humanism. During the Italian Renaissance, the topics that people wrote about changed. So did their style of writing and the language in which they wrote.

In medieval times, literature usually dealt with religious topics. Most writers used a formal, impersonal style. Most Italian writers wrote in Latin. Their work could be read only by a few highly educated people.

In contrast, Renaissance writers were interested in individual experience and in the world around them. Writing about **secular,** or non-religious, topics became more common. Writers used a more individual style, and they expressed thoughts and feelings about life. By the end of the Renaissance, most writers were writing in their own dialect instead of Latin. As a result, far more people could read their work.

Dante Alighieri, a native of Florence, was the first well-known writer to create literature in his native language. His best-known work, *The Divine Comedy,* was written in the early 1300s. This long poem describes Dante's imaginary journey through the places where Christians believed that souls went in the afterlife. With the spirit of the ancient Roman poet Virgil as his guide, Dante witnesses the torments of souls condemned to Inferno, or hell. Virgil also takes him to Purgatory, a place between heaven and hell where souls await entry into heaven. Then a beautiful woman named Beatrice shows him Paradise, or heaven.

Like other humanist art, *The Divine Comedy* highlights strong emotions and the experiences of individuals. Dante's poem is a social commentary, too. It is filled with real people. The inhabitants of hell included people Dante disapproved of. People he admired appeared in heaven.

Dante's work became a model for other Renaissance writers. He strongly influenced two important Florentine writers, Petrarch and Boccaccio. They described people's lives with a new intensity of feeling. Like Dante, they wrote using the local dialect, so their words touched many more people.

secular relating to earthly life rather than to religion or spiritual matters

Dante, a Renaissance writer in Florence, wrote a long poem called *The Divine Comedy.* Dante is painted here with scenes of heaven and hell as described in his poem.

29.7 Advances in Science and Mathematics

The Renaissance was not just a time of progress in the arts. Scholars and others also made great advances in science and mathematics.

Before the Renaissance, most of what people believed about the natural world was based on ideas in ancient Greek and Roman texts. As the humanist spirit took hold, people started questioning old ideas. They began carefully observing the world around them. Instead of relying on old books and theories, scientists began to perform experiments. They analyzed the results using mathematics and logic. This approach to research changed the study of science.

One of the most creative Renaissance thinkers was Leonardo da Vinci. Leonardo was an artist, a scientist, and an inventor. He studied under art masters in Florence and did his early work there. It is said that he was often to be found thinking and sketching at his favorite church, Orsanmichele.

Leonardo was endlessly curious. He did not accept anything as true until he had proved it himself. In his notebooks, he sketched and wrote about an amazing variety of topics. He wrote about geometry, engineering, sound, motion, and architecture. He studied anatomy, including the **circulation** of blood and the workings of the eye. He learned about the effects of the moon on Earth's tides. He was the first person to draw maps from a bird's-eye view (above the ground). As an inventor, he designed bridges, weapons, and many other machines. Among his many farsighted ideas was an underwater diving suit.

Other Italian scientists and mathematicians made breakthroughs as well. Girolamo Cardano solved complex equations in algebra. Cardano, who was interested in gambling, also did pioneering work in probability, the science of chance. Galileo Galilei did important experiments concerning gravity. He proved that a heavier object and a lighter object fall at the same rate. If the two objects are dropped from the same height, they reach the ground at the same time. Galileo also built the first telescope that could be used to look into space. He used his telescope to discover sunspots and the moons of the planet Jupiter. By emphasizing observation and experiment, Galileo and other Renaissance scientists paved the way for modern science.

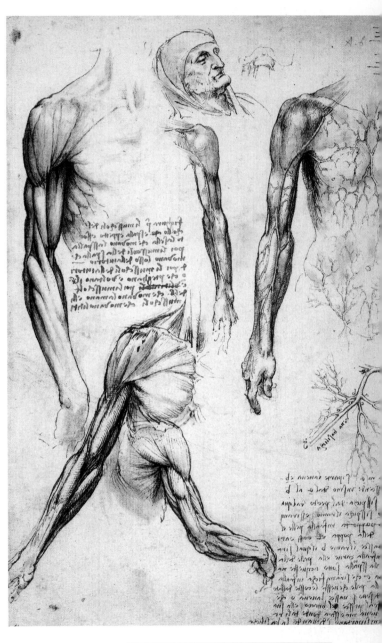

Leonardo da Vinci studied many things, including human anatomy. These sketches of the muscles of the arm are from his notebooks.

circulation the movement of blood through the body

29.8 Florentine Politics

The local government of Florence was housed in the Palazzo Vecchio. Like other Italian city-states, Florence was ruled by a governing board. As you learned in Chapter 28, however, these boards were often controlled by rich families. The powerful Medici family controlled Florence for nearly three centuries.

The Medicis maintained their power in a number of ways. They built palaces and kept a strong military. They were involved in all aspects of life in the city. They were great supporters of artists, writers, and musicians. The Medicis also defeated enemies who plotted against the family or even to murder some of its members.

One of the most powerful members of the Medicis was Lorenzo the Magnificent. A leading patron of art and scholarship, Lorenzo ruled Florence for more than 20 years, from 1469 until his death in 1492. Two years later, a revolution forced the Medicis into temporary exile. In 1512, the family regained power.

A Florentine statesman and historian, Niccolo Machiavelli, watched these struggles for power. During the Medicis' exile, he reorganized the city's defenses. He also served as a diplomat and spent time observing the actions of other Italian rulers.

Machiavelli drew on his experiences in a famous book called *The Prince*. The book was a frank account of how politics and government really worked. Machiavelli advised rulers to make their states strong by doing what worked best, rather than by being good or moral. He said that they should even lie if it helped them to rule. In his view, the end, or purpose, justified the means (the actions taken to achieve a certain purpose). Rulers, he wrote, should be feared rather than loved.

The Prince seems to contradict humanist ideals about people's goodness. Its cold realism shocked many readers. Yet in other ways the book shows the influence of humanist ideas. It was the product of one individual's careful observation and thinking. It was concerned with how things really worked in the world. It also separated ideas about government from religion. In this respect, *The Prince* was a very modern work.

Florins were the most valuable coins in all of Europe during the Renaissance.

The Procession of the Magi is a fresco from one of the Medici family's palaces in Florence.

29.9 Florentine Commerce and Trade

As you have learned, one reason that Florence became a cultural center was the wealth that trade and commerce brought to the city. Let's conclude our visit to Renaissance Florence with a look at this part of the city's life.

The economy of Florence was unusually flexible. Its first great industry was woolen-cloth making, but people often worked in several kinds of business. The owner of a cloth factory might also deal in banking and real estate. A grain dealer might also be a lawyer. People often belonged to several of Florence's guilds at once.

The shift to a money economy during the Renaissance helped create a thriving banking industry in Florence. The Medicis, for example, started out as merchants and moneylenders. Over time, Florence became Europe's banking hub. The Medicis became one of the wealthiest families in Italy, and Florence became richer than the largest kingdoms in Europe. Popes and kings borrowed money from its 80 banks.

There were two market centers in the city. At the Mercato Vecchio (Old Market), people bought everyday items like vegetables, fruits, bread, fish, meat, medicine, and shoes. The Mercato Vecchio was crowded, noisy, and smelly. Still, people from all over Europe came there to buy and sell goods.

The Mercato Nuovo (New Market) was built in the mid 1500s as a center for the cloth and banking industries. City officials banned food and weapons from this new market. They wanted it to be clean and orderly as a sign that commerce was highly regarded in Florence.

The Mercato Nuovo became one of the largest financial marketplaces in Europe. People traveled from far and wide to get loans or to convert their money into florins, which could be used anywhere in Europe.

Florence's Mercato Nuovo (New Market) was much cleaner and nicer than the city's Mercato Vecchio (Old Market). The Mercato Nuovo represented Florence's high status in Europe as a center of commerce.

29.10 Chapter Summary

In this chapter, you visited Florence to learn about Renaissance advances in a number of fields. You saw how humanism influenced artists and thinkers like Michelangelo and Leonardo da Vinci. You also learned about Machiavelli's political ideas and Florentine trade and commerce.

In the next chapter, you will learn how Renaissance ideas spread from Italy across Europe. Then you will meet 10 leading figures of the Renaissance—people who changed the world with their ideas.

CHAPTER 30

◄ ◄ Renaissance artist Albrecht Dürer painted this self-portrait at the age of 26.

Leading Figures of the Renaissance

30.1 Introduction

In the last chapter, you visited Florence to explore some of the major advances of the Renaissance. Now you will learn how Renaissance ideas spread from Italy across Europe. Then you will study the lives and work of 10 leading figures of the Renaissance.

From the 14th through the 16th centuries, Europe crackled with energy. Trade and commerce boomed. Cities grew. Artists and writers experimented with their crafts and created wonderful works of art and literature. New ways of thinking led to inventions and scientific discoveries. Rulers and wealthy patrons supported the work of artists, scientists, and explorers.

Why was there so much creative energy during the Renaissance? One reason was the Renaissance ideal that people should be educated in many areas. People who studied art or music, for example, were also interested in science. To this day we still use the phrase "Renaissance person" to describe someone who is skilled and knowledgeable in many fields.

You have already met the best example of this Renaissance ideal: Leonardo da Vinci. Leonardo trained as a painter, but he was also a scientist, engineer, musician, and architect. He designed fortifications, waterways, and machines. He studied and drew plants, animals, and people. In his notebooks he sketched ideas for inventions that were far ahead of his time.

Leonardo is one of the 10 Renaissance **artists, scientists, monarchs,** and **writers** you will study in this chapter. First, though, let's look at how the Renaissance spread throughout Europe from its birthplace in Italy.

Use a bust and pedestal as a graphic organizer to help you remember what you learn about leading figures of the Renaissance.

The Renaissance spread from Italy throughout Europe. In Flanders, an early painter of the northern Renaissance was Jan van Eyck, shown here in his studio.

30.2 The Renaissance Spreads Through Europe

As you have learned, the Renaissance began in Italy. From there it spread to France, Germany, Flanders (modern-day Belgium), Holland, England, and Spain.

Renaissance ideas were spread through trade, travel, and education. Italy was the gateway to Europe for much of the trade from Asia, Africa, and the Greek-speaking cities of the east. Traders moved through Italy to the rest of Europe, bringing a rich flow of new ideas along with their goods.

Visitors to Italy also helped spread Renaissance ideas. People from all over Europe traveled to Italy to learn as well as to trade. Scholars went to study humanism. Artists studied Italian painting and sculpture to learn new styles and techniques.

When these travelers returned home, many of them founded art schools and universities. Artists taught others what they had learned in Italy. Scholars began to teach the new ideas of experimentation and logical thinking.

The spread of ideas was made even easier by the invention of the printing press. This machine presses inked type or plates onto paper to create many copies of a work. Recall from your study of China that the Chinese had learned to make paper and to print using wooden blocks. Gradually, knowledge of papermaking and examples of Chinese printing blocks reached Europe.

In about 1450, a German named Johannes Gutenberg dramatically improved on existing printing methods. He invented a printing press that used movable type—characters that could be rearranged and used over again on other printing jobs. Unlike the Chinese, who used wooden blocks for printing, Gutenberg cast his type in metal.

Before Gutenberg's invention, most books were written and copied by hand. It could take four or five months to copy a 200-page book. The new press could produce 300 pages in a single day. As a result, books and short works called *pamphlets* could be made much more quickly and cheaply.

The number of printers in Europe soon increased rapidly. People used printed matter to spread new ideas, discoveries, and inventions. And since printed material was more widely available, more people learned to read.

As new ideas spread, people in more countries were swept up in the spirit of the Renaissance. Let's look now at 10 leading Renaissance figures and their accomplishments.

After Gutenberg's invention of the printing press, print shops such as this one created books and pamphlets quickly and easily.

30.3 Michelangelo, Italian Sculptor and Painter

You met Michelangelo (1475– 1564) in Chapter 29. Michelangelo was born in a small village near Florence. He grew up to become one of the greatest painters and sculptors in history.

Personality and Training

Historians say that Michelangelo had a difficult childhood. His mother died when he was six years old. His father was stern and demanding. Perhaps this troubled early life contributed to Michelangelo's famously bad temper. Although he was very religious, he was known to use fierce words when he was angry. He was also intensely ambitious.

When Michelangelo was 13, he became an apprentice to a painter in Florence. At 15, he began studying under a sculptor who worked for the powerful Medici family. Michelangelo lived for a time in the Medici household. There he met many leading thinkers, artists, and writers.

Talents and Achievements

Michelangelo was amazingly gifted in both sculpture and painting. His art combines ideal beauty with emotional expressiveness. To other artists, Michelangelo's talent seemed almost godlike.

Michelangelo's sculptures show his amazing talent for bringing life to figures carved from giant blocks of marble. When he was just 24, he carved his famous *Pieta*. A pieta is a depiction of Mary, the mother of Jesus, mourning over her crucified son. Michelangelo's *Pieta* shows Mary tenderly holding the body of Jesus on her lap.

Two other magnificent sculptures by Michelangelo are his *David* and *Moses*. As you learned in Chapter 29, *David* is 17 feet tall. The statue combines great beauty with the intense look of a youth who is about to go into battle. Michelangelo's *Moses* is also a strong, powerful figure. In the Bible, Moses receives the Ten Commandments from God. Meanwhile his people, the Hebrews, are worshiping false gods. The expression of Michelangelo's *Moses* is a mixture of compassion and anger.

Michelangelo is perhaps best known for painting the ceiling of the Sistine Chapel, the pope's **chapel** in Rome. Michelangelo labored for almost four years on a high platform to complete this work. He covered the curved ceiling with brilliantly colored scenes from the Bible. The scenes contain over 300 figures and continue to awe visitors to Rome today.

In this famous scene from the ceiling of the Sistine Chapel, God is reaching out to touch the finger of Adam, the first man in the Bible story of creation. Adam seems to be coming to life under God's touch.

chapel a room, sometimes inside a larger church, set aside for prayer and worship

Michelangelo

This is one of many portraits of Emperor Charles V that Titian painted during his years as court painter of Italy.

Titian

30.4 Titian, Italian Painter

Titian (about 1488–1576) was born in a village in the Italian Alps. The exact date of his birth is uncertain. Early in life, Titian's talent took him to the wealthy society of Venice. He became the city's greatest Renaissance painter.

Personality and Training   As a boy, Titian was sent to Venice to train with famous painters. As a young man he worked with an artist named Giorgione, a master of fresco painting. (A fresco is painted on the wet plaster of a wall or ceiling.) Titian also studied examples of art from Rome and Florence. In time, he outgrew the influence of his teachers and created his own style.

Titian was a persuasive man. According to legend, long after he was rich and famous, he persuaded patrons to support his art by claiming to be poor. But he was also said to be quite generous with his friends.

Talents and Achievements
Titian's early work was precise and detailed. Later he developed a freer style. He used blobs of paint to create vivid forms, colors, and textures. He was known for his inspired use of color and for loose, lively brushwork that made his pictures appear to be alive. His work also shows a flair for expressing human personality.

Titian painted many classical myths and Bible stories. As a court painter, he created portraits of the rich and powerful. In 1516, he was named the official painter of Venice. Later, Holy Roman emperor Charles V made him court painter of Italy. Titian made many portraits of Charles V and other royalty.

Charles greatly admired Titian's work. There is a story that the emperor once picked up a paintbrush that had fallen to the floor. Titian protested, "I am not worthy of such a servant." The emperor replied, "Titian is worthy to be served by Caesar," referring to the emperor of ancient Rome. Charles even made Titian a knight—a first-time honor for a painter.

Titian is often described as a "painter's painter" because of his influence on other artists' use of color and brush strokes. Centuries later, many painters still try to copy his techniques.

30.5 Albrecht Dürer, German Artist

Albrecht Dürer (1471–1528) was born in the German city of Nuremberg. He earned fame for his paintings, drawings, prints, and writings on art.

Personality and Training As a boy, Dürer received a varied education. The son of a goldsmith, he learned his father's trade. At 15, he began training with a well-known painter and printmaker. (A printmaker uses printing to make copies of works of art.) He also studied math, Latin, and classical literature.

As a young man, Dürer traveled through Germany, Italy, and the Netherlands. He became friends with many humanist artists, writers, and thinkers. He studied classical sculpture for years to learn ideal human **proportions**. He wanted to be able to show the parts of the human body correctly sized in relation to each other.

Dürer's self-portraits show him to be a fashionable, confident man. He had an intellectual approach to life and art. He asked himself, "What is beauty?" His art was an attempt to answer that question.

Talents and Achievements In his painting, Dürer blended the detailed style of Germany with the perspective and idealized beauty that he learned from Italian painting. He encouraged artists to study measurement and geometry as the keys to understanding Renaissance and classical art.

Dürer was especially skilled at making **engravings** and **woodcuts**. These are prints made from an original that is specially prepared for printing. The original may be etched, or engraved, in metal, or it may be cut into a block of wood. Then it is inked to make copies. In Renaissance times, printers used engravings and woodcuts to illustrate books.

Much of Dürer's art shows religious figures. He also painted subjects from myths and did a series of self-portraits. Like other artists of his time, he did many portraits of royalty and wealthy patrons. He worked for years as a court artist for Holy Roman emperor Maximilian I.

Dürer's work is widely admired, particularly his beautiful engravings and woodcuts. These works set a new standard in printing because of their clarity, expressiveness, and fine detail. Dürer also wrote influential books about human proportions in art. Many modern artists still read these writings.

proportion the relative sizes of things, such as the length of an arm compared to the overall size of the human body

engraving a print of an image that has been engraved, or etched, in a hard surface, such as metal

woodcut a print of an image that has been carved in wood

Dürer's woodcut *The Four Horsemen of the Apocalypse* illustrates a vision of the end of the world that is described in the Christian Bible.

Albrecht Dürer

Since ancient times, most people believed that Earth was at the center of the universe. This engraving illustrates Copernicus's theory that Earth and the other planets travel around the sun.

axis an imaginary line drawn through a sphere, or ball, such as Earth

Nicolaus Copernicus

30.6 Nicolaus Copernicus, Polish Scientist

Nicolaus Copernicus (1473–1543) was born in Torun, Poland. He is often called the father of modern astronomy.

Personality and Training

When Copernicus was 10 years old, his father died. His uncle, a Catholic bishop, became his guardian. He made sure that Copernicus received a good education.

As a young man, Copernicus attended Poland's University of Krakow. Then he went to Italy to study medicine and church law. In Italy he rented rooms at an astronomy teacher's house. Soon he became fascinated by astronomy.

Copernicus's scientific work would show that he was highly creative. He was also a free thinker, unafraid to question accepted beliefs.

Talents and Achievements
Copernicus was skilled in mathematics and observation. He based his thinking on what he truly saw, rather than on what he thought he *should* see.

Like others of his day, Copernicus had been taught that Earth was at the center of the universe. According to this idea, the sun, stars, and planets traveled around Earth.

As Copernicus studied the motion of the planets, he became dissatisfied with this explanation. He proposed a revolutionary idea. People, he said, had it backward. In reality, Earth and the other planets revolve (travel) around the sun. Earth rotates, or turns, on its **axis**. This turning is what makes the sun and other objects in the heavens seem to move across the sky.

In 1514, Copernicus printed a booklet that outlined his theory. Then he began years of work on a full-length book. He called it *On the Revolutions of the Celestial Spheres*. (*Celestial* means "heavenly.") According to legend, he saw his book in print just a few hours before his death in 1543.

Copernicus dedicated his book to the pope. However, the idea of Earth traveling around the sun went against the church's belief that God had placed humans at the center of the universe. In 1616, the church forbade people to read Copernicus's book.

Despite the church's disapproval, Copernicus's theory had a major influence on a few key scientists. Eventually it was proved to be correct. Today the Copernican theory is part of the basis of modern astronomy.

30.7 Andreas Vesalius, Belgian Scientist

Andreas Vesalius (1514–1564) was born in Brussels, in what is now Belgium. He became an outstanding scientist. His work changed medicine and the study of anatomy.

Personality and Training

Vesalius came from a family of doctors and pharmacists. (Pharmacists are people who prepare medicines.) He was always interested in living things, and especially in anatomy. As a young boy, he studied stray dogs and cats.

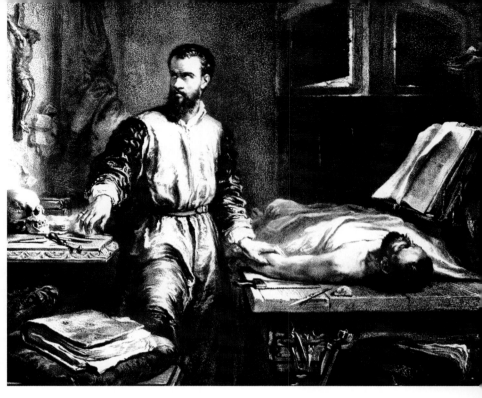

Vesalius dissected dead bodies to study human anatomy. He insisted on performing dissections himself rather than relying on untrained assistants.

Vesalius attended universities in Belgium, France, and Italy. In 1537, he earned his medical degree, specializing in anatomy. Later he became a personal doctor for Italian and Spanish royalty.

Vesalius was hardworking, curious, and confident. He was also said to be gloomy and distant at times.

Talents and Achievements

Vesalius was a talented observer and an independent thinker. He also had the artistic skill to draw his observations.

In Vesalius's day, physicians' understanding of human anatomy was based on the works of the ancient Greek physician Galen. Vesalius studied Galen, but he soon broke with this tradition. Like Copernicus, he was determined to observe things for himself.

Vesalius began **dissecting,** or cutting open, dead human bodies. His research showed that Galen's work had relied on studies of animals. As a result, it had many errors when applied to humans.

dissect to cut and separate the parts of a living thing for scientific study

Vesalius made many discoveries about the human body. For example, he showed that that the human heart has four hollow areas, called *chambers*. His discoveries led him to write his own seven-volume textbook of anatomy.

Vesalius called his book *On the Structure of the Human Body*. It explained the construction of the body and how the body functions. The book contained prints by artists that were based on Vesalius's drawings of the body.

Vesalius's book was a major breakthrough. It changed what people knew about human anatomy and how they studied it. It also changed physicians' understanding of medicine. Today his book is seen as the world's first modern medical textbook.

Andreas Vesalius

Queen Isabella I helped sponsor Christopher Columbus's attempt to find a route across the Atlantic Ocean to Asia. Instead of Asia, Columbus found the Americas. In this painting, Isabella wishes Columbus a safe and successful voyage.

New World the name given by Europeans to the Americas, which were unknown in Europe before the voyages of Christopher Columbus

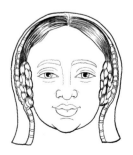

Queen Isabella I

30.8 Isabella I, Queen of Spain

Queen Isabella I (1451–1504) was born in the Spanish kingdom of Castile. She is best remembered for helping to unify Spain and for sponsoring the voyages of Christopher Columbus.

Personality and Training   Isabella was the daughter of the king of Castile. She was highly intelligent, strong-willed, and a devoted Catholic. Girls at that time received little education, so Isabella's schooling was limited. In adulthood she educated herself by learning Latin. As queen, she supported scholarship and art, collected fine paintings, and built schools.

When her father died, Isabella's half-brother, Henry, became king. At 13, Isabella was brought to Henry's court. There she learned about court affairs.

Talents and Achievements   Isabella was a forceful woman who could hold her own in court politics. Against Henry's wishes, in 1469 she married Ferdinand of Aragon, prince of the other major kingdom in Spain at that time. When Henry died five years later, Isabella became queen of Castile. In 1479, Ferdinand inherited the throne of Aragon. The two monarchs now ruled jointly over a united Spain.

Isabella and Ferdinand actively encouraged exploration. Isabella gave her support to Christopher Columbus, an Italian who proposed to find a new sea route to Asia. In 1492, Columbus sailed across the Atlantic and stumbled upon the Americas. His discovery of this *"New World"* would lead to a Spanish empire and create great wealth for Spain. You will learn more about his voyages and their impact in Unit 8.

Isabella and Ferdinand also sought to further unify Spain as a Catholic country. Jews who refused to convert to Catholicism were forced to leave the country. This harsh action cost Spain many of its most talented and productive citizens. For the Spanish Jews, it was a tragedy.

30.9 Elizabeth I, Queen of England

Queen Elizabeth I (1533–1603) was one of England's most popular and successful monarchs. Born in London, she was the daughter of King Henry VIII and his second wife, Anne Boleyn.

Personality and Training   When Elizabeth was two years old, King Henry lost interest in her mother, Queen Anne. Claiming that Anne had been unfaithful to him, he had her beheaded.

Elizabeth was raised in a separate household, away from the royal court. An English scholar became her teacher and educated her as a possible future monarch. Elizabeth was a gifted student. She became highly educated and learned to speak Greek, Latin, French, and Italian.

Elizabeth was strong-minded ruler, but she was not stubborn. As queen she was willing to listen to good advice, and she was always devoted to England.

Talents and Achievements   Elizabeth became queen at age 25 and reigned for 45 years, until her death. She never married, because she feared that a husband would take her power. She said she was married to the people of England.

Elizabeth was a conscientious and able ruler. She was strong and independent, but she was also flexible. She was willing to change unpopular policies. She showed political skill in balancing the interests of different people in her court. She inspired great love and loyalty from her **subjects,** who called her "Good Queen Bess."

Elizabeth's long reign is often called England's Golden Age. Culture thrived under her. She supported theater, fashion, literature, dance, and education. Poets and **playwrights** composed some of the greatest works in the English language.

Elizabeth worked to strengthen England's economy, and she encouraged trade and commerce. She authorized English trading companies in Africa, Asia, and the Americas. Her funding of sea exploration helped England gain a foothold in North America. In 1588, the English navy defeated the Spanish **Armada,** a mighty fleet that tried to attack England. This victory sparked a national celebration and further strengthened England's sea power. By the time Elizabeth died, England was one of the strongest and richest countries in the world.

subject a person under the rule of a monarch
playwright an author of plays
armada a large fleet of ships

Queen Elizabeth I welcomed artists, writers, dancers, musicians, and other cultural figures to her court. One frequent visitor was poet and playwright William Shakespeare.

Queen Elizabeth I

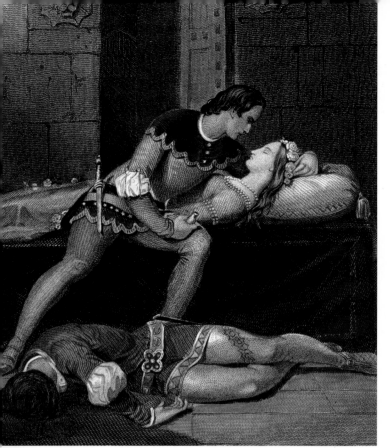

Shakespeare wrote about life with both humor and drama. This tragic scene is from his play *Romeo and Juliet*.

comedy an amusing play with a happy ending
tragedy a serious play with a sad ending

William Shakespeare

30.10 William Shakespeare, English Poet and Playwright

William Shakespeare (1564–1616) was born in the English town of Stratford-on-Avon. He was a major figure in the English Renaissance. He is often called the world's greatest playwright and one of its finest poets.

Personality and Training Shakespeare's father was a glove maker. As a boy, William studied Latin and classical literature in grammar school. He never went to a university. His plays, however, show a broad knowledge of many subjects, from history and politics to music and art.

In his early 20s, Shakespeare became an actor with a theater company in London. He learned about drama by performing and writing plays for the company. Many of his plays were first presented at the Globe Theatre.

Shakespeare had a reputation for being quiet and a bit mysterious. His writings show that he was curious and keenly observant. He thought deeply about life and its sufferings. Yet he also had a sense of humor and found much to laugh at in life.

Talents and Achievements Shakespeare was a skilled actor, but he was an even greater poet and playwright. He had an enormous talent for expressing thoughts and feelings in memorable ways. His plays show that he had a deep understanding of human behavior and emotions. Above all, he had the skill to present his understanding through vivid characters and exciting drama.

Shakespeare's poetry is widely admired, especially the 14-line poems called *sonnets*. Many of his sonnets are beautiful love poems. He is best known, however, for his plays. He wrote both **comedies** and **tragedies**. Many of his 38 plays are still performed today around the world. Among the most popular are *Romeo and Juliet, Hamlet, Macbeth,* and *The Merchant of Venice*.

Shakespeare's plays cover a broad range of subjects. He wrote about history, romance, politics, prejudice, murder, suicide, and war. His plays remain popular in part because he wrote about timeless themes such as love, jealousy, power, ambition, hatred, and fear.

Shakespeare has had a deep influence on writers. He also left a lasting mark on the English language. Many common sayings come from Shakespeare, such as "Love is blind" and "All's well that ends well." People often quote his witty, wise lines, sometimes without knowing that they owe their graceful words to Shakespeare.

30.11 Miguel Cervantes, Spanish Writer

Miguel Cervantes (1547–1616) was born near Madrid, Spain. He is best known for his comic novel *Don Quixote*.

Personality and Training   Little is known of Cervantes' education. He may have studied with priests influenced by humanism. It is certain that he loved to read.

Much of Cervantes' education came through hard experience. At 23, he became a soldier. In a battle at sea, he was shot twice in the chest. He also injured his left hand so badly that the hand became useless. Several years later, he was taken prisoner at sea by pirates. He spent five years as a slave in North Africa until his family bought his freedom.

Cervantes' early life shows that he was adventurous and courageous. His sense of humor could be biting, but he also turned it on himself. He once bragged that the public liked his plays enough not to boo them off the stage or throw vegetables at the actors.

Cervantes' life also had a shady side. He was imprisoned twice for disputes involving money and was once a suspect in a murder.

Talents and Achievements   A gifted writer, Cervantes wrote many plays, poems, and novels. He had a particular talent for **satire**. His masterpiece, *Don Quixote,* pokes fun at romantic stories of heroic knights as well as Spanish society. The main character in the novel, Don Quixote, is a tall, thin, elderly man who has read too many tales of glorious knights. Although the age of knights is past, he dresses up in rusty armor and sets out to do noble deeds. With him is short, stout Sancho Panza. Sancho is an ordinary farmer who rides a mule, but Don Quixote sees him as his faithful squire.

Together the two men have a series of comic adventures. In Don Quixote's imagination, country inns turn into castles and windmills into fearsome giants. While his adventures are very funny, there is something noble about the way he bravely fights evil, even if his deeds are only in his mind.

Don Quixote was very popular in Spain. King Philip III supposedly saw a man reading and laughing so hard that he was crying. The king said, "That man is either crazy or he is reading *Don Quixote*." Today, *Don Quixote* is considered one of the masterpieces of world literature.

Don Quixote, shown here with his armor, is the hero of Cervantes' comic novel by the same name.

satire a work that uses sharp humor to attack people or society

Miguel Cervantes

30.12 Leonardo da Vinci, Italian Renaissance Person

Leonardo da Vinci (1452–1519) was born in a village near Florence. His wide range of interests and accomplishments made him a true Renaissance person.

Personality and Training As a teenager, Leonardo trained in Florence under a master sculptor and painter. All his life he studied many subjects, including art, music, math, anatomy, botany, architecture, and engineering.

Leonardo spent much of his life in Florence and Milan. He worked as an artist, engineer, and architect for kings, popes, and wealthy patrons. A handsome, brilliant man, he had a special love of animals. Sometimes he bought caged animals at the market and set them free. He also was a vegetarian (he ate no meat), which was quite unusual at the time.

As you can see from all the topics he studied, Leonardo was endlessly curious. He was a careful observer and liked to figure things out for himself.

Talents and Achievements Leonardo was gifted in many fields. He was an accomplished painter, sculptor, architect, engineer, and inventor.

Mona Lisa is one of Leonardo da Vinci's best-known paintings. This surprisingly small painting—only about 20 by 30 inches—has had a huge and lasting influence on artists to this day.

Leonardo da Vinci

Leonardo's notebooks show him to be one of the greatest creative minds of all time. Like Albrecht Dürer, he closely studied proportions. He made precise drawings of people, animals, and plants. He also sketched out ideas about geometry and mechanics, the science of motion and force. He designed weapons, buildings, and a variety of machines. Many of the inventions he drew, such as a helicopter and a submarine, were centuries ahead of their time.

Leonardo's paintings are among the world's greatest works of art. One of his masterpieces is the *Mona Lisa,* a painting of a woman with a mysterious smile. It is one of the most famous paintings in the world. Like his other paintings, it displays a remarkable use of perspective, balance, and detail. The rich effects of light, shade, and color reveal Leonardo's close study of light. Students of his art also detect how principles of geometry helped him organize the space in his paintings.

Leonardo's art inspired other great artists, such as Michelangelo. With his many interests and talents, Leonardo is a nearly perfect example of the spirit of the Renaissance.

30.13 Chapter Summary

In this chapter, you learned how the Renaissance spread from Italy across Europe. You learned that trade, travel, education, and the printing press all helped to spread Renaissance ideas. Then you studied the lives and accomplishments of 10 Renaissance people.

Renaissance artists like Michelangelo, Titian, and Dürer created many kinds of art. Each displayed humanist ideals of realism and beauty. Through their observations and fresh thinking, scientists like Copernicus and Vesalius dramatically increased human knowledge. Queen Isabella and Queen Elizabeth were strong monarchs who supported the arts and encouraged exploration. Shakespeare and Cervantes created masterpieces of world literature. Leonardo da Vinci was a creative genius. His many interests made him a true Renaissance person.

The spirit of the Renaissance led people to question many ideas and practices. Some of these questions were directed at the church. In the next chapter, you will learn about a time of religious unrest in Europe called the Reformation.

Pope Julius II ordered artists Bramante, Michelangelo, and Raphael to construct the Vatican and St. Peter's cathedral.

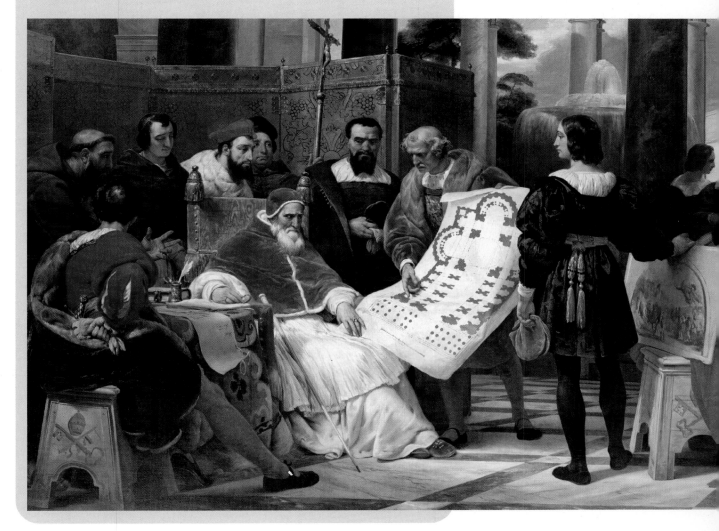

CHAPTER 31

◄ Corruption in the church led to questions about the morals of church officials.

The Reformation Begins

31.1 Introduction

In the last chapter, you met 10 leading figures of the Renaissance. At the height of the Renaissance, western Europe was still Roman Catholic. In this chapter, you will learn about the beginnings of the **Reformation**. This historic movement led to the start of many new Christian churches that broke away from the Catholic Church.

The Reformation began in the early 1500s and lasted into the 1600s. Until then, all Christians in western Europe were Catholics. But even before the Reformation, the church's religious and moral authority was starting to weaken.

One reason for the weakening of the church was the humanism of the Renaissance. Humanists often were very secular (non-religious) in their thinking. They believed in free thought and questioned many accepted beliefs.

Problems within the church added to this spirit of questioning. Many Catholics were dismayed by worldliness and corruption (immoral and dishonest behavior) in the church. Bishops and clergy often seemed devoted more to comfort and good living than to serving God. Sometimes they used questionable practices to raise money for the church. Some popes seemed more concerned with power and money than with spiritual matters.

These problems led a number of Catholics to cry out for reform. They questioned the authority of church leaders and some of the church's teachings. Some broke away from the church entirely. They became known as **Protestants** because of their protests against the Catholic Church. The establishment of Protestant churches divided Christians into many separate groups.

In this chapter, you will learn more about the problems that weakened the Catholic Church. You'll meet early reformers who tried to change the church. Then you will learn how a German priest, Martin Luther, ignited the movement that ended the religious unity of Europe. Finally, you'll read about other early leaders of the Reformation.

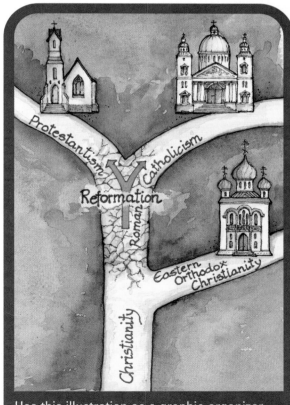

Use this illustration as a graphic organizer to help you explore the causes and spread of the Reformation.

31.2 The Weakening of the Catholic Church

By the Late Middle Ages, two major problems were weakening the Catholic Church. The first was worldliness and corruption within the church. The second was political conflict between the pope and European monarchs.

Worldliness and Corruption Within the Church   During the Middle Ages, the Catholic Church united the Christians of western Europe in a single faith. But the church was a political and economic institution as well as a religious one. By the 1300s, many Catholics felt that the church had become far too worldly and corrupt.

Too often, people who were supposedly dedicated to the church failed to live up to their role as spiritual leaders. For example, priests, monks, and nuns made vows, or solemn promises, not to marry or have children. Yet many broke these vows. Some seemed to ignore Christian values and morals. Church leaders often behaved like royalty instead of humble servants of God. Popes, cardinals, and bishops lived in elegant palaces and wore jeweled robes.

People were also troubled by the way many church officials tried to get money to support the church. One practice was the selling of **indulgences**. An indulgence was a release from punishment for sins. During the Middle Ages, the church granted indulgences in return for gifts to the church and other good works. People who received indulgences did not have to perform good deeds to make up for their sins. Over time, popes and bishops began selling indulgences as a way of raising money. This practice made it seem that people could buy forgiveness for their sins. Many Catholics were deeply disturbed by the abuse of indulgences.

The church also sold offices, or leadership positions. This practice is called **simony**. Instead of being chosen for their merit, buyers simply paid for their appointments. Buying an office was worthwhile because it could be a source of even more income. Often people acquired multiple offices in different places without actually going there to perform their duties.

People questioned other practices as well. Some clergy charged pilgrims to see holy objects, such as the relics of saints. In addition, all Catholics paid taxes to the church. Many people resented having to pay taxes to Rome as well as to their own governments.

indulgence a grant by the Catholic Church that released a person from punishment for sins

simony the buying and selling of spiritual or holy things

The selling of indulgences made it seem as though people could buy forgiveness for their sins. This and other moneymaking practices led people to distrust the church.

Political Conflicts with European Rulers   In medieval times, the pope became a powerful political figure as well as a religious leader. The church also accumulated vast wealth. Its political and economic power presented a problem for monarchs, because the church claimed to be independent of their control.

As kings and queens tried to increase their own power, they often came into conflict with the pope. They quarreled with the pope over church property and the right to make appointments to church offices. Popes also became entangled in other political conflicts.

These disputes added to the questioning of the pope's authority. At times they led to scandals that damaged the church's reputation.

One dramatic crisis unfolded in France in 1301. When King Philip IV tried to tax the French clergy, the pope threatened to excommunicate him. In response, soldiers hired by the king kidnapped the pope. The elderly pope was soon released, but he died a few weeks later.

When Pope Clement V moved his headquarters from Italy to France, the quarrel between King Philip IV and the pope ended.

The quarrel with the king ended under Pope Clement V. In 1309, Clement moved his headquarters from Rome to the French city of Avignon. He appointed 24 new cardinals during his reign, 22 of whom were French. The next six popes also lived in Avignon and named still more French cardinals. Many Europeans believed that France's kings now controlled the **papacy** (the office of the pope). As a result, they lost respect for the pope as the supreme head of the church.

An even worse crisis developed after Pope Gregory XI moved the papacy back to Rome in 1377. The next year, Gregory died, and an Italian was elected pope. The new pope refused to move back to Avignon. A group of cardinals, most of them French, left Rome and elected a rival pope. The church now had two popes, one in Rome and one in Avignon. Later a church council elected a third pope. Each pope claimed to be the real head of the church.

papacy the office, or position, of pope as head of the Catholic Church

This division in the church is called the Great Schism. For nearly 40 years, the various lines of popes denounced each other as impostors. Catholics were divided and confused. The Great Schism lessened people's respect for the papacy and sparked calls for reform.

31.3 Early Calls for Reform

As you have seen, by the 1300s the church was beginning to lose some of its moral and religious standing. Many Catholics, including clergy, criticized the corruption and abuses that plagued the church. They challenged the authority of the pope. Some began to question church teachings and express new forms of Christian faith.

Reformers wanted to purify the church, not destroy it. By challenging the church's practices and teachings, however, they helped pave the way for the dramatic changes of the Reformation. In this section, you will meet four of these early reformers.

John Wycliffe (About 1330–1384)   John Wycliffe was a scholar in England. Wycliffe challenged the church's right to money that it demanded from England. When the Great Schism began, he publicly questioned the pope's authority. He also attacked indulgences and immoral behavior on the part of the clergy.

During the Middle Ages, church officials tried to control interpretations of the Bible. Wycliffe believed that the Bible, not the church, was the supreme source of religious authority. Against church tradition, he had the Bible translated from Latin into English so that common people could read it.

The pope accused Wycliffe of **heresy,** or opinions that contradict church **doctrine**. Wycliffe's followers were persecuted, and some of them were burned to death. After his death, the church had his writings burned. Despite the church's opposition, Wycliffe's ideas had a wide influence.

heresy beliefs that contradict the official teachings of a religion or church; one who holds such beliefs is called a *heretic*

doctrine the official teachings of a religion or church

Priest Jan Hus was an early reformer who agreed with Wycliffe's ideas and spoke against the pope. For this, he was burned at the stake as a heretic.

Jan Hus (About 1370–1415) Jan Hus was a priest in Bohemia (today's Czech Republic). He read Wycliffe's writings and agreed with many of his ideas. Hus criticized the vast wealth of the church and spoke out against the pope's authority. The true head of the church, he said, was Jesus Christ.

Hus wanted to purify the church and return it to the people. He called for an end to corruption among the clergy. He wanted both the Bible and the mass to be offered in the common language of the people instead of Latin.

In 1414, Hus was arrested and charged with heresy. In July 1415, he was burned at the stake.

Like Wycliffe, Hus had a major influence on future reformers. Martin Luther would later say that he and his supporters were "all Hussites without knowing it."

Catherine of Siena (1347–1380) Catherine of Siena was an Italian **mystic**. She was extraordinarily devoted and felt that she had a direct experience of God. Even as a child, she had visions of Jesus and promised to be his "bride."

Catherine spent long hours deep in prayer and wrote many letters about spiritual life. She also involved herself in church affairs. Her pleas helped convince Pope Gregory XI to move the papacy back to Rome from Avignon. Later she traveled to Rome to try to end the Great Schism.

Catherine was a faithful Catholic, and in 1461 the church declared her a saint. Yet her example showed that people could lead spiritual lives that went beyond the usual norms of the church. She and other mystics emphasized personal experience of God more than formal observance of church practices. This approach to faith helped prepare people for the ideas of the Reformation.

Desiderius Erasmus (1466–1536) Desiderius Erasmus was a humanist from Holland. A priest and devoted Catholic, he was one of the most outspoken figures in the call for reform.

In 1509, Erasmus published a book called *The Praise of Folly*. (*Folly* means "foolishness.") The book was a sharply worded satire of society, including abuses by clergy and church leaders. Erasmus argued for a return to simple Christian goodness.

Erasmus wanted to reform the church from within. He angrily denied that he was really a Protestant. Yet perhaps more than any other individual, he helped to prepare Europe for the Reformation. His attacks on corruption in the church contributed to many people's desire to leave Catholicism. For this reason it is often said that "Erasmus laid the egg, and Luther hatched it."

Catholic priest Erasmus of Holland was perhaps the most influential person in spreading the ideas of reform before the Reformation.

mystic a person who is devoted to religion and has spiritual experiences

Luther nailed his list of 95 arguments, called the Ninety-Five Theses, to a church door in Wittenberg. Church leaders condemned the ideas in this document.

31.4 Martin Luther Breaks Away from the Church

By the early 1500s, there was considerable turmoil in the church. In Germany, then part of the Holy Roman Empire, a priest named Martin Luther became involved in a serious dispute with church authorities. Condemned by the church, Luther broke away and began the first Protestant church. The Reformation had begun.

Luther's Early Life   Luther was born in Germany in 1483. Raised as a devout Catholic, he planned a career in law. As a young man, he was badly frightened when he was caught in a violent thunderstorm. As lighting flashed around him, he vowed that if he survived, he would become a monk.

Luther kept his promise and joined an order of monks. Later he became a priest. He studied the Bible thoroughly and earned a reputation as a scholar and teacher.

Luther Pushes for Change in the Catholic Church   Like many Christians of his time, Luther asked the question, "What must I do to be saved?" The church stressed that keeping the sacraments and living a good life were the keys to salvation. Luther's studies of the Bible led him to a different answer. No one, he believed, could earn salvation. Instead, salvation was a gift from God that people received in faith. People, he said, were saved by their faith, not good works.

Luther's views brought him into conflict with the church over indulgences. In 1517, Pope Leo X needed money to finish building St. Peter's, the grand cathedral in Rome. He sent preachers around Europe to sell indulgences. Buyers were promised pardons of all of their sins and those of friends and family. Luther was outraged. He felt that the church was selling false salvation to uneducated people.

Luther posted a list of arguments, called *theses,* against indulgences and church abuses on the church door in the town of Wittenberg. He also sent the list, called the Ninety-Five Theses, to church leaders.

Luther's theses caused considerable controversy. Many people were excited by his ideas, while the church condemned them. Gradually, he was drawn into more serious disagreements with church authorities.

In response to critics, Luther published pamphlets that explained his thinking. He argued that the Bible—not the pope or church leaders—was the ultimate source of religious authority. The only true sacraments, he said, were baptism and the Eucharist. The church's other five sacraments had no basis in the Bible. Moreover, all Christians were priests, and all should study the Bible for themselves. "Faith alone," Luther wrote, "and the efficacious [effective] use of the word of God bring salvation."

In the eyes of church leaders, Luther was attacking fundamental truths of the Catholic religion. In January 1521, he was excommunicated (no longer allowed to be a member of the church). The church also pressured the authorities in Germany to silence him once and for all.

In April, Luther was brought before the Diet, an assembly of state leaders, in the city of Worms. At the risk of his life, he refused to take back his teachings. The Holy Roman emperor declared Luther a heretic and forbade the printing or selling of his writings. For a time Luther went into hiding. But the movement he had started continued to spread.

Luther Starts His Own Church   Many Germans saw Luther as a hero. As his popularity grew, he continued to develop his ideas. Soon he was openly organizing a new Christian **denomination** known as Lutheranism. The new church emphasized study of the Bible. Luther translated the Bible into German. He also wrote a baptism service, a mass, and new hymns (sacred songs) in German.

Having rejected the church's hierarchy, Luther looked to German princes to support his church. When a peasants' revolt broke out in 1524, the rebels expected Luther to support their demands for social and economic change. Instead, Luther denounced the peasants and sided with the rulers. He needed the help of Germany's rulers to keep his new church growing. By the time the uprising was crushed, tens of thousands of peasants had been brutally killed. Many peasants rejected Lutheranism.

Several princes, however, supported Luther, and Lutheranism continued to grow. Over the next 30 years, Lutherans and Catholics were often at war in Germany. These religious wars ended in 1555 with the Peace of Augsburg. According to this treaty, each prince within the Holy Roman Empire could determine the religion of his subjects.

The Peace of Augsburg was a major victory for Protestantism. Christian unity was at an end, and not only in Germany. As you will learn next, by this time a number of other Protestant churches had sprung up in northern Europe.

denomination a particular religious grouping within a larger faith; for example, the Lutheran church is a denomination of Christianity

At the Diet of Worms, Charles V declared Luther a heretic and forbade the printing of his writings.

31.5 Other Early Leaders of the Reformation

The movement begun by Martin Luther soon swept across much of Europe. Many people who were dismayed by abuses in the church remained loyal Catholics. Others, however, were attracted to new forms of the Christian faith. The printing press helped spread new ideas, as well as translations of the Bible, faster than ever before. In addition, government leaders had learned from Luther's experience that they could win religious independence from the church. The Reformation succeeded most where rulers embraced Protestant faiths.

Booksellers helped to spread the ideas of the Reformation by selling books and pamphlets in public marketplaces.

Many reformers contributed to the spread of Protestantism. Let's take a look at four early leaders of the Reformation.

Huldrych Zwingli (1484–1531) Huldrych Zwingli was a Catholic priest in Zurich, Switzerland. Zwingli was influenced by both Erasmus and Luther. After reading Luther's work, he persuaded the local government to ban any form of worship that was not based on the Bible. In 1523, Zurich declared its independence from the authority of the local Catholic bishop.

Zwingli wanted Christians to focus solely on the Bible. He attacked the worship of relics, saints, and images. In Zwinglian churches, there were no religious statues or paintings. Services were very simple, without music or singing.

Zwingli took his ideas to other Swiss cities. In 1531, war broke out between his followers and Swiss Catholics. Zwingli died in the war, but the new church lived on.

John Calvin (1509–1564) In the late 1530s, John Calvin, a French humanist, started another Protestant branch in Geneva, Switzerland. His book, *Institutes of the Christian Religion,* became one of the most influential works of the Reformation.

Calvin emphasized that salvation came only from God's grace. He said that the "saved" whom God elected (chose) lived according to strict standards. He believed firmly in hard work and thrift (the careful use of money). Success in business, he taught, was a sign of God's grace. Calvin tried to establish a Christian state in Geneva that would be ruled by God through the Calvinist Church.

Calvin influenced many other reformers. One of them was John Knox, a Scotsman who lived in Geneva for a time. Knox led the Protestant reform that established the Presbyterian Church in Scotland.

King Henry VIII (1491–1547) England's Protestant Reformation was led by King Henry VIII. In 1534, Henry formed the Church of England (also called the Anglican Church), with himself as its head.

Unlike Luther and Calvin, King Henry did not have major disagreements with Catholic teachings. His reasons for breaking with the church were personal and political. On a personal level, he wanted to end his first marriage, but the pope had denied him a divorce. On a political level, he no longer wanted to share power and wealth with the church. In 1536, Henry closed down Catholic monasteries in England and took their riches.

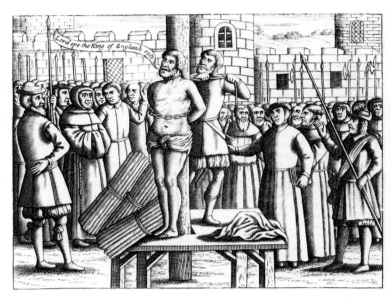

Writer and scholar Tyndale was burned at the stake for his Protestant views.

William Tyndale (About 1491–1536) William Tyndale was an English priest, scholar, and writer. Tyndale traveled to Germany and met Martin Luther. His views became more and more Protestant. He attacked corruption in the Catholic Church and defended the English Reformation. After being arrested by Catholic authorities in the city of Antwerp (in present-day Belgium), he spent over a year in prison. In 1536, he was burned at the stake.

Tyndale was especially important for his translations of books from the Bible. To spread knowledge of the Bible, he translated the **New Testament,** and parts of the **Old Testament,** into English. In the early 1600s, his work was used in the preparation of the King James, or Authorized, Version of the Bible. Famed for its beautiful language, the King James Bible had an enormous influence on English worship and literature.

New Testament the second part of the Christian Bible, which includes the Gospels and other writings of the early Christian church

Old Testament the first part of the Christian Bible, corresponding to the Jewish Bible

31.6 Chapter Summary

In this chapter, you learned how the Reformation began. By the Late Middle Ages, the Catholic Church had been weakened by corruption and political struggles. Early reformers hoped to purify the church. Martin Luther, however, broke with the church completely. Luther started the first Protestant church. Other reformers soon followed.

In the next chapter, you'll take a closer look at three Protestant faiths: Lutheranism, Calvinism, and Anglicanism. You will also learn how the Catholic Church responded to the challenge of Protestantism.

CHAPTER 32

◄ ◄ Catholic leaders worked to strengthen the church in response to the Reformation.

The Spread and Impact of the Reformation

32.1 Introduction

In the last chapter, you learned how the Reformation began. Now you'll learn more about the Protestant churches that emerged in the 1500s. You'll also explore the impact of the Reformation on the Catholic Church and on the history of Europe.

As Protestantism spread, it branched out in a number of directions. By the start of the 1600s, there were many different Christian churches in Europe.

Each Protestant **sect,** or group, had its own beliefs and practices. But all Protestants had much in common. They shared a belief in the Bible, individual conscience, and the importance of faith. They were also united in their desire to reform Christianity.

The growth of Protestantism helped to spur reform within the Catholic Church as well. This Catholic reform movement is called the **Counter-Reformation**. Church leaders worked to correct abuses. They clarified and defended Catholic teachings. They condemned what they saw as Protestant errors. They also tried to win back areas of Europe that had been lost to the church.

The many divisions among Christians led to a series of wars and persecutions (violent attacks on groups of people). Catholics fought Protestants, and Protestants fought one another. These struggles involved political, economic, and cultural differences as well as deep religious beliefs.

The Reformation brought much strife to Europe, but it also created many new forms of the Christian faith. In this chapter, you'll learn more about the varieties of Protestantism by exploring the beliefs and practices of three important sects: **Lutheranism, Calvinism,** and **Anglicanism**. Next you'll learn about the Catholic Counter-Reformation. Finally, you'll look at some of the lasting effects of the Reformation.

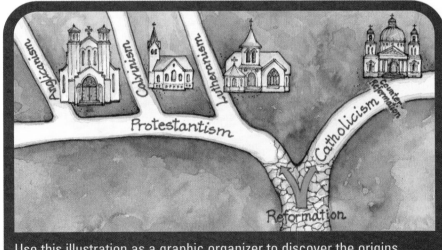

Use this illustration as a graphic organizer to discover the origins, beliefs, and practices of three Protestant churches of the Reformation.

The Augsburg Confession, or statement of faith, was prepared by German reformer Melanchthon in 1530 with Luther's approval. The Confession spelled out Lutheran beliefs. In its modern form, it is the basis of Lutheranism for millions of people around the world.

32.2 Lutheranism

The first major Protestant sect was Lutheranism. As you learned in Chapter 31, Lutheranism began in Germany after Martin Luther was excommunicated by the Catholic Church in 1521.

Luther was a Catholic priest and scholar. He taught **scripture** and theology (the study of religious truth) at the University of Wittenberg. As he studied the Bible, Luther became troubled. He could not find a basis in the Bible for many church teachings and practices. He was also upset about corruption in the church, especially the sale of indulgences.

Luther tried to work out his differences with the church. But after his views were condemned, he started the movement that became Lutheranism.

Beliefs About Sin and Salvation Luther and his followers disagreed with the Catholic Church about sin and salvation. Catholics believed that people earned salvation by following the teachings and practices of the church. Taking part in the sacraments was essential. For example, the sacrament of baptism wiped away **original sin**. In Christian belief, this was the sinful state passed on to all people by Adam, the first man created by God in the Bible. Once they were baptized, people needed to pray, take the sacraments, follow rules laid down by the church, and perform good works.

Lutherans denied that people could do anything to earn their salvation. Salvation, they said, was God's gift, which people received in faith. People would be "justified," or saved, if they sincerely believed in Jesus Christ, were sorry for their sins, and accepted the words of the

scripture sacred writings; in Christianity, the Bible

original sin in Christian belief, the sinful state into which all people are born

Bible as truth. Luther called this "justification by faith." Those who have faith perform good works and avoid sin because God commands them to, not in order to earn salvation.

Ultimate Source of Authority   Lutherans rejected traditional sources of religious authority, such as church councils and the pope. They believed that the Bible was the only true source of religious guidance. Reading the Bible was the only way to learn how to lead a good life and gain faith in God. Lutherans published the Bible in several languages so that people could read it for themselves.

Rituals and Worship   Lutheran church services combined Catholic practices with new Lutheran ones. Lutherans met in church buildings that had originally been Catholic. Like Catholics, they used an altar, candles, and a crucifix (a representation of Jesus on a cross).

In many ways, Lutheran services resembled the Catholic mass. The services included **Holy Communion** (the Eucharist), Bible readings, and sermons, in which clergy explained the day's lesson from the Bible. Like Catholics, Lutherans sang hymns. Luther believed in the power of music. He wrote hymns for his followers to sing. He used German words and often set hymns to popular tunes so everyone could sing them.

Other parts of Lutheran worship were different from Catholic practice. Prayers were written and spoken in German, not in Latin, so that everyone could take part. Instead of having seven sacraments, as Catholics did, Lutherans had just two: baptism and the Eucharist. Luther believed that these were the only two sacraments that are clearly named in the Bible.

Community Life   Luther gave his followers certain rules for how to live. Over time, he preached less about the Bible. He began to put more importance on strict discipline and strong families. He said that fathers should teach their children religion by having them pray before meals and before bed. "Unless they [pray]," he said, "they should be given neither food nor drink." He also thought that women should get married and give birth to as many children as possible. He believed that these rules would help Lutheran communities to grow and to be strong.

Unlike Catholic priests, Lutheran ministers (clergy) were free to marry. Luther himself married a former nun.

> **Holy Communion** in Christian ritual, the sharing of bread and wine that has been consecrated by a priest or minister (also called the Eucharist)

This painting of a Reformation church shows Lutheran clergy ministering the sacraments of baptism (far left) and the Eucharist (center). Luther preaches from the altar at right.

John Calvin led a Reformation church in Geneva, Switzerland. Calvinists lived by strict rules to help them be good Christians.

32.3 Calvinism

Calvinism was founded by John Calvin, a French humanist who did his most influential work in Geneva, Switzerland. In 1541, Calvin took over the leadership of the church reform movement in Geneva. He tried to make Geneva a model Christian state.

Beliefs About Sin and Salvation Calvinists agreed with Lutherans that people depended entirely upon God to be saved. No one deserved salvation, and no one could "force" God to grant salvation by doing good works. Instead, God chose certain people—the "elect"—to be saved and to enjoy eternal life. Religious faith and salvation were God's gifts to the elect. Everyone else was doomed to spend eternity in hell.

Calvin maintained that God knew from the beginning of time who would be saved and who would be condemned. This idea is called **predestination**. There was nothing people could do to change their destiny. Everything, Calvin said, is under God's control.

Calvinists believed that the elect could be known by their actions. The world, they believed, was full of opportunities to sin. But only people who were destined not to be saved would actually sin. Good behavior showed that a person was one of the elect who was destined for heaven. The reason for good behavior was to honor God, not to "buy" one's salvation.

Calvinists had many strict rules defining what good behavior was. For example, singing, dancing, playing cards, and wearing fancy clothing were all forbidden. Many people followed these rules to show that they believed they were saved.

Ultimate Source of Authority Like Lutherans, Calvinists thought that the Bible was the only true source of religious guidance. Part of the task of church leaders was to interpret the Bible and make laws from it. Calvinists believed that all of life should be lived according to God's law. Consequently, in a Calvinist state, religious rules also became laws for the government. Anyone who sinned was also committing a crime. A lawbreaker was punished first by Calvinist clergy and then by the local court system. Sins such as **blasphemy** (showing disrespect to God) were punished as serious crimes.

Rituals and Worship Calvinist churchgoers attended services up to five times a week. Services included sermons that lasted for hours. The sermons explained how to live according to the Bible.

Calvinist church buildings showed Calvin's belief in simplicity. Churches were paneled in plain wood, and people sat on long wooden benches. There were no paintings, statues, or stained glass windows. The minister preached from a **pulpit** in the middle of the room. Men sat on one side, and women and children sat on the other side. Children had to be ready to answer questions from the minister at a moment's notice. Failure to answer correctly would bring shame or even punishment.

Like Lutherans, Calvinists used only the two sacraments they found in the Bible: baptism and the Eucharist, or Communion. Calvinists were not allowed to sing any words except those found in the Bible. At services, they sang verses from the Bible set to popular tunes. Some Bible songs had new melodies written for them. These verses could also be sung during prayers at home.

Community Life Calvinists believed that each community should be a **theocracy,** or a state governed by God through religious leaders. Calvinists had a duty to try to establish communities in which church and state were united.

Calvinist communities had strict laws based on the Bible. Parents could name babies only certain Christian names from the Bible. Guests at local inns had to be in bed by nine o'clock at night. They were not allowed to swear, dance, play cards, or insult anyone else at the inn. Inn owners had to report anyone who broke these rules. The same rules applied to people in their homes. Church leaders could inspect homes yearly to see whether families were living by the strict Calvinist laws. Offenders were punished severely. Some were even banished from their hometowns.

blasphemy an act of disrespect toward God

pulpit a platform or other structure in a church from which a priest or minister preaches

theocracy a government or state in which God is the supreme ruler and religious officials govern in God's name

Calvinist churches were simple and practical with no decorations.

Despite the pope's refusal to grant Henry VIII a divorce from his first wife, Henry secretly married his second wife, Anne Boleyn, in early 1533. Their marriage signaled Henry's clear break with the Catholic Church.

32.4 Anglicanism

Anglicanism was founded in 1534 by King Henry VIII in England. Recall from the last chapter that Henry was not a religious reformer like Luther or Calvin. Instead, he broke away from the Catholic Church for political and personal reasons.

Politically, Henry did not want to share either his power or his kingdom's wealth with the church. Personally, he wanted to get a divorce so that he could marry another woman, Anne Boleyn. Not only was he fascinated with Anne, but he wanted a son for an heir, and he and his wife had failed to have a male child.

When the pope refused to grant permission for a divorce, Henry took matters into his own hands. He had Parliament, England's lawmaking body, declare him the head of the English church. So began the Church of England, or Anglican Church, with the king at its head.

Under Henry, the Church of England greatly resembled the Catholic Church. Over time, it blended elements of Catholicism and Protestantism.

Beliefs About Sin and Salvation Anglican beliefs had much in common with those of the Catholic Church. Like Catholics, Anglicans believed that baptism washed away original sin and began the Christian life. Anglicans, however, were also influenced by Protestant ideas. Unlike Catholics, they accepted Luther's idea of justification by faith. To go to heaven, all people needed was to believe in God, regret their sins, and receive God's mercy.

Anglicans believed that people should have privacy in how they practiced religion. It was up to individuals to figure out how to live by their religious beliefs.

Ultimate Source of Authority Anglicans based their beliefs on the Bible. However, the English monarch, as head of the church, was the main interpreter of the Bible's meaning. The highest-ranking bishop in England, the Archbishop of Canterbury, helped the monarch with this task.

Beneath the archbishop, other clergy helped spread the monarch's ideas about religion. In practice, local clergy and churchgoers could interpret church beliefs in their own ways as long as they were loyal to the king or queen.

Rituals and Worship   Anglican services had similarities to both Catholic and Lutheran services. Two versions of the Anglican Church service developed. The High Church service was much like the Catholic mass and very formal. The Low Church service was similar to the Lutheran service. The style of Low Church services varied from place to place, depending on the beliefs of the local pastor, or minister.

Anglican services were held in former Catholic church buildings. Most of the paintings, statues, and other decorations were removed. The inside of each church was painted white, and the Ten Commandments were painted on a plain white wall. Churchgoers sang simple hymns with English words and easy melodies. The hymns were accompanied by musical instruments.

Like other Protestant groups, Anglicans used only two sacraments: baptism and the Eucharist. English slowly replaced Latin in Anglican services. Under King Edward VI, an official prayer book, the *Book of Common Prayer,* was published. It provided English-language prayers for services and morning and evening prayers. It also expressed the basic ideas of Anglican doctrine. In the early 1600s, King James I had a committee of scholars prepare a new English translation of the Bible, known as the Authorized Version, or the King James Version.

Community Life   Anglican communities were not all alike. High Church communities were made up mostly of wealthy people. Low Church communities were usually made up of middle-class and working-class people.

Henry VIII's daughter, Queen Elizabeth I, said that no one should be forced to believe or practice a particular kind of Anglicanism. People could choose how to worship as long as they obeyed the laws of England and were loyal to the monarch. Heresy ceased to be a crime. However, citizens had to take care not to attack the monarch or the Anglican Church's place as the official church of England.

Baptism and the Eucharist are the only two sacraments mentioned in the Bible.

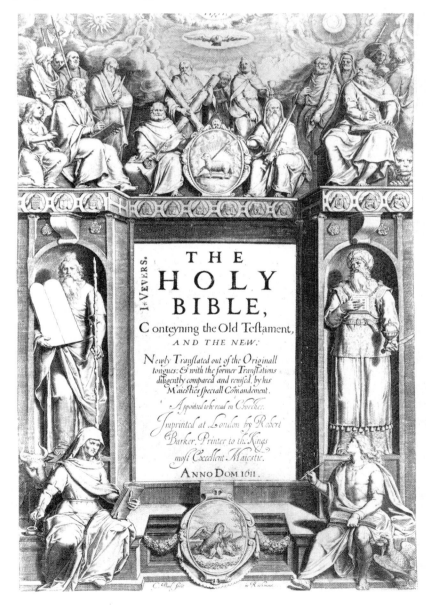

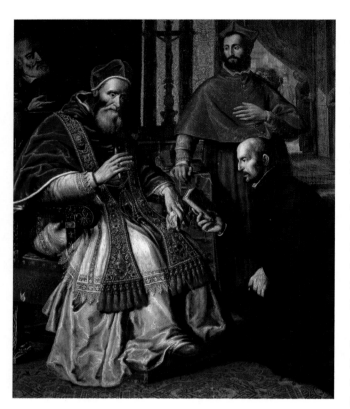

The Jesuits became the most important new religious order of the Counter-Reformation. In this 16th-century painting, Ignatius of Loyola kneels before Pope Paul III, who officially recognized the Jesuits in 1540.

32.5 The Catholic Response: The Counter-Reformation

As Protestantism spread, the Catholic Church responded with a program of serious reform. It clarified its teachings, corrected abuses, and tried to win people back to Catholicism. This movement within the Catholic Church is called the Counter-Reformation.

The Council of Trent A major part of the Counter-Reformation was the Council of Trent. The council was a meeting of church leaders that began in Trent, Italy, in 1545. Pope Paul III summoned the council to combat corruption in the church and to fight Protestantism. The council continued its work in more than 20 sessions over the next 18 years.

In response to Protestant ideas, the council gave a more precise statement of Catholic teachings. It rejected predestination, declaring that individuals do have a role to play in deciding the fate of their souls. The council agreed with Protestants that faith was important and that salvation was God's gift. But it rejected justification by faith alone. The council insisted that faith, good works, and the sacraments were all necessary for salvation. It reaffirmed the Catholic belief in seven sacraments.

The council acknowledged the importance of the Bible. It insisted, however, on the church's authority to interpret the Bible. It said that the Latin Bible was the only official scripture.

Besides stating Catholic teachings, the council took action to make needed changes in the church. It required better education and training of clergy. It called for priests and bishops to spend more time preaching. It corrected many of the abuses involving money and church offices. And it set down rules for church services so that they would be more alike everywhere.

The Council of Trent went a long way toward achieving the goals of Pope Paul III. The council's work brought a higher standard of morality to the church's clergy and leadership. Its statements of Catholic belief and practices helped unify the church. The reformed church was better able to compete with Protestantism for the loyalties of Christians.

Catholic Reformers and Missionaries The spirit of reform brought new life to the Catholic Church. Many individuals and groups helped to reform the church and spread its message. For example, Teresa of Avila, a nun and mystic, started a new religious order in Spain and helped reform the lives of priests and nuns. Her example and writings inspired many Catholics to return to the values taught by Jesus.

Other new orders were formed to preach, to educate people, and to perform services such as feeding the poor. The most important of these orders was the Society of Jesus, also known as the Jesuits.

The Jesuits were founded by Ignatius of Loyola, a Spanish nobleman. As a young soldier Ignatius had his leg shattered by a cannonball in a battle. While he was recovering, he read about the lives of saints. He vowed to become a "soldier for Jesus."

After years of study, Ignatius started the order that became the Jesuits. The Jesuits were dedicated teachers and **missionaries**. They founded schools and colleges, and they brought many Europeans back to the church. They worked to spread Catholicism in Africa, Asia, and the Americas. They became the largest order in the church and actively supported the pope.

missionary a person who works to spread a religion and make converts

Fighting the Spread of Protestantism   The Catholic Church also fought the spread of Protestantism by condemning beliefs that it considered to be errors and dealing harshly with those it labeled heretics. It looked to Catholic rulers to support its efforts and to win back lands lost to Protestantism.

To deal with heresies during the Middle Ages, the church had established the Inquisition. This body was made up of churchmen called *inquisitors* who sought out and tried heretics. Inquisitors could order various punishments, including fines and imprisonment. Sometimes they turned to civil rulers to put heretics to death.

As you learned in Unit 2, King Ferdinand and Queen Isabella used the Spanish Inquisition against Jews. With the start of the Reformation, the Spanish Inquisition also fought the spread of Protestantism. In Rome, the pope established a new Inquisition. The Roman Inquisition sought out and condemned people, including churchmen, whose views were considered dangerous. The church also published a list of books that it said offended Catholic faith or morals. Catholics were forbidden to read any of the books on the list.

This view of the Council of Trent was painted in 1633.

32.6 Effects of the Reformation

The Reformation brought lasting change to Europe. Through the influence of Europeans, it also affected other parts of the world.

Religious Wars and Persecution   The religious divisions of the Reformation led to a series of wars and persecutions during the 16th and 17th centuries. Catholics and Protestants alike persecuted members of other sects. Many people died for their beliefs. Others, like the French Protestants who moved to Switzerland, fled to different countries.

Civil wars erupted in many countries. In France, wars between Catholics and Protestants left over a million dead between 1562 and 1598. Several **massacres** added to the horror of these wars.

The wars in France were not just about religion. They were also about the power of the Catholic monarchy. Similarly, the last major war of the Reformation was both political and religious. Called the Thirty Years' War (1618–1648), it was fought mainly in Germany. The war pitted Catholics against Protestants, and Protestants against each other. But it was also a struggle for power that involved most of the nations of Europe. Nations fought for their own interests as well as for religious reasons. Catholic France, for example, sided with Protestants to combat the power of the Holy Roman Empire.

The Thirty Years' War ended with the signing of the Peace of Westphalia in 1648. This treaty called for peace between Protestants and Catholics. By deciding the control of territory, it set boundaries between Catholic and Protestant lands. Most of northern Europe, including much of Germany, was Protestant. Spain, Portugal, Italy, and France remained Catholic. So did Bohemia, Austria, and Hungary. This religious division survived into modern times.

The Rise of Nationalism and Democratic Practices
The spread of Protestantism went hand in hand with growing **nationalism**. More and more, people identified with their nation. Throughout Europe, official state religions strengthened national unity.

Along with nationalism, monarchy was also growing stronger. Protestant rulers claimed authority over religious as well as secular matters. Even Catholic rulers became increasingly independent of the pope.

massacre the killing of many helpless or unresisting people

nationalism identification with, and devotion to, the interests of one's nation

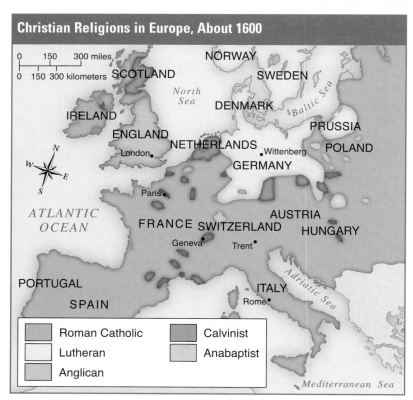

Christian Religions in Europe, About 1600

These changes led to a period that is often called "The Age of Kings and Queens." Monarchs revived the old idea of the divine right of kings. According to this idea, rulers received their authority directly from God. This way of thinking reached its height in France, where kings established an **absolute monarchy**.

Yet the Reformation also planted the seeds of democratic ideas and practices. Beginning with Martin Luther, Protestants emphasized being true to the Bible and to their own conscience. This belief made people more willing to resist authority.

Some persecuted groups sought freedom to worship in their own ways. For example, **Puritans** fled from England to America in search of religious liberty. Congregationalists insisted on the right of local church groups, or congregations, to control their own affairs. In addition, the leaders of Protestant churches were elected instead of being appointed by a central authority like the pope. Such beliefs about religious freedom and church government helped prepare the way for democracy.

The Spread of Christianity By the time of the Reformation, Europeans had embarked upon a great age of exploration. As they voyaged around the world, both Catholics and Protestants worked to spread their faith. By the 1700s, there were missionary societies in several European countries.

Jesuit missionaries were particularly active in spreading Catholicism. Jesuits traveled to India, China, Japan, and southeast Asia. Protestant missionaries worked in Ceylon, India, and Indonesia.

The religious divisions in Europe were repeated in areas controlled by countries around the world. This was especially true in the Americas. Most of the people in the English colonies of North America were Protestant. Missionaries and settlers from France brought Catholicism to parts of Canada and the Mississippi valley. The Spanish and Portuguese brought Catholicism to the American southwest, Mexico, and South America. As in Europe, these patterns of religious faith are still evident today.

absolute monarchy a monarchy in which the ruler's power is unlimited

Puritan a Protestant who wanted to "purify" the Anglican Church of Catholic elements

32.7 Chapter Summary

In this chapter, you read about three branches of Protestantism. You studied the practices and beliefs of Lutheranism, Calvinism, and Anglicanism. You also learned about the Catholic response to the Reformation and looked at some of the Reformation's lasting effects.

By the end of the religious wars that followed the Reformation, medieval Europe was largely a thing of the past. In the next unit, you will learn about the beginnings of what historians call the early modern era.

About 1450

Johannes Gutenberg begins using the newly invented printing press in Mainz, Germany.

1400 C.E.	**1425** C.E.	**1450** C.E.	**1475** C.E.	**1500** C.E.

1517

Martin Luther posts his Ninety-Five Theses on the church door in Wittenberg, Germany, an act that leads to the Reformation.

THE HOLY BIBLE

1525

William Tyndale translates the Bible into English.

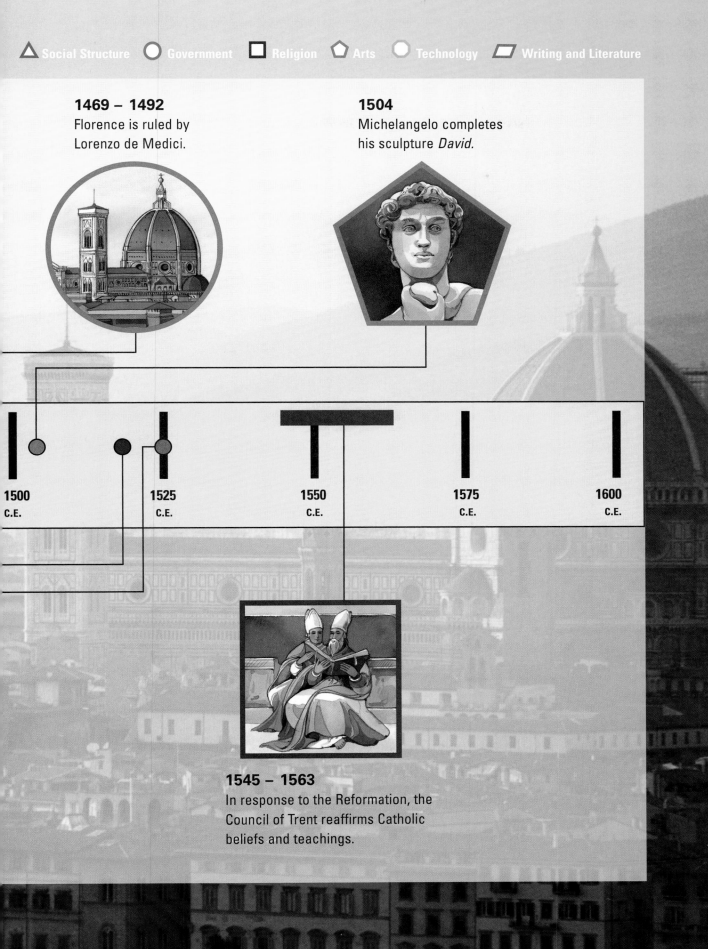

△ Social Structure ◯ Government ◻ Religion ⬠ Arts ◯ Technology ▱ Writing and Literature

1469 – 1492
Florence is ruled by
Lorenzo de Medici.

1504
Michelangelo completes
his sculpture *David.*

1500
C.E.

1525
C.E.

1550
C.E.

1575
C.E.

1600
C.E.

1545 – 1563
In response to the Reformation, the
Council of Trent reaffirms Catholic
beliefs and teachings.

UNIT 8

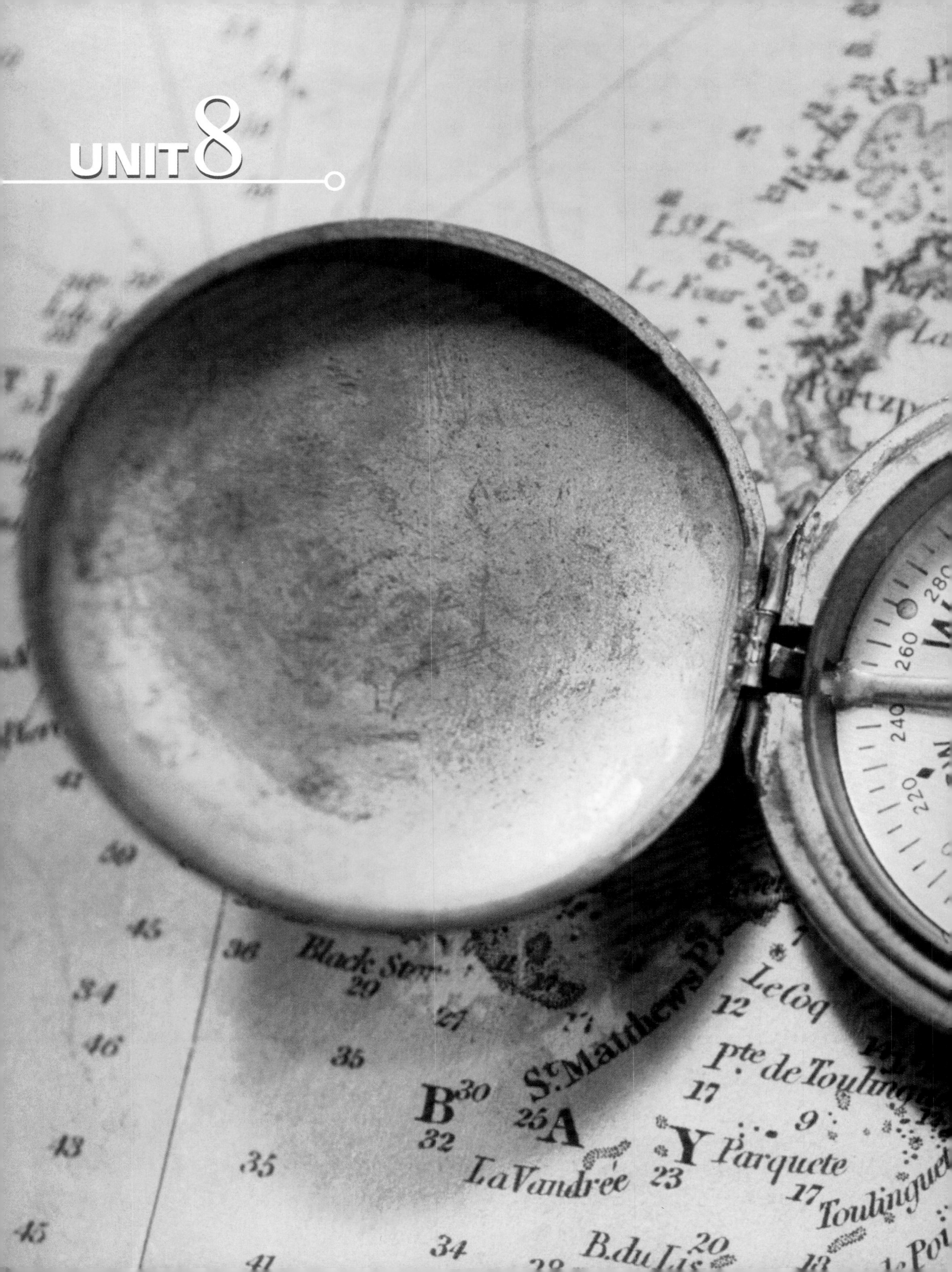

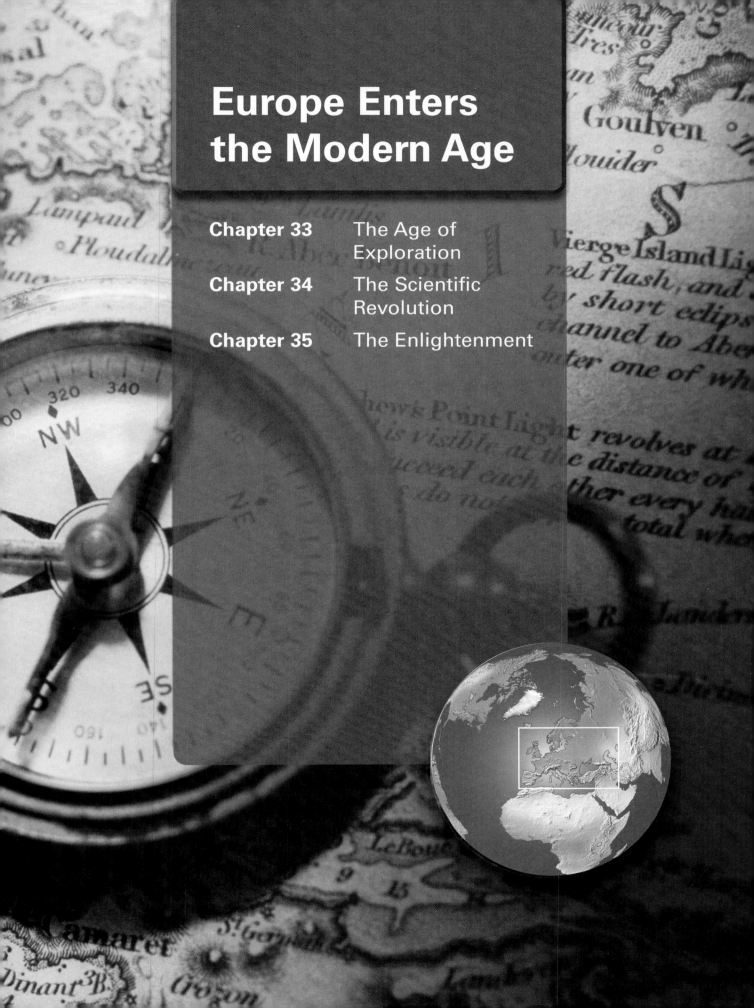

Europe Enters the Modern Age

Setting the Stage

Europe Enters the Modern Age

In the last unit, you learned about the Renaissance and the Reformation. In this unit, you'll learn about Europe during the early modern age. This period lasted from the 1400s to the 1700s.

The early modern age was a time of major discoveries and new ways of thinking. It began with a series of voyages by European explorers during the 1400s, 1500s, and early 1600s. Historians call this time the Age of Exploration.

Before the 1400s, Europeans had only limited knowledge of other continents. Beginning in about 1418, several countries sent explorers by sea to other parts of the world. Portugal and Spain led the way. They were followed

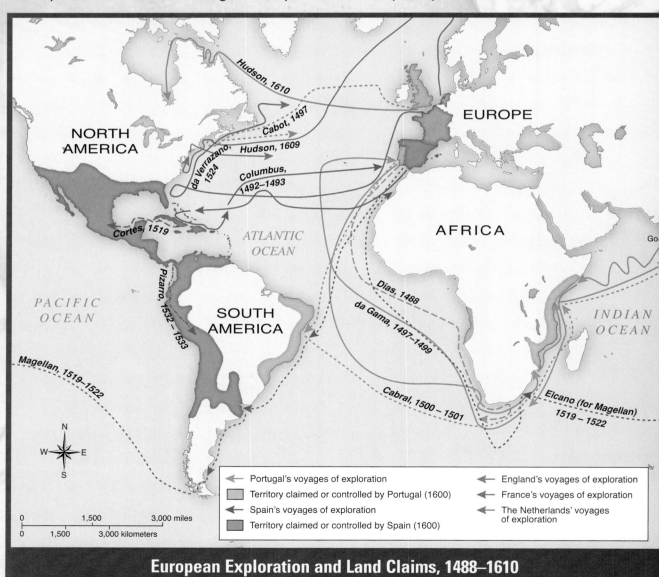

European Exploration and Land Claims, 1488–1610

by England, France, and the Netherlands. Their journeys took explorers to Africa, Asia, and North and South America. Their discoveries changed Europeans' knowledge of the world forever.

Countries raced to take advantage of this new knowledge. They sought riches through trade. They also claimed large parts of the world for themselves. As they competed with one another, Europeans had an enormous impact on people living in distant lands.

A second great change during this period was the Scientific Revolution. Between 1500 and 1700, scientists used observations, experiments, and logic to make dramatic discoveries. For example, Isaac Newton formulated the laws of gravity. These laws explained both the movement of physical objects on Earth and the motions of planets in the heavens. The methods used by Newton and other scientists led to rapid progress in many fields.

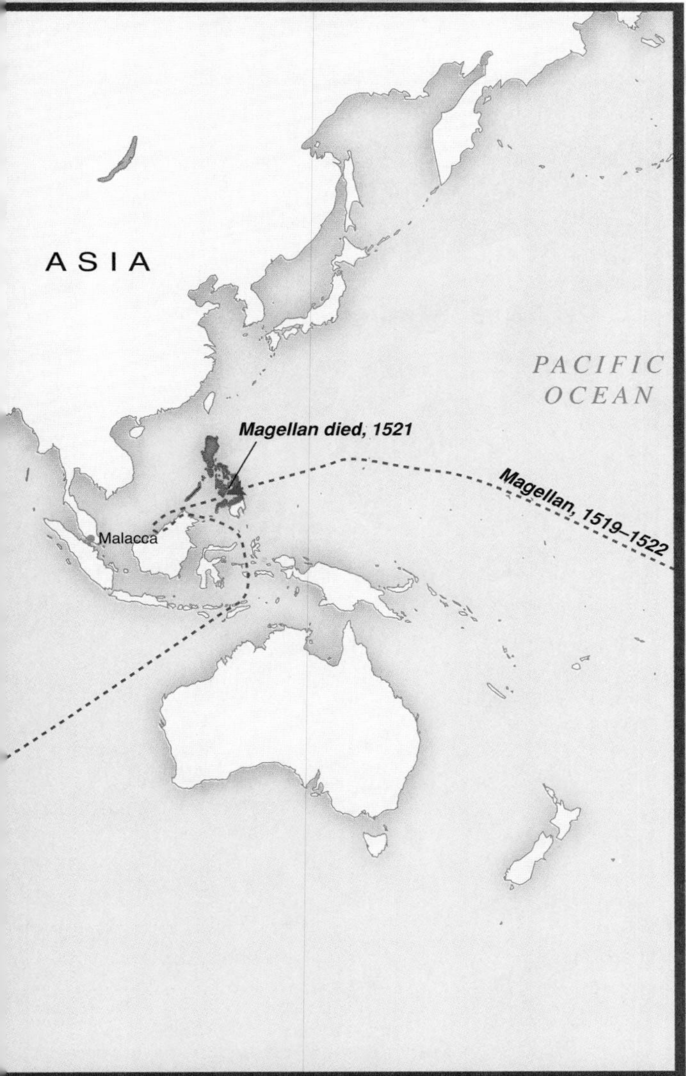

Advances in science helped pave the way for a period called the Enlightenment. The Enlightenment began during the 1600s. It was a time of optimistic faith in progress based on reason (rational thinking). In fact, it is often called the Age of Reason.

Enlightenment thinkers wanted to apply observation and reason to problems in human society. This approach led to new ideas about government, human nature, and people's rights as human beings.

The far-reaching changes of the early modern age helped to shape the world we live in today. Let's begin our study of this important time with the voyages of discovery that took place during the Age of Exploration.

ASIA

PACIFIC OCEAN

Magellan died, 1521

Magellan, 1519–1522

Malacca

CHAPTER 33

Explorer Christopher Columbus plants
Spain's flag in the Americas.

The Age of Exploration

33.1 Introduction

In this chapter, you will learn about the Age of Exploration. This period of discovery lasted from about 1418 to 1620. During this time, European **explorers** made many daring voyages that changed world history.

A major reason for these voyages was the desire to find sea routes to east Asia, which Europeans called the Indies. When Christopher Columbus sailed west across the Atlantic Ocean, he was looking for such a route. Instead, he landed in the Americas. Columbus thought he had reached the Indies. In time, Europeans would realize that he had found what they called the **"New World."** European nations soon rushed to claim lands in the Americas for themselves.

Early explorers often suffered terrible hardships. In 1520, Ferdinand Magellan set out with three ships to cross the Pacific Ocean from South America. He had guessed, correctly, that the Indies lay on the other side of the Pacific. But Magellan had no idea how vast the ocean really was. He thought his crew would be sailing for a few weeks at most. Instead, the crossing took three months. While the ships were still at sea, the crew ran out of food. One sailor wrote about this terrible time. "We ate biscuit… swarming with worms…. We drank yellow water that had been putrid [rotten] for days... and often we ate sawdust from boards."

Why did explorers brave such dangers? In this chapter, you will discover some of the reasons for the Age of Exploration. Then you will learn about the voyages of explorers from Portugal, Spain, and other European countries. You will also learn about the **impact** of their discoveries on Europe and on the lands they explored.

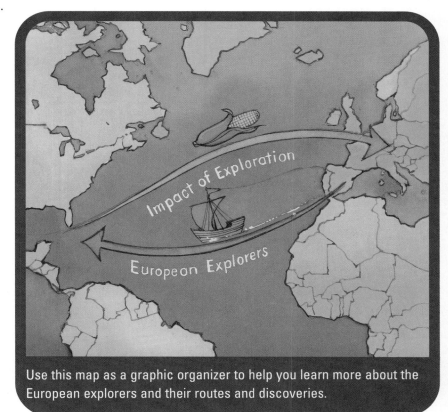

Use this map as a graphic organizer to help you learn more about the European explorers and their routes and discoveries.

33.2 Reasons for the Age of Exploration

Why did European exploration begin to flourish in the 1400s? Two main reasons stand out. First, Europeans of this time had several motives for exploring the world. Second, advances in knowledge and technology helped make voyages of discovery possible.

Motives for Exploration For early explorers, one of the main motives for exploration was the desire to find new trade routes to Asia. By the 1400s, merchants and crusaders had brought many goods to Europe from Africa, the Middle East, and Asia. Demand for these goods increased the desire for trade.

Europeans were especially interested in spices from Asia. They had learned to use spices to help preserve food during winter and to cover up the taste of food that was no longer fresh.

Trade with the East, however, was expensive and difficult. Muslims and Italians controlled the flow of trade. Muslim traders carried goods to the east coast of the Mediterranean Sea. Italian merchants then brought the goods to Europe. Problems arose when Muslim rulers sometimes closed the trade routes from Asia to Europe. Also, the goods went through many hands, and each trading party raised their price.

European monarchs and merchants wanted to break the hold that Muslims and Italians had on trade. One way to do so was to find a sea route to Asia. Portuguese sailors looked for a route that went around Africa. Christopher Columbus tried to reach Asia by sailing west across the Atlantic.

Mapmakers created better, more accurate maps by using navigational tools and information from explorers.

Other motives also came into play. Many people were excited by the opportunity for new knowledge. Explorers saw the chance to earn fame and glory as well as wealth. Some craved adventure. And as new lands were discovered, nations wanted to claim the lands' riches for themselves.

A final motive for exploration was the desire to spread Christianity. As you learned in Unit 7, both Protestant and Catholic nations were eager to make new converts. Missionaries followed the path blazed by explorers, sometimes using force to bring native peoples into their faiths.

Advances in Knowledge and Technology   The Age of Exploration began in the midst of the Renaissance. As you have learned, the Renaissance was a time of new learning. A number of advances made it easier for explorers to venture into the unknown.

One key advance was in **cartography,** the art and science of mapmaking. In the early 1400s, an Italian scholar translated an ancient book called *Guide to Geography* from Greek into Latin. The book had been written by Ptolemy in the second century C.E. Printed copies of the book inspired new interest in cartography. European mapmakers used Ptolemy's work to draw more accurate maps.

Discoveries by explorers gave mapmakers new information to work with. The result was a dramatic change in Europeans' view of the world. By the 1500s, globes showed Earth as a sphere, or ball. In 1507, a German cartographer made the first map that clearly showed North and South America separated from Asia.

In turn, better maps helped explorers by making navigation easier. The most important Renaissance geographer, Gerardus Mercator, created maps using improved lines of **longitude** and **latitude**. Mercator's mapmaking technique was a great help to navigators.

An improved ship design also helped explorers. By the 1400s, Portuguese and Spanish shipbuilders were making **caravels**. These ships were small, fast, and easy to maneuver. Their shallow bottoms made it easier for explorers to travel along coastlines where the water was not deep. Caravels also used lateen (triangular) sails, an idea borrowed from Muslim ships. These sails could be positioned to take advantage of the wind no matter which way it blew.

Along with better ships, new navigational tools helped sailors to travel more safely on the open seas. By the end of the 15th century, the compass was much improved. Sailors used compasses to find their bearing, or direction of travel. The astrolabe, which you read about in Unit 2, helped sailors figure out their distance north or south from the equator.

Finally, improved weapons gave Europeans a huge advantage over the people they met in their explorations. Sailors could fire their cannons at targets near the shore without leaving their ships. On land, the weapons of native peoples often were no match for European guns, armor, and horses.

Europe's Age of Exploration produced important advances in cartography and navigation. This 15th-century map of the world is drawn according to the work of 2nd-century Greek geographer Ptolemy.

cartography the art and science of mapmaking

longitude a measure of how far east or west a place on Earth is from an imaginary line that runs between the North and South Poles

latitude a measure of how far north or south a place on Earth is from the equator

caravel a light sailing ship that is easy to maneuver and can sail in shallow water

33.3 Portugal Begins the Age of Exploration

The Age of Exploration began in Portugal. This small country is located on the southwestern tip of Europe. Its rulers sent explorers first to nearby Africa and then around the world.

Key Explorers   The key figure in early Portuguese exploration was Prince Henry, the son of King John I. Nicknamed "the Navigator," Henry was not an explorer himself. Instead, he encouraged exploration and directed many important expeditions.

Beginning in about 1418, Henry sent explorers to sea almost every year. He also started a school of navigation where sailors and mapmakers could learn their trades. His cartographers made new maps based on the information captains brought back.

Henry's early expeditions focused on the west coast of Africa. He wanted to continue the crusades against the Muslims, find gold, and take part in trade.

Gradually, Portuguese explorers made their way farther and farther south. In 1488, Bartolomeu Dias became the first European to go around the southern tip of Africa. Later, Dias died in a storm at sea.

Prince Henry the Navigator encouraged Portuguese exploration and began a school of navigation.

Vasco da Gama

In July 1497, Vasco da Gama set sail with four ships to chart a sea route to India. Da Gama's ships rounded Africa's southern tip and then sailed up the east coast of the continent. With the help of a sailor who knew the route to India, they crossed the Indian Ocean.

Da Gama arrived in the port of Calicut, India, in May 1498. There he obtained a load of cinnamon and pepper. On the return trip to Portugal, da Gama lost half of his ships. Many of his crewmembers died of hunger or disease. Still, the valuable cargo he brought back paid for the voyage many times over. His trip made the Portuguese even more eager to trade directly with Indian merchants.

In 1500, Pedro Cabral set sail for India with a fleet of 13 ships. Cabral first sailed southwest to avoid calms (areas where there are no winds to fill sails). But he sailed so far west that he reached the east coast of present-day Brazil. After claiming this land for Portugal, he sailed east and rounded Africa. Arriving in Calicut, he established a trading post and signed trading treaties. He returned to Portugal in June 1501 after battling several Muslim ships.

The Impact of Portuguese Exploration

Portugal's explorers changed Europeans' understanding of the world in several ways. They explored the coasts of Africa and brought back gold and slaves. They also found a sea route to India. From India, explorers brought back spices like cinnamon and pepper and goods such as porcelain, incense, jewels, and silk.

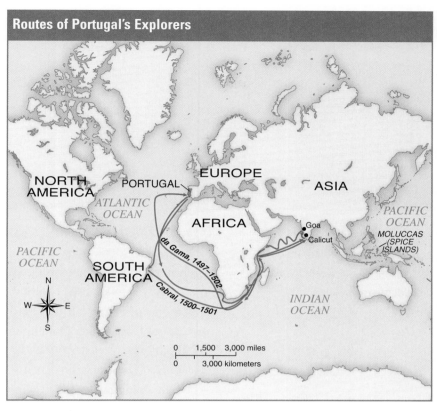

Routes of Portugal's Explorers

After Cabral's voyage, the Portuguese took control of the eastern sea routes to Asia. They seized the seaport of Goa in India and built forts there. They attacked towns on the east coast of Africa. They also set their sights on the Moluccas, or Spice Islands, in what is now Indonesia. In 1511, they attacked the main port of the islands and killed the Muslim defenders. The captain of this expedition explained what was at stake. If Portugal could take the spice trade away from Muslim traders, he wrote, then Cairo and Makkah "will be ruined." As for Italian merchants, "Venice will receive no spices unless her merchants go to buy them in Portugal."

Portugal's control of the Indian Ocean broke the hold of Muslims and Italians on Asian trade. The prices of Asian goods like spices and fabrics dropped, and more people in Europe could afford to buy them.

During the 1500s, Portugal also began to establish **colonies** in Brazil. The native people of Brazil suffered greatly as a result. The Portuguese tried to get the native people to give up their religion and convert to Christianity. They also forced them to work on sugar **plantations**. Missionaries sometimes tried to protect them from abuse, but countless numbers died from overwork and European diseases. Others fled into the interior of Brazil.

The colonization of Brazil also had an impact on Africa. As the native population of Brazil decreased, the Portuguese needed more laborers. Starting in the mid 1500s, they turned to Africa. Over the next 300 years, ships brought millions of enslaved West Africans to Brazil.

colony a country or an area ruled by another country
plantation a large farm where crops such as sugar, rubber, or tobacco are grown

Pedro Cabral

Explorer Christopher Columbus convinced King Ferdinand and Queen Isabella of Spain to support his westward voyages.

33.4 Spain's Early Explorations

In the late 1400s, King Ferdinand and Queen Isabella of Spain were determined to make their country a powerful force in Europe. One way to do this was to sponsor explorations and claim new lands for Spain.

Key Explorers It was Ferdinand and Isabella who sponsored the voyages of Christopher Columbus. The Italian-born Columbus thought that the Indies, or eastern Asia, lay on the other side of the Atlantic Ocean. He believed sailing west would be the easiest route to the Indies.

When Columbus failed to win Portuguese support for his idea, he turned to Spain. Ferdinand and Isabella agreed to pay for the risky voyage. They wanted to beat Portugal in the race to control the wealth of Asia. They also wanted to spread Christianity.

In August 1492, three ships left Spain under Columbus's command. For the crew, venturing into the open ocean was frightening. As the weeks went by, some of the men began to fear they would never see Spain again.

Then, on October 12, a lookout cried "Land!" Columbus went ashore on an island in the Caribbean Sea. Thinking he had reached the Indies, Columbus claimed the island for Spain.

For three months, Columbus and his men explored nearby islands with the help of native islanders, whom the Spanish called Taino. Thinking they were in the Indies, the Spanish soon called all the local people "Indians."

In March 1493, Columbus arrived back in Spain. He proudly reported that he had reached Asia. Over the next 10 years, he made three more voyages to what he called the West Indies. He died in Spain in 1506, still insisting that he had sailed to Asia.

Many Europeans, however, believed that Columbus had actually found a land mass that lay between Europe and Asia. One of these people was Ferdinand Magellan, a Portuguese explorer.

Magellan believed he could sail west to the Indies if he found a **strait,** or channel, through South America. The strait would connect the Atlantic and Pacific Oceans, allowing ships to continue on to Asia.

Magellan won Spain's backing for a voyage to find the strait. In August 1519, he set sail with five ships and about 250 men.

strait a narrow body of water that connects two seas

Christopher Columbus

Magellan looked for the strait all along South America's east coast. He finally found it at the southern tip of the continent. Today it is called the Strait of Magellan.

After passing through the strait, Magellan reached the Pacific Ocean in November 1520. It took another three months to cross the Pacific. During the crossing, Magellan's men ran out of food and were plagued by disease and thirst. They reached an island in the western Pacific just in time.

Continuing west, Magellan visited the Philippines. There he became involved in a battle between two local chiefs. In April 1521, Magellan was killed in the fighting.

Magellan's crew sailed on to the Spice Islands. Three years after the expedition began, the only ship to survive the expedition returned to Spain, loaded with cloves. The 18 sailors on board were the first people to **circumnavigate** the globe.

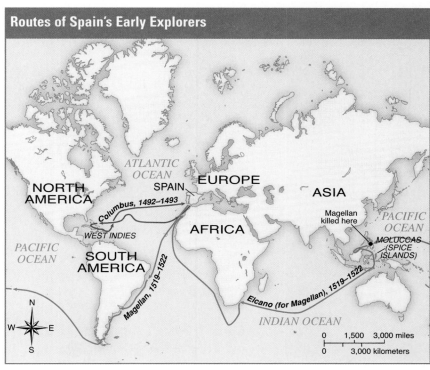

Routes of Spain's Early Explorers

The Impact of Early Spanish Exploration   Early Spanish exploration changed Europeans' view of the world. The voyages of Columbus revealed the existence of the Americas. Magellan's expedition opened up a westward route to the Indies. It showed that it was possible to sail completely around the world. And it proved that Columbus had indeed found a "New World"—one they hadn't realized was there.

Columbus's voyages were the beginning of Spanish settlement in the West Indies. Spain earned great wealth from its settlements. Settlers mined for precious minerals and started sugar plantations. The Spanish also sent Europe new crops, such as sweet potatoes and pineapples.

For the native people of the West Indies, Spanish settlement was devastating. Priests forced many of them to become Christians. Native people were forced to work as slaves in the mines and on the plantations. When the Spanish arrived, perhaps 1 or 2 million Taino lived on the islands. Within 50 years, fewer than 500 were left. The rest had died of starvation, overwork, or European diseases.

Like Portugal, Spain looked to West Africa for new sources of laborers. From 1518 through the mid 1800s, the Spanish brought millions of enslaved Africans to work in their American colonies.

circumnavigate to travel completely around something, such as Earth

Ferdinand Magellan

When Spanish explorer Cortes first entered Mexico, he was welcomed by the Aztec ruler, Montezuma.

Hernan Cortes

33.5 Later Spanish Exploration and Conquest

After Columbus's voyages, Spain was eager to claim lands in the New World. To explore and conquer "New Spain," the Spanish turned to adventurers called *conquistadors* (conquerors). The conquistadors were allowed to establish settlements and seize the wealth of natives. In return, the Spanish government claimed one fifth of the treasures they found.

Key Explorers In 1519, Spanish explorer Hernan Cortes and a band of conquistadors set out to explore present-day Mexico. From native people, Cortes learned about the Aztecs. As you discovered in Unit 6, the Aztecs had built a large and wealthy empire in Mexico.

With the help of a native woman named Malinche, Cortes and his men reached the Aztec capital, Tenochtitlan. The Aztec ruler, Montezuma, welcomed the Spanish with great honors. Determined to break the power of the Aztecs, Cortes took Montezuma hostage.

Cortes now controlled the Aztec capital. In 1520, he left Tenochtitlan to battle a rival Spanish force. While he was gone, a group of conquistadors attacked the Aztecs in the midst of a religious celebration. In response, the Aztecs rose up against the Spanish. The soldiers had to fight their way out of the city. Many of them were killed during the escape.

The following year, Cortes mounted a siege of the city, aided by thousands of native allies who resented Aztec rule. The Aztecs ran out of food and water, yet they fought desperately. After several months, the Spanish captured their leader, and Aztec resistance collapsed. The city was in ruins. The mighty Aztec Empire was no more.

Four factors contributed to the defeat of the Aztec Empire. First, Aztec legend had told of the coming of a white-skinned god. When Cortes appeared, the Aztecs welcomed him because they thought he might be their god Quetzalcoatl. Second, Cortes was able to make allies of the Aztecs' native enemies. Third, their horses, armor, and superior weapons gave the Spanish an advantage in battle. The Aztecs had never seen any of these things before. Fourth, the Spanish carried diseases that caused deadly **epidemics** among the Aztecs.

Aztec riches inspired Spanish conquistadors to continue their search for gold. In the 1520s, Francisco Pizarro received permission from Spain to conquer the Inca Empire in South America. As you learned in Unit 6, the Incas ruled an empire that ran along most of the Andes Mountains. By the time Pizarro arrived, however, a civil war had weakened the empire.

In April 1532, the Inca emperor, Atahualpa, greeted the Spanish as guests. Following Cortes's example, Pizarro launched a surprise attack and kidnapped the emperor. Although the Incas paid a roomful of gold and silver for Atahualpa's ransom, the Spanish killed him the following year. Without their leader, the Incas' empire quickly fell apart.

The Impact of Later Spanish Exploration and Conquest

The explorations and conquests of the conquistadors transformed Spain. The Spanish rapidly expanded foreign trade and overseas colonization. For a time, wealth from the Americas made Spain one of the world's richest and most powerful countries.

Besides gold and silver, ships brought corn and potatoes from the New World to Spain. These crops grew well in Europe. By increasing the food supply, they helped spur a population boom. Conquistadors also introduced Europeans to new luxury items, such as chocolate and tobacco.

In the long run, gold and silver from the Americas hurt Spain's economy. **Inflation,** or an increase in the supply of money compared to goods, led to higher prices. Monarchs and the wealthy spent their riches wastefully instead of building up Spain's industries.

The Spanish conquests had a major impact on the New World. The Spanish introduced new animals to the Americas, such as horses, cattle, sheep, and pigs. But they also destroyed two advanced civilizations. The Aztecs and Incas lost much of their culture along with their wealth. Many became laborers for the Spanish. Millions died from disease. In Mexico, for example, there were about 25 million native people in 1519. By 1605, this number had dwindled to 1 million.

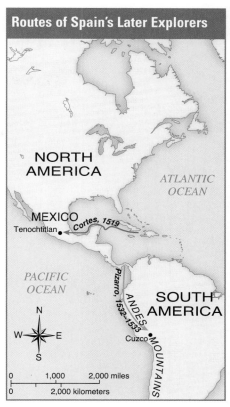

Routes of Spain's Later Explorers

NORTH AMERICA

ATLANTIC OCEAN

MEXICO

Tenochtitlan • Cortes, 1519

PACIFIC OCEAN

Pizarro, 1532–1533

SOUTH AMERICA

Cuzco •

ANDES MOUNTAINS

N W E S

0   1,000   2,000 miles
0   2,000 kilometers

epidemic an outbreak of a disease that affects many people within a geographic area

inflation an increase in the supply of money compared to goods, resulting in higher prices

Francisco Pizarro

33.6 European Exploration of North America

Spain and Portugal dominated the early years of exploration. Rulers in rival nations wanted their own share of trade and new lands in the Americas. Soon England, France, and the Netherlands all sent expeditions to North America.

Key Explorers Explorers often sailed for any country that would pay for their voyages. The Italian sailor John Cabot made England's first voyage of discovery. Cabot believed he could reach the Indies by sailing northwest across the Atlantic. In 1497, he landed in what is now Canada. Believing he had reached the northeast coast of Asia, he claimed the region for England.

The next year, Cabot set out on another voyage with five ships. The fate of this expedition is uncertain. Cabot may have returned to England, or he may have been lost at sea.

Another Italian, Giovanni da Verrazano, sailed under the French flag. In 1524, da Verrazano explored the Atlantic coast from present-day North Carolina to Canada. His voyage gave France its first claims in the Americas. Like many explorers, however, he met an unhappy end. On a later trip to the West Indies, he was killed and eaten by native people.

English explorer Henry Hudson traded with native North Americans.

Sailing for the Netherlands, English explorer Henry Hudson journeyed to North America in 1609. Hudson wanted to find a **northwest passage** through North America to the Pacific Ocean. Such a water route would allow ships to sail from Europe to Asia without entering waters controlled by Spain.

Hudson did not find a northwest passage, but he did explore what is now called the Hudson River. Twenty years later, Dutch settlers (people from the Netherlands) began arriving in the Hudson River valley.

The next year Hudson tried again, this time under the flag of his native England. Searching farther north, he sailed into a large bay in Canada that is now called Hudson Bay. He spent three months looking for an outlet to the Pacific, but there was none.

northwest passage a water route through North America connecting the Atlantic and Pacific Oceans

John Cabot

After a hard winter in the icy bay, some of Hudson's crew rebelled. They set him, his son, and seven loyal followers adrift in a small boat. Hudson and the other castaways were never seen again. Hudson's voyage, however, laid the basis for later English claims in Canada.

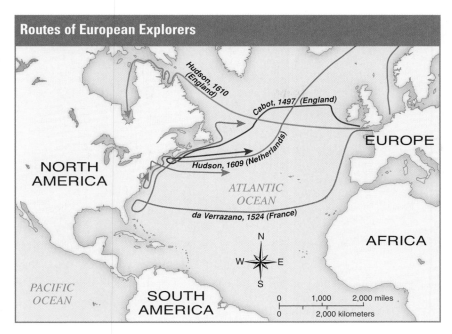

Routes of European Explorers

Hudson, 1610 (England)

Cabot, 1497 (England)

EUROPE

NORTH AMERICA

Hudson, 1609 (Netherlands)

ATLANTIC OCEAN

da Verrazano, 1524 (France)

AFRICA

N W E S

PACIFIC OCEAN

SOUTH AMERICA

0   1,000   2,000 miles

0   2,000 kilometers

The Impact of European Exploration of North America

Unlike the conquistadors in the south, northern explorers did not find gold and other treasure. As a result, there was less interest at first in starting colonies.

Canada's shores did offer rich resources of cod and other fish. Within a few years of Cabot's trip, fishing boats regularly visited the region. Europeans were also interested in trading with Native Americans for otter skins, whale oil, and beaver and fox furs. By the 1600s, Europeans had set up a number of trading posts in North America.

English exploration also contributed to a war between England and Spain. As English ships roamed the seas, some captains, nicknamed "sea dogs," began raiding Spanish ports and ships to take their gold. Between 1577 and 1580, Francis Drake sailed around the world. He also claimed part of what is now California for England, ignoring Spain's claims to the area.

The English raids added to other tensions between England and Spain. In 1588, King Philip II of Spain sent an armada, or fleet, to invade England. With 130 heavily armed vessels and about 31,000 men, the Spanish Armada seemed an unbeatable force. But the smaller English fleet was fast and well armed. Their guns had a longer range, so they could attack from a safe distance. After several battles, a number of the armada's ships had been sunk or driven ashore. The rest turned around but faced terrible storms on the way home. Fewer than half of the ships made it back to Spain.

The defeat of the Spanish Armada marked the start of a shift in power in Europe. By 1630, Spain no longer dominated the continent. With Spain's decline, other countries—particularly England and the Netherlands—took an active role in trade and colonization around the world.

Giovanni da Verrazano

Henry Hudson

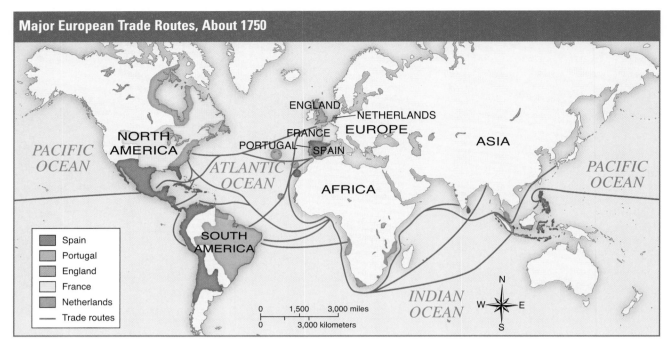

Major European Trade Routes, About 1750

Spain
Portugal
England
France
Netherlands
— Trade routes

0   1,500   3,000 miles
0   3,000 kilometers

33.7 The Impact of Exploration on European Commerce and Economies

The voyages of explorers had a dramatic impact on European commerce and economies. As a result of exploration, more goods, raw materials, and precious metals entered Europe. Mapmakers carefully charted trade routes and the locations of newly discovered lands. By the 1700s, European ships traveled trade routes that spanned the globe. New centers of commerce developed in the port cities of the Netherlands and England, which had colonies and trading posts in faraway lands.

Exploration and trade contributed to the growth of **capitalism**. This economic system is based on investing money for profit. Merchants gained great wealth by trading and selling goods from around the world. Many of them used their profits to finance still more voyages and to start trading companies. Other people began investing money in these companies and shared in the profits. Soon this type of shared ownership was applied to other kinds of business.

Another aspect of the capitalist economy concerned the way people exchanged goods and services. Money became more important as precious metals flowed into Europe. Instead of having a fixed price, items were sold for prices that were set by the open market. This meant that the price of an item depended on how much of the item was available and how many people wanted to buy it. Sellers could charge high prices for scarce items that many people wanted. If the supply of an item was large and few people wanted it, sellers lowered the price. This kind of system is called a **market economy**.

Labor, too, was given a money value. Increasingly, people began working for hire instead of directly providing for their own needs.

capitalism an economic system based on investment of money (capital) for profit

market economy an economy in which prices are determined by the buying and selling decisions of individuals in the marketplace

Merchants hired people to work in their own cottages, turning raw materials from overseas into finished products. This growing **cottage industry** was especially important in the making of textiles. Often entire families worked at home, spinning wool into thread or weaving thread into cloth. Cottage industry was a step toward the system of factories operated by capitalists in later centuries.

A final result of exploration was a new economic policy called **mercantilism**. European rulers believed that piling up wealth was the best way to build their countries' power. For this reason, they tried to reduce the things they bought from other countries and increase the items they sold.

Having colonies was a key part of this policy. Nations looked to their colonies to supply raw materials for their industries. They profited by turning the materials into finished goods that they could sell to other countries and to their own colonies. To protect the valuable trade with their colonies, rulers often forbade colonists from trading with other nations.

Weaving cloth became a growing cottage industry as families set up looms and workshops in their homes.

cottage industry a small-scale business in which people work mostly at home

mercantilism an economic policy by which nations try to gather as much gold and silver as possible by controlling trade and establishing colonies

33.8 Chapter Summary

In this chapter, you learned about the Age of Exploration. Beginning in the 1400s, European explorers went on great voyages of discovery. Their voyages had a major impact on Europe and on the lands they explored.

European explorers sought wealth, land, knowledge, and adventure. They also wanted to spread Christianity. A number of advances in knowledge and technology made their journeys possible.

The Portuguese explored Africa's coasts, charted a sea route to Asia, and claimed Brazil. The voyages of Christopher Columbus led to Spanish colonization in the Americas. England, France, and the Netherlands sent explorers to North America.

Millions of people living in the Americas died as a result of European colonization and conquest. The Inca and Aztec Empires were destroyed. West Africans suffered greatly when they were brought to the Americas to work as slaves.

The Age of Exploration vastly increased Europeans' knowledge of the world. In the next chapter, you will learn about another source of new knowledge: the Scientific Revolution.

CHAPTER 34

The Scientific Revolution

34.1 Introduction

In the last chapter, you read about the Age of Exploration. You learned that voyages of discovery changed how Europeans saw the world. Now you will learn about another major shift in thinking, the **Scientific Revolution**.

Between 1500 and 1700, modern science emerged as a new way of gaining knowledge about the natural world. Before this time, Europeans relied on two main sources for their understanding of nature. One was the Bible. The other was the work of classical thinkers, especially the philosopher Aristotle.

During the Scientific Revolution, scientists challenged traditional teachings about nature. They asked fresh questions, and they answered them in new ways. Inventions like the telescope showed them a universe no one had imagined before. Careful observation also revealed errors in accepted ideas about the physical world.

A good example is Aristotle's description of falling objects. Aristotle had said that heavier objects fall to the ground faster than lighter ones. This idea seemed logical, but the Italian scientist Galileo Galilei questioned it.

According to his first biographer, one day Galileo performed a demonstration in the city of Pisa, where he was teaching. He dropped two balls of different weights from the city's famous Leaning Tower.

The results shocked the watching crowd of students and professors. They expected the heavier ball to land first. Instead, the two balls landed at the same time.

Galileo's demonstration is an example of the **scientific method**. As you will learn, the scientific method uses both logic and observation to help people find out how the natural world works.

The work of thinkers like Galileo gave birth to modern science. In this chapter, you will first learn about the roots of the Scientific Revolution. Then you'll meet some of the key **scientists** of this period. You'll find out about their major **discoveries** and **inventions**. You'll also learn how their work gave rise to the scientific method.

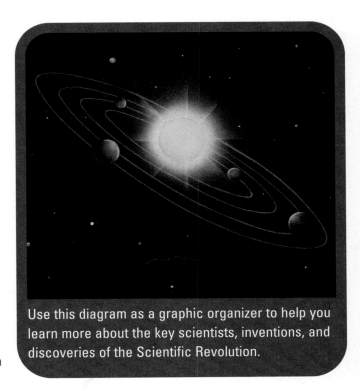

Use this diagram as a graphic organizer to help you learn more about the key scientists, inventions, and discoveries of the Scientific Revolution.

34.2 Roots of the Scientific Revolution

Humans have asked questions about nature since ancient times. What was different about the Scientific Revolution of the 16th and 17th centuries? And what factors helped to bring it about?

Humanist studies from the Renaissance influenced later scientific discoveries. Da Vinci's drawing *Vitruvian Man* (detail) is a famous study of the human body from this period.

rationalism belief in reason and logic as the primary source of knowledge

During the Middle Ages, two major sources guided most Europeans' thinking about the natural world. The first was the Bible. For Christians, the Bible was the word of God. Whatever the Bible seemed to say about nature, then, must be true.

The second source was the teachings of Aristotle. This Greek philosopher had written about nature in the 300s B.C.E. In the late Middle Ages, thinkers like Thomas Aquinas combined Aristotle's thinking with Christian faith. The result was a view of the world that seemed to be a satisfying whole.

During the Renaissance, many thinkers began to question this worldview. As you have learned, Renaissance scholars rediscovered more of the culture of ancient Greece and Rome. A number of ancient texts came to Europe by way of Muslim lands, where they had been preserved during the Middle Ages. Arab, Christian, and Jewish scholars in the Muslim world translated many classical works. They also made advances of their own in such fields as medicine, astronomy, and mathematics.

From the works of these scholars, Europeans learned about a greater variety of ideas than just those of Aristotle. Many thinkers were influenced by Greek **rationalism**. This was the belief that reason (logical thought) could be used to discover basic truths about the world. Renaissance thinkers also observed nature for themselves. You may remember how Vesalius cut up corpses to test ancient ideas about the body. Trust in reason and observation became a key part of modern science.

The voyages of explorers also helped spur the growth of science. For instance, in the second century C.E., Ptolemy had stated that there were only three continents: Europe, Africa, and Asia. Explorers who visited the Americas proved that he was wrong. Such discoveries encouraged Europeans to question traditional teachings.

Gradually, scientists developed a new method for probing nature's mysteries. As you will see, their work led to many dramatic discoveries.

34.3 Copernicus and Kepler: A New View of the Universe

The Scientific Revolution began with the work of Polish astronomer Nicolaus Copernicus. You met Copernicus when you read about the Renaissance. Let's see how his work led to a new view of the universe.

For almost 2,000 years, most people believed that Earth was the center of the universe. According to this **geocentric** theory, the sun, stars, and planets traveled around a motionless Earth.

Aristotle had taught this theory. The Bible seemed to support it as well. For example, in one Bible story God stops the sun from moving across the sky. The geocentric theory also seemed to make sense. After all, the sun and stars do look like they travel around Earth.

Aristotle had also taught that all heavenly bodies move in circles. Unfortunately, this belief made it hard to explain the observed movements of planets such as Mars and Jupiter. In the second century C.E., Ptolemy created a complicated theory to account for these observations.

Both ancient and medieval writers, including Muslim scientists, pointed out problems with Ptolemy's theory. In the early 1500s, Copernicus tackled these problems. Using observations and mathematics, he proposed a very different idea. His **heliocentric** theory put the sun at the center of the universe. Earth and the other planets, he said, traveled in circles around the sun. Earth also turned on its own axis every 24 hours. This turning explained why heavenly objects seemed to move across the sky.

Like Ptolemy, Copernicus had trouble predicting the movement of planets with perfect accuracy. Still, he thought his theory was simpler and more satisfying than Ptolemy's. In 1543, he published a book describing his idea. The book convinced very few people. Some church officials and scientists attacked it.

Then, in the early 1600s, German scientist Johannes Kepler improved on Copernicus's theory. After studying detailed records of planetary observations, Kepler figured out that the **orbits** (paths) of the planets were ellipses (ovals), not circles. With this insight, he wrote precise mathematical laws describing the movements of the planets around the sun.

Kepler's laws agreed beautifully with actual observations. This agreement was evidence that the Copernican theory was correct. Once the theory took hold, people would never see the universe in the same way again.

geocentric having Earth at the center (*Geo* is Greek for "Earth.")
heliocentric having the sun at the center (*Helios* is Greek for "sun.")
orbit the path that one heavenly body (such as a planet) follows around another (such as the sun)

Copernicus's heliocentric theory put the sun at the center of the universe. Before this, people thought all planets revolved around Earth.

34.4 Galileo and the Copernican Theory

Galileo lived at the same time as Johannes Kepler. Galileo explored many questions. He was especially interested in problems of motion. As you have read, he disproved Aristotle's theory that heavy objects fall faster than lighter ones. He made other discoveries about motion as well. For example, he used mathematics to describe the paths of **projectiles**.

Galileo's biggest impact came when he turned his curiosity to the heavens. What he learned made him a champion of the Copernican theory.

Galileo's Discoveries   In 1609, Galileo was teaching in Padua, Italy, when he heard about an invention from the Netherlands: the telescope. The telescope used glass lenses to make distant objects appear much closer.

Galileo decided to build his own telescope. He figured out how telescopes worked. He learned how to grind glass. Soon he was building more and more powerful telescopes.

That fall, Galileo began studying the heavens through a telescope. He saw things no one had seen before. He saw that the moon's surface was rough and uneven. He discovered four moons revolving around the planet Jupiter.

Galileo also observed the planet Venus. To the naked eye, Venus looks like a bright star. Galileo saw something new. You know from looking at the moon that it goes through phases. It takes on what appear to be different shapes, from a thin sliver to the full moon. With his telescope, Galileo could see that Venus also passed through phases. Sometimes it was brightly lit. At other times it was partially dark.

Galileo's discoveries contradicted the traditional view of the universe. For example, Aristotle had taught that the moon was perfectly smooth. Galileo saw that it wasn't. Aristotle had said that Earth was the only center of motion in the universe. Galileo saw moons going around Jupiter. Aristotle believed that Venus and other planets traveled around Earth. Galileo realized that the phases of Venus meant that it was traveling around the sun. As seen from Earth, sometimes only part of Venus was lit by the sun.

Galileo already believed in the Copernican theory of the universe. What he saw through his telescope only convinced him more.

projectile an object that is fired or launched, such as a cannonball

Galileo's work with telescopes helped him discover new information about the planets that supported Copernicus's theories about the universe.

Conflict with the Church

Galileo's discoveries led him into a bitter conflict with the Catholic Church. Church leaders saw the Copernican theory as both wrong and dangerous. To them, the idea that Earth was the center of the universe was part of an entire system of belief approved by the church. Church officials feared that attacks on the geocentric theory could lead people to doubt the church's teachings. In 1616, the church warned Galileo not to teach the Copernican theory.

Galileo refused to be silenced. In 1632, he published a book called *Dialogue on the Two Chief World Systems*. The book described an imaginary conversation about the theories of Ptolemy and Copernicus. Galileo did not openly take sides, but the book was really a clever argument for the Copernican theory. The character who upheld the geocentric theory was portrayed as foolish. The one who believed the heliocentric theory was logical and convincing.

Galileo's *Dialogue* caused an uproar. In 1633, the pope called Galileo to Rome to face the church court known as the Inquisition.

At Galileo's trial, church leaders accused him of heresy. They demanded that he confess his error. At first Galileo resisted. In the end, the court forced him to swear that the geocentric theory was true. He was forbidden to write again about the Copernican theory.

Galileo's Influence

The church's opposition could not stop the spread of Galileo's ideas. Scientists all over Europe read his witty *Dialogue*. The book helped convert many people to the Copernican theory. The Inquisition ordered the burning of the *Dialogue*.

Galileo's studies of motion also advanced the Scientific Revolution. Like Kepler, he used observation and mathematics to solve scientific problems. Galileo's theory of motion described how objects moved on Earth. Kepler's laws described the movements of the planets. The next scientist you will meet united these ideas in a single great theory.

Galileo was brought before the Inquisition, Rome's court, because his new beliefs were unacceptable to the church. Church officials demanded that he agree that Earth is at the center of the universe.

34.5 Isaac Newton and the Law of Gravity

Isaac Newton was born in 1642, the same year Galileo died. Newton became a brilliant scientist and mathematician. His greatest discovery was the law of gravity.

In later life, Newton told a story about his discovery. He was trying to figure out what kept the moon traveling in its orbit around Earth. Since the moon was in motion, why didn't it fly off into space in a straight line? Then Newton saw an apple fall from a tree. He wondered if the same force that pulled the apple to the ground was tugging on the moon. The difference was that the moon was far away, and Newton reasoned that the force was weaker there. It was just strong enough to bend the moon's motion into a nearly circular path around Earth.

This was Newton's great insight. A single force explained a falling apple on Earth and the movements of heavenly bodies as well. Newton called this force *gravity*.

Newton stated the law of gravity in a simple formula. All physical objects, he said, had a force of attraction between them. The strength of the force depended on the **masses** of the objects and the distance between them. For example, the moon and Earth tugged on each other. At a certain point in space, these "tugs" canceled each other out. The result was that the moon was trapped in its orbit around Earth. In contrast, an apple had a small mass and was very close to Earth, so gravity dragged it to the ground.

In 1687, Newton published a book known as the *Principia* (Principles). The book presented the law of gravity. It also described three laws of motion. Newton's laws provided a physical explanation for what earlier scientists had discovered. For example, others had shown that the planets moved around the sun. Newton's laws explained why. Just as gravity kept the moon traveling around Earth, it kept the planets traveling around the sun.

Newton's laws dramatically changed people's picture of the universe. Many people began to see the universe as a beautifully designed machine. Some compared it to a well-built clock. The same mathematical laws applied everywhere. All people had to do was discover them.

Inspiration for new ideas and discoveries often comes when the ordinary is seen in a new way. Isaac Newton gained insight into the laws of nature after observing an apple fall to the ground.

mass the amount of matter in an object

34.6 The Scientific Method

A key outcome of the Scientific Revolution was the development of the scientific method. Two philosophers who influenced this development were Francis Bacon and Rene Descartes.

Francis Bacon was born in England in 1561. Bacon distrusted much of the traditional learning of the Middle Ages. He said people could gain knowledge only if they rid their minds of false beliefs. He outlined a method of scientific investigation that depended on close observation.

Rene Descartes was born in France in 1596. Descartes prized logic and mathematics. To gain knowledge that was certain, he said, people should doubt every statement until logic proved it to be true. Descartes also saw the physical universe as obeying universal mathematical laws.

These ideas helped create a new approach to science. Over time, scientists developed this approach into the scientific method.

The scientific method combines logic, mathematics, and observation. It has five basic steps:

1. The scientist states a question or problem.
2. The scientist forms a **hypothesis,** or assumption, about the problem.
3. The scientist designs and conducts an experiment to test the hypothesis.
4. The scientist measures the **data,** or information, produced by the experiment and records the results.
5. The scientist analyzes the data to determine whether the hypothesis is correct.

Galileo's demonstration with falling objects shows how this method works. Galileo wondered whether objects of different weights fall at the same speed. He formed a hypothesis that they did. Then he designed and conducted an experiment. He dropped a heavy and a light ball from a tower and saw that they landed at the same time. This result showed that his hypothesis was correct.

Scientists still use this basic method today. An advantage of the method is that any trained scientist can repeat what another has done. In this way, scientists can test others' ideas for themselves.

In one way, the spread of the scientific method marked a break with the past. Fewer and fewer people looked to traditional authorities for the answers to scientific problems. But that did not mean they discarded all their old beliefs. For example, thinkers such as Descartes and Newton were deeply religious. For many, science was a way to better understand the world God had made.

Galileo tested his hypotheses about gravity by dropping two different-size balls from the top of the Leaning Tower of Pisa.

hypothesis an idea or assumption to be tested in an experiment

data facts or information

Steps in the Scientific Method

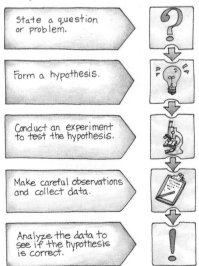

State a question or problem.

Form a hypothesis.

Conduct an experiment to test the hypothesis.

Make careful observations and collect data.

Analyze the data to see if the hypothesis is correct.

Antonie van Leeuwenhoek observed microorganisms through microscopes that he designed.

34.7 Key Inventions

The Scientific Revolution spurred the invention of new tools for studying nature. These tools helped scientists discover new facts and measure data more accurately.

One example of such a tool is the telescope, which makes distant objects seem closer. A similar invention was the **microscope,** which makes small objects appear much larger.

The microscope was invented by Dutch lens makers in the late 1500s. In the mid 1600s, the Dutchman Antonie van Leeuwenhoek designed his own powerful microscopes. He became the first person to see bacteria. Leeuwenhoek was amazed to find a tiny world of living things. He exclaimed, "All the people living in our United Netherlands are not so many as the living animals that I carry in my own mouth this very day!"

Another important tool was the **barometer**. A barometer measures changes in the pressure of the atmosphere. Evangelista Torricelli invented the barometer in the 1640s. Torricelli filled a glass tube with a heavy liquid called *mercury*. Then he placed the tube upside down in a dish.

Over the next few days, Torricelli watched the tube. He saw that the height of the mercury did not stay the same. The column of mercury moved up and down as the pressure in the atmosphere changed. The barometer soon proved to be a valuable tool in studying and predicting the weather.

Galileo likely made the first **thermometer**. In the early 1700s, a German scientist, Daniel Gabriel Fahrenheit, made thermometers more accurate. He put mercury in a glass tube. As the mercury grew warmer, it expanded and rose up the tube. The height of the mercury provided a measure of temperature. Fahrenheit also designed a new temperature scale. In the United States, we still measure temperature using Fahrenheit degrees.

With new tools and the scientific method, scientists made rapid advances in their understanding of nature. Their work had many practical results, such as the invention of the steam engine. As new technologies developed, Europeans used them to become the commercial and industrial leaders of the world. Science is one of the most powerful forces shaping our world today.

34.8 Chapter Summary

In this chapter, you learned about the Scientific Revolution. This movement marked a major shift in the way people thought about the natural world.

Several factors contributed to the Scientific Revolution. Renaissance thinkers questioned traditional learning and observed nature for themselves. Translations of classical texts exposed scholars to new ideas. Discoveries by explorers showed that accepted ideas could be wrong.

The Scientific Revolution began when Copernicus proposed the daring idea that Earth and the other planets traveled around the sun. Kepler built on this work by correctly describing the planets' orbits. Galileo's discoveries supported the Copernican theory.

Newton took all this work a giant step forward. His law of gravity explained why planets orbited the sun. Newton also showed that the same laws applied everywhere in the known universe.

The ideas of Bacon and Descartes helped to shape the scientific method, which proved to be a powerful way of testing ideas about nature. New tools like the microscope and the thermometer also aided scientific progress.

Europeans were dazzled by rapid advances in science. Many were inspired to take a similar approach to problems of human life and society. You'll learn about these thinkers in the next chapter.

Today's high-powered microscopes are based on the first designs from the 1600s. Scientific research would not be possible without such inventions.

CHAPTER 35

◄ ◄ In the 18th century, French philosophers gathered in salons to discuss new ideas.

The Enlightenment

35.1 Introduction

In the last chapter, you learned about the Scientific Revolution. In this chapter, you will explore the **Enlightenment**.

The word Enlightenment refers to a change in outlook among many educated Europeans that began during the 1600s. The new outlook put great trust in **reason** as the key to human progress. In the 1700s, this way of thinking became widespread in Europe.

Enlightenment thinkers were inspired by the example of scientists such as Galileo and Newton. Scientists used observation and logic to understand the physical world. Their methods were rapidly overturning old beliefs. Now thinkers wanted to take a similar approach to problems of human life. Forget the teachings of the past, they said. A new age of reason is dawning. In this new age, governments and social institutions will be based on rational understanding, not the "errors and superstitions" of earlier times.

A Frenchman, Bernard de Fontenelle, expressed this optimistic faith in reason and progress. In 1702, he wrote that the new century "will become more enlightened day by day, so that all previous centuries will be lost in darkness by comparison."

In France, thinkers called *philosophes* (French for "philosophers") championed these ideas. Philosophes often gathered in informal meetings called **salons**. There they exchanged and debated ideas.

Many salons were organized by women. The painting on the facing page shows a salon in the home of Madame Geoffrin in the 1750s. Gatherings like these helped to shape and spread the ideas of the Enlightenment.

In this chapter, you will first learn about the roots of the Enlightenment. Then you will meet five **philosophers** whose ideas influenced the Enlightenment. You will see how their work led to new thinking about **government** and **individual rights**. Finally, you'll meet several women who played important roles in the Enlightenment.

Use this illustration as a graphic organizer to help you remember the ideas of five philosophers whose thinking influenced the Enlightenment.

35.2 The Roots of the Enlightenment

Enlightenment thinkers wanted to examine human life in the light of reason. Rational understanding, they felt, would lead to great progress in government and society.

These thinkers believed they were making a major break with the past. Like all people, however, they were influenced by what had come before them. In this section, we'll first look at some of the roots of the Enlightenment. Then we'll consider ways in which the new ideas of the Enlightenment clashed with old beliefs.

The Scientific Revolution   Enlightenment thinking grew out of the Scientific Revolution. In science, observation and reason were revealing laws that applied throughout the physical world. The thinkers of the Enlightenment wanted to apply this approach to human life. They asked questions like these: What natural law governs the way people should live? How well do our institutions agree with natural law? Does natural law give all people certain rights? What is the best form of government?

Philosophers did not always agree about the answers to these questions. For example, some of them defended the right of kings to rule. Others argued that people should have more say in their own government. What they all shared was a way of thinking about such questions. Like scientists, they placed their trust in reason and observation as the best sources of understanding and progress.

The Renaissance and the Reformation   The Enlightenment also had roots in the Renaissance and the Reformation. The humanists of the Renaissance questioned accepted beliefs. They celebrated the dignity and worth of the individual. During the Reformation, Protestants rebelled against the Catholic Church. They put individual conscience ahead of the authority of the church. Enlightenment thinkers went even farther in rejecting authority and upholding the freedom of individuals to think for themselves.

Classical and Christian Influences   Like the humanists of the Renaissance, many Enlightenment thinkers were inspired by classical culture. Trust in reason, for example, goes all the way back to the ancient Greeks. So does the idea that people should have a say in their government. Philosophers who argued for this idea could point to the democracy of ancient Athens or the republic of ancient Rome.

Erasmus was a humanist scholar of the Renaissance who challenged the authority of the Catholic Church and paved the way for later Enlightenment thinkers.

Christian ideas also colored Enlightenment thinking. Enlightenment philosophers preferred rational understanding to faith based on the Bible. Yet most of them continued to believe in God. They saw the laws of nature as the work of an intelligent Creator. They saw human progress as a sign of God's goodness. Often their approach to moral problems reflected Christian values, such as respect for others and for a moral law.

New Ideas Versus Old Beliefs   The thinkers of the Enlightenment prized reason over authority. They questioned the basis of religion, morality, and government. Everything, they said, must be examined anew in the light of reason. This outlook led to many clashes with accepted beliefs.

Christian faith, for example, was based largely on trust in the Bible as God's word. Enlightenment thinkers believed that humans were perfectly able to discover truth for themselves. Some of them even questioned the existence of God. Others sought a "natural religion" based on reason. To these thinkers, the order in the universe was proof enough of an intelligent Creator. There was no need to base belief in God on revelations in holy books. Similarly, ideas about right and wrong should be based on rational insight, not on the teachings of religious authorities.

Enlightenment thinkers also criticized accepted ideas about government. Some questioned the long-held belief in the divine right of kings to rule. Many stressed individual rights that governments must respect. Toward the end of the 18th century, these ideas played a major role in revolutions in both America and France.

The Enlightenment helped to shape modern views of human nature, society, and government. Let's take a closer look at five thinkers whose ideas were influential during the Enlightenment.

Ideas from ancient Athens and the republic of ancient Rome, such as the idea of a democratic government, inspired Enlightenment philosophers.

Hobbes compared society to a giant "artificial man" that he called Leviathan.

Thomas Hobbes

35.3 Thomas Hobbes: Absolute Rule by Kings

Thomas Hobbes was born in England in 1588. He wrote about many subjects, including politics and government. He tried to give a rational basis for absolute (unlimited) rule by kings.

The son of a clergyman, Hobbes studied at Oxford University. As an adult, he traveled to other European countries, where he met many writers, scientists, and philosophers. He studied mathematics and science as well as history and government. His studies inspired him to take a scientific approach to problems of human society.

Hobbes's thinking about society was greatly influenced by events in England in the mid 1600s. The king was struggling for power with Parliament, England's lawmaking body. In 1642, civil war broke out between supporters of the monarch and Parliament. Hobbes sided with the king.

In 1649, the king was beheaded. For the next several years, England was ruled by Parliament's House of Commons. But disorder and discontent continued. Finally, in 1660, the monarchy was restored.

The chaos of these years had a powerful impact on Hobbes. What, he asked, is the basis of social order? To answer this question, he tried to reason from his observations of human nature.

In Hobbes's view, human beings were naturally cruel, selfish, and greedy. In 1651, he published a book called *Leviathan*. In this book, he wrote that people are driven by a restless desire for power. Without laws or other social controls, people would always be in conflict. In such a "state of nature," life would be "nasty, brutish and short."

Governments, Hobbes said, were created to protect people from their own selfishness. Because people were selfish by nature, they could not be trusted to make decisions that were good for society as a whole. Only a government that has a ruler with absolute authority could maintain an orderly society.

Later Enlightenment thinkers came to quite different conclusions about human nature and the best form of government. Hobbes was important, however, because he was one of the first thinkers to apply the tools of the Scientific Revolution to problems of politics. His philosophy may sound harsh, but he believed it was based on objective observation and sound reasoning.

35.4 John Locke: Natural Rights

John Locke was born in England in 1632. His thinking about government and people's rights had a major impact on the Enlightenment.

Thomas Hobbes had argued that kings should have absolute power. In contrast, Locke favored **constitutional monarchy**. In this type of government, a basic set of laws limits the ruler's power.

Locke's ideas reflected a long tradition in England. Recall how English barons forced King John to accept the Magna Carta in 1215. The Magna Carta favored nobles rather than common people, but it established the idea of rights and liberties that the king had to respect.

Over time, Parliament became the main check on the king's power. During the civil war of the 1640s, Locke's father fought on the side of Parliament. The young Locke was greatly influenced by his father's beliefs.

In the 1680s, another crisis developed. The new king, James II, was Catholic. His enemies in Protestant England feared that he wanted to put Catholics in power. In 1688, they forced James to flee the country.

The next year, Parliament gave the crown to a Protestant, King William III. Parliament also passed a **bill of rights**. The English Bill of Rights strengthened the power of Parliament as the representative of the people. For example, it forbade the king to keep a standing army in peacetime or to levy taxes without Parliament's consent. It also listed individual rights. Among them were protection in court cases from excessive fines and "cruel and unusual punishment."

Locke approved of these changes in England. In 1690, he published *Two Treatises of Government.* In this book, he offered a theory of government that justified Parliament's actions.

Locke denied the divine right of kings to rule. The true basis of government, he wrote, was a **social contract,** or agreement, among free people. The purpose of government was to protect people's **natural rights**. These included the right to life, liberty, and property. In exchange for this protection, people gave government the power to make and enforce laws.

In Locke's theory, a government's authority was based on the consent of the governed. If the government failed to respect people's rights, it could be overthrown.

Locke's view of government had a wide influence. In 1776, his ideas would be echoed in the American Declaration of Independence.

constitutional monarchy
a form of government in which the monarch's power is limited by a basic set of laws, or constitution

bill of rights a list of basic human rights that a government must protect

social contract an agreement in which people give up certain powers in return for the benefits of government

natural rights rights that belong to people "by nature," that is, simply because they are human beings

John Locke wrote about theories of government.

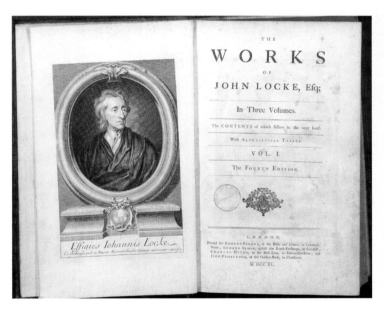

John Locke

Montesquieu was powerful and well respected.

35.5 Baron de Montesquieu: Separation of Powers

Charles-Louis de Secondat was born in France in 1689. He is better known by his title, the Baron de Montesquieu.

In his youth, Montesquieu attended a Catholic school. Later he became a lawyer. When his uncle died in 1716, Montesquieu inherited the title of baron along with his uncle's fortune. He also became president of the local parliament.

In 1721, Montesquieu achieved fame as a writer with a book called *Persian Letters*. The book described French society as seen by fictional travelers from Persia. It used humor to criticize French institutions, including the king's court and the Catholic Church. It quickly became very popular, and Montesquieu became an admired guest in the salons of Paris.

Montesquieu's most famous book was *The Spirit of Laws,* published in 1748. In this book, he described his theory of how governments should be organized.

Like John Locke, Montesquieu was concerned with how to protect political liberty. The best way to do this, he argued, was to divide power among three branches of government. In such a system, the legislative branch made the laws. The executive branch enforced the laws. The judicial branch interpreted the laws. The three branches should be separate but equal. In this way, no one branch would be too powerful. Montesquieu called this concept the **separation of powers**.

separation of powers the division of powers among separate branches of government
despotism rule by a despot, or tyrant

Baron de Montesquieu

Montesquieu's theory reflected his admiration for the English system of government. In England, lawmaking was the job of Parliament. The king enforced the laws, and courts interpreted them. Each branch of government checked (limited) the power of the others. When powers were not separated in this way, Montesquieu warned, liberty was soon lost. Too much power in the hands of any one person or group led to **despotism** (tyranny).

Montesquieu's ideas had a powerful impact on later thinkers. Among them were the men who wrote the U.S. Constitution. They made the separation of powers a key part of the American system of government.

35.6 Voltaire: Religious Tolerance and Free Speech

Francois-Marie Arouet was born in France in 1694. Under the **pen name** Voltaire, he became one of the most celebrated writers of the Enlightenment.

As a young man, Voltaire attended a Catholic college in Paris. After college, he settled on a career in literature. He soon earned fame as a writer and as a witty participant in Paris salons.

Voltaire believed passionately in reforming society in the name of justice and human happiness. He warred against what he saw as superstition, error, and **oppression**. With biting humor, he attacked the French court and the power of the Catholic clergy.

One of Voltaire's most popular books was a humorous novel called *Candide*. The novel poked fun at the idea that the world made by God must necessarily be "the best of all possible worlds." Such a belief, Voltaire thought, prevented people from fighting the evils in the world.

Like Montesquieu, Voltaire admired England's constitutional monarchy and separation of powers. In his view, the English were governed by law, not by the arbitrary wishes of a single ruler. To be governed by law, he said, was "man's most cherished right."

Voltaire was especially concerned with freedom of thought and expression. He championed religious **tolerance**. This meant allowing people to profess religion in their own ways. Religious strife, he thought, was one of the main sources of evil in the world. In reality, no single religion possessed all the truth. At the same time, there was a core of truth in all religions. This core was the "natural religion" that reason made available to everyone.

Voltaire also spoke out for the right of free speech. Once he wrote a letter to a man he strongly disagreed with. He said that he would give his life so that his opponent could continue to write. A later writer expressed Voltaire's feeling in the words, "I disapprove of what you say, but I will defend to the death your right to say it."

Throughout his life, Voltaire criticized intolerance and oppression wherever he saw them. His outspoken ways often led to conflicts with authorities. Twice he spent time in prison. Several times he was forced to flee to another city or country when his opinions made him unwelcome.

Voltaire was a passionate and outspoken writer who believed strongly in freedom of thought and expression. Here he is shown reading aloud to Frederick the Great.

pen name a name used in place of a writer's real name
oppression cruel or unjust treatment
tolerance the acceptance of different beliefs and customs

Voltaire

35.7 Cesare Beccaria: The Rights of the Accused

Cesare Beccaria was born in Milan, Italy, in 1738. He was a pioneer in the field of **criminology**. His work stressed the rights of accused people to fair treatment.

The son of an aristocrat, Beccaria attended a Catholic school as a boy. In 1758, he received a degree in law from the University of Pavia. When he finished his studies, he returned to Milan. There he was soon caught up in the intellectual excitement of the Enlightenment.

In 1763, Beccaria began a study of criminal law and the justice system. He was upset by the harsh practices that were common in his day. Torture was often used to get confessions from accused persons or statements from witnesses to a crime. People might have their thumbs crushed in a device called a *thumbscrew*. Or they might have their bodies stretched on a device called a *rack* until their bones were separated.

Beccaria argued against forms of punishment that had been in use for centuries, such as stretching a man on a rack.

Beccaria objected to other practices as well. It wasn't unusual for trials to be held in secret. Judges were often corrupt. People found guilty of crimes were often sentenced to death.

Beccaria attacked these practices in a famous book called *On Crimes and Punishments*. He argued that laws exist to preserve security and order. Punishments, he said, should be designed to serve this purpose. Like other people, criminals made rational decisions. To stop people from committing crimes, punishment did not have to be brutal. It only had to be certain and just severe enough to outweigh the potential benefits of the crime.

Beccaria also argued for other specific rights. A person accused of a crime, he said, should receive a fair and speedy trial. Torture should never be used. In addition, it was wrong to punish some people more harshly than others for the same crime. Punishment, he said, should fit the seriousness of the crime. And **capital punishment** (putting someone to death) should be done away with completely.

Beccaria's book encouraged the scientific study of crime. His ideas about rights and punishment influenced reform movements throughout Europe. In the United States, many laws concerning crime reflect his ideas.

criminology the scientific study of crime and punishment
capital punishment punishment by death; also called the *death penalty*

Cesare Beccaria

35.8 The Impact of the Enlightenment on Government

Enlightenment thinkers proposed new ideas about human nature and the best forms of government. Let's take a look at the influence of these ideas in Europe and America.

Enlightened Rule by Monarchs Several European monarchs tried to apply Enlightenment ideas during the 1700s. Among them were Frederick the Great of Prussia, Catherine the Great of Russia, and Joseph II of Austria. These rulers became known as "enlightened monarchs." They are also called "benevolent despots." (*Benevolent* means having people's best interests at heart.)

Enlightened monarchs founded universities and scientific societies. They introduced reforms such as greater religious tolerance and an end to torture and capital punishment. But these rulers pushed change only so far. They did not want to anger the noble classes, whose support they needed. Nor did they want to lose their own power.

The American and French Revolutions Enlightenment ideas had a major influence on the leaders of the American Revolution. English colonists in America shared with John Locke the traditions of the Magna Carta and the English Bill of Rights. When the colonists rebelled in 1775, they pointed to the abuse of their rights by the English king. The Declaration of Independence echoed Locke's ideas on natural rights and the purpose of government.

Other Enlightenment ideas can be seen in the U.S. Constitution. America's basic law includes Montesquieu's idea of separation of powers. The Bill of Rights protects the freedom of religion and speech championed by Voltaire. It also supports some of the rights promoted by Beccaria, such as the right to a speedy trial.

Enlightenment ideas had a great influence on the writing of America's Declaration of Independence.

In 1789, revolution broke out in France. The National Assembly adopted the Declaration of the Rights of Man and Citizen. This document proclaimed liberty and equality. It upheld the rights to own property and to resist oppression. It also guaranteed freedom of speech and religion. All these ideas grew out of the Enlightenment.

Soon, however, the French Revolution unleashed terrible passions and violence. Thousands of aristocrats and other supposed enemies of the revolution were sent to the guillotine. (The guillotine was a machine that cut off people's heads.) The bloody chaos brought a strange end to the Enlightenment dream of peaceful progress based purely on reason.

35.9 Women of the Enlightenment

The women of the 1700s did not enjoy the same rights or status as men. Yet a number of women played an important role in the Enlightenment. Some helped nurture and spread Enlightenment thinking by hosting salons. Others extended ideas about rights and equality to women. Let's meet a few of these women.

Madame Geoffrin   One of the most prominent sponsors of salons was Madame Marie-Therese Rodet Geoffrin. Beginning in the mid 1700s, the brightest talents in Europe met in her home for lively talk about the latest ideas. Madame Geoffrin also gave financial support to the Encyclopedists, a group of men who put together the first encyclopedia.

In support of the Enlightenment, Madame Geoffrin invited artists, writers, and philosophers to meet and discuss new ideas in her home.

At Madame Geoffrin's salons, princes and politicians mingled with artists, writers, and philosophers. Madame led these gatherings with a firm hand. She reserved Mondays for artists and Wednesdays for writers and philosophers. When discussions became heated, she would say, "There, that will do." The men quickly shifted their conversation to another topic.

Abigail Adams   Abigail Adams was married to John Adams, a leader of the American Revolution. Abigail firmly supported the movement for independence from England. She reminded John not to forget women. "Remember all men would be tyrants if they could," she wrote. "If particular care and attention is not paid to the Ladies, we are determined to foment [start] a Rebellion." Women, she went on, "will not hold ourselves bound by any Laws in which we have no voice." Abigail also spoke out for a woman's right to education.

Olympe de Gouges   The Frenchwoman Olympe de Gouges was the daughter of a butcher. Despite being poorly educated, she became a writer and social reformer. In 1791, she published the Declaration of the Rights of Woman and the Female Citizen. This document was her answer to the National Assembly's Declaration of the Rights of Man and Citizen. De Gouges argued for women's equality with men in every aspect of public and private life. Women, she said, should have the right to vote, hold office, own property, and serve in the military. They should have equal power to men in family life and in the church.

The French revolutionaries mocked de Gouges's ideas and her efforts to organize women. When she spoke out against the bloodshed of the revolution, they branded her a traitor. In 1793, she was sent to the guillotine.

Mary Wollstonecraft English writer Mary Wollstonecraft was another early leader in the struggle to gain equal rights for women. In an essay published in 1792, she argued that women deserved the same rights and opportunities as men. "Let woman share the rights," she wrote, "and she will emulate [imitate] the virtues of men, for she must grow more perfect when emancipated [free]."

Wollstonecraft believed that education was the key to gaining equality and freedom. She called for reforms to give women the same education as men. In the 19th century, her ideas about equality for women inspired early leaders of the women's rights movement in the United States.

Writer Mary Wollstonecraft believed in equal education for all.

35.10 Chapter Summary

In this chapter, you learned about the Enlightenment. This change in outlook grew out of the Scientific Revolution. It also had roots in earlier periods of history. Much Enlightenment thinking, however, challenged accepted beliefs.

Enlightenment philosophers wanted to apply reason to problems of government and society. Thomas Hobbes upheld the absolute power of kings. John Locke championed the rights to life, liberty, and property. Montesquieu argued for a separation of powers in government. Voltaire championed religious tolerance and free speech. Cesare Beccaria called for reforms in criminal law to protect the rights of the accused.

Enlightenment thinking influenced monarchs in Europe and revolutions in America and France. A number of women extended ideas of liberty and equality to women's rights. Modern views of people and government owe a great deal to these and other Enlightenment thinkers.

Our exploration of the medieval world and beyond ends here, at the very beginning of the modern world. Throughout your journey, you have seen how events in the past help to shape the future. You have also discovered how cultures influence one another. Your own life has been deeply affected by those who came before you. So, too, will your actions and thoughts have an influence on those who come after you.

Modern Europe Timeline

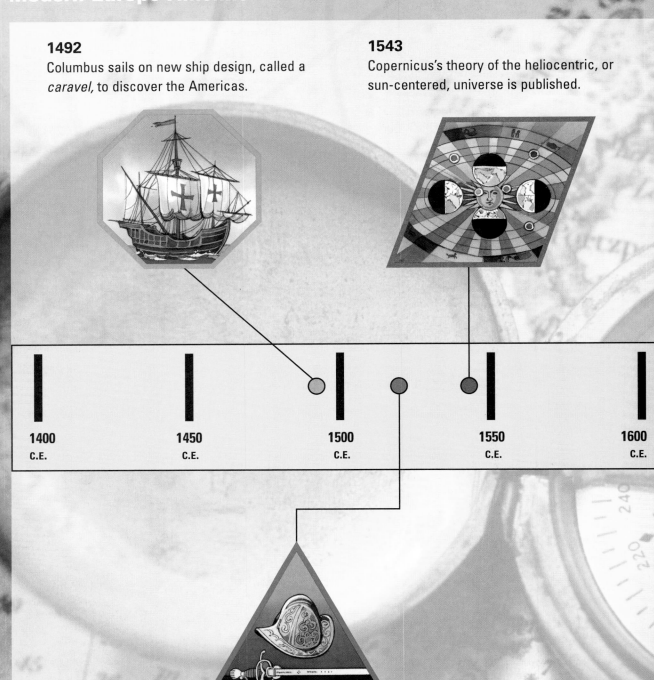

1492
Columbus sails on new ship design, called a *caravel,* to discover the Americas.

1543
Copernicus's theory of the heliocentric, or sun-centered, universe is published.

1400 C.E.

1450 C.E.

1500 C.E.

1550 C.E.

1600 C.E.

1519 – 1521
Cortes conquers the Aztec Empire.

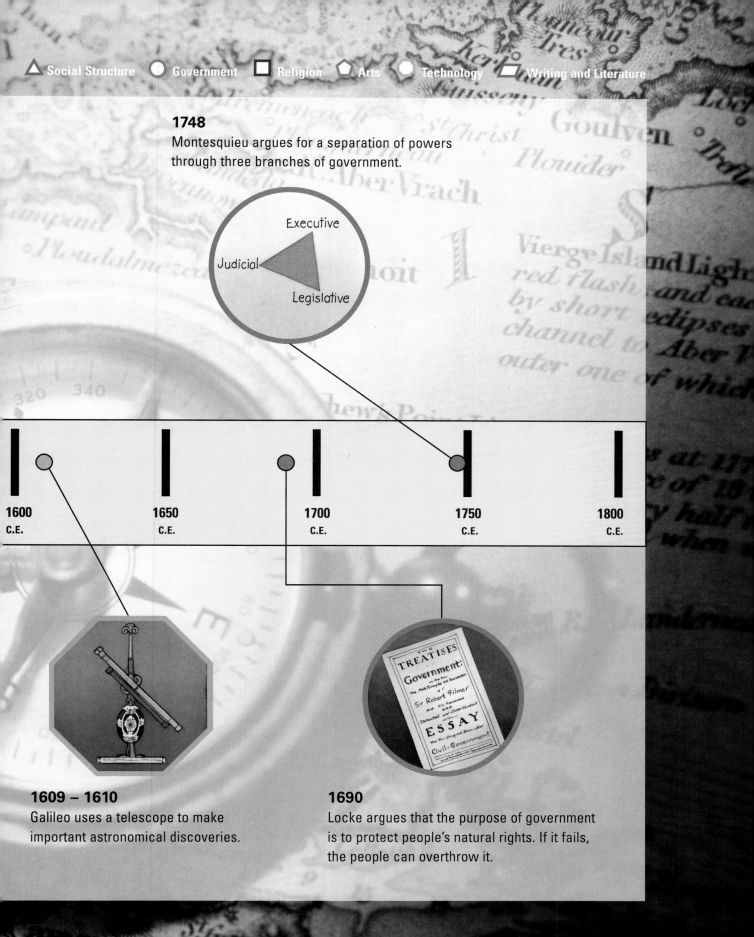

1748

Montesquieu argues for a separation of powers through three branches of government.

Executive

Judicial

Legislative

| 1600 C.E. | 1650 C.E. | 1700 C.E. | 1750 C.E. | 1800 C.E. |

1609 – 1610

Galileo uses a telescope to make important astronomical discoveries.

1690

Locke argues that the purpose of government is to protect people's natural rights. If it fails, the people can overthrow it.

RESOURCES

History Alive! The Medieval World and Beyond Timeline

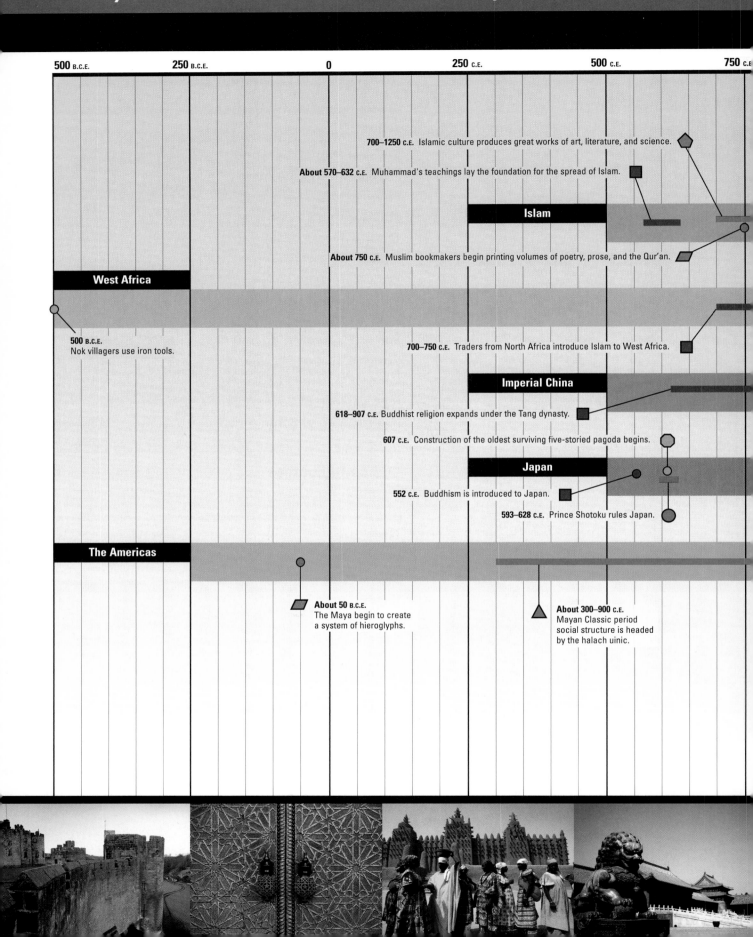

500 B.C.E.   250 B.C.E.   0   250 C.E.   500 C.E.   750 C.E.

700–1250 C.E. Islamic culture produces great works of art, literature, and science.

About 570–632 C.E. Muhammad's teachings lay the foundation for the spread of Islam.

Islam

About 750 C.E. Muslim bookmakers begin printing volumes of poetry, prose, and the Qur'an.

West Africa

500 B.C.E.
Nok villagers use iron tools.

700–750 C.E. Traders from North Africa introduce Islam to West Africa.

Imperial China

618–907 C.E. Buddhist religion expands under the Tang dynasty.

607 C.E. Construction of the oldest surviving five-storied pagoda begins.

Japan

552 C.E. Buddhism is introduced to Japan.

593–628 C.E. Prince Shotoku rules Japan.

The Americas

About 50 B.C.E.
The Maya begin to create
a system of hieroglyphs.

About 300–900 C.E.
Mayan Classic period
social structure is headed
by the halach uinic.

▲ **Social Structure**　● **Government**　■ **Religion**　⬠ **Arts**　⬡ **Technology**　▰ **Writing and Literature**

750 C.E.　　**1000** C.E.　　**1250** C.E.　　**1500** C.E.　　**1750** C.E.　　**2000** C.E.

Medieval Europe

About 800 C.E.
Scholars begin to write with
lowercase letters.

1066 C.E.
William the Conqueror introduces
feudalism to England.

1194 C.E.　Construction of present-day Chartres Cathedral begins in France.

1215 C.E.　King John puts his seal to the Magna Carta.

1346 C.E.
English archers use longbows to defeat the
French at Crecy in the Hundred Year's War.

1054 C.E.
Schism leads to two separate Christian churches:
Roman Catholic and Eastern Orthodox.

1492 C.E.
The Spanish conquer Granada, the
last Muslim-held city in Spain.

About 750 C.E.　Muslims begin using water power.

850 C.E.　Ghana becomes a rich empire.

1096–1291 C.E.　A series of crusades are fought in the Middle East.

1325 C.E.　Al-Saheli builds a new mosque at Timbuktu.

1350 C.E.
Timbuktu becomes a center for the study
of Arabic language and literature.

920 C.E.　First record of foot binding.

1312 C.E.　The rule of Mansa Musa in Mali begins.

About 1050 C.E.　Movable type is invented in China.

1405–1433 C.E.
Zheng He's voyages gain new tributary states for China.

850 C.E.　Tang Dynasty invents gunpowder.

1065 C.E.　Song dynasty begins regular civil service exams.

800–900 C.E.　Hiragana writing develops.

1192 C.E.
The first shogun is appointed.

794–1185 C.E.
Aristocrats lead a golden age of culture during the Heian period.

1325–1519 C.E.　The Aztecs practice human sacrifice in religious rituals.

1438–1532 C.E.
The Incas create a system of roads.

Early 1500s C.E.
The Inca Empire stretches over 2,500 miles
with an estimated 10 million people.

1325 C.E.　The Aztecs begin building Tenochtitlan using chinampas.

1469–1492 C.E.　Florence is ruled by Lorenzo de Medici.

Renaissance and Reformation

1517 C.E.　Martin Luther posts his 95 Theses.

About 1450 C.E.　Johannes Gutenberg begins using the printing press.

1545–1563 C.E.
Council of Trent reaffirms Catholicism.

1504 C.E.　Michelangelo completes his sculpture *David*.

1543 C.E.
Copernicus's theory of the
universe is published.

1525 C.E.　William Tyndale translates the Bible into English.

1748 C.E.
Montesquieu argues
for separation of powers
in three branches
of government.

Modern Europe

1492 C.E.　Columbus sails to discover the Americas.

1519–1521 C.E.　Cortes conquers the Aztec Empire.

1690 C.E.　Locke argues for people's rights.

1609–1610 C.E.　Galileo uses the telescope.

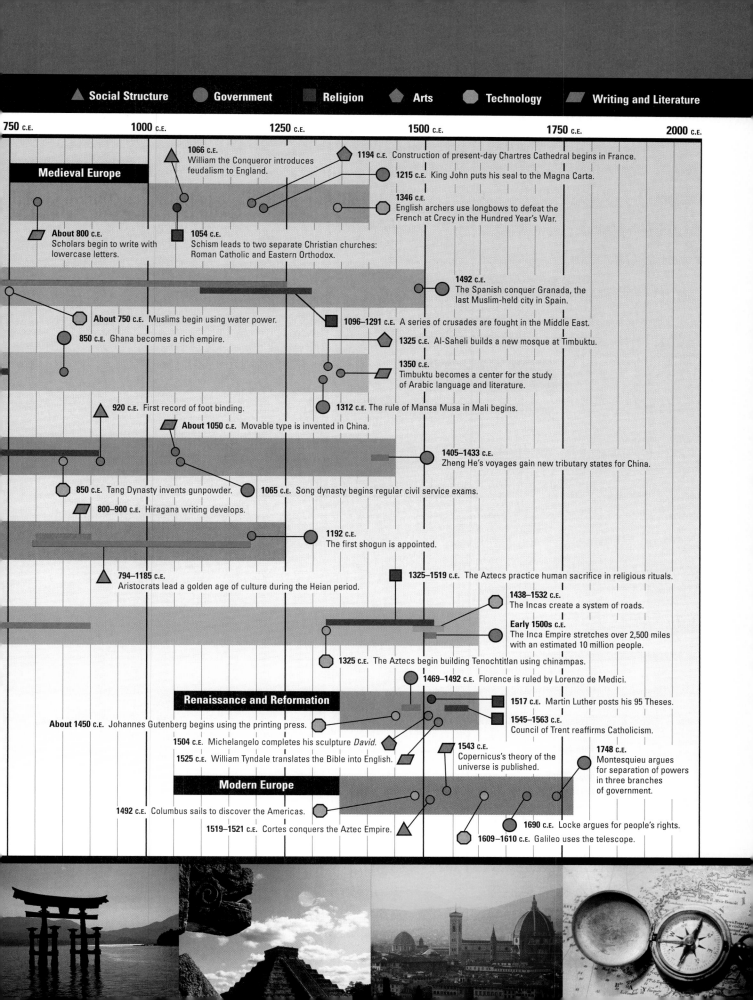

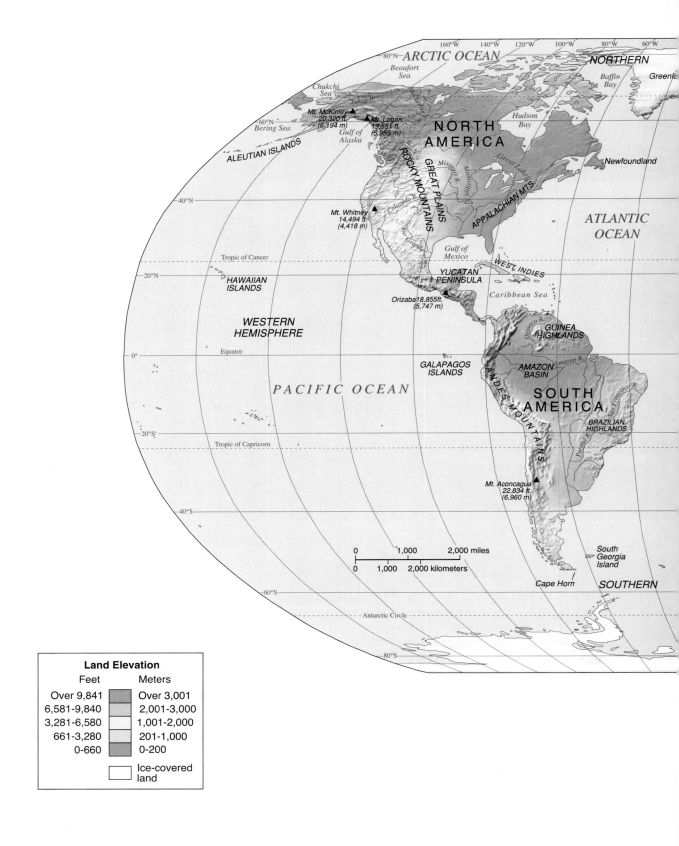

160°W   140°W   120°W   100°W   80°W   60°W

80°N ARCTIC OCEAN   NORTHERN

Beaufort
Sea

Chukchi
Sea   Baffin   Greenl
                                        Bay

Yukon R.

Mt. McKinley   Hudson
20,320 ft.   Bay
(6,194 m)   Mt. Logan
60°N   19,551 ft.   NORTH
Bering Sea   (5,959 m)   AMERICA
Gulf of
Alaska

ALEUTIAN ISLANDS

Newfoundland

Missouri R.   Great Lakes

ROCKY MOUNTAINS   Mississippi R.

GREAT PLAINS

40°N   ATLANTIC
Mt. Whitney   APPALACHIAN MTS.   OCEAN
14,494 ft.   Colorado R.
(4,418 m)
Rio Grande   Gulf of
Mexico   WEST INDIES

Tropic of Cancer   YUCATAN
PENINSULA
20°N
HAWAIIAN   Orizaba 18,855ft.   Caribbean Sea
ISLANDS   (5,747 m)

WESTERN
HEMISPHERE   Orinoco R.   GUINEA
HIGHLANDS
Equator   GALAPAGOS   Amazon R.
0°   ISLANDS   AMAZON
BASIN
San Francisco R.
PACIFIC OCEAN   ANDES MOUNTAINS   SOUTH
AMERICA
BRAZILIAN
20°S   HIGHLANDS
Paraná R.
Tropic of Capricorn

Mt. Aconcagua
22,834 ft.
(6,960 m)

40°S
1,000   2,000 miles   South
0   Georgia
0   1,000   2,000 kilometers   Island

Cape Horn   SOUTHERN
60°S

Antarctic Circle

80°S

Land Elevation

Feet	Meters
Over 9,841	Over 3,001
6,581–9,840	2,001–3,000
3,281–6,580	1,001–2,000
661–3,280	201–1,000
0–660	0–200
	Ice-covered land

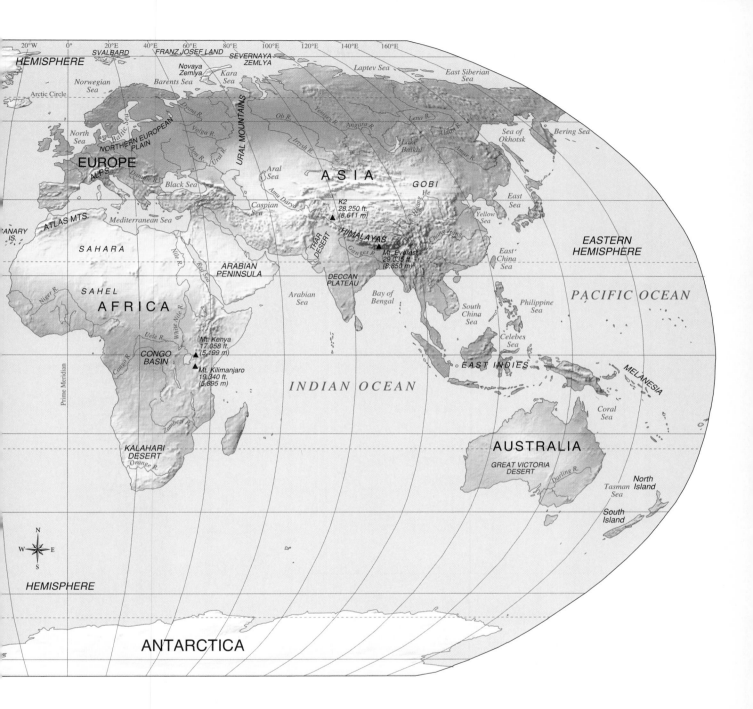

20°W 0° 20°E 40°E 60°E 80°E 100°E 120°E 140°E 160°E

SVALBARD   FRANZ JOSEF LAND   SEVERNAYA ZEMLYA

Novaya Zemlya   Kara Sea

Norwegian Sea

Barents Sea

Arctic Circle

Laptev Sea   East Siberian Sea

Duina R.

North Sea

Baltic Sea

NORTHERN EUROPEAN PLAIN

Ob R.

Yenisey R.

Angara R.

Lena R.

Aldan R.

Sea of Okhotsk

Bering Sea

EUROPE

ALPS

Danube R.

Don R.

Ural R.

URAL MOUNTAINS

Volga R.

Irtysh R.

Lake Baikal

Amur R.

Black Sea

Aral Sea

A S I A

GOBI

East Sea

CANARY IS.

ATLAS MTS.

Mediterranean Sea

Caspian Sea

Amu Darya

K2
28,250 ft.
(8,611 m)

Huang He

Chang Jiang

Yellow Sea

EASTERN HEMISPHERE

SAHARA

Red Sea

THAR DESERT

HIMALAYAS

Mt. Everest
29,035 ft.
(8,850 m)

East China Sea

Nile R.

ARABIAN PENINSULA

Ganges R.

SAHEL

AFRICA

Niger R.

DECCAN PLATEAU

Arabian Sea

Bay of Bengal

South China Sea

Philippine Sea

PACIFIC OCEAN

White Nile R.

Uele R.

Mt. Kenya
17,058 ft.
(5,199 m)

Celebes Sea

Congo R.

CONGO BASIN

Mt. Kilimanjaro
19,340 ft.
(5,895 m)

EAST INDIES

MELANESIA

Prime Meridian

INDIAN OCEAN

Zambezi R.

Coral Sea

KALAHARI DESERT

Orange R.

AUSTRALIA

GREAT VICTORIA DESERT

Darling R.

North Island

Tasman Sea

South Island

N
W   E
S

ANTARCTICA

Political Map of the World

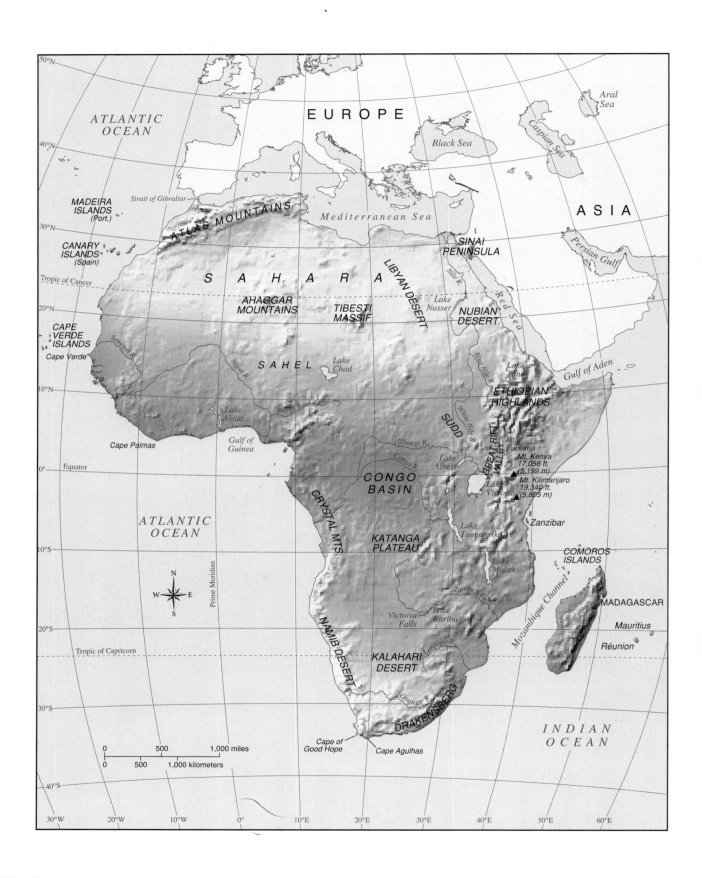

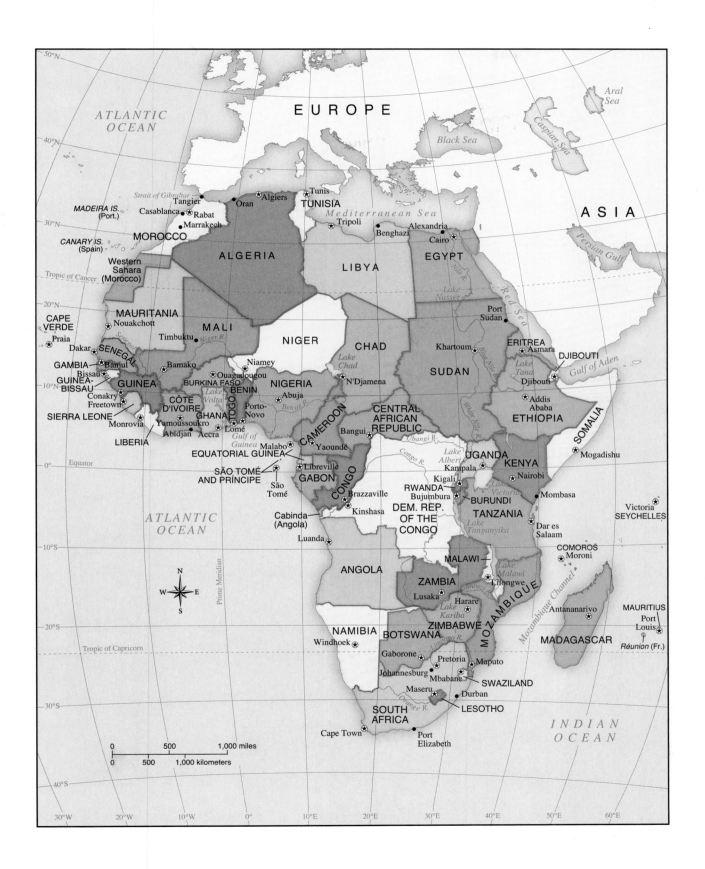

50°N

ATLANTIC OCEAN

E U R O P E

Aral Sea

A S I A

40°N

Black Sea

Caspian Sea

MADEIRA IS. (Port.)

Strait of Gibraltar

Tangier ✪ Algiers ✪ Tunis

Oran ● **TUNISIA**

Casablanca ✪ Rabat

Mediterranean Sea

30°N

Marrakech ● Tripoli ✪

MOROCCO

Benghazi ● Alexandria ●

Cairo ✪ **EGYPT**

Persian Gulf

CANARY IS. (Spain)

Western Sahara (Morocco)

ALGERIA

LIBYA

Tropic of Cancer

20°N

Port Sudan ●

Nile R.

Lake Nasser

Red Sea

MAURITANIA

Nouakchott ✪

MALI

NIGER

CHAD

Khartoum ✪

ERITREA

Asmara ✪

DJIBOUTI

CAPE VERDE

Praia ✪

Timbuktu ●

Niger R.

Blue Nile

Lake Tana

Gulf of Aden

Dakar ✪

SENEGAL

Bamako ●

Niamey ●

SUDAN

Djibouti ●

GAMBIA Banjul ✪

Ouagadougou ●

NIGERIA

N'Djamena ●

Addis Ababa ✪

10°N

Bissau ✪ **BURKINA FASO**

Lake Chad

GUINEA-BISSAU

GUINEA

BENIN

Abuja ●

Porto-Novo

Benue R.

ETHIOPIA

SOMALIA

Conakry ✪

Lake Volta

CENTRAL AFRICAN REPUBLIC

Freetown ✪

CÔTE D'IVOIRE

GHANA

TOGO

SIERRA LEONE

Yamoussoukro ●

Lomé ●

Bangui ●

White Nile

Monrovia ●

Accra ●

CAMEROON

Abidjan ●

Gulf of Guinea

Yaoundé ●

Obangi R.

Lake Albert

UGANDA

KENYA

Mogadishu ✪

LIBERIA

Malabo ●

EQUATORIAL GUINEA

Kampala ✪

Nairobi ✪

0° Equator

SÃO TOMÉ AND PRÍNCIPE

Libreville ●

Congo R.

Kigali ●

Lake Victoria

São Tomé ●

GABON

CONGO

RWANDA

Bujumbura ●

Mombasa ●

VICTORIA SEYCHELLES

Brazzaville ●

BURUNDI

Kinshasa ●

TANZANIA

Cabinda (Angola)

DEM. REP. OF THE CONGO

Lake Tanganyika

Dar es Salaam ●

10°S

ATLANTIC OCEAN

Luanda ●

COMOROS

Moroni ●

MALAWI

Lake Malawi

Prime Meridian

ANGOLA

ZAMBIA

Lilongwe ●

MAURITIUS

Port Louis ✪

Lusaka ●

MOZAMBIQUE

Antananarivo ●

N

Harare ●

Lake Kariba

MADAGASCAR

20°S

W E

S

NAMIBIA

ZIMBABWE

Réunion (Fr.)

BOTSWANA

Zambezi R.

Tropic of Capricorn

Windhoek ●

Limpopo R.

Gaborone ●

Pretoria ✪

Maputo ●

Johannesburg ●

Mbabane ●

SWAZILAND

30°S

Maseru ●

Durban ●

SOUTH AFRICA

Orange R.

LESOTHO

INDIAN OCEAN

Cape Town ✪

Port Elizabeth ●

0   500   1,000 miles

0   500   1,000 kilometers

40°S

30°W   20°W   10°W   0°   10°E   20°E   30°E   40°E   50°E   60°E

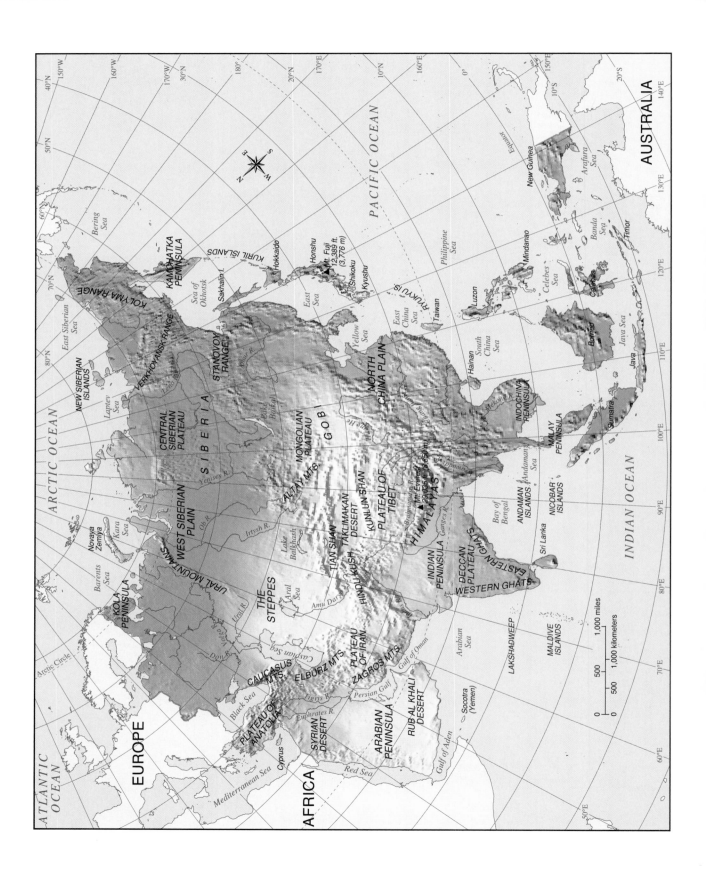

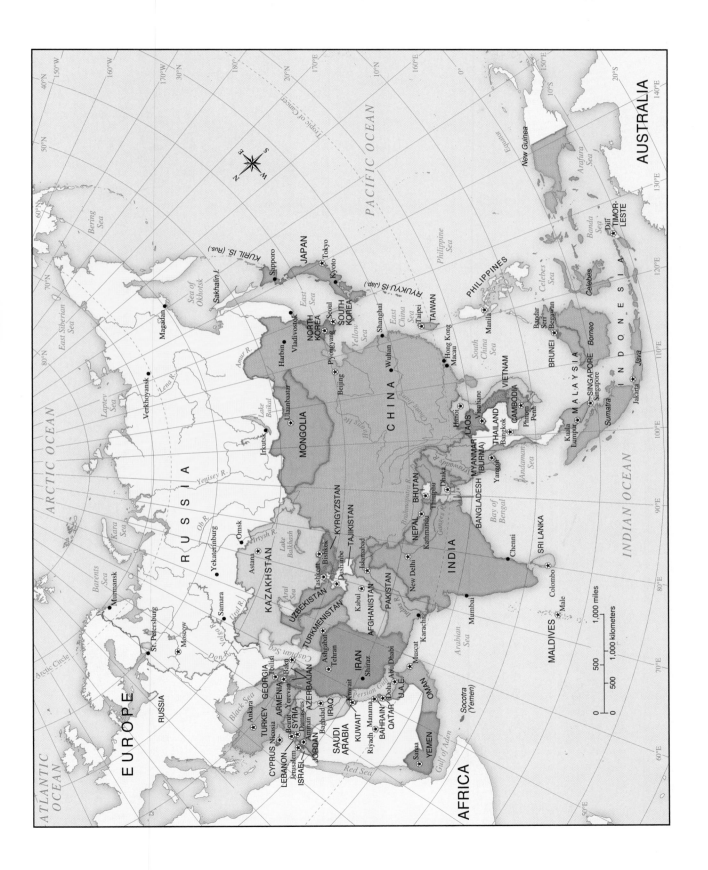

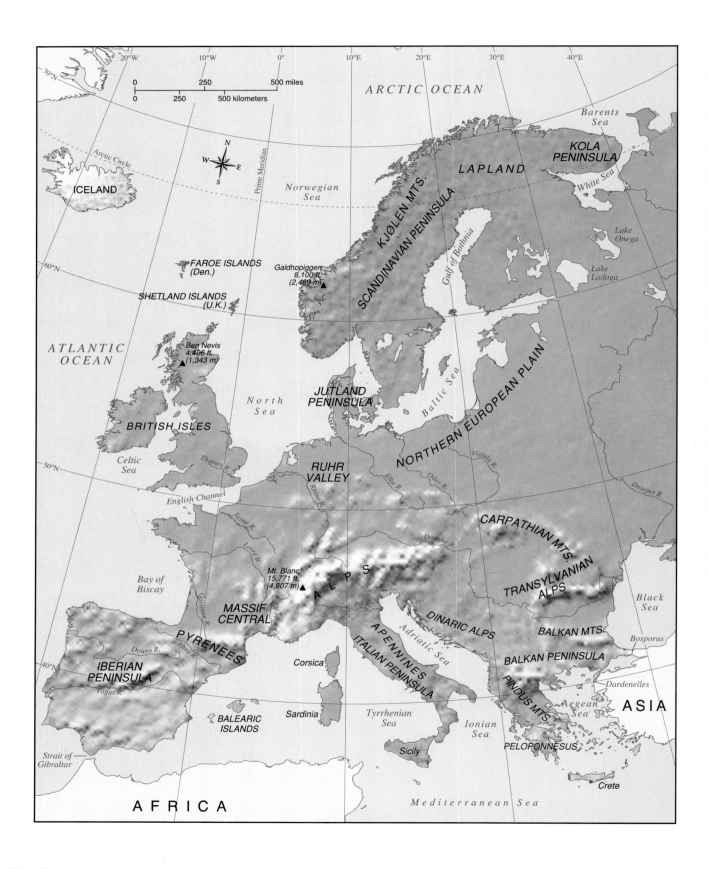

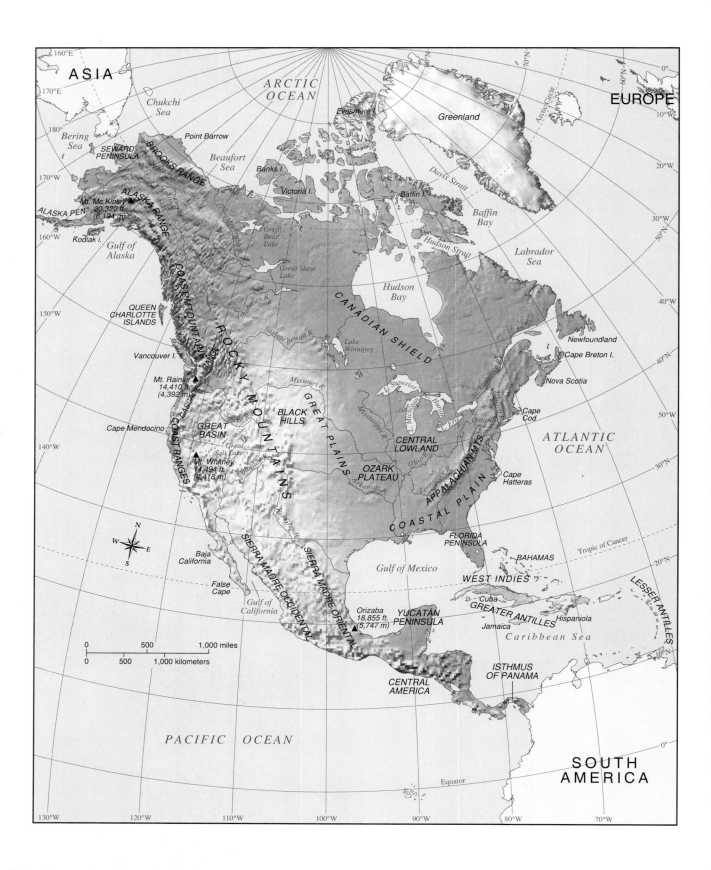

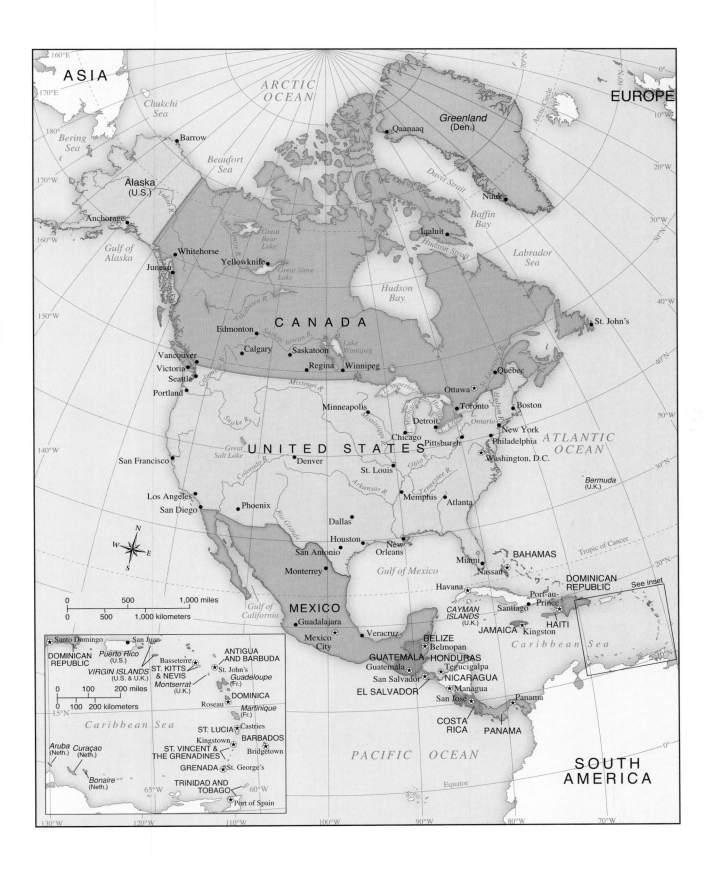

Physical Map of Oceania

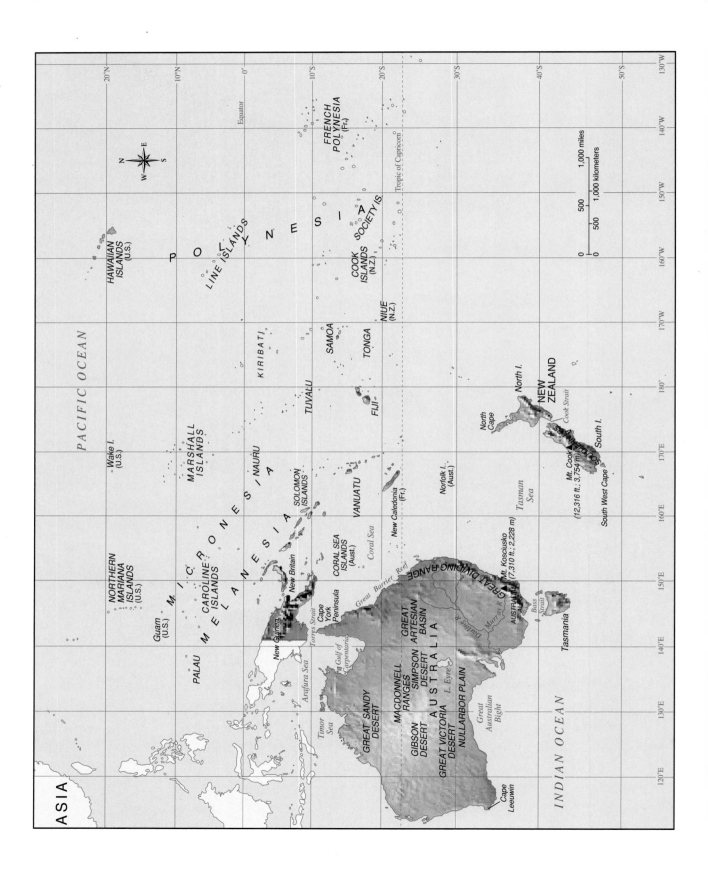

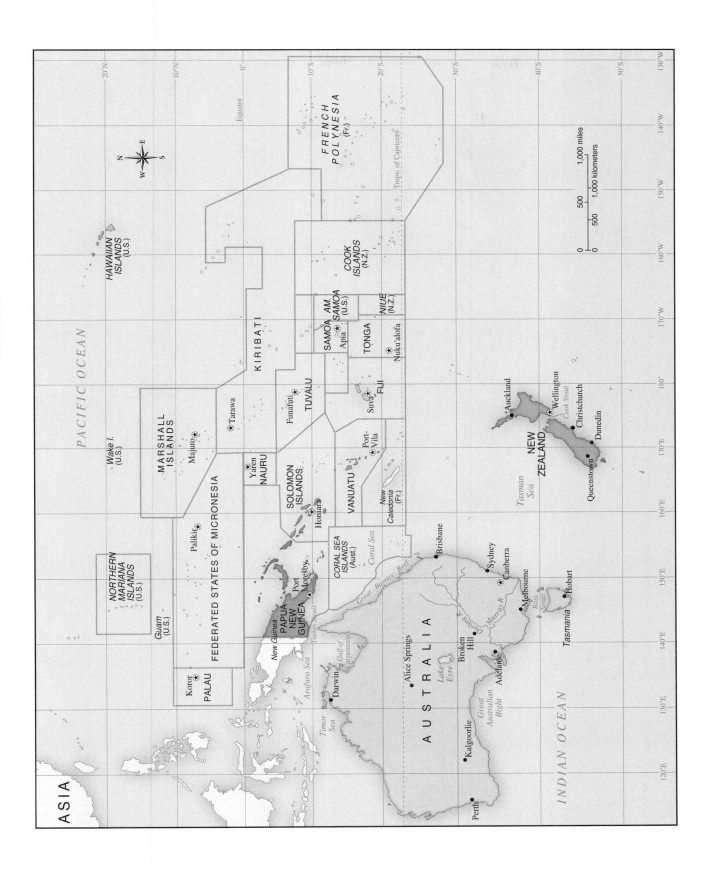

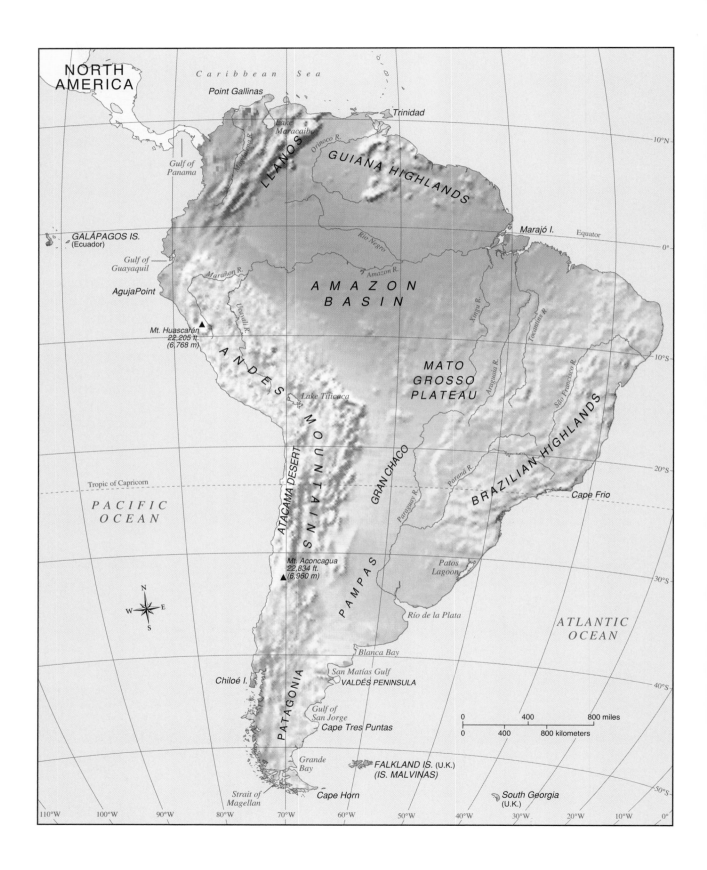

NORTH
AMERICA

Caribbean Sea

Point Gallinas

Trinidad

Lake
Maracaibo

Orinoco R.

LLANOS

GUIANA HIGHLANDS

Gulf of
Panama

Magdalena R.

GALÁPAGOS IS.
(Ecuador)

Marajó I.

Equator

Gulf of
Guayaquil

Río Negro

AMAZON
BASIN

Amazon R.

Marañón R.

AgujaPoint

Ucayali R.

Xingu R.

Tocantins R.

Mt. Huascarán
22,205 ft.
(6,768 m)

A N D E S

MATO
GROSSO
PLATEAU

Araguaia R.

São Francisco R.

Lake Titicaca

10°N

0°

10°S

M O U N T A I N S

ATACAMA DESERT

GRAN CHACO

BRAZILIAN HIGHLANDS

Paraná R.

20°S

Tropic of Capricorn

PACIFIC
OCEAN

Paraguay R.

Cape Frio

Mt. Aconcagua
22,834 ft.
(6,960 m)

PAMPAS

Patos
Lagoon

30°S

N
W E
S

Río de la Plata

ATLANTIC
OCEAN

Blanca Bay

Chiloé I.

San Matías Gulf
VALDÉS PENINSULA

40°S

PATAGONIA

Gulf of
San Jorge
Cape Tres Puntas

0   400   800 miles
0   400   800 kilometers

Grande
Bay

FALKLAND IS. (U.K.)
(IS. MALVINAS)

50°S

Strait of
Magellan

Cape Horn

South Georgia
(U.K.)

110°W   100°W   90°W   80°W   70°W   60°W   50°W   40°W   30°W   20°W   10°W   0°

NORTH
AMERICA

Caribbean Sea

Barranquilla
Cartagena
Maracaibo
Valencia
Lake Maracaibo
Caracas

GUYANA
Georgetown
SURINAME
Paramaribo
Cayenne
French Guiana
(Fr.)

VENEZUELA

Orinoco R.

Magdalena R.

Medellín
Bogotá
Cali

COLOMBIA

Gulf of Panama

GALÁPAGOS IS.
(Ecuador)

Quito

ECUADOR

Gulf of Guayaquil

Guayaquil
Iquitos

Río Negro

Manaus

Belém

Equator

Amazon R.

Marañón R.

Trujillo

Ucayali R.

Lima
Callao

PERU

Cuzco

Lake Titicaca

Arequipa

La Paz

BOLIVIA

Sucre

B R A Z I L

Xingu R.

Tocantins R.

Araguaia R.

São Francisco R.

Recife

Brasília

Salvador

Belo
Horizonte

Tropic of Capricorn

Antofagasta

PARAGUAY

Asunción

Tucumán

CHILE

Paraná R.

Paraguay R.

São Paulo
Rio de Janeiro

Pôrto Alegre

Córdoba

Patos Lagoon

Valparaíso
Santiago

Rosario

URUGUAY

Buenos Aires
Montevideo

Río de la Plata

Concepción

ARGENTINA

Bahía Blanca
Blanca Bay

San Matías Gulf

PACIFIC OCEAN

ATLANTIC OCEAN

N
W   E
S

Gulf of San Jorge

800 miles
400
400   800 kilometers

Grande Bay

FALKLAND IS. (U.K.)
(IS. MALVINAS)

Punta Arenas

Strait of Magellan

10°N
0°
10°S
20°S
30°S
40°S
50°S

110°W 100°W 90°W 80°W 70°W 60°W 50°W 40°W 30°W 20°W 10°W 0°

Online Resources

The Online Resources at www.teachtci.com/historyalive provide the following resources and assignments linked to the content of each unit in *History Alive! The Medieval World and Beyond*:

- biographies of people important in the history of each area of the world
- excerpts from primary sources and literature
- Internet research projects and links to related Web sites for more in-depth exploration
- enrichment essays and activities

Below are brief descriptions of the biographies and excerpts from primary sources and literature for each unit.

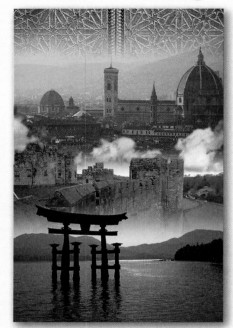

Unit 1: Europe During Medieval Times

Biography: Empress Theodora (c. 497–548). A peasant by birth, Theodora became the wife of Justinian I and empress of the Byzantine Empire. She is credited with saving Justinian's dynasty and with creating many laws protecting women's rights. (Chapter 6: The Byzantine Empire)

Primary Source: *Medieval Fairs and Markets.* This is an account of the Great Fair at Thessalonica, in Greece, as it was in the mid-12th century. (Chapter 4: Life in Medieval Towns)

Literature: *The Canterbury Tales* by Geoffrey Chaucer (c. 1340–1400). During the Middle Ages, religious faith led many people to make a pilgrimage, or journey to a holy site. This work by English writer Geoffrey Chaucer is a book of verse about a group of fictional pilgrims. (Chapter 3: The Role of the Church in Medieval Europe)

Unit 2: The Rise of Islam

Biography: Suleyman I (c. 1494–1566). The Ottoman Empire reached its peak in the 16th century under Suleyman I. He expanded the empire and was a great supporter of the arts. (Chapter 11: From the Crusades to New Muslim Empires)

Primary Source: *Travels in Asia and Africa* by Ibn Battutah (c. 1304–1368). Ibn Battutah was a Muslim with an incredible passion for travel. His book taught many people about the Muslim world. (Chapter 10: Contributions of Muslims to World Civilization)

Literature: *Shahnama (Epic of Kings)* by Ferdowsi (c. 940–1020). This epic history of Persia, written by poet Ferdowsi, is part legend and part history. (Chapter 10: Contributions of Muslims to World Civilization)

The Rubaiyat by Omar Khayyam (1048–1123). Khayyam, a Sufi mystic, is credited with writing and compiling this collection of poetic verses. *The Rubaiyat* is one of the most widely translated pieces of literature in the world. (Chapter 10: Contributions of Muslims to World Civilization)

Unit 3: The Culture and Kingdoms of West Africa

Biography: Askia Muhammad Toure (?–1538). Toure was the ruler of the Songhai empire at its height. (Chapter 14: The Influence of Islam on West Africa)

Primary Source: *Account of Ghana* by Abu Ubayd Al-Bakri. Al-Bakri was a Muslim geographer who wrote about Ghana. (Chapter 13: Ghana: A West African Trading Empire)

Literature: *West African Oral Story.* Oral stories can be very entertaining. They are also used to pass along history and to teach young people morals and values. This one is about a hyena. (Chapter 15: The Cultural Legacy of West Africa)

Unit 4: Imperial China

Biography: Empress Wu Chao (625–705). The first woman to rule as emperor in Chinese history, Wu Chao made many contributions to the Tang dynasty and is known for her ruthless political tactics. (Chapter 16: The Political Development of Imperial China)

Primary Source: *The Travels of Marco Polo* told by Marco Polo (1254–1324). Italian merchant and adventurer Marco Polo was one of the most famous travelers to China. He claimed to have served Kublai Khan, the ruler of the Mongol Empire. (Chapter 19: China's Contacts with the Outside World)

Literature: *Poetry from the Tang Dynasty.* This explores a poem by Wang Wei, one of the most famous poets of the Tang dynasty. (Chapter 19: China's Contacts with the Outside World)

Unit 5: Japan During Medieval Times

Biography: Lady Murasaki Shikibu (c. 978–1030). Shikibu is the author of *The Tale of Genji,* often called the first novel ever written. (Chapter 21: Heian-kyo: The Heart of Japan's Golden Age)

Primary Source: *The Seventeen Article Constitution* by Prince Shotoku (574–622). Japan's earliest code of law, this work is based on ideas from Chinese philosopher Confucius. (Chapter 20: The Influence of Neighboring Cultures on Japan)

Literature: *Poems About Warriors*. This piece explores a Japanese haiku and an excerpt from *Beowulf,* an English epic poem. (Chapter 22: The Rise of the Warrior Class in Japan)

Unit 6: Civilizations of the Americas

Biography: Pachacuti Inca Yupanqui (1438–1471). This Inca ruler expanded the empire, built roads, and made many reforms. (Chapter 26: The Incas)

Primary Source: Excerpt from *Popul Vuh.* This Mayan document is part mythology and part history and includes a Mayan creation story. (Chapter 23: The Maya)

Literature: Poem by Nezahualcoytl (1402–1472), an Aztec leader and poet. (Chapter 25: Daily Life in Tenochtitlan)

Unit 7: Europe's Renaissance and Reformation

Primary Source: *Renaissance Children.* This is an excerpt from Hugh Rhodes' *Boke of Nurture,* a well-known book about child rearing published in 1577. (Chapter 30: Leading Figures of the Renaissance)

Literature: *Don Quixote* by Miguel Cervantes (1547–1616). Cervantes is best known for this comic novel. (Chapter 30: Leading Figures of the Renaissance)

Unit 8: Europe Enters the Modern Age

Primary Source: *Freedom of Thought and Religion* by Baruch Spinoza (1632–1677). This is an excerpt from the Jewish philosopher's writing. (Chapter 35: The Enlightenment)

Literature: *Robinson Crusoe* by Daniel Defoe (c. 1660–1731). This story of a shipwrecked sailor was published in 1719. (Chapter 33: The Age of Exploration)

Glossary

Teal words are defined in the margins of *History Alive! The Medieval World and Beyond*.
Red words are key concepts in the chapter introductions.

A

Abassid member of a Muslim ruling family descended from Abbas, an uncle of Muhammad

absolute monarchy a monarchy in which the ruler's power is unlimited

achievement an accomplishment

adaptation a change in a way of life that allows people to survive in a particular environment

advance improvement

agricultural techniques farming methods

agriculture the business of farming

alchemy a combination of science, magic, and philosophy that was practiced in medieval times

algebra a branch of mathematics that solves problems involving unknown numbers

alliance a group of countries, city-states, or other entities who agree to work together, often to fight common enemies

almsgiving the giving of money, food, or other things of value to the needy

amulet a piece of jewelry or other object used as a charm to provide protection against bad luck, illness, injury, or evil

Anatolia a large peninsula at the western edge of Asia; also called Asia Minor

Anglicanism a Protestant sect of the Christian faith

anti-Semitism prejudice toward Jews

appliqué a technique in which shaped pieces of fabric are attached to a background fabric to form a design or picture

apprentice a person who works for an expert in a trade or craft in return for training

aqueduct a pipe or channel built to carry water between distant places

Arabian Peninsula a peninsula located in southwest Asia, between the Red Sea and the Persian Gulf

architecture the art of designing buildings

aristocracy a ruling class of noble families

armada a large fleet of ships

armor a covering, usually made of metal or leather, worn to protect the body during fighting

art human creations intended to express beauty and convey messages

artist a person who creates art

astrolabe an instrument used to observe and measure the position of the sun and other heavenly bodies

astronomy the science of the stars, planets, and other objects in the universe

aviary an enclosed space or cage for keeping birds

axis an imaginary line drawn through a sphere, or ball, such as Earth

ayllu an Inca clan (group of related families), the basic unit of Inca society

Aztecs a Mesoamerican people who built a vast empire in central Mexico that flourished from 1428 to 1519 C.E.

B

barbarian a person belonging to a tribe or group that is considered uncivilized

barge a long boat with a flat bottom

barometer an instrument used for measuring changes in the pressure of the atmosphere

barter to buy and sell by trading goods or services rather than money

bill of rights a list of basic human rights that a government must protect

blasphemy an act of disrespect toward God

bookmaking the process and art of making books

boycott a refusal to do business with an organization or group

bubonic plague a deadly contagious disease caused by bacteria and spread by fleas; also called the Black Death

bureaucracy a highly organized body of workers with many levels of authority

Byzantine Empire a great empire that straddled two continents, Europe and Asia, and lasted from about 500 to 1453 C.E.

C

caliph a title taken by Muslim rulers who claimed religious authority to rule

call and response a song style in which a singer or musician leads with a call and a group responds

calligraphy the art of beautiful handwriting

Calvinism a Protestant sect of the Christian faith

canal lock a gated chamber in a canal used to raise or lower the water level

capital punishment punishment by death; also called the *death penalty*

capitalism an economic system based on investment of money (capital) for profit

caravan a group of people traveling together for mutual protection, often with pack animals such as camels

caravel a light sailing ship that is easy to maneuver and can sail in shallow water

cartography the art and science of mapmaking

catapult a slingshot-like war machine used for shooting rocks, shells, and other objects

cathedral a large and important church

causeway a raised road built across water or low ground

center of medieval life in western Europe, the Roman Catholic Church

chain pump a pump with containers attached to a loop of chain to lift water and carry it where it is wanted

chapel a room, sometimes inside a larger church, set aside for prayer and worship

charter a written grant of rights and privileges by a ruler or government to a community, class of people, or organization

chivalry the medieval knight's code of ideal behavior, including bravery, loyalty, and respect for women

Christianity a religion based on the life and teachings of Jesus Christ

circulation the movement of blood through the body

circumference the distance around a circle

circumnavigate to travel completely around something, such as Earth

citizenship membership in a community

city a community that is larger than a town

city building the planning and construction of a city

civil service examination a test given to qualify candidates for positions in the government

clan a group of related families

class structure the organization of groups of people within a society

classical art art influenced by the styles and techniques of ancient Greece and Rome

clergy the body of people, such as priests, who perform the sacred functions of a church

coastal plain an area of flat land bordering a sea or ocean

code of conduct rules of behavior

colony a country or an area ruled by another country

comedy an amusing play with a happy ending

Glossary

coming-of-age ceremony a ceremony that celebrates the end of childhood and acceptance into the adult community

commerce the buying and selling of goods

common law a body of rulings made by judges that become part of a nation's legal system

commoner a person who is not of noble rank

communal shared by a community or group

conservatory an advanced school of music

Constantinople city on the eastern edge of Europe that the emperor Constantine made the capital of the Byzantine Empire in 330 C.E.

constitutional monarchy a form of government in which the monarch's power is limited by a basic set of laws, or constitution

convent a community of nuns; also called a *nunnery*

convert a person who adopts new beliefs, especially those of a religious faith

corruption dishonest or illegal practices, especially involving money

cottage industry a small-scale business in which people work mostly at home

Counter-Reformation a movement of the Roman Catholic Church following the Reformation in which church leaders worked to correct abuses, to clarify and defend Catholic teachings, to condemn what they saw as Protestant errors, and to win back members to the Catholic Church

courtier a member of a ruler's court

crime and punishment a community's system of defining crimes and their consequences

criminology the scientific study of crime and punishment

crossbow a medieval weapon made up of a bow that was fixed across a wooden stock (which had a groove to direct the arrow's flight) and operated by a trigger

crusades a series of religious wars launched against Muslims by European Christians

cultural diffusion the spread of cultural elements from one society to another

cultural exchange the sharing, or borrowing, of cultural elements between societies

culture a characteristic of civilization that includes the beliefs and behaviors of a society or group of people

currency the form of money used in a country

D

daily life the elements of everyday existence in a society, including religion, recreation, housing, food and drink, and education

daimyo a local lord in Japan in the era of the samurai

data facts or information

decline of feudalism the weakening of the economic and political system that developed in Europe during the Middle Ages

decorative arts everyday, useful objects created as art such as furniture, ceramics, and textiles

denomination a particular religious grouping within a larger faith; for example, the Lutheran church is a denomination of Christianity

deposit a layer or mass of a material found in rock or in the ground

desert a geographic area with an extremely warm and dry climate

despotism rule by a despot, or tyrant

dialect a regional variety of a language

dike a wall or dam built to hold back water and prevent flooding

discovery something seen or learned about for the first time

disease an illness or medical condition

disease prevention methods to help people avoid getting sick

dissect to cut and separate the parts of a living thing for scientific study

divination the art of telling the future or finding hidden knowledge through religious means

divine right of kings the belief that God gives monarchs the right to rule

doctrine the official teachings of a religion or church

domain the land controlled by a ruler or lord

dome a roof shaped like a half-circle or hemisphere

dowry a gift of money or goods presented to a man or a woman upon marriage

duke the highest type of European noble, ranking just below a prince

dynasty a line of rulers descended from the same family

E

Eastern Orthodox Church a Christian religion that arose in the Byzantine Empire

economy a system of managing the wealth and resources of a community or region

education a system of learning

elements of culture objects, ideas, and customs of a particular culture

empire a large territory in which several groups of people are ruled by a single leader or government

engineering the science of building structures and the like

engraving a print of an image that has been engraved, or etched, in a hard surface, such as metal

Enlightenment a period beginning in the 1600s in which educated Europeans changed their outlook on life by seeing reason as the key to human progress

environment the water, topography (shape of the land), and vegetation (plant life) of an area or region

epidemic an outbreak of a disease that affects many people within a geographic area

everyday object a common item used by most people in their daily lives

evolution the process by which different kinds of animals and other living things develop

excavate in archeology, to carefully dig out an ancient site

excommunicate to formally deprive a person of membership in a church

exploration travel in new areas

explorer a person who travels to unfamiliar places in order to learn what they are like and to describe them with words, pictures, and maps

expulsion removal by force

extended family an immediate family (parents and their children) plus other close relatives, such as grandparents, aunts, uncles, and cousins

F

family life the daily interaction of members of a family

family-based community a small community in which all the members are related; in early societies, people lived in family-based communities before there were villages and towns

Fatimid dynasty a Muslim ruling family in Egypt and North Africa that was descended from Fatimah, Muhammad's daughter

feudalism the economic and political system that developed in Europe during the Middle Ages

fief land granted by a lord to a vassal in exchange for loyalty and service

Five Pillars of Faith the most basic acts of worship for Muslims: faith, prayer, charity, fasting, and making a pilgrimage to Makkah

folktale a story that is usually passed down orally and becomes part of a community's tradition

Glossary

food something people eat to stay alive and healthy

foreign contacts interaction with people from different cultures or parts of the world

fresco a picture painted on the moist plaster of a wall or ceiling

friar a member of a certain religious order devoted to teaching and works of charity

G

garrison a place where a group of soldiers is stationed for defensive purposes

genealogy an account of the line of ancestry within a family

geocentric having Earth at the center (*Geo* is Greek for "Earth.")

geography the physical features of an area

glyph a symbol or character in a hieroglyphic system of writing

golden age a time of great prosperity and achievement

government the people or groups that rule a particular region

government by foreigners when people from one country have power in another country's government

guild an organization of people who work in the same craft or trade

gunpowder an explosive powder made of saltpeter and other materials

H

habeas corpus the principle that accused persons cannot be held in jail without the consent of a court

hadith accounts of Muhammad's words or actions that are accepted as having authority for Muslims

harrow a farm tool used to break up and even out plowed ground

headdress a decorative covering worn on the head, often as a sign of rank

Heian period a period of Japanese history that lasted from 794 to 1185

heliocentric having the sun at the center (*Helios* is Greek for "sun.")

hereditary passed on from parent to child; inherited

heresy beliefs that contradict the official teachings of a religion or church; one who holds such beliefs is called a *heretic*

heretic a person who holds beliefs that are contrary to the teachings of a church or other group

hierarchy a system of organizing people into ranks, with those of higher rank having more power and privileges

hieroglyphic writing that uses pictures as symbols

hoist a mechanical device used to lift people or heavy objects

Holy Communion in Christian ritual, the sharing of bread and wine that has been consecrated by a priest or minister (also called the Eucharist)

Holy Land the area between Egypt and Syria that was the ancient homeland of Jews and the place where Jesus Christ had lived; also called Palestine

homes and households the buildings and structures where people live

humanism a philosophy that emphasizes the worth and potential of all individuals and tries to balance religious faith with belief in the power of the human mind

Hundred Years' War a series of wars fought by France and England between 1337 and 1453

hypothesis an idea or assumption to be tested in an experiment

I

Iberian Peninsula a peninsula in southwestern Europe that today is divided between Spain and Portugal

icon a type of religious image typically painted on a small wooden panel and considered sacred by Eastern Orthodox Christians

illuminated manuscript a handwritten book decorated with bright colors and precious metals

imagery descriptive or imaginative language, especially when used to inspire mental "pictures"

imam a leader of prayer in a mosque

immortal able to live forever

immune system the body's natural defense against disease

impact a lasting effect

imperial belonging or related to an emperor

imperial China China under the rule of emperors

Inca Empire a great society in the Andes Mountains of South America that arose in the 1400s C.E. and lasted until 1532

individual rights the privileges of the people in a society

indulgence a grant by the Catholic Church that released a person from punishment for sins

industry a business that manufactures a particular product

inflation an increase in the supply of money compared to goods, resulting in higher prices

inoculate to protect against disease by transmitting a disease-causing agent to a person, stimulating the body's defensive reactions

Inquisition a judicial body established by the Catholic Church to combat heresy and other forms of religious error

invention a new tool, device, or process created after scientific study and experimentation

irrigate to bring water to a dry place in order to grow crops

Islam the religious faith of Muslims; also the civilization based on the Islamic religion and the group of modern countries where Islam is the main religion

J

Jew a descendant of the ancient Hebrews, the founders of the religion of Judaism; also, any person whose religion is Judaism

jihad represents Muslims' struggle with challenges within themselves and the world as they strive to please God

journeyman a person who has learned a particular trade or craft but has not become an employer, or master

K

kingdom a country or territory ruled by a monarch

knight an armed warrior

L

language the means of verbal and written communication; an aspect of culture

latitude a measure of how far north or south a place on Earth is from the equator

law a legal system

learning knowledge gained from study or experience

legend a popular myth or story passed on from the past

leisure and entertainment a time when people are free from work and have fun

leprosy a skin and nerve disease that causes open sores on the body and can lead to serious complications and death

literature writing in prose or verse that is excellent in form and expresses ideas of interest to a wide range of people; an aspect of culture

Glossary

litter a seat or chair on which a person is carried; a kind of carriage for high-ranking people

liturgy a sacred rite of public worship

longbow a large bow used for firing feathered arrows

longitude a measure of how far east or west a place on Earth is from an imaginary line that runs between the North and South Poles

lord a ruler or a powerful landowner

Lutheranism a Protestant sect of the Christian faith

M

Magna Carta a written agreement from 1215 that limited the English king's power and strengthened the rights of nobles

manor a large estate, including farmland and villages, held by a lord

maritime relating to the sea

market economy an economy in which prices are determined by the buying and selling decisions of individuals in the marketplace

market a place to buy and sell goods

marriage a legal agreement entered into by two people that unites them as family

martial arts styles of fighting or self-defense, such as modern-day judo and karate, that mostly began in Asia

mass the amount of matter in an object

massacre the killing of many helpless or unresisting people

mass-produce to make similar items in quantity by using standardized designs and dividing labor among workers

mathematics the science of numbers

matrilineal based on a woman's family line

Mayan civilization a great civilization that lasted from about 2000 B.C.E. to 1500 C.E. and at its peak included present-day southern Mexico and large portions of Central America

medical treatment some form of medicine provided to cure or control a disease or physical condition

medicine the science of healing the body and preventing disease

meditation a spiritual discipline that involves deep relaxation and an emptying of distracting thoughts from the mind

mercantilism an economic policy by which nations try to gather as much gold and silver as possible by controlling trade and establishing colonies

mercenary a soldier who is paid to fight for another country or group

meritocracy rule by officials of proven merit

Mesoamerica "Middle America," the region extending from modern-day Mexico through Central America

microscope an instrument that uses lenses to make small objects appear larger

middlemen people who fill in for or represent others in business dealings; agents

military related to soldiers and warfare

military technology knowledge and tools used to accomplish military goals

minstrel a singer or musician who sang or recited poems to music played on a harp or other instrument

miracle play a type of religious drama in the Middle Ages based on stories about saints

missionary a person who works to spread a religion and make converts

moat a deep, wide ditch, often filled with water

monarch a ruler, such as a king or queen

monastery a community of monks

monasticism a way of life in which men and women withdraw from the rest of the world in order to devote themselves to their faith

monk a man who has taken a solemn vow to devote his life to prayer and service in a monastery

monotheism belief in a single God

mosaic a picture made up of small pieces of tile, glass, or colored stone

mountain range a single line of mountains that are connected

movable type individual characters made of wood or metal that can be arranged to create a job for printing and then used over again

Muhammad a man born in about 570 C.E. who taught the faith of Islam

mural a painting on a wall

music vocal and instrumental sounds having rhythm, melody, or harmony

Muslim a follower of the Islamic faith

mystery play a type of religious drama in the Middle Ages based on stories from the Bible

mystic a person who is devoted to religion and has spiritual experiences

mysticism a form of religious belief and practice involving sudden insight and intense experiences of God

N

nationalism identification with, and devotion to, the interests of one's nation

natural law the concept that there is a universal order built into nature that can guide moral thinking

natural rights rights that belong to people "by nature," that is, simply because they are human beings

navigation the science of guiding ships and other vehicles of transportation from one place to another

New Testament the second part of the Christian Bible, which includes the Gospels and other writings of the early Christian church

New World the name given by Europeans to the Americas, which were unknown in Europe before the voyages of Christopher Columbus

noble a person of high rank by birth or title

Noh theater a classic form of Japanese drama involving heroic themes, a chorus, and dance

nomad a person who moves from place to place, often in search of water and vegetation

northwest passage a water route through North America connecting the Atlantic and Pacific Oceans

nun a woman who has taken a sacred vow to devote her life to prayer and service to the church

O

oasis a place where water can be found in a desert

observatory a building designed for observing the stars and planets

Old Testament the first part of the Christian Bible, corresponding to the Jewish Bible

oppression cruel or unjust treatment

oracle a person through whom a god or spirit is believed to speak

oral traditions the art of storytelling to record a culture's history

orbit the path that one heavenly body (such as a planet) follows around another (such as the sun)

original sin in Christian belief, the sinful state into which all people are born

P

pagoda a tower-shaped structure with several stories and roofs

painting artwork created with paint on a flat surface such as paper or canvas

papacy the office, or position, of pope as head of the Catholic Church

patriarch in the Eastern Orthodox Church, the bishop of an important city

patrilineal based on a man's family line

Glossary

patron a person who supports the arts or other activities by supplying money for them

peasant in feudalism, a person who worked the land

pen name a name used in place of a writer's real name

persecute to cause a person to suffer because of his or her beliefs

perspective the appearance of distance or depth on a flat surface, as in a painting

pharmacist a person who prepares medications for use in healing

philosopher a scholar or thinker

philosophy the study of wisdom, knowledge, and the nature of reality

pictograph a written symbol that represents an idea or object

pilgrimage a journey to a holy site

plantation a large farm where crops such as sugar, rubber, or tobacco are grown

plateau a raised area of flat land

playwright an author of plays

plaza a public square or other open area in a city where people can gather

pok-a-tok a Mayan ball game that had religious significance

politics the science of government

polygamy marriage in which a man or a woman has more than one spouse

polytheist a person who believes in more than one god

pope the bishop of Rome and supreme leader of the Roman Catholic Church

porcelain a hard, white pottery; also called *china*

porter a person who is hired to carry loads for travelers

predestination the belief that the fate of each soul was decided by God at the beginning of time

projectile an object that is fired or launched, such as a cannonball

prophet a person who speaks or interprets for God to other people

proportion the relative sizes of things, such as the length of an arm compared to the overall size of the human body

Protestant originally, people who broke away from ("protested" against) the Catholic Church

proverb a popular saying that is meant to express something wise or true

province a division of a country or an empire

public works construction projects built by a government for public use, such as buildings, roads, and bridges

pulpit a platform or other structure in a church from which a priest or minister preaches

Puritan a Protestant who wanted to "purify" the Anglican Church of Catholic elements

Q

Qur'an the holy book of the religion of Islam

R

rainforest an area of lush vegetation and year-round rainfall

Ramadan the ninth month of the Islamic calendar, during which Muslims are required to fast

ransom money paid in exchange for the release of prisoners

rationalism belief in reason and logic as the primary source of knowledge

reason the ability to think logically about something

recreation activities people do as hobbies and for relaxation

Reformation a historic movement from the early 1500s to the 1600s that led to the start of many new Christian churches

regent one who rules in the name of another

relations with other peoples the interaction of one culture with another

relic an object considered holy because it belonged to, or was touched by, a saint or other holy person

religion a set of spiritual beliefs, values, and practices

religious beliefs ideas held to be true by a particular religion

religious order a brotherhood or sisterhood of monks, nuns, or friars

religious practices the rites and rituals of a religion

Renaissance a great flowering of culture, toward the end of the Middle Ages, that began in Italy and spread throughout Europe

rhetoric the study of persuasive writing and speaking

ritual a set of actions that is always performed the same way as part of a religious ceremony

Roman Catholic Church the Christian church headed by the pope in Rome

Roman Empire empire that, at its height, around 117 C.E., spanned the whole of the Mediterranean world, from northern Africa to the Scottish border, from Spain to Syria

S

sacrament a solemn rite of Christian churches

sacrifice a gift of an animal for slaughter as a way to honor gods

salon in France, an informal meeting of philosophers during the Enlightenment

samurai a powerful warrior class in Japan

satire a work that uses sharp humor to attack people or society

scaffolding a framework used to support workers and materials during the construction or repair of a building

schism a formal division in a church or religious body

scholarship the act of and knowledge gained through being a scholar

science knowledge of the physical world

scientific method a five-step process of gaining knowledge

Scientific Revolution a major shift in thinking between 1500 and 1700, in which modern science emerged as a new way of gaining knowledge about the natural world

scientist an expert in some aspect of science

scribe a person trained to write or copy documents by hand

scripture sacred writings; in Christianity, the Bible

sculpture the art of creating three-dimensional figures from such materials as wood, stone, and clay

sect a religious group that has its own beliefs and practices

secular relating to earthly life rather than to religion or spiritual matters

sedentary permanently settled in one place

segmental arch bridge a bridge supported by arches that are shallow segments (parts) of a circle

segregation the forced separation of one group from the rest of a community

semidivine more than human but not fully a god

separation of powers the division of powers among separate branches of government

shah a ruler in certain Middle East lands, especially Persia (modern-day Iran)

shari'ah the body of Islamic law based on the Qur'an and the Sunnah

Glossary

shogun the head of the military government of Japan in the era of the samurai

siege an attempt to surround a place and cut off all access to it in order to force a surrender

simony the buying and selling of spiritual or holy things

slash-and-burn agriculture a farming technique in which vegetation is cut away and burned to clear land for growing crops

social contract an agreement in which people give up certain powers in return for the benefits of government

social pyramid a social structure in the shape of a pyramid, with layers representing social classes of different rank or status

solar year the time it takes Earth to travel once around the sun

stele a stone slab or pillar with carvings or inscriptions

strait a narrow body of water that connects two seas

subject a person under the rule of a monarch

succession inheritance of the right to rule

sultan the sovereign ruler of a Muslim state

Sunnah the example that Muhammad set for Muslims about how to live

suspension bridge a bridge whose roadway is held up by cables that are anchored on each end of the bridge

syllable a unit of sound in a word; for example, *unit* has two syllables, "u" and "nit"

synagogue a Jewish house of worship

T

technology the use of tools and other inventions for practical purposes

Tenochtitlan a city built on an island in Lake Texcoco that became the center of the Aztec Empire

terrace a flat strip of ground on a hillside used for growing crops

terra-cotta a baked clay often used to make pottery and sculptures

textile a woven cloth

theocracy a government or state in which God is the supreme ruler and religious officials govern in God's name

theology the study of God and religious truth

thermometer an instrument used for measuring temperature

tolerance the acceptance of different beliefs and customs

Torah the Jewish scriptures, or Bible. The word Torah is often used to mean to the first five books of the Bible, traditionally said to have been written by Moses.

town a community smaller than a city and larger than a village

trade the business of buying and selling or exchanging items

tragedy a serious play with a sad ending

trans-Saharan trade trade that requires crossing the Sahara Desert

travel to journey to other places

trephination a type of surgery that involves penetrating the skull

tribe a social group that shares a common ancestry, leadership, and traditions

tributary a ruler or country that pays tribute to a conqueror

tribute a payment made by one ruler or country to another for protection or as a sign of submission

truce an agreed-upon halt in fighting

U

university a school of advanced learning

urbanization the growth of cities

V

vaccine a substance used to immunize people against a disease

vault an arched structure used to hold up a ceiling or a roof

village a small community

visual arts artforms that are viewed with the eyes, such as paintings and sculpture

W

ward a neighborhood that is a political unit within a city

warlord a military leader operating outside the control of the government

woodcut a print of an image that has been carved in wood

woodland forest an area of abundant trees and shrubs

writer someone who expresses ideas and stories with written words and language

writing letters, words, and symbols formed on a surface, such as paper, using an instrument

written traditions the particular forms of writing used to record a culture's history

Z

zoology the scientific study of animals

Index

A

Index

Index

Index

Index

mercenary, 272, 273

merchant guilds, 45, 46

merchants/merchant class
- in China, 191
- in Mayan society, 263

meritocracy, 183

Mesoamerica, 260

Michelangelo, 324, 335
- ceiling of the Sistine Chapel, 11
- *David,* 327

microscope, 396

military leaders, in Aztec society, 280

Ming dynasty, 180, 184
- foreign contacts under, 210–211

minstrel, 50

miracle play, 50

missionaries, 365
- to China, 208
- protection of natives against colonizers, 379

moat, 24

Model Parliament, 55

Mona Lisa (da Vinci), 344

monarchs/monarchy, 22
- absolute, 367
- constitutional, 403
- enlightened, 407
- during feudal times, 23

monasteries, 32

monasticism, 40

Mongols
- foreign contacts under, 208–209
- invasion of Muslim empires, 127
- rule of China, 184

monks, 32, 40–41

monotheism, 86, 94, 96

Montesquieu, Baron de, 404

Montezuma, 382

mosaics, 10

Moses, 94, 96

mosque, 107

motte, 24

mountains, in the Arabian Peninsula, 80

movable type, 198–199

Mughal Empire, 129

Muhammad, 72, 75, 83
- call to prophethood, 86
- early life, 85
- migration to Madinah and end of life, 88
- rejection of teaching of, 87

murals, 10

Murasaki Shikibu, *The Tale of Genji,* 236–237, 239

Musa, Mansa, 156, 162

music
- influence of Central Asia on Chinese, 206
- influence on Japanese, 226
- Muslim Spain, 115
- West African, 168–169

Muslims, 83
- impact of crusades on, 125
- invasion of Ghana's empire, 148
- unification under caliph Uthman, 89

mystery play, 50

mysticism, 113

N

Nara, Japan capital, 222, 230

nationalism, Protestantism and, 366–367

natural law, 38, 400

natural rights, 403

nave, 36–37

navigation, Muslim scholars and, 110

Nero, 8

New Testament, 355

Newton, Isaac, 373, 394

ngoni, 168

Niger River, 138

Noah, 94, 96

nobility
- in Aztec society, 280
- in Inca society, 292
- in Mayan society, 262
- *See also* lords and ladies; monarchs/monarchy

noble, 23

Noh theatre, 239

Nok people, 140

nomads, Arabian Peninsula, 77, 78

North America, European exploration of, 384–385

numerals, use of Roman, 15

nun, 35, 40–41

Index

Correlation of History Alive! Materials to State History–Social Science Standards

Below is a correlation of *History Alive! The Medieval World and Beyond* to California Content Standards. For correlations to state standards, go to http://www.teachtci.com.

California History Social Science Standards, Seventh Grade	Where Standards Are Addressed
7.1 Students analyze the causes and effects of the vast expansion and ultimate disintegration of the Roman Empire.	
1. Study the early strengths and lasting contributions of Rome (e.g., significance of Roman citizenship; rights under Roman law; Roman art, architecture, engineering, and philosophy; preservation and transmission of Christianity) and its ultimate internal weaknesses (e.g., rise of autonomous military powers within the empire, undermining of citizenship by the growth of corruption and slavery, lack of education, and distribution of news).	pp. 7–17, 32 (Christianity)
2. Discuss the geographic borders of the empire at its height and the factors that threatened its territorial cohesion.	pp. 7, 8, 9
3. Describe the establishment by Constantine of the new capital in Constantinople and the development of the Byzantine Empire, with an emphasis on the consequences of the development of two distinct European civilizations, Eastern Orthodox and Roman Catholic, and their two distinct views on church-state relations.	pp. 8–9, 61–67 Online Resources: Ch. 6 Biographies
7.2 Students analyze the geographic, political, economic, religious, and social structures of the civilizations of Islam in the Middle Ages.	
1. Identify the physical features and describe the climate of the Arabian peninsula, its relationship to surrounding bodies of land and water, and nomadic and sedentary ways of life.	pp. 75–91
2. Trace the origins of Islam and the life and teachings of Muhammad, including Islamic teachings on the connection with Judaism and Christianity.	pp. 83–88, 93–103
3. Explain the significance of the Qur'an and the Sunnah as the primary sources of Islamic beliefs, practice, and law, and their influence in Muslims' daily life.	pp. 86 (origins of Qur'an), 93–103 Online Resources: Ch. 9 Primary Sources
4. Discuss the expansion of Muslim rule through military conquests and treaties, emphasizing the cultural blending within Muslim civilization and the spread and acceptance of Islam and the Arabic language.	pp. 84, 87–90, 101, 105–106, 127–128, 155–163 Online Resources: Ch. 11 Biographies
5. Describe the growth of cities and the establishment of trade routes among Asia, Africa, and Europe, the products and inventions that traveled along these routes (e.g., spices, textiles, paper, steel, new crops), and the role of merchants in Arab society.	pp. 72–73, 76–79, 106
6. Understand the intellectual exchanges among Muslim scholars of Eurasia and Africa and the contributions Muslim scholars made to later civilizations in the areas of science, geography, mathematics, philosophy, medicine, art, and literature.	pp. 105–117 Online Resources: Ch. 10 Literature

California History Social Science Standards, Seventh Grade	Where Standards Are Addressed
7.3 Students analyze the geographic, political, economic, religious, and social structures of the civilizations of China in the Middle Ages.	
1. Describe the reunification of China under the Tang Dynasty and reasons for the spread of Buddhism in Tang China, Korea, and Japan.	pp. 180–181, 206–207, 219–220, 222–223 Online Resources: Ch. 16 Biographies
2. Describe agricultural, technological, and commercial developments during the Tang and Song periods.	pp. 187–193, 195–203, 206–207
3. Analyze the influences of Confucianism and changes in Confucian thought during the Song and Mongol periods.	pp. 183–184, 192–193
4. Understand the importance of both overland trade and maritime expeditions between China and other civilizations in the Mongol Ascendancy and Ming Dynasty.	pp. 208–211 Online Resources: Ch. 19 Primary Sources
5. Trace the historic influence of such discoveries as tea, the manufacture of paper, wood.	pp. 188–189 (tea), 190–191 (compass), 195–203 (including more on compass)
6. Describe the development of the imperial state and the scholar-official class.	pp. 179–185
7.4 Students analyze the geographic, political, economic, religious, and social structures of the sub-Saharan civilizations of Ghana and Mali in Medieval Africa.	
1. Study the Niger River and the relationship of vegetation zones of forest, savannah, and desert to trade in gold, salt, food, and slaves; and the growth of the Ghana and Mali empires.	pp. 134–135, 137–143, 145–153, 156–157 Online Resources: Ch. 14 Primary Sources
2. Analyze the importance of family, labor specialization, and regional commerce in the development of states and cities in West Africa.	pp. 139–142
3. Describe the role of the trans-Saharan caravan trade in the changing religious and cultural characteristics of West Africa and the influence of Islamic beliefs, ethics, and law.	pp. 153, 155–163
4. Trace the growth of the Arabic language in government, trade, and Islamic scholarship in West Africa.	pp. 160–161 Online Resources: Ch. 14 Biographies
5. Describe the importance of written and oral traditions in the transmission of African history and culture.	pp. 166–167 Online Resources: Ch. 15 Literature
7.5 Students analyze the geographic, political, economic, religious, and social structures of the civilizations of Medieval Japan.	
1. Describe the significance of Japan's proximity to China and Korea and the intellectual, linguistic, religious, and philosophical influence of those countries on Japan.	pp. 219–227
2. Discuss the reign of Prince Shotoku of Japan and the characteristics of Japanese society and family life during his reign.	pp. 219–221 Online Resources: Ch. 20 Primary Sources

California History Social Science Standards, Seventh Grade	Where Standards Are Addressed
3. Describe the values, social customs, and traditions prescribed by the lord-vassal system consisting of shogun, daimyo, and samurai and the lasting influence of the warrior code in the twentieth century.	pp. 241–251 Online Resources: Ch. 22 Literature
4. Trace the development of distinctive forms of Japanese Buddhism.	pp. 222–223, 247
5. Study the ninth and tenth centuries' golden age of literature, art, and drama and its lasting effects on culture today, including Murasaki Shikibu's *Tale of Genji*.	pp. 229–239 Online Resources: Ch. 21 Biographies
6. Analyze the rise of a military society in the late twelfth century and the role of the samurai in that society.	pp. 241–249 Online Resources: Ch. 22 Literature
7.6 Students analyze the geographic, political, economic, religious, and social structures of the civilizations of Medieval Europe.	
1. Study the geography of the Europe and the Eurasian landmass, including their location, topography, waterways, vegetation, and climate and their relationship to ways of life in Medieval Europe.	pp. 4–5, 44
2. Describe the spread of Christianity north of the Alps and the roles played by the early church and by monasteries in its diffusion after the fall of the western half of the Roman Empire.	pp. 20–21, 32–33, 40–41
3. Understand the development of feudalism, its role in the medieval European economy, the way in which it was influenced by physical geography (the role of the manor and the growth of towns), and how feudal relationships provided the foundation of political order.	pp. 9–29, 43–44, 46
4. Demonstrate an understanding of the conflict and cooperation between the Papacy and European monarchs (e.g., Charlemagne, Gregory VII, Emperor Henry IV).	pp. 20–21, 32–33
5. Know the significance of developments in medieval English legal and constitutional practices and their importance in the rise of modern democratic thought and representative institutions (e.g., Magna Carta, parliament, development of habeas corpus, an independent judiciary in England).	pp. 49, 54–55
6. Discuss the causes and course of the religious Crusades and their effects on the Christian, Muslim, and Jewish populations in Europe, with emphasis on the increasing contact by Europeans with cultures of the Eastern Mediterranean world.	pp. 35 (mention), 119–126 Online Resources: Ch. 11 Enrichment Essay 3
7. Map the spread of the bubonic plague from Central Asia to China, the Middle East, and Europe and describe its impact on global population.	pp. 56–57
8. Understand the importance of the Catholic church as a political, intellectual, and aesthetic institution (e.g., founding of universities, political and spiritual roles of the clergy, creation of monastic and mendicant religious orders, preservation of the Latin language and religious texts, St. Thomas Aquinas's synthesis of classical philosophy with Christian theology, and the concept of "natural law").	pp. 31–41
9. Know the history of the decline of Muslim rule in the Iberian Peninsula that culminated in the Reconquista and the rise of Spanish and Portuguese kingdoms.	pp. 123, 340 Online Resources: Ch. 11 Enrichment Essay 3

California History Social Science Standards, Seventh Grade	Where Standards Are Addressed
7.7 Students compare and contrast the geographic, political, economic, religious, and social structures of the Meso-American and Andean civilizations.	
1. Study the locations, landforms, and climates of Mexico, Central America, and South America and their effects on Mayan, Aztec, and Incan economies, trade, and development of urban societies.	pp. 256–257; 260–263, 268–269 (Maya); 272–275 (Aztecs); 290–291 (Incas)
2. Study the roles of people in each society, including class structures, family life, warfare, religious beliefs and practices, and slavery.	pp. 259–269 (Maya); 276–277, 279–287 (Aztecs); 292–299 (Incas)
3. Explain how and where each empire arose and how the Aztec and Incan empires were defeated by the Spanish.	pp. 260–261 (Maya); 272–273, 276–277, 304–305 (Aztecs); 290–291, 299 (Incas); 382–383 Online Resources: Ch. 26 Biographies
4. Describe the artistic and oral traditions and architecture in the three civilizations.	pp. 260–261, 302–303 (Maya); 274–275, 304–305 (Aztecs); 306–307 (Incas) Online Resources: Unit 6 Primary Sources; Unit 6 Literature
5. Describe the Meso-American achievements in astronomy and mathematics, including the development of the calendar and the Meso-American knowledge of seasonal changes to the civilizations' agricultural systems.	pp. 260–261, 266–269, 302–303 (Maya); 304–305 (Aztecs)
7.8 Students analyze the origins, accomplishments, and geographic diffusion of the Renaissance.	
1. Describe the way in which the revival of classical learning and the arts fostered a new interest in humanism (i.e. a balance between intellect and religious faith).	pp. 315–317, 320–321, 324–330
2. Explain the importance of Florence in the early stages of the Renaissance and the growth of independent trading cities (e.g., Venice), with emphasis on the cities' importance in the spread of Renaissance ideas.	pp. 318, 319, 323–331
3. Understand the effects of the reopening of the ancient "Silk Road" between Europe and China, including Marco Polo's travels and the location of his routes.	pp. 187, 208–209, 318 Online Resources: Ch. 19 Primary Sources
4. Describe the growth and effects of new ways of disseminating information (e.g., the ability to manufacture paper, translation of the Bible into the vernacular, printing).	pp. 334; 350–355 (Bible)
5. Detail advances made in literature, the arts, science, mathematics, cartography, engineering, and the understanding of human anatomy and astronomy (e.g., by Dante Alighieri, Leonardo da Vinci, Michelangelo di Buonarroti Simoni, Johann Gutenberg, William Shakespeare).	pp. 325–329, 335–339, 342–345, 376–377 (cartography) Online Resources: Ch. 30 Investigating Literature
7.9 Students analyze the historical developments of the Reformation.	
1. List the causes for the internal turmoil in and weakening of the Catholic church (e.g., tax policies, selling of indulgences).	pp. 347–349
2. Describe the theological, political, and economic ideas of the major figures during the Reformation (e.g., Desiderius Erasmus, Martin Luther, John Calvin, William Tyndale).	pp. 350–355, 358–363
3. Explain Protestants' new practices of church self-government and the influence of those practices on the development of democratic practices and ideas of federalism.	pp. 366–367 Online Resources: Ch. 32 Enrichment Essay 4

California History Social Science Standards, Seventh Grade	Where Standards Are Addressed
4. Identify and locate the European regions that remained Catholic and those that became Protestant and explain how the division affected the distribution of religions in the New World.	pp. 366–367
5. Analyze how the Counter-Reformation revitalized the Catholic church and the forces that fostered the movement (e.g., St. Ignatius of Loyola and the Jesuits, the Council of Trent).	pp. 364–365
6. Understand the institution and impact of missionaries on Christianity and the diffusion of Christianity from Europe to other parts of the world in the medieval and early modern periods; locate missions on a world map.	pp. 366–367 Online Resources: Ch. 32 Enrichment Essay 5
7. Describe the Golden Age of cooperation between Jews and Muslims in medieval Spain that promoted creativity in art, literature, and science, including how that cooperation was terminated by the religious persecution of individuals and groups (e.g., the Spanish Inquisition and the expulsion of Jews and Muslims from Spain in 1492).	pp. 106, 114–115, 123, 340, 365
7.10 Students analyze the historical developments of the Scientific Revolution and its lasting effect on religious, political, and cultural institutions.	
1. Discuss the roots of the Scientific Revolution (e.g., Greek rationalism; Jewish, Christian, and Muslim science; Renaissance humanism; new knowledge from global exploration).	pp. 106, 108–112, 390–391
2. Understand the significance of the new scientific theories (e.g., those of Copernicus, Galileo, Kepler, Newton) and the significance of new inventions (e.g., the telescope, microscope, thermometer, barometer).	pp. 391–396
3. Understand the scientific method advanced by Bacon and Descartes, the influence of new scientific rationalism on the growth of democratic ideas, and the coexistence of science with traditional religious beliefs.	pp. 395
7.11 Students analyze political and economic change in the sixteenth, seventeenth, and eighteenth centuries (the Age of Exploration, the Enlightenment, and the Age of Reason).	
1. Know the great voyages of discovery, the locations of the routes, and the influence of cartography in the development of a new European worldview.	pp. 372–373, 375–385
2. Discuss the exchanges of plants, animals, technology, culture, and ideas among Europe, Africa, Asia, and the Americas in the fifteenth and sixteenth centuries and the major economic and social effects on each continent.	pp. 375–387 Online Resources: Ch. 33 Enrichment Essay 6
3. Examine the origins of modern capitalism; the influence of mercantilism and cottage industry; the elements and importance of a market economy in seventeenth-century Europe; the changing international trading and marketing patterns, including their locations on a world map; and the influence of explorers and mapmakers.	pp. 386–387
4. Explain how the main ideas of the Enlightenment can be traced back to such movements as the Renaissance, the Reformation, and the Scientific Revolution and to the Greeks, Romans, and Christianity.	pp. 399–401
5. Describe how democratic thought and institutions were influenced by Enlightenment thinkers (e.g., John Locke, Charles-Louis Montesquieu, American founders).	pp. 402–409 Online Resources: Ch. 35 Primary Sources
6. Discuss how the principles in the Magna Carta were embodied in such documents as the English Bill of Rights and the American Declaration of Independence.	pp. 403, 407

Historical and Social Science Analysis Skills

In addition to the content standards, students demonstrate the following intellectual reasoning, reflection, and research skills, which are reinforced throughout the program.

Chronological and Spatial Thinking
1. Students explain how major events are related to one another in time.
2. Students construct various time lines of key events, people, and periods of the historical era they are studying.
3. Students use a variety of maps and documents to identify physical and cultural features of neighborhoods, cities, states, and countries and to explain the historical migration of people, expansion and disintegration of empires, and the growth of economic systems.

Historical Research, Evidence, and Point of View
1. Students frame questions that can be answered by historical study and research.
2. Students distinguish fact from opinion in historical narratives and stories.
3. Students distinguish relevant from irrelevant information, essential from incidental information, and verifiable from unverifiable information in historical narratives and stories.
4. Students assess the credibility of primary and secondary sources and draw sound conclusions from them.
5. Students detect the different historical points of view on historical events and determine the context in which the historical statements were made (the questions asked, sources used, author's perspectives).

Historical Interpretation
1. Students explain the central issues and problems from the past, placing people and events in a matrix of time and place.
2. Students understand and distinguish cause, effect, sequence, and correlation in historical events, including the long- and short-term causal relations.
3. Students explain the sources of historical continuity and how the combination of ideas and events explains the emergence of new patterns.
4. Students recognize the role of chance, oversight, and error in history.
5. Students recognize that interpretations of history are subject to change as new information is uncovered.
6. Students interpret basic indicators of economic performance and conduct cost-benefit analyses of economic and political issues.

Notes

Chapter 8
p. 86: Ammer Ali, *The Spirit of Islam* (London: Christopher Publishing, 1922), 52.

Chapter 10
p. 113: Huston Smith, *The Illustrated World's Religions: A Guide to Our World's Traditions* (San Francisco: Harper San Francisco, 1994).

Chapter 13
pp. 146–147: A. Adu Boahen and Alvin M. Josephy, *The Horizon History of Africa* (New York: American Heritage, 1971), 182.

Chapter 14
p. 157: Patricia McKissack and Frederick McKissack, *The Royal Kingdoms of Ghana, Mali, and Songhay: Life in Medieval Africa* (New York: Henry Holt, 1995), p. 60.
p. 158: Editors of Time-Life Books, *Africa's Glorious Legacy* (Alexandria, VA: Time-Life Books, 1994), 18.

Chapter 19
p. 205: Joanna Waley-Cohen, *The Sextants of Beijing: Global Currents in Chinese History* (New York: W.W. Norton, 1999), 36
p. 210: *Planet Time,* http://planet.time.net.mt/CentralMarket/melaka101/chengho.htm.

Chapter 20
p. 224: Edwin O. Reischauer and Albert M. Craig, *Japan: Tradition and Transformation,* rev. ed. (Cambridge, MA: Harvard University Press, 1989), 27.

Chapter 21
p. 237: Ivan Morris, trans. and ed., *The Pillow Book of Sei Shonagon* (New York: Columbia University Press, 1991).

Chapter 22
p. 245: Yamamoto Tsunetomo, *Hagakure: The Book of the Samurai,* trans. William Scott Wilson, rev. ed. (Tokyo: Kodansha International, 1992).
p. 246: Hiroaki Sato and Burton Watson, eds., *From the Country of Eight Islands: An Anthology of Japanese Poetry* (Garden City, NY: Anchor Books, 1981).

Chapter 27
p. 305: Jacques Soustelle, *Daily Life of the Aztecs,* trans. Patrick O'Brian (London: Phoenix Press, 1961), 237.

Chapter 34
p. 396: Julie M. Fenster, *Mavericks, Miracles, and Medicine: The Pioneers Who Risked Their Lives to Bring Medicine into the Modern Age* (New York: Carroll and Graf, 2003), 63.

Chapter 35
p. 399: *Encyclopedia Britannica Online,* "Europe, history of," http://www.britannica.com/.
p. 402: *Tom Bridges, Philosophy and Religion Department, MSU,* "Hobbes's Leviathan," http://www.msu.org/ethics/content_ethics/texts/hobbes/hobbes_leviathan.html.
p. 405, first, second: Paul Edwards, ed., *Encyclopedia of Philosophy,* Vol. 7, "Voltaire" (New York, Macmillan, 1967), 269.
p. 405, third: John Bartlett, *Familiar Quotations,* 16th ed. (Boston: Little, Brown, 1992), p 307.
p. 408: John Bartlett, *Familiar Quotations,* "Letter to John Adams, March 31, 1776," 16th ed. (Boston: Little, Brown, 1992), 347.
p. 409: Mary Wollstonecraft, *A Vindication of the Rights of Women with Structures on Political and Moral Subjects* (Boston: Peter Edes, 1792).

Chapter 1
pp. 2–3: Rubberball Productions/Getty Images. pp. 4–5, background: Rubberball Productions/Getty Images. p. 6: © James L. Amos/Corbis. p. 7: Len Ebert. p. 8: North Wind Picture Archives. p. 10, left: Louvre, Paris/Bridgeman Art Library. p. 10, right: New-York Historical Society, New York/Bridgeman Art Library. p. 11: Museo Archeologico Nazionale, Naples, Italy/Bridgeman Art Library. p. 12: © Scala/Art Resource, NY. p. 13, upper: © Peter Guttman/Corbis. p. 13, lower: WDC013/Royalty Free/Corbis. p. 14: © SEF/Art Resource, NY. p. 16: The Art Archive/Museo Capitolino, Rome/Dagli Orti. p. 17: © David Butow/Corbis SABA.

Chapter 2
p. 18: Musée Conde, Chantilly/Réunion des Musées Nationaux/Art Resource, NY. p. 19: Len Ebert. p. 20: Bibliothèque Municipale, Castres, France/Bridgeman Art Library. p. 21: The Granger Collection, New York. p. 22: The Art Archive/Real Biblioteca de lo Escorial/Dagli Orti. p. 23: The Art Archive/Musée de la Tapisserie, Bayeux, France/Dagli Orti. p. 24: © Archivo Iconografico, S.A./Corbis. p. 25: © Archivo Iconografico, S.A./Corbis. p. 26: The Art Archive/University Library, Heidelberg, Germany/Dagli Orti. p. 27: © Archivo Iconografico, S.A./Corbis. p. 28: The Art Archive/Torre Aquila. p. 29: ©The Pierpont Morgan Library, New York/Art Resource, NY.

Chapter 3
p. 30: © National Gallery Collection. By kind permission of the Trustees of the National Gallery, London/Corbis. p. 31: Susan Jaekel. p. 32: © Craig Lovell/Corbis. p. 33: © Bettmann/ Corbis. p. 34: © Archivo Iconografico, S.A./Corbis. p. 35: The Granger Collection, New York. p. 36, upper: © Paul Maeyaert/Bridgeman Art Library. p. 36, lower: Monica Lau/PhotoDisc. p. 37: The Art Archive/Dagli Orti. p. 38: © Leonard de Selva/Corbis. p. 39: © Erich Lessing/Art Resource, NY. p. 40: © Bettmann/Corbis. p. 41: The Granger Collection, New York.

Chapter 4
p. 42: © Bettmann/Corbis. p. 43: Susan Jaekel. p. 45: © Stock Montage, Inc. p. 46: Castello di Issogne, Val d'Aosta, Italy/Bridgeman Art Library. p. 47: © Araldo de Luca/Corbis. p. 48: © Bettmann/Corbis. p. 49: © Archivo Iconografico, S.A./Corbis. p. 50: The Art Archive. p. 51: Bibliotea Estense, Modena, Italy/Giraudon/Bridgeman Art Library.

Chapter 5
p. 52: Musée Conde, Chantilly/Réunion des Musées Nationaux/Art Resource, NY. p. 53: Len Ebert. p. 54: © Bettmann/Corbis. p. 55: The Granger Collection, New York. p. 57: © Bettmann/Corbis. p. 58: Collection of the Earl of Leicester, Holkham Hall, Norfolk/Bridgeman Art Library. p. 59: Musée des Beaux-Arts, Orleans, France/Giraudon/Bridgeman Art Library.

Chapter 6
p. 60: © Jean-Leon Huens/National Geographic Image Collection. p. 61: Len Ebert. p. 62: The Art Archive/Marine Museum, Lisbon/Dagli Orti. p. 63: © Archivo Iconografico, S.A./Corbis. p. 64: © Ruggero Vanni/Corbis. p. 65: Dave G. Houser/Corbis. p. 66: The Art Archive/Biblioteca Nazionale, Palermo/Dagli Orti. p. 67: © Bettmann/Corbis. pp. 68–69, background: Rubberball Productions/Getty Images. pp. 68–69, details: Len Ebert.

Chapter 7
pp. 70–71: © Royalty-Free/Corbis. pp. 72–73, background: © Royalty-Free/Corbis. p. 74: © WorldStat International Inc., 2001. All rights reserved. p. 75: Doug Roy. p. 77: © Peter Stephenson/Envision. p. 78: © Robert Azzi/Woodfin Camp & Associates. p. 79: Aramco World. p. 80: © Robert Azzi/Woodfin Camp & Associates. p. 81: ©Yann Arthus-Bertrand/Corbis.

Chapter 8
p. 82: Musée Condé, Chantilly, France/Giraudon/Bridgeman Art Library. p. 82, background: PhotoSpin. p. 83: Susan Jaekel. p. 84: Bradford Art Galleries and Museums, West Yorkshire, UK/Bridgeman Art Library. p. 85: Collection of Andrew McIntosh Patrick, UK/Bridgeman Art Library. p. 86: © Peter Sanders Photography. p. 87: © Marvin Newman/Woodfin Camp & Associates. p. 88: © Peter Sanders Photography. p. 89: © Archivo Iconografico, S.A./Corbis. p. 90: © Peter Sanders Photography. p. 91: Glen Allison, PhotoDisc.

Chapter 9
p. 92: Khaled al-Hariri © Reuters/Corbis. p. 93: Doug Roy. p. 94: © Peter Turnley/Corbis. p. 95: © Shezad Noorani/Woodfin Camp & Associates. p. 96: © Peter Sanders Photography. p. 97: © Ludovic Maisant/Corbis. p. 98: © Peter Sanders Photography. p. 99: © Peter Sanders Photography. p. 100: © Nabeel Turner/Stone/Getty Images. p. 101: The Art Archive/Museum of Islamic Art, Cairo/Dagli Orti. p. 102: The Granger Collection, New York. p. 103: R Strange/PhotoLink, PhotoDisc.

Chapter 10
p. 104: © Vittoriano Rastelli/Corbis. p. 105: Doug Roy. p. 106: Lauros/Giraudon/Bridgeman Art Library. p. 107: © Abilio Lope/Corbis. p. 108: The Art Archive/Topkapi Museum, Istanbul/Dagli Orti. p. 109: © Elio Ciol/Corbis. p. 110: Bibliothèque Nationale de Cartes et Plans, Paris/Bridgeman Art Library. p. 111: © Peter Sanders Photography. p. 112: © Werner Forman Archive/Art Resource, NY. p. 113: Bildarchiv Preusslscher Kulturbesitz/Art Resource, NY. p. 114: © Marvin Newman/Woodfin Camp & Associates. p. 115: Bibliothèque Nationale, Paris/Bridgeman Art Library. p. 116: The Art Archive/Real Biblioteca de lo Escorial/Dagli Orti. p. 117: © Bettmann/Corbis.

Chapter 11
p. 118: The Art Archive/Uppsala University Library, Sweden/Dagli Orti. p. 119: Len Ebert. p. 120: © A. Ramey/Woodfin Camp & Associates. p. 122: Stock Montage, Inc. p. 123: Stock Montage, Inc. p. 124: Stock Montage, Inc. p. 125: Bibliothèque Nationale, Paris/Snark/Art Resource, NY. p. 126: © Christel Gerstenberg/Corbis. p. 127: Bibliothèque Nationale, Paris/Bridgeman Art Library. p. 128: The Stapleton Collection/Bridgeman Art Library. pp. 130–131, background: © Royalty-Free/Corbis. p. 130, details: Len Ebert.

Chapter 12
pp. 132–133: PhotoDisc. pp. 134–135, background: PhotoDisc. p. 136: © Rod McIntosh. p. 137: Doug Roy. p. 138: ©Yann Arthus-Bertrand/Corbis. p. 139: © W. Robert Moore/National Geographic Image Collection. p. 140: © Brian A. Vikander/Corbis. p. 141: © Rod McIntosh. p. 142: © Michael & Patricia Fogden/Corbis. p. 143: © Charles & Josette Lenars/Corbis.

Chapter 13
p. 144: © James L. Stanfield/National Geographic Image Collection. p. 145: Len Ebert. p. 146: Len Ebert. p. 148: © David Parker/Photo Researchers, Inc. p. 150: American Numismatic Society. p. 151: © Robert Holmes/Corbis. p. 152: © George Gerster/Photo Researchers Inc. p. 153: © Bernard and Catherine Desjeux/Corbis.

Chapter 14
p. 154: John Elk Photography. p. 155: Doug Roy. p. 156: © Michael S. Lewis/Corbis. p. 157: The Art Archive/John Webb. p. 158: © Paul Almasy/Corbis. p. 159: © Liba Taylor/Corbis. p. 160: The Granger Collection, New York. p. 161: ©Wolfgang Kaehler/Corbis. p. 162: © Charles & Josette Lenars/Corbis. p. 163: © Paul Almasy/Corbis.

Chapter 15
p. 164: © Margaret Courtney-Clarke/Corbis. p. 165: Len Ebert. p. 166: © Michael & Patricia Fogden/Corbis. p. 167: © M&E Bernheim/Woodfin Camp & Associates.

Credits

Chapter 27

p. 300, upper: © Bettmann/Corbis. **p. 300, lower left:** ©Werner Forman Archive/Art Resource, NY. **p. 300, lower right:** © Gianni Dagli Orti/Corbis. **p. 301:** Renate Lohmann. **p. 302:** © AFP Photo/Jorge Uzon/Corbis. **p. 303:** © Jack Fields/Corbis. **p. 303, inset:** ©Werner Forman Archive/Art Resource, NY. **p. 304:** © Steve Vidler/SuperStock. **p. 305:** © Royalty-Free/Corbis. **p. 306:** © Loren McIntyre/Woodfin Camp & Associates. **p. 307:** © Dave G. Houser/Corbis. **pp. 308–309, background:** © Royalty-Free/Corbis. **pp. 308–309, details:** Len Ebert.

Chapter 28

pp. 310–311: PhotoDisc. **pp. 312–313, background:** PhotoDisc. **p. 314:** Vatican Museums and Galleries, Vatican City, Italy/Giraudon/Bridgeman Art Library. **p. 315:** Susan Jaekel. **p. 316:** © Scala/Art Resource, NY. **p. 317, upper:** Lauros/Giraudon/Bridgeman Art Library. **p. 317, lower:** Vatican Museums and Galleries, Vatican City, Italy/Giraudon/Bridgeman Art Library. **p. 318:** © Philip de Bay/Historical Picture Archive/Corbis. **p. 319:** © Scala/Art Resource. **p. 320:** © Erich Lessing/Art Resource, NY. **p. 321:** © Archivo Iconografico, S.A./Corbis.

Chapter 29

p. 322: © Scala/Art Resource, NY. **p. 323:** Renate Lohmann. **p. 324:** Topkapi Palace Museum, Istanbul, Turkey/Bridgeman Art Library. **p. 325:** © Jim Zuckerman/Corbis. **p. 326:** Francis G. Mayer/Corbis. **p. 327, upper:** © Scala/Art Resource, NY. **p. 327, lower:** © Scala/Art Resource, NY. **p. 328:** © Scala/Art Resource, NY. **p. 329:** The Granger Collection, New York. **p. 330, upper:** ©Ted Spiegel/Corbis. **p. 330, lower:** © Massimo Listri/Corbis. **p. 331:** DJ Simison.

Chapter 30

p. 332: © Arte & Immagini srl/Corbis. **p. 333:** Len Ebert. **p. 334, upper:** © Musée de Brou, Bourg-en-Bresse, France/Photo by Michele Bellot/Réunion des Musées Nationaux/Art Resource, NY. **p. 334, lower:** © Bettmann/Corbis. **p. 335, upper:** © Sistine Chapel, Vatican Palace, Vatican State, Rome/Scala/Art Resource, NY. **p. 335, lower:** Rosiland Solomon. **p. 336, upper:** © Scala/Art Resource, NY. **p. 336, lower:** Rosiland Solomon. **p. 337, upper:** © Foto Marburg/Art Resource, NY. **p. 337, lower:** Rosiland Solomon. **p. 338, upper:** © Victoria & Albert Museum, London/Art Resource, NY. **p. 338, lower:** Rosiland Solomon. **p. 339, upper:** © Bettmann/Corbis. **p. 339, lower:** Rosiland Solomon. **p. 340, upper:** © Gianni Dagli Orti/Corbis. **p. 340, lower:** Rosiland Solomon. **p. 341, upper:** © Stapleton Collection/Corbis. **p. 341, lower:** Rosiland Solomon. **p. 342, upper:** The Granger Collection, New York.

p. 342, lower: Rosiland Solomon. **p. 343, upper:** © Bettmann/Corbis. **p. 343, lower:** Rosiland Solomon. **p. 344, upper:** Musée du Louvre, Paris © Réunion des Musées Nationaux/Art Resource, NY. **p. 344, lower:** Rosiland Solomon. **p. 345:** Musée du Louvre, Paris/Giraudon/Bridgeman Art Library.

Chapter 31

p. 346: © Bettmann/Corbis. **p. 347:** Renate Lohmann. **p. 348:** The Granger Collection, New York. **p. 349:** British Library, London/Bridgeman Art Library. **p. 350:** Stock Montage, Inc. **p. 351:** © Musée du Louvre, Paris/Réunion des Musées Nationaux/Art Resource, NY. **p. 352:** © Stock Montage, Inc. **p. 353:** Bibliothèque Nationale, Paris/Bridgeman Art Library. **p. 354:** © Bettmann/Corbis. **p. 355:** © Hulton-Deutsch Collection/Corbis.

Chapter 32

p. 356: © Archivo Iconografico, S.A./Corbis. **p. 357:** Renate Lohmann. **p. 358:** Georgenkirche, Eisenach, Germany/Bridgeman Art Library. **p. 359:** Nationalmuseet Copenhagen, Denmark/© Archivo Iconografico, S.A./Corbis. **p. 360:** Bibliothèque de l'Histoire du Protestantisme, Paris/Snark/Art Resource, NY. **p. 361:** The Art Archive/University Library Geneva/Dagli Orti. **p. 362:** © Culver Pictures, Inc. **p. 363:** The Pierpont Morgan Library, New York/Art Resource, NY. **p. 364:** The Art Archive/Chiesa del Gesu, Rome/Dagli Orti (A). **p. 365:** © Scala/Art Resource, NY. **pp. 368–369, background:** PhotoDisc. **pp. 368–369, details:** Len Ebert.

Chapter 33

pp. 370–371: PhotoDisc. **pp. 372–373, background:** PhotoDisc. **p. 374:** Library of Congress. **p. 375:** Len Ebert. **p. 376:** Mary Evans Picture Library. **p. 377:** © Gianni Dagli Orti/Corbis. **p. 378, upper:** © Bettmann/Corbis. **p. 378, lower:** © Stapleton Collection/Corbis. **p. 379:** © Corbis. **p. 380, upper:** The Granger Collection, New York. **p. 380, lower:** The Metropolitan Museum of Art, New York/Bridgeman Art Library. **p. 381:** © Gianni Dagli Orti/Corbis. **p. 382, upper:** © Bettmann/Corbis. **p. 382, lower:** © Archivo Iconografico, S.A./Corbis. **p. 383:** © Bettmann/Corbis. **p. 384, upper:** © Bettmann/Corbis. **p. 384, lower:** © Bettmann/Corbis. **p. 385, upper:** © Bettmann/Corbis. **p. 385, lower:** © Bettmann/Corbis. **p. 387:** Frans Hals Museum, Haarlem, the Netherlands/Bridgeman Art Library.

Chapter 34

p. 388: © Pinacoteca, Vatican Museums, Rome/Scala/Art Resource, NY. **p. 389:** Rosiland Solomon. **p. 390:** © Bettmann/Corbis. **p. 391:** © Stefano Bianchetti/Corbis. **p. 392:** ©Tribuna di Galileo, Museo della

Scienza/Scala/Art Resource, NY. **p. 393:** © Musée du Louvre, Paris/Erich Lessing/Art Resource, NY. **p. 394:** The Royal Institution, London/Bridgeman Art Library. **p. 395, upper:** © Bettmann/Corbis. **p. 395, lower:** Doug Roy. **p. 396:** © Bettmann/Corbis. **p. 397:** © John Paul Kay/Peter Arnold, Inc.

Chapter 35

p. 398: Musée des Beaux-Arts, Rouen, France/Erich Lessing/Art Resource, NY. **p. 398, background:** Photolink. **p. 399:** Len Ebert. **p. 400:** © Archivo Iconografico, S.A./Corbis. **p. 401:** © Scala/Art Resource, NY. **p. 402, upper:** © Bettmann/Corbis. **p. 402, lower:** Rosiland Solomon. **p. 403, upper:** © Archivo Iconografico, S.A./Corbis. **p. 403, lower:** Rosiland Solomon. **p. 404, upper:** The Art Archive/Musée du Louvre, Paris/Dagli Orti (A). **p. 404, lower:** Rosiland Solomon. **p. 405, upper:** © Bettmann/Corbis. **p. 405, lower:** Rosiland Solomon. **p. 406, upper:** © Bettmann/Corbis. **p. 406, lower:** Rosiland Solomon. **p. 407:** © Bettmann/Corbis. **p. 408:** Chateaux de Versailles et deTrianon, Versailles, France/ Réunion des Musées Nationaux/Art Resource, NY. **p. 409, left:** ©Tate Gallery, London/Art Resource, NY. **p. 409, right:** Mary Evans Picture Library. **pp. 410–411, background:** PhotoDisc. **pp. 410–411, details:** Len Ebert.